# To Improve the Academy

*Resources for Faculty, Instructional, and
Organizational Development*

VOLUME 24

**Sandra Chadwick-Blossey, Editor**
Rollins College

**Douglas Reimondo Robertson, Associate Editor**
Northern Kentucky University

NETWORK
Professional and Organizational Development Network in Higher Education

ANKER PUBLISHING COMPANY, INC.
Bolton, Massachusetts

**To Improve the Academy**
*Resources for Faculty, Instructional, and Organizational Development*

VOLUME 24

ISBN 1-882982-89-4

Composition by Lyn Rodger, Deerfoot Studios
Cover design by Boynton Hue Studio

Anker Publishing Company, Inc.
563 Main Street
P.O. Box 249
Bolton, MA 01740-0249 USA

www.ankerpub.com

# To Improve the Academy

# To Improve the Academy

*To Improve the Academy* is published annually by the Professional and Organizational Development Network in Higher Education (POD) through Anker Publishing Company, and is abstracted in ERIC documents and in Higher Education Abstracts.

## Ordering Information

The annual volume of *To Improve the Academy* is distributed to members at the POD conference in the autumn of each year. To order or to obtain ordering information, contact:

Anker Publishing Company, Inc.
P. O. Box 249
Bolton, MA 01740-0249
Voice     978-779-6190
Fax       978-779-6366
Email     info@ankerpub.com
Web       www.ankerpub.com

## Permission to Copy

The contents of *To Improve the Academy* are copyrighted to protect the authors. Nevertheless, consistent with the networking and resource-sharing functions of POD, readers are encouraged to reproduce articles and cases from *To Improve the Academy* for educational use, as long as the source is identified. This permission excludes Figure 16.1 in Chapter 16, "Practicing What We Preach: Transforming the TA Orientation" by Patricia Armstrong, Peter Felten, Jeffrey Johnston, and Allison Pingree. Permission to reproduce this figure should be directed to the Association for Supervision and Curriculum Development, 1703 N. Beauregard Street, Alexandria, VA 22311-1714, www.ascd.org.

## Instructions to Contributors for the Next Volume

Anyone interested in the issues related to instructional, faculty, and organizational development in higher education may submit manuscripts. Manuscripts are submitted to the current editors in December of each year and sent through a blind peer review process. Correspondence, including requests for information about guidelines and submission of manuscripts for Volume 25, should be directed to:

Douglas Reimondo Robertson, Ph.D.
Assistant Provost, Professional Development Programs
Northern Kentucky University
Steely Library 220
Highland Heights, KY 41099
Voice    859-572-1354
Mobile  859-630-4467
Fax       859-572-1387
Email    robertsond2@nku.edu

## Mission Statement

As revised and accepted by the POD Core Committee, April 2, 2004.

### Statement of Purpose

The Professional and Organizational Development Network in Higher Education is an association of higher education professionals dedicated to enhancing teaching and learning by supporting educational developers and leaders in higher education.

The Professional and Organizational Development Network in Higher Education encourages the advocacy of the ongoing enhancement of teaching and learning through faculty, TA, instructional, and organizational development. To this end, it supports the work of educational developers and champions their importance to the academic enterprise.

### Vision Statement

During the 21st century, the Professional and Organizational Development Network in Higher Education will expand guidelines for educational development, build strong alliances with sister organizations, and encourage developer exchanges and research projects to improve teaching and learning.

### Values

The Professional and Organizational Development Network in Higher Education is committed to:

• Personal, faculty, instructional, and organizational development

- Humane and collaborative organizations and administrations

- Diverse perspectives and a diverse membership

- Supportive educational development networks on the local, regional, national, and international levels

- Advocacy for improved teaching and learning in the academy through programs for faculty, administrators, and graduate students

- The identification and collection of a strong and accessible body of research on development theories and practices

- The establishment of guidelines for ethical practice

- The increasingly useful and thorough assessment and evaluation of practice and research

## Programs, Publications, and Activities

The Professional and Organizational Development network in Higher Education offers members and interested individuals the following benefits:

- An annual conference designed to promote professional and personal growth, nurture innovation and change, stimulate important research projects, and enable participants to exchange ideas and broaden professional networks

- An annual membership directory and networking guide

- Publications in print and in electronic form

- Access to the POD web site and listserv

## Membership, Conference, and Programs Information

For information contact:
Frank and Kay Gillespie, Executive Directors
The POD Network
P. O. Box 271370
Fort Collins, CO 80527–1370
Voice   970-377-9269
Fax     970-377-9282
Email   podnetwork@podweb.org

# About the Authors

## The Editors

*Sandra Chadwick-Blossey* is director of the Christian A. Johnson Institute for Effective Teaching at Rollins College. She teaches undergraduate and graduate courses in organizational development and learning organizations. Prior to her nine years at Rollins, she was director of the Learning Assistance Program at Wake Forest University. She can be reached at sblossey@rollins.edu.

*Douglas Reimondo Robertson* is assistant provost for professional development programs and professor of educational leadership at Northern Kentucky University. He has helped to start or reorganize four university professional development centers (Portland State University, University of Nevada Las Vegas, Eastern Kentucky University, and Northern Kentucky University). He chairs the Faculty Development Work Group for the Commonwealth of Kentucky's Council for Postsecondary Education. He is a Fulbright Senior Specialist and a frequent consultant and speaker at colleges and universities. His most recent book is *Making Time, Making Change: Avoiding Overload in College Teaching* (New Forums Press, 2003). He can be reached at robertsond2@nku.edu.

## The Contributors

*Patricia Armstrong* is assistant director of the Center for Teaching at Vanderbilt University. She teaches French language courses and writing, and her current research interests include teaching writing outside the composition classroom and teaching reading across the disciplines. She can be reached at patricia.armstrong@vanderbilt.edu.

*Raoul A. Arreola* is professor of health sciences administration and director of institutional research, assessment, and planning at the University of Tennessee Health Science Center. For the last 35 years Dr. Arreola has worked and published in the fields of faculty evaluation, faculty development, distance education, and student learning outcomes assessment. He has taught in the areas of statistics, instructional research, educational psychology, and academic administrative leadership, and has served as a consultant to more than 250 colleges and universities in assisting with the design, development, and operation of large-scale faculty evaluation and development systems. His book, *Developing a Comprehensive Faculty Evaluation System* (Anker, 2000), has become the standard in the field and is used by many colleges and universities in guiding the development of their faculty evaluation and development programs. He can be reached at rarreola@utmem.edu.

*Dorothe J. Bach* is assistant professor and faculty consultant in the Teaching Resource Center at the University of Virginia (U.Va.), where she coordinates the Excellence in Diversity Fellows Program, among others. Born and raised in Germany, she received a master's degree in German literature and physical education from the Albert-Ludwigs-Universität in Freiburg. As a DAAD fellow at the Hebrew University, Jerusalem, she researched German-Jewish autobiographies. She holds a Ph.D. in German literature from the U.Va., where she has taught various language, literature, and culture courses. Her research interests include Jewish-German relations, polemical literature, and young adult and children's literature. She can be reached at bach@virginia.edu.

*Marva A. Barnett,* founding director of the Teaching Resource Center, holds the rank of professor at the University of Virginia (U.Va.), where she teaches French literature and composition. Her current research focuses on the work and life of Victor Hugo, including an anthology. As the Thomas Jefferson Visiting Fellow at Downing College, Cambridge University (2000), she pursued a cross-cultural analysis of thinking skills, values, and expectations in the context of the humanities in the U.S., France, and England. Other research interests include second-language reading and writing processes, foreign-language methodology, and teacher training. She is also winner of the 2002 U.Va. Elizabeth Zintl Leadership Award. She can be reached at marva@virginia.edu.

*Leora Baron* is director of the Teaching and Learning Center at the University of Nevada Las Vegas. She leads a unique center that combines pedagogical faculty support with learning technologies teaching/learning faculty support. The center works with graduate teaching assistants as well. She held previous positions as center director, director of academic-corporate partnerships, and director of entrepreneurship education. These experiences, as well as her previous experience as a K–12 principal, inform her approach to faculty development, including the broader role of faculty development in the institution's organizational development, and her current scholarly activities. She holds a doctorate in education from the University of Massachusetts Amherst. She can be reached at leora.baron@ccmail.nevada.edu.

*Andrea L. Beach* is an assistant professor in the Department of Teaching, Learning, and Leadership at Western Michigan University, where she teaches in the Higher Education Leadership Doctoral Program. She received her Ph.D. in higher, adult, and lifelong education from Michigan State University and her master's degree in adult and continuing education. Her research centers on issues of organizational climate in universities, teaching and learning, and faculty development. She is coauthor of *Creating the Future of Faculty Development* (Anker, 2006) and is currently external evaluator on three grants addressing faculty development and faculty learning communities. She can be reached at andrea.beach@umich.edu.

*Philip E. Bishop* is professor of humanities at Valencia Community College. He was a member of the original Teaching/Learning Academy design team and has served on many peer review panels. He is the author of two humanities textbooks, *Adventures in the Human Spirit* (Prentice Hall, 2004, fourth edition) and *A Beginner's Guide to the Humanities* (Prentice Hall, 2002), and also serves as a regular art critic for the *Orlando Sentinel.* He can be reached at pbishop@valenciacc.edu.

*Chris Carlson-Dakes* is associate director for the Delta Program for Research, Teaching, and Learning at the University of Wisconsin–Madison (UW–Madison). He holds bachelor's and master's degrees in mechanical engineering from Carnegie Mellon University and Penn State University, respectively, and a doctoral degree in industrial engineering from UW–Madison. He also works in the private sector as an organizational development specialist with Affiliated Engineers, Inc. His work in both settings centers on researching, designing, and implementing professional development opportunities to create and sustain organizational structures for people to reconsider their approaches to work in a healthy, safe, respectful, and collaborative environment. He can be reached at cgcarlso@wisc.edu.

*Helen M. Clarke* is founding coordinator and director of the Teaching/Learning Academy (TLA) at Valencia Community College. She is coauthor of the chapter "Preparing Today's Faculty for Tomorrow's Students: One College's Faculty Development Solution" that appeared in Volume 19 of *To Improve the Academy* (Anker, 2001) and describes Valencia's efforts that helped set the foundation for the TLA. She can be reached at hclarke@valenciacc.edu.

*Patricia Cranton* is visiting professor at Saint Francis Xavier University in Nova Scotia, Canada. She has been involved in faculty development at several universities across Canada since 1976. Her current research interests are in the areas of transformative learning, including faculty development as a transformative process, and authenticity in teaching. Beginning in August 2005, she will be at Penn State Harrisburg.

*Marc Cutright* is associate professor of higher education at Ohio University. His career in higher education includes 20 years as a chief public affairs officer for several institutions. He is a research fellow of the Policy Center on the First Year of College. Dr. Cutright is the editor of *Chaos Theory and Higher Education* (Peter Lang, 2001) and a coauthor of *Achieving and Sustaining Institutional Excellence for the First Year of College* (Jossey-Bass, 2005). He can be reached at cutrighm@ohio.edu.

*Phyllis Worthy Dawkins* is director of the Faculty Development Program, dean of the College of Professional Studies, and associate professor of physical education at Johnson C. Smith University (JCSU). She directs a comprehensive campus-based faculty development program around six strands: learning communities, learning across the curriculum, instructional technology, pedagogy, new faculty orientation, and discussion series. She is co-director of the Historically Black Colleges and Universities Faculty Development Network and serves as a faculty development consultant, evaluator, and presenter. The JCSU Faculty Development Program received a Theodore M. Hesburgh Certificate of Excellence for Faculty Development in 1994. She can be reached at pdawkins@jcsu.edu.

*James Downey* has been president of three Canadian universities: Carleton University, the University of New Brunswick, and the University of Waterloo. He is currently professor of English and director of the Waterloo Centre for the Advancement of Co-operative Education at the University of Waterloo. He can be reached at jdowney@waterloo.ca.

*Harriet Fayne* is a professor in the education department at Otterbein College, where she teaches courses in educational psychology and research methods. Her research interests involve faculty development and program evaluation both in K–12 schools and at the collegiate level. She is internal evaluator for the Learning Communities Project underwritten by the McGregor Fund. She can be reached at hfayne@otterbein.edu.

*Peter Felton,* founding director of the Center for the Advancement of Teaching and Learning, is an associate professor at Elon University. He teaches in history, focusing on issues of race and education. His current research explores how emotion shapes service-learning experiences and how students learn from images in traditionally text-based disciplines. He can be reached at pfelton@elon.edu.

*Sherwood C. Frey* is Ethyl Corporation Professor of Business Administration in the Darden Graduate School of Business at the University of Virginia. As a member of the Darden faculty since 1979, Sherwood teaches, researches, writes, and consults in the areas of negotiation and proactively managing risks in major capital commitments. He is actively involved in Darden's MBA and Executive Development Programs as well as a wide variety of private activities, both domestic and international. He has been honored on a number of occasions by Darden and the university for his teaching and service to the community. He serves as faculty advisor to the Black Business Students Forum and to Darden Outreach as well as a member of the board of several community and national organizations. Prior to Darden, he was a member of the faculty of the Harvard Business School and a consultant to the Department of Defense. He holds an A.B. in mathematics and M.S. in engineering science from the University of California–Berkeley and a Ph.D. in operations research from The Johns Hopkins University. He can be reached at scf@virginia.edu.

*José D. Fuentes* is an associate professor in the Department of Environmental Sciences at the University of Virginia. His research seeks to define and quantify the surface-atmosphere exchanges of energy and materials such as pollutants and greenhouse gases. He pursues both theoretical and field research in places as distant and exotic as the North Pole, the Brazilian rain forest, and the Florida Everglades. During the last 10 years, he has guided many minority students to pursue geoscience as their professional careers. He can be reached at jf6s@virginia.edu.

*Sherril B. Gelmon* is professor of public health at Portland State University and Campus Compact Engaged Scholar on Assessment. Her scholarly interests focus on two areas: assessment of higher education, with a particular emphasis on community-based learning and community-university partnerships, and applications of improvement theory to professional education and health workforce preparation. She was formerly executive director of the Accrediting Commission on Education for Health Services Administration, and coordinator of planning and policy development for the University of Toronto Faculty of Medicine. She can be reached at gelmons@pdx.edu.

*Linda C. Hodges* is director of the Harold W. McGraw, Jr. Center for Teaching and Learning at Princeton University. A biochemist by training, she spent more than 20 years as a professor in undergraduate education. Her last position was at Agnes Scott College where she was the William Rand Kenan, Jr. Professor. In 1999 she was chosen by the Carnegie Foundation for the Advancement of Teaching as a Carnegie Scholar of the Pew National Fellowship Program. This experience spurred her transition to the field of faculty development, and in 2001 she came to Princeton as associate director of the center. She writes on her pedagogical research as well as reflective pieces on teaching and faculty development. She can be reached at lhodges@princeton.edu.

*Jacqueline A. Isaacs* is an associate professor in the Department of Mechanical and Industrial Engineering at Northeastern University. She received her M.S. and Sc.D. from Massachusetts Institute of Technology in metallurgy and materials science. She chairs the working group that creates the *Chalk Talk* columns, and was also a member of the GE Master Teachers Team at its inception. She received a university-wide teaching award in 2000. Currently, she is responsible for the education and outreach activities at Northeastern University for the National Science Foundation-sponsored Nanoscale Science and Engineering Center, the Center for High-rate Nanomanufacturing—a collaborative partnership among Northeastern University, University of Massachusetts–Lowell, and the University of New Hampshire. She can be reached at jaisaacs@coe.neu.edu.

*Jeffrey Johnston* is assistant director of the Center for Teaching at Vanderbilt University and serves as a liaison between the center and STEM (science, technology, engineering, and math) departments at Vanderbilt. His current research interests include the connection between the principles of information design and analytical thinking. He can be reached at jeffrey.johnston@vanderbilt.edu.

*Kevin J. Kecskes* is director for Community-University Partnerships for Learning at Portland State University, where he oversees faculty and department development for community engagement as well as institutional civic engagement initiatives and events. His research and scholarship interests include community-university partnership development, faculty development for service-learning and civic engagement, and institutional transformation in higher education. He is currently editing a book on the engaged department for Anker Publishing. He can be reached at kecskesk@pdx.edu.

*George Keller* is a leading scholar of higher education and an award-winning writer, editor, and strategic planner. A former faculty member, college dean, and presidential assistant, he is the former chair of higher education studies at the University of Pennsylvania Graduate School of Education. He is the author of more than 100 articles and reviews and several books including the influential *Academic Strategy* (Johns Hopkins University Press, 1983). His numerous awards include the 2003 James L. Fisher Award from the Council for Advancement and Support of Education. He can be reached at georgkell@aol.com.

*Chantal S. Levesque* is associate professor of psychology and faculty associate to the Academic Development Center at Missouri State University (MSU). She teaches courses in statistics and research methods at the undergraduate and graduate level. Her scholarly work is in the area of human motivation generally and integrative learning theory specifically. She conducts basic research in motivation and social psychology and applied research in education and learning. She is active in the Teaching Fellowship program at MSU which supports and mentors faculty interested in the scholarship of teaching and learning (SoTL). She can be reached at chl131f@missouristate.edu.

*Barbara J. Millis,* director of the Excellence in Teaching Program at the University of Nevada Reno, received her Ph.D. in English literature from Florida State University. Former director of faculty development at the U.S. Air Force Academy (USAFA), she has conducted workshops at more than 300 colleges and universities as well as at professional conferences. She publishes articles on a variety of faculty development topics such as cooperative learning, peer classroom observation, the teaching portfolio, microteaching, syllabus construction, classroom assessment/research, critical thinking, writing for publication, focus groups, writing across the curriculum, academic games, and course redesign. She has published *Enhancing Learning—and More!—Through Cooperative Learning* (an IDEA paper series), *Cooperative Learning for Higher Education Faculty* with coauthor Philip Cottell (Oryx, 1998), and *Using Simulations to Enhance Learning in Higher Education* coauthored with John Hertel (Stylus, 2002), which will be followed by a book on academic games. While at USAFA, she won both a teaching award and a research award, and after the Association of American Colleges and Universities (AAC&U) selected USAFA as a Leadership Institution in Undergraduate Education in 2001, she began serving as the liaison to the AAC&U's Greater Expectations Consortium on Quality Education. In 2002, she was Visiting Scholar at Victoria University in Wellington, New Zealand. She can be reached at millis@unr.edu.

*Bonnie B. Mullinix* coordinates the Faculty Resource Center (FRC) within Instructional Technology Services at Monmouth University. An adult educator with more than 25 years of national and international experience, she has actively supported faculty development at Monmouth over the past five years. Her work has culminated in several key initiatives including the development of the FRC and, with the Office of Academic Program Initiatives, the design of the Center for Excellence in Teaching and Learning. Prior to her current position, she served as Visiting Assistant Professor in the School of Social Work (2001–2002) and the Millicent Fenwick Research Professor in Education and Public Issues in the School of Education (1999–2001). Her work in higher education and elsewhere has involved active exploration of educational technologies and integration of participatory, learner-centered approaches. She can be reached at bmullini@monmouth.edu.

*Leslie Ortquist-Ahrens* is director of the Center for Teaching and Learning at Otterbein College, where she also teaches an integrative studies freshman seminar and a senior year experience course. Currently, her research interests involve faculty learning communities and initiatives to encourage the success of new faculty members. She is project director for the Learning Communities Project underwritten by the McGregor Fund. She can be reached at lortquist-ahrens@otterbein.edu.

*Alice Pawley* is a Ph.D. student in industrial and systems engineering and a research assistant and program facilitator for the Delta Program for Research, Teaching, and Learning at the University of Wisconsin–Madison (UW–Madison). She received her undergraduate degree in chemical engineering at McGill University and her master's degree in industrial engineering at UW–Madison. Her doctoral research focuses on the influence of academia-related institutions on the structure of engineering and engineering practice, and the gendered character of engineering's disciplinary boundaries. She can be reached at pawley@cae.wisc.edu.

*Allison Pingree* is director of the Center for Teaching at Vanderbilt University. She teaches courses in English, American, and southern studies, and women's studies, and her current research interests include emotion in the classroom, one-on-one teaching and mentoring, and leadership and organizational change. She can be reached at allison.pingree@vanderbilt.edu.

*Deborah L. Pollack* is TA instructional consultant in the Center for Teaching Excellence at Duquesne University. She is also a Ph.D. candidate in clinical psychology at Duquesne, where she received her M.A. in psychology. Her dissertation research is a feminist, qualitative study of the emotional expression and relational patterns of bulimic women. She can be reached at pollackd@duq.edu.

*Donna M. Qualters* is director of the Center for Effective University Teaching and associate professor of education at Northeastern University. She has been a faculty developer at comprehensive, liberal arts, and research intensive institutions. Her research focuses on teaching, learning, and assessment, as well as nontraditional areas such as ethical inquiry, dialogue for meaning, and spirituality in the classroom. She is also program director for the Massachusetts Board of Directors for the American Council of Education National Network of Women Leaders which promotes the development of women in higher education. She serves as the mentoring chair for the Professional and Organizational Development Network in Higher Education and is a previous winner of the Bright Idea Award. She can be reached at d.qualters@neu.edu.

*Stephen L. Rozman* is professor of political science and director of the Center for Civic Engagement and Social Responsibility at Tougaloo College. He is also founder and co-director of the Historically Black Colleges and Universities Faculty Development Network. He can be reached at srozman@aol.com.

*Peter Seldin* is Distinguished Professor of Management Emeritus at Pace University. A specialist in the evaluation and development of faculty and administrative performance, he has been a consultant on higher education issues to more than 300 colleges and universities throughout the United States and in 40 countries around the world. His 14 well-received books include, most recently, *The Teaching Portfolio* (Anker, 2004, third edition), *The Administrative Portfolio* (Anker, 2002, with Mary Lou Higgerson), and *Changing Practices in Evaluating Teaching* (Anker, 1999). He has contributed numerous articles on the teaching profession, student ratings, educational practice, and academic culture to such publications as *The New York Times, The Chronicle of Higher Education,* and *Change*. Among recent honors, he was named by the World Bank as a Visiting Scholar to Indonesia. In addition, he was elected a Fellow of the College of Preceptors, London, England. He currently serves as co-director of the International Conference on Improving University Teaching. He can be reached at pseldin@pace.edu.

*G. Roger Sell* is professor and director of the Academic Development Center at Missouri State University. He also has been involved in the initiation of faculty development centers at the University of Northern Iowa and Ohio State University. He is a past president of the Professional and Organizational Development Network in Higher Education. He can be reached at RogerSell@missouristate.edu.

*Thomas C. Sheahan* is an associate professor in the Department of Civil and Environmental Engineering at Northeastern University. He received his M.S. and Sc.D. from Massachusetts Institute of Technology in geotechnical engineering. Since 1997, he has served as undergraduate program director for the department and is the faculty advisor for the department's undergraduate students. He has received teaching awards at the department and college levels and was a member of the GE Master Teachers Team. He is currently the principal investigator for a GE Fund project on quantitative assessment methods for engineering student learning. He is an American Society of Civil Engineers

Fellow and co-editor of the ASTM (American Society for Testing and Materials) *Geotechnical Testing Journal.* He can be reached at t.sheahan@coe.neu.edu.

*Amy Spring* is assistant director for Community-Based Learning at Portland State University, where she facilitates campus-community partnership development and delivers training and technical assistance to faculty, departments, students, and community-based organizations on service-learning pedagogy and other civic engagement strategies. Her research and scholarly interests include student leadership development, assessing service-learning impact, and the scholarship of engagement. She can be reached at springa@pdx.edu.

*Laurel Willingham-McLain* is associate director of the Center for Teaching Excellence at Duquesne University, where she supports faculty and TAs in their teaching and professional development. She provides campus-wide leadership in student-learning assessment and has helped Duquesne implement faculty-led assessment planning. Her current research interests include teaching awards, particularly their intersection with evidence of student learning. She earned a Ph.D. in French linguistics from Indiana University, and as a graduate student she had a special interest in how people learn languages and served as editorial assistant for *Studies in Second Language Acquisition.* She can be reached at willingham@duq.edu.

*James A. Zimmerman* is assistant professor of chemistry and faculty associate to the Academic Development Center at Missouri State University (MSU). He teaches undergraduate and graduate courses in general, nuclear, and physical chemistry. His scholarly agenda consists of experimental nuclear chemistry, integrative learning theory, and more traditional chemistry education research. His professional development activities include participation in the MSU Teaching Fellowship program that supports faculty interested in scholarship of teaching and learning studies, the mentoring of university and college faculty team projects designed to improve science and mathematics education with an emphasis on addressing issues that often discourage women and minorities from pursuing study in the sciences or mathematics, and presenting the National Science Foundation-sponsored Multi-Initiative Dissemination (MID) project curriculum to cohorts of science faculty from a wide range of academic institutions. He can be reached at jaz878f@missouristate.edu.

# Table of Contents

## Section II: Innovations and Outcomes

# Preface

*To Improve the Academy* is the annual publication of POD, the Professional and Organizational Development Network in Higher Education. This growing alliance of professionals promotes excellence in teaching and learning through faculty and organizational development. Members of POD include college and university administrators, faculty developers, instructional technologists, educational consultants, and full- and part-time faculty from all disciplines who are involved in research and teaching. POD members gather for the annual meeting each fall. Some of the chapters in this volume were inspired by presentations or conversations at the November 2004 meeting in Montreal, titled *Culture, Creativity, Community.* More information about POD can be found at podnetwork.org.

The production of *To Improve the Academy, Volume 24* was a yearlong process involving collaboration of ideas, thoughtful writing, submission of manuscripts, peer review, multiple revisions, and careful editing. More than 100 people were involved, and all were volunteers who care about the improvement of teaching and learning. I particularly want to thank Associate Editor Doug Robertson, whose meticulous editing, thoughtful suggestions, and consistent good humor contributed considerably to the quality of this volume. In addition, I want to thank Brianne Clair, my work-study student, for her tireless efforts which made my work on this volume a pleasure. For their thoughtful and timely work, I thank the reviewers: Ron Ayers, Danilo Baylen, Donna Bird, Phyllis Blumberg, Jeanette Clausen, Cynthia Desrochers, Joseph Eng, Becky Glass, Judy Grace, Jace Hargis, Timothy Hickman, Eric Hobson, Wayne Jacobson, Frances Johnson, Kathleen Kingston, Joseph LaLopa, Jean Layne, Alice Macpherson, Vilma Mesa, Johon Noakes, Ed Nuhfer, Leslie Ortquist-Ahrens, Bunny Paine-Clemes, Gary Parnell, Calvin Piston, Nancy Polk, Judy Silvestrone, Kathleen Smith, Margaret Snooks, Lydia Soliel, Karen St. Clair, and Mary Wright. Ultimately, the decisions among many excellent manuscripts regarding inclusion and arrangement were mine.

Carolyn Dumore, of Anker Publishing, was most responsive and helpful with my many questions. And, as always, I am grateful for the good ideas and constant support of my husband, Professor Erich C. Blossey, D. J. and J. M. Cram Chair of Chemistry at Rollins College.

*Sandra Chadwick Blossey*
Rollins College
Winter Park, Florida
April 2005

# Introduction

My primary goal for this volume, as for Volume 23, is to increase the readership of this important publication by selecting high-quality articles of wide appeal to academic administrators, faculty developers, full- and part-time faculty, instructional technologists, educational consultants, and institutional researchers. As in previous volumes of *To Improve the Academy*, many of the chapters were inspired by workshops, presentations, and conversations at the November 2004 national meeting of POD, the Professional and Organizational Network in Higher Education. However, this publication is also well known outside of POD, and there were numerous submissions from authors who are not members. Chapters were accepted on the basis of the reviewers' ratings and comments, as well as their appropriateness to the mission of POD and this publication.

## Contents Overview

Chapter 1. A highlight of the November 2004 POD Conference was the keynote address by James Downey on the conference theme, *Culture, Creativity, and Communication*. Dr. Downey's presentation was so inspiring that there were many requests to publish it. He graciously consented, and although the written form lacks the humor and occasional drama of his delivery, it is an appropriate way to continue the POD conversations through print.

### Section I: Reflections and Propositions

Chapter 2. Raoul A. Arreola directs our attention to a paradigm shift in the basic support for higher education. His impassioned writing offers revolutionary changes for the academy's survival and success.

Chapter 3. Leora Baron provides a systemic and practical approach to the reciprocal relationship between organizational development and faculty development.

Chapter 4. Marc Cutright introduces us to a different way of looking more deeply at strategic planning using chaos theory and metaphors.

Chapter 5. Esteemed consultant George Keller reflects on the changes he has seen in higher education and considers what this means for faculty, programs, and ways of teaching.

Chapter 6. Authenticity is a recently emerging concept in pedagogical literature. Patricia Cranton explains her research project in the light of a developmental continuum for an authentic practice of teaching.

Chapter 7. Chantal S. Levesque, G. Roger Sell, and James A. Zimmerman propose an integrative model for learning and motivation to move students from external regulation to self-determination.

Chapter 8. Phyllis Worthy Dawkins, Andrea L. Beach, and Stephen L. Rozman describe the rich history as well as the accomplishments and challenges of Historically Black Colleges and Universities (HBCUs). The results of their survey of HBCUs are compared with data from POD.

Chapter 9. Linda Hodges completes Section I with a discussion of a deeply personal issue for faculty: fear. She examines how fears such as risk-taking or failure impede pedagogical change and proposes strategies to overcome fear and embrace change.

## Section II: Innovations and Outcomes

Chapter 10. Distinguished professor and consultant Peter Seldin provides the research background and practical suggestions for faculty development activities that are designed for sequential career stages.

Chapter 11. Kevin J. Kecskes, Sherril B. Gelmon, and Amy Spring describe a successful program that encourages faculty participation in civic engagement initiatives by focusing on academic departments. The resulting engaged departments reap multiple rewards.

Chapter 12. Dorothe J. Bach, Marva A. Barnett, José D. Fuentes, and Sherwood C. Frey discuss the Fellows Program at the University of Virginia, which is designed for a diverse beginning faculty. This supportive program promotes intellectual community and professional growth through networks and partnerships.

Chapter 13. Bonnie Mullinix describes a web-facilitated approach for scheduling faculty sessions that meet their needs and interests. This project received the 2003 POD Bright Idea Award, as well as a POD grant in 2004 to expand the project.

Chapter 14. Donna M. Qualters, Thomas C. Sheahan, and Jacqueline A. Isaacs describe the development of an electronically distributed advice column for building a teaching community among instructors of first-year engineering students.

Chapter 15. Veteran workshop leader Barbara J. Millis shares her knowledge and experience by describing planned sequenced assignments and activities that faculty developers can use to connect theory, research, and practice for more effective teaching.

Chapter 16. Patricia Armstrong, Peter Felten, Jeffrey Johnston, and Allison Pingree describe and assess the transformation of their TA orientation program.

Chapter 17. Laurel Willingham-McLain and Deborah Pollack explore best practices from the literature on teaching awards and describe how they modified such practices to create the Duquesne University Graduate Student Award for Teaching Excellence.

Chapter 18. Chris Carlson-Dakes and Alice Pawley outline a low-risk, low-cost, high-impact professional development program they call expeditionary learning.

Chapter 19. Harriet Fayne and Leslie Ortquist-Ahrens piloted a yearlong learning community program for first-year faculty. Their case study tracks the developmental path leading to a focus on student learning.

Chapter 20. Helen M. Clarke and Philip E. Bishop describe their work in faculty development and institutional change. Their model describes a program with direct impact on faculty careers, student learning outcomes, and institutional transformation.

# 1

# An Adventure on POD's High Cs: Culture, Creativity, and Communication in the Academy: A Humanist Perspective

Keynote address given at the November 2004 POD Conference in Montreal, Quebec.

James Downey
University of Waterloo

First, let me say how honored I feel to have been invited to give a keynote address at this conference. I admire POD (Professional and Organizational Development Network in Higher Education) and believe the work its members do in faculty development and the enhancement of teaching and learning is vital to the ability of our universities to meet the challenge of contemporary society and, even more important, to fulfill our timeless purpose of educating men and women into better, fuller, and more satisfying lives.

When it comes to speeches, university presidents have a reputation to live down to. I assume, however, that if the organizers of this conference had wished a dog and pony show they would have invited an animal trainer, not an ink-stained humanist who has spent nearly all his adult life dispensing words, first as an academic, then as an administrator. And I emphasize the two modes. For, to paraphrase Saint Paul: When I was an academic I spake as an academic, I thought as an academic, I understood as an academic. But when I became an administrator I put away academic things. Now I see through a glass darkly and speak only in generalities.

*Culture, communication, and creativity:* Just to say it kind of sucks all the air out of the room. The primary colors of meaning have run so badly in all

*1*

these nouns that each has become a semantic Rorschach. Most thinking people prefer to avoid them.

Take *culture,* for example. *The Closing of the American Mind* by Allan Bloom (1987) was, you will painfully recall, a requiem for the academy. Compared to the high ideals of Plato's Lyceum, the modern university was a world of fallen arches. Rubble had accumulated at the mouth of the cave inhabited by self-serving professors and time-serving students. The culture of the academy had been corrupted. The word *culture* itself, he said, had become part of "empty talk, its original imprecision now carried to the point of pathology."

> Anthropologists can't define it although they are sure there is such a thing. Artists have no vision of the sublime, but they know culture (i.e., what they do) has a right to the honor and support of civil society. Sociologists and the disseminators of their views, the journalists of all descriptions, call everything a culture—the drug culture, the rock culture, the street gang culture, and so on endlessly and without discrimination. (p. 184)

*Creativity,* according to Bloom, has fared no better. The concept has been trivialized by indiscriminate application: "[A word] meant to describe and encourage Beethoven and Goethe [is] now applied to every school child. It is in the nature of democracy to deny no one access to good things" (p. 183). "Thus," Bloom concludes of the use of both culture and creativity, "what was intended as an elevation of taste and morality has become grist for our mill while sapping the mill's foundation" (pp. 183–184). I can only conclude that Professor Bloom is spinning like a top in his grave as we open this conference.

Whatever one might think of the thesis of Bloom's famous book, it is hard not to grant his point about the leaching of meaning out of these two ubiquitous words, *culture* and *creativity.* (What he might have said about communication, had he thought to anatomize it, is not hard to imagine.) Others, who do not share Bloom's opinion of the academy, have agreed with him. Stephen Greenblatt (2004), author of a splendid new book on Shakespeare, said that culture "is a term that is repeatedly used without meaning much of anything at all, a vague gesture toward a dimly perceived ethos" (p. 225).

And yet, and yet, we cannot avoid using those words. In fact, truth to tell, we love 'em. We love their elasticity, their malleability. We love the way they expand and contract to accommodate whatever cargo we want them to carry. Perhaps it's too late to try to impose any kind of lexical discipline on them, but it does seem necessary, at the beginning of a conference that has chosen these words for its title, that we should reflect on their provenance.

Culture and creativity, as secular concepts at least, have their origins in ideals of human freedom and potential forged during the Enlightenment. Both words speak to a humanistic transcendence in human intelligence and character, religious transcendence having given rise to too many blood feuds in the not-too-distant past. Both words were intended to elevate human accomplishment and self-esteem: the one collectively, the other individually. Together they represented both the means of production and the finest finished products of the human mind: "The best that is known and thought in the world" (p. 17), as Matthew Arnold (1865) would put it in his *Essays in Criticism* a century later.

But a caveat. In one sense culture and creativity are products of Enlightenment philosophy; in another, they were a protest against it. A product, because they grow out of a more optimistic view of humans and what they can achieve both individually and collectively. A protest, because together they helped to counterbalance the intellectual hegemony of materialistic, deterministic science which, for all the technological progress it made possible, seemed to strip humans of their claims to uniqueness and freedom. The twin concepts of culture and creativity were an affirmation that people were beings of nurture, not just creatures of nature. And on this there was a multilingual and multinational consensus: Rousseau and Voltaire, Locke and Hume, Paine and Jefferson, not to mention the man who likely coined the word *culture*, Immanuel Kant, all contributed to the ideas of progress and freedom and the right to dissent—in other words, of individual and collective agency and responsibility—on which modern democratic society was built.

And with it the modern university, for the university as we have inherited it is also a creature of the Enlightenment, and the academy's broad aims are entirely resonant with Enlightenment ideals. As the unofficial poet laureate of American higher education, Bart Giamatti (1990), once put it:

> The university is something made, not born, cradling those individual acts of shaping that it figures forth. It is our culture's assertion that what is made by the mind has value and can convey values. Thus the university, rooted in history, open to every new impulse, insists on its centrality to culture and on its uniqueness. Thus it is so powerful and so fragile, the foe of the merely random, insisting on order while urging freedom, convinced that the human mind, out of nature, can fashion shapes and patterns nature never bore, and convinced that it is prime among the artifacts. (p. 49)

To the extent that culture and creativity speak to the primacy of the acquired over the natural, they speak to the essence of the university as it has developed in the years since the Enlightenment. In fact, I would argue that it is those twin concepts, culture and creativity, that, when properly understood, provide us with our most unique and important *raison d'etre*.

"When properly understood" includes their relation to the primary instrument of both culture and creativity: language—which also happens to be the primary instrument of communication. Let's look at our triumvirate of high Cs in reverse order, perhaps the better to understand how together they define what is most essential and inspiring in what we do.

## Communication

Communication may have other connotations but it begins and ends with language. The study of language is in the first instance, and above all, a quest to understand what is most definingly human, that which sets us most distinctively apart from the rest of animal nature. To study language and its products, therefore, is to explore the complexity and diversity of our minds and emotions. What is the relation between language and culture? Between language and ethnicity? Between language and creativity? Between language and religious experience? Between language and critical judgment? Between language and feeling? What does it mean, since we're in Quebec, to speak of linguistic rights? To what extent does the language we speak and write condition perception and shape experience? What are syntactic and grammatical structures and how are they learned? Under what social and political conditions does language become debased, and what is the consequence of that debasement? How can words be combined to produce aesthetic pleasure? Why do words wound? How can words heal?

Such questions are of interest not just to professional humanists but also to all who teach, learn, or work in universities. We sometimes hear language referred to as a vehicle of communication. And it is that, of course. But it's much more. It is the primary means for discovering what we think and feel. The relationship of language to thought is not that of dress to body but of body to soul.

A humanistic interest in language goes beyond the attempt to understand how it works, to a concern for the way in which it is used. To think and speak and write clearly are important to self-expression; they are also the precondition of effective citizenship in a democratic society. They are as well, and increasingly, important to career success in a knowledge economy. Facility with language is to some degree a gift, but it is also an art that can be taught, learned, and cultivated.

I am not one of those who believes that there has been some recent fall from grace in the quality of writing and speaking of the young, but I know there are forces at work—some social, some technological, some pedagogical—that militate against clear, direct, and effective writing and speaking. This is as true in our universities as in society at large. Some of it is manifest in what Richard Dawkins (2003), in *A Devil's Chaplain,* has called "metatwaddle," the process by which an academic subject expands to fill the vacuum of its intrinsic simplicity. He explains:

> Physics is a genuinely difficult and profound subject, so physicists need to—and do—work hard to make their language as simple as possible. . . . Other academics . . . want to be thought profound, but their subject is rather easy and shallow, so they have to language it up to redress the balance. (p. 51)

This may not be the whole truth; there is, however, an embarrassing measure of truth in it.

But it's not just the obscurantism of academics; it's the prophylactic prose that is the warp and weft of bureaucracies everywhere, prose that is designed to prevent meaning from seeping through. As I say, bureaucratic prudence, in universities as much as anywhere, fosters reliance on such language, but let there be no mistake about it, it has a debilitating effect on culture and community alike. The stream of our public discourse is often eloquent without being articulate, a muddy trickle of clichés and half-truths. Many in our society make a handsome living by manipulating and distorting language. Universities have a special responsibility for ensuring the wellsprings of language and communication are purified by disciplined study and disciplined usage.

## Creativity

It is expected of universities that they should celebrate the great works of human creativity in all their multifarious originality. For Professor Northrop Frye (1988), the purpose of education is the training of the imagination so that we can create out of the world we live in a picture of the world we wish to live in. Frye wasn't, of course, talking about some minor pictive or fictive faculty of the human mind, but about the power we all possess to go beyond the constraints of our lives and work and envision a better society, a better world.

> Every person with any function in society at all will have some kind of ideal vision of that society in the light of which he operates. One

> can hardly imagine a social worker going out to do case work with-
> out thinking of her as having, somewhere in her mind, a vision of a
> better, cleaner, healthier, more emotionally balanced city, as a kind of
> mental model inspiring the work she does. One can hardly imagine
> in fact any professional person not having such a social model—a
> world of health for the doctor or of justice for the judge—nor would
> such a social vision be confined to the professions.
>
> It seems to me in fact that a Utopia should be conceived, not as an
> impossible dream of an impossible ideal, but as the kind of working
> model of society that exists somewhere in the mind of every sane
> person who has any social function at all. (p. 70)

Is this a fantasy world, a gauzy abstraction? On the contrary, I believe, with
Frye, that it is the real world, the only abiding, dependable world. Consider
the so-called real world for a moment. I was born just at the outbreak of
World War II. Here, as described by Frye, is how it was then:

> Japan was a totalitarian enemy and China was a bourgeois friend, the
> King of England was Emperor of India, Nazi Germany ruled the most
> powerful empire the world has ever seen. . . . When we look back on
> that world we realize that what we are living in, the world of current
> events and news, is actually a kind of phantasmagoria. (p. 93)

Contrary to the usual notion, the real world is the one created by education,
and thus "it is not the relation of education to the world that matters, it is the
relation of the world to education" (p. 95).

I believe, with Frye, that it is the empowering of this idealism that is the
overarching purpose of our universities. But, to repeat and reinforce the
point, the end of such study of the works of human creativity is not to stand
in awe of the genius of a few great people, but to help educate our own and
our students' minds so that we and they are less gullible, less susceptible to
slick and facile assumptions and beliefs; to build standards of judgment and
taste by which to measure our society and culture; to render our students and
ourselves more our own men and women, less vulnerable to political and
commercial hucksterism, less comfortable with clichés and cant, more alive to
life's possibilities for achievement and service.

Does all this sound utopian? I would hope so. After the kind of dystopian
century we have recently exited, and given the way we have begun a new one, we
are not in danger of overdosing on optimism anytime soon. Utopias of course
do not exist. That's the point of them. They are not strategic plans for political
implementation, but expressions of unreal possibility, meant to stir hope and

spur action, rude intrusions of creativity and ideals into human thought and affairs. Our universities should be rain forests for the growth of utopian dreams, providing the culture, the context, the communication, the connectivity, and the creativity to build the society and world we want to live in.

## Culture

All human societies exist within an envelope of culture—of social, legal, and religious practices that, for the most part, are distilled into words. Culture has many expressions but our common understanding of the term takes three forms. There is culture as lifestyle, the way people dress or prepare food or dance. It will not take you long in Montreal to observe that a distinctive culture in that sense is alive and well in Quebec. Then there is culture as a common heritage of historical memories and customs shared through a common language. There are varying translations of the inscription you will see on Quebec license plates, *je me souviens* (I remember), but its deepest resonance is with culture in this second sense. Finally, there is culture as the form of what is genuinely created by a society in its literature, its art, its music, its science, its architecture, its engineering. While universities should and do provide for the study of the first two kinds of culture, it is the advancing of this third kind that lies at the heart of the university's purpose.

At the center of culture in this sense is a concern for how people live, the purposes and standards they set for themselves, the qualities and values to which they attach significance, and the principles by which they have sought and seek to give meaning to their lives and order to their communities. The mode and mood of inquiry are interrogative. Whence arise our notions of good and evil, right and wrong? By what criteria should we evaluate systems of thought, courses of action, methods of governing, works of art, each other? What other value systems and symbols have evolved in other times and places, and how may a knowledge of them clarify and enrich our own? What do we need to know and to do—in this time, in this place—to live ethically and to exercise our full rights and responsibilities in our private and public lives?

There's a story that, if apocryphal, still bears repeating. Sometime in the 1930s Albert Einstein was giving an examination to some of his Ph.D. students. As he was passing out the tests, his assistant pulled him aside to inform him that a terrible mistake had been made. It appeared that Einstein was passing out the same test he had given them once before. "That's all right," he said and smiled. "The questions may be the same, but the answers have all changed." The answers to scientific questions do indeed change, and sometimes very fast. In some other spheres of human endeavor the concept of progress does not apply in the same way, but there too it is essential to ask the timeless and telling questions, refining and rephrasing them to fit our current preoccupations and the state of knowledge we have arrived at.

The primary mission of the university, I believe, is not to train (though training is essential to all learning) but also to educate; not to prepare students for jobs (though that in itself is noble) but to make them wiser and more discerning people. And this is true for all students, even those learning the technical and mental skills of a profession. I like the way Cyril Belshaw (1974) put it in *Towers Besieged:*

> A university is only justified in giving a medical or engineering, or any other, degree, if in the process the doctor or engineer has learned to question and inquire, to exercise relevant intellectual and moral judgment, and to add to knowledge if the opportunity and circumstances of his [or her] career permit. This means that the university has helped to develop [a student's] powers of intellectual awareness, . . . to know what is needed to provide answers (as distinct from jumping to conclusions or accepting what one is told); and to be mature, disciplined and wise in making judgments. (p. 22)

A bit idealistic no doubt. But "without a vision the people perish." And certainly, without a sense of its higher purpose the university loses what most makes it unique among our social institutions.

In Alistair Cooke's (1952) *One Man's America,* there is a story that seems appropriate here. On the 19th of May, 1780, in Hartford, Connecticut, the skies at noon turned from blue to gray and by mid-afternoon had blackened over so densely that, in that more religious age, people fell on their knees and begged a final blessing before the end came. The Connecticut House of Representatives was in session, and as some of the delegates fell down in the darkened chamber and others clamored for an immediate adjournment, the speaker of the house, one Colonel Davenport, came to his feet. He silenced the din with these words: "The Day of Judgment is either approaching—or it is not. If it is not, there is no cause for adjournment. If it is, I choose to be found doing my duty. I wish, therefore, that candles may be brought."

What our universities need most of all at the moment—more than we need new facilities or larger appropriations or better performance indicators or even, God forgive me for saying so in this company, better faculty development programs, important as all of these are—are more enthusiastic and dedicated candle-bringers: people who believe with conviction in human agency, who believe we are not trapped in systems of thought or feeling or governance which we cannot change, who believe that ideals of justice and equality—and their affiliates, liberty and learning—still resonate with people all over the world. The change and the excellence we seek will not come about by grand design but through the countless daily acts of people who can look beyond the university's utilitarian function to catch a glimpse of its deeper culture and higher possibilities.

So what if those who learn, teach, research, and serve in the university too frequently fall short of the standards implicit in that deeper culture? A Montrealer, Leonard Cohen (1993), had the best answer to that: "Ring the bells that still can ring, / Forget your perfect offering. / There is a crack in everything, / That's how the light gets in" (p. 373).

Our sustained fascination with Leonard Cohen (at 70 he is having yet another renaissance) is evidence that culture may be mediated not only by the arguments we make, but by the songs we sing and the stories we tell. In the fall 2002 issue of *The Presidency,* Robert Birnbaum said that the challenge of universities in our time is not to argue a better case but to tell a better story. Stories compete with stories in the marketplace of narratives. And there is no shortage of competing narratives about the role of the contemporary university. Some portray an institution standing in very much the same relationship to its users as banks, supermarkets, and utility companies do to theirs, providing convenient, dependable, and quality service. Some tell of an institution that is already past its best-before date and will largely disappear within the next generation. They are simplistic narratives, but nonetheless effective for that. They may or may not be true, but they resonate widely.

Birnbaum cautions, "you cannot dispel a narrative merely by criticizing it or presenting logical arguments against it. A narrative can be displaced only by another narrative that is as easy to understand and tells a better story" (p. 38). Where do we get better, more compelling narratives? Birnbaum suggests we start with the past.

> Our narratives once told of education for democracy, for social justice, for the whole person, for the perpetuation of civilization. That is what people came to believe colleges and universities did.... Our narratives now increasingly talk about being the engines of the economy. We are, of course, but I don't believe that a utilitarian narrative alone excites the imagination of the public, or commits faculty, staff, or administrators to their institution and its success, or connects the university to our deepest human needs. (pp. 37–38)

As I was writing this address it was announced that Wangari Maathi, African environmentalist and women's rights crusader, was the 2004 winner of the Nobel Peace Prize. I quote from an account printed in the *Globe and Mail* on October 9, 2004: "Mrs. Maathi's husband, a politician, divorced her in the 1980s on the grounds that she was 'too educated, too strong, too successful, too stubborn and too hard to control.'" Let me repeat that: "too educated, too strong, too successful, too stubborn and too hard to control." What a narrative is inherent in that!

Listen again to Northrop Frye (1969):

> But it seems to me that the university is a kind of Moses, who comes to people stuck in Egypt, trying to make bricks without straw, and says to them: "I think I can get you out of this, if you have the intelligence and persistence to go with me. It's a long and dusty walk, one step after another: it will take forty years and you will often lose your way. I can take you to the boundary of a better country. It belongs to you; it's your home; all you have to do is enter and take possession. But I will not go with you, because I have to go back to Egypt for more slaves. (p. 67)

O, to be able to catch a glimpse of that profoundly liberational and celebrational vision from time to time, to feel that *this* is the cause of which we are a part, this is the culture we are creating; this is the narrative we are asked to communicate; to sense our pulses quickened and our spirits lifted by the realization that all around us fresh insights are being discovered, minds illumined, and lives liberated by the knowledge and skills being imparted, by people like us.

## References

Arnold, M. (1865). The function of criticism at the present time. In *Essays in criticism* (pp. 1–41). London, England: Macmillan.

Belshaw, C. S. (1974). *Towers besieged: The dilemma of the creative university.* Toronto, Canada: McClelland and Stewart.

Birnbaum, R. (2002, Fall). The president as storyteller: Restoring the narrative of higher education. *The presidency*, 33–39.

Bloom, A. (1987). *The closing of the American mind.* New York, NY: Simon & Schuster.

Cohen, L. (1993). Anthem. In *Stranger music: Selected poems and songs* (pp. 373–374). Toronto, Canada: McClelland and Stewart.

Cooke, A. (1952). *One man's America.* New York, NY: Alfred A. Knopf.

Dawkins, R. (2003). *A devil's chaplain: Reflections on hope, lies, science, and love.* New York, NY: Houghton Mifflin.

Frye, N. (1969). *The ethics of change.* Toronto, Canada: Canadian Broadcasting Corporation.

Frye, N. (1988). *On education.* Toronto, Canada: Fitzhenry & Whiteside.

Giamatti, A. B. (1990). *A free and ordered space: The real world of the university.* New York, NY: W. W. Norton & Company.

Greenblatt, S. (2004). *Will in the world: How Shakespeare became Shakespeare.* New York, NY: W. W. Norton & Company.

# Section I

# Reflections and Propositions

# 2

# Monster at the Foot of the Bed: Surviving the Challenge of Marketplace Forces on Higher Education

Raoul A. Arreola
University of Tennessee Health Science Center

*The impact of technology on society has caused a paradigm shift in the basic support for higher education. Where higher education was traditionally supported as a function of government, the knowledge explosion and global economy resulting from the impact of computer and other technologies is moving the underlying support of higher education to the marketplace. There is evidence that traditional academic strategies and practices that were successful under the old paradigm may no longer be working. Twelve suggestions are offered for revolutionary changes that the academy must make in order to survive, even thrive, in the new paradigm.*

## Introduction

At the 2004 annual POD (Professional and Organizational Development Network in Higher Education) meeting held in Montreal, I had the privilege and great pleasure of participating in a session dealing with the question of whether students were customers of higher education. The session, structured as a mock trial before a panel of "supreme court justices," gave participants the opportunity to testify and argue for one side or the other. I was fortunate to be selected to serve as one of the judges. The deliberations among the judges and the participants led to a tentative conclusion that society as a whole was the customer of higher education, and, as members of society, students were part of that customer base.

What was especially fascinating, however, was the aspect of the discussion that considered higher education as a part of the larger economic engine of American society. This perspective on higher education is one that has been of particular interest to me during the last few years since my university, like many others across the nation, continues to experience annual declines in its state budget. When one examines higher education as a social enterprise within the larger context of the American culture and economy of the 21st century, it is clear that the academy is experiencing a significant shift in the paradigm within which it must operate.

## Monster Under the Bed

In 1994, two businessmen, Stan Davis and Jim Botkin, authored a particularly prescient book entitled *The Monster Under the Bed: How Business Is Mastering the Opportunity of Knowledge for Profit*. The "monster" under the bed was seen as the paradigm shift being brought about by the impact of technology on all segments of American society—especially education. While chronicling the various social, political, economic, and religious forces that impact education, the authors make one major point that is of particular interest here, namely, that education, as a social enterprise, has historically been supported by different segments of society and that a shift in that support is once again occurring—perhaps to the academy's detriment.

> Through successive periods of history, different institutions have borne the major responsibility for education. Changes in education take a very long time to evolve. They are a consequence of greater transformations, often social, political, economic, or religious, and therefore are always a few steps behind the demands of the society they are designed to serve. But today schools are more than a few steps behind, and many feel they are on the wrong path altogether. (Davis & Botkin, 1994, p. 23)

Davis and Botkin point out that from an historical perspective, organized educational efforts originated as a function of the church. Later, especially in America, the responsibility for supporting education moved to the government (when an educated populace was seen as necessary for the successful functioning of a free, democratic society). Now, with the ubiquity of the computer, the Internet, and the resultant knowledge explosion and global economy, the underlying support for education is moving from the government to the marketplace. The social paradigm under which higher education has successfully functioned, and been supported for generations, is undergoing a significant change. In short, I believe the monster has moved out from under the bed, yanked off the covers, and is gnawing at the academy's vitals.

## The Monster

The term *paradigm shift* was defined and popularized by Thomas Kuhn (1970) in his seminal work *The Structure of Scientific Revolution*. Kuhn defined a paradigm shift as a "series of peaceful interludes punctuated by intellectually violent revolutions . . . [where] one conceptual world view is replaced by another" (p. 10). The literature on paradigm shifts suggests that an enterprise often must lose a considerable amount of its resources before it realizes that the shift has occurred. In addition, as an enterprise begins to feel the pain of losing resources, it frequently *increases* those activities that brought it success in the past. By the very fact of the shift in paradigm, however, those activities are precisely the ones most likely to contribute to the enterprise's decline and demise under the new paradigm.

There is little doubt that higher education as a social enterprise is experiencing a loss of resources. During the 2004 calendar year, the *Chronicle of Higher Education* published numerous accounts of state budget cuts to higher education. In some instances colleges merged together to remain economically viable; in others, colleges were reported to simply have declared bankruptcy and closed down. More recently, colleges have been encouraged to privatize so as to tap into commercial resources (Mangan, 2005; Schmidt, 2003). Predictably, the higher education enterprise has doubled and redoubled those activities that, under the old paradigm, brought great success, namely, intensifying development (fundraising) efforts and pushing faculty to bring in more research grant money.

> Although the major goal of the U.S. universities is the advancement and dissemination of knowledge, universities also need funding to support their activities. A university must seek revenue from a variety of sources and more and more, faculty members are encouraged to generate income. (Howard Hughes Medical Institute, 2004, p. 27)

The response of intensifying development programs clearly indicates that colleges and universities have internalized their status as professional begging institutions. However, the new market-driven paradigm is moving the money elsewhere—witness the recent government evisceration of the

Fund for the Improvement of Post Secondary Education (FIPSE), and the changes in the federal formula that reduces student aid (Burd, 2005; Field, 2005; Selingo, 2003).

What is going on here? Just as the invention of the printing press created a paradigm shift that precipitated the move of support for higher education from the church to government, the advent of the Internet, the global economy, and the emergence of knowledge businesses (i.e., corporate universities, commercial online universities, etc.) is shifting the support base of higher education from the government to the marketplace (maybe students *are* the customers). This means that colleges and universities must compete not only with one another, but also with other, non-educational societal interests and priorities. In short, the rules under which higher education has successfully operated for so long have changed and, if the academy is to continue to thrive—indeed if it is to survive as we have known it—it must adapt to the new rules.

I don't presume to be an expert on the paradigm shift phenomenon, the complexity of the full impact of computer technology on society, or even on all the operational aspects of colleges and universities. However, as an active participant in the higher education enterprise for the last 35 years, I would like to offer a few observations relative to the pains or losses the Academy is experiencing under the new paradigm—a look into the jaws of the monster, as it were.

## The Jaws of the Monster

In August 2000, the Council for Higher Education Accreditation, the umbrella organization for higher education accrediting agencies, issued an occasional paper prepared by the National Center for Higher Education Management Systems titled *The Competency Standards Project: Another Approach to Accreditation Review*. This paper was one of those "intellectually violent events" Kuhn (1970) described that serve to define a paradigm shift. At its most fundamental level, this report proposed shifting the accreditation process from one of evaluating processes to one of evaluating outcomes. The question asked of higher education was about to change from "What resources do you have and what are you doing with them?" to "How much have your students learned and what can they actually do as a result of the experience you gave them?" Institutions that have just completed or are currently undergoing an accreditation review are intensely familiar with the pain and cost resulting from this element of the paradigm shift. The shift was so enormous it cannot be overstated—it essentially redefined what society specifically expects of the professoriate—it rewrote the social contract between the academy and society, between the professor and the student.

Under the old paradigm, the academy was expected to serve a "filtering" function. A personal case in point: on my first day as a freshman at Arizona State University in 1961, I and all the other freshmen were brought into a large auditorium to listen to a speech from the dean. The speech ended with the dean saying, "Look to your left, look to your right, one of you won't be here next semester." I, like everyone else at the time, took this to be an expression of the quality and rigor of the institution and felt a sense of pride and confidence, sure that I would be one of the survivors.

What the dean was conveying to us was the essence of the contract the academy had with society: It was expected to sort students into various levels—from the ablest to the least able. From this paradigm comes the tradition of grading on the curve. Each faculty member, in each course, each year, would flunk a certain percentage of students, so that by the senior year, the students that were left were the "survivors." That is, they constituted that segment of the population that could learn no matter what obstacles and challenges were put before them. A college graduate, then, was known by society to be the best and the brightest that could be produced. College graduates were valued and, mostly, paid appropriately.

This type of filtering contract even extended down into high school where students were sorted, on the basis of standardized tests, into one of three tracks: the college preparatory track, the general education track, or the vocational education track (students were responsible for their own self-esteem in those days). The college prep students were those destined to go to college (although not necessarily survive); the general education track students would go to work upon graduation (they could go to college if they wanted but were not expected to survive); and the vocational education track students became electricians, mechanics, plumbers, secretaries, and so on. It was a matter of common knowledge, as well as some research, that college graduates would make a lot more money during their lifetime than those that did not finish or never went to college. However, a sure sign that the paradigm was beginning to shift was when more and more millionaires started emerging from the vocational education track. Of course, Bill Gates, the richest man in the world (as of this writing), is a college dropout.

The new paradigm moves the academy from a filtering function to, ironically, a true instructional/teaching function. That is, instead of sorting the bright from the not-so-bright, the talented from the not-so-talented, the persistent from the not-so-persistent, society is now demanding that the academy accept virtually anyone who comes in the door and take them from whatever level of ignorance and ability they possess upon entrance up to some *specified level* of *employable competence*. Moreover, society is expecting the academy to do this in a timely and cost-effective manner (evidence of the corporate just-in-time-training influence).

Under the old paradigm, scholarship was the sine qua non of the professoriate's activities and responsibilities. Within this paradigm, research was the most highly valued activity. However, as the new paradigm began to take hold, the demand for accountability in teaching grew. Valuing teaching under the traditions and beliefs of the old paradigm proved to be extraordinarily difficult. Even given the Herculean intellectual and philosophical efforts of Ernest Boyer (1990) to raise the value of teaching up to that of research by defining scholarship as including teaching, research has remained the most valued professional activity among the professoriate because it can generate money. Research has been highly valued because, under the old paradigm, it produced both increased funds for the institution and increased prestige for the institution and the scholar. In short, it made both the institution and the scholar appear worthy of societal support.

In Boyer's work, under the old paradigm, the presumption is made that teaching is an extension of research (scholarship). Under the new paradigm, teaching is seen as a separate, high-level profession in and of itself, requiring not only the content expertise of the traditional scholar, but expertise in instructional design, instructional delivery (including the use of computer and communication technology), and instructional assessment (Arreola, Aleamoni, & Theall, 2001; Arreola, Theall, & Aleamoni, 2003). Those institutions in the knowledge business, such as Phoenix University and the various corporate universities, recognize this new paradigm and use teams of individuals with these different areas of expertise to produce and deliver their instructional experiences. However, as the professoriate persists in those activities and traditions that made the academy successful under the old paradigm, certain losses are beginning to be felt across higher education. The academy is beginning to feel the monster's fangs.

## The Monster's Fangs

One of the more visible signs of the effect of the paradigm shift is what might be called the Rodney Dangerfield Effect. That is, the professoriate, traditionally treated as elite members of society, has lost much of the respect it enjoyed in years past. Part of the reason for this, I believe, is the easy access to information provided by technology, especially the Internet.

When information was difficult to come by, the college professor, as a guardian and producer of knowledge, as a pedagogical priest, was valued and perhaps even revered. Under the old paradigm the teacher/scholar was the center of the teaching/learning universe. The teacher/scholar conducted the research to discover or develop new knowledge and shared that knowledge with those who were willing and able to learn.

Ironically, over the last decade or so we in academe have given much lip service to the concept of a student-centered learning experience. We have conducted research, designed new teaching strategies, developed new methods and materials, and published politically correct articles about the need for a learning community and putting the student at the center of the teaching/learning experience. Throughout all this discussion, however, somehow the teacher/scholar remains as the central mover or actor or core, because of our inability to escape from the ways of thinking that have been rewarded under the old paradigm.

More and more, however, I have started to come across faculty who have had the experience of a student in class citing more recent information (found on the Internet before class) than what the professor was presenting, thus making the professor appear (perhaps correctly) to be less informed than the student. Under the new paradigm we finally have what we wished for—a true student-centered learning environment. Thanks to the Internet, instant messaging, camera phones, satellite phones, and CNN, the learner sits at the center of an information-rich environment in which the college professor is only one of many different sources of information. We may argue about the validity, reliability, and accuracy of that information, or even bring up that old chestnut about the difference between information, knowledge, and wisdom, but the point is that the teacher/scholar, or even the traditional library, is no longer the only game in town insofar as the student/learner is concerned. With this shift in the teaching/learning paradigm has come a decline in society's respect for the professoriate.

## The Post-Tenure Review Phenomenon

Another element of pain being felt within the academy is the move to post-tenure review. Under the old paradigm, tenured faculty were considered the core of the academy—those senior, seasoned paragons of the pedagogical priesthood—upon which the success and reputation of the institution depended. Tenure, originally intended to protect faculty from being punished for teaching a "truth" that contradicted church doctrine or popular societal beliefs, became, in the government-supported paradigm (and the resultant litigiously oriented society), essentially a lifetime guarantee of employment regardless of the quality of performance.

Under the new marketplace paradigm, tenured faculty are seen as an economic albatross hung around the budgetary neck of the educational institution. More and more colleges and universities are moving toward the use of part-time, adjunct, and limited-contract faculty. In fact, I have seen some institutions where more than 80% of the entire curriculum was taught by part-time or adjunct faculty. The increased use of nontenure earning faculty positions, along with the growth of the post-tenure review phenomenon would appear to signal the decline, if not the demise, of tenure. In the new, outcomes-oriented, market-driven paradigm there appears to be no place for tenure.

## Devaluation of the College Degree

Under the old paradigm the amount of information available on any subject was assumed to grow very slowly. So, curricula were developed based on a fixed period of time to learn a relatively fixed amount of information. A bachelor's degree in virtually any field was expected to be completed in four years (with summers off so students could work in the fields to help plant and bring in the harvest). Under the old paradigm students taking longer than four years to complete a degree were traditionally seen as evidence of some sort of problem or failure.

In today's paradigm the amount of information in virtually every field is growing exponentially. Yet our degree programs (with a few exceptions) continue to be designed essentially as fixed-time experiences. Faculty, concerned about trying to get the latest research information into their fixed number of courses, are assigning more readings, moving more quickly through dense PowerPoint slides, and generally trying to cover more material in the time allotted—all the while agonizing over the fear that their student ratings will be lowered if they make their courses too hard. Students, on the other hand, are reporting greater stress because of the content-overloaded courses, and some are increasingly responding with the psychologically predictable response of cheating.

The academy is responding slowly by adding new layers of degrees. In some fields where a bachelor's degree was considered an appropriate entry-level degree into a profession, it has now moved to the master's degree. In other areas, where a master's degree was sufficient for certification, now a doctoral degree is required. Ironically, the effect of this has been a certain devaluing of the college degree. A bachelor's degree is now often considered in the same way that a high school diploma used to be considered.

Even though certain fields have added layers of degrees to try to accommodate the knowledge explosion, within higher education we generally continue with the fixed-time-variable-learning format. We often simply push more and more information into the time allotted, easing up on our grading standards so we don't have the majority of students failing. This is especially serious in the sciences since there is a veritable tsunami of new research information coming out every year that faculty must try to fit into their courses—and students must try to learn and master. For example, in the medical school on my campus it is common to hear among both faculty and students the expression "by the time you graduate half of everything you know will be wrong." This is not so much an assessment of the quality of teaching, but simply a recognition of the exponential growth in information within the biomedical and health sciences.

Our curricular designs have persisted in the tradition of keeping time constant and letting the amount of learning vary. However, the demands of the new paradigm require that time be flexible and that the amount of learning meet a specific level. On more than one occasion I have heard a president or vice president of a college or university publicly state that they are no longer interested in equality of opportunity but, rather, equality of outcome. If a student is admitted to an institution of higher learning there is an obligation, growing pressure, for that institution to award them a degree. However, since the academy's tradition is to hold time constant and allow the amount of learning to vary, the only way it can meet this obligation is to lower the standards for degrees. We can see evidence of this in the phenomenon of grade inflation and, in some cases, the systematic reduction of the number of hours required to get a degree. All this, of course, contributes to the social devaluing of the college degree and the consequent devaluing of the entire higher education enterprise as a function society is willing to support with public monies.

## Emergence of Survival Learners

The impact of technology on everyday life has had an interesting consequence on the knowledge business and has produced a whole new cadre of what might be called survival learners. That is, people who need to learn specific information or acquire a specific skill to get ahead in their job or even to remain employed.

When I was a young boy I had an uncle who had only a third grade education but worked as a "shade tree mechanic" repairing cars in his backyard. This work enabled him to own his own (small) house and support my aunt and cousin. The automotive technology of the time was of such a nature that it was possible for a relatively uneducated person to learn how to repair and maintain an automobile. Today's automotive technology is so complex that it requires highly specialized training to use the sophisticated computerized equipment involved in an automobile's repair and maintenance. Thus, during my lifetime the knowledge necessary to maintain the technology that moves people in a motorized carriage from point A to point B has grown to the point that some form of advanced education and skill is needed to maintain it. Interestingly, the same phenomenon is impacting virtually every aspect of the work world—from ditch digger to secretary to physician to college professor.

This phenomenon has resulted in a whole new spectrum of learners that might be called survival learners. That is, individuals who are not particularly interested in getting a degree but instead, have a very short time to learn a specific body of knowledge or gain a specific skill in order to simply hold on to their job. Traditionally, higher education has dealt with that relatively small percentage of the population (18–21 year olds) who had the time to spend in a diffused or semi-focused learning/maturation experience. However, with an aging populace and the impact of technology on employability, there has emerged a large body of learners which, by and large, the academy is ignoring but from which marketplace-oriented institutions (i.e., Phoenix University, DeVry Institute, etc.) are profiting. Of course, many public community and technical colleges are much more attuned to this growing segment of the learning population and are, accordingly, tapping into the resultant financial benefits. They are learning to ride the monster.

## Riding the Monster

As noted earlier, Thomas Kuhn (1970) defined a paradigm shift as a "series of peaceful interludes punctuated by intellectually violent revolutions ... [where] one conceptual world view is replaced by another" (p. 10). It is clear that the academy is no longer in a "peaceful interlude" and that certain "intellectually violent revolutions" are taking place. To succeed and thrive in the new paradigm brought about by these revolutions, I offer the following list of equally revolutionary (and, I'm sure some would consider academically blasphemous) changes that the academy must undertake if it is to survive and thrive under the new paradigm. I do not defend these suggestions here (that is for another time) but simply offer them as the conclusions I have drawn based on the elements of the paradigm shift just described.

- Abolish the practice of hiring into significant academic administrative positions (department chair and above) those individuals whose primary accomplishment is research and the obtaining of research grants. It is important to recognize that the successful administration of a large, complex multimillion-dollar enterprise requires professional-level skills in such areas as leadership, budgeting, personnel management, conflict management, public speaking, fundraising, and policy analysis and development. The skills required to be a successful and productive researcher overlap very little with, and are sometimes antithetical to, those skills required to be a successful academic administrator.

- Within the academy organizationally separate the functions of instruction and assessment. Ideally, centers for the assessment of learning outcomes should be established as key academic support resources that provide faculty with valid, reliable, criterion-referenced measures of their students' learning and provide knowledge and skill certification services that formally confirm the competency an individual may already possess in a specific area, regardless of how or where they gained that competency.

- Within all degree programs, develop modularized curricula that are time independent but learning-outcome constant. That is, establish curricular programs through which students may proceed at their own pace to gain specific knowledge and skills required to pass an objective, criterion-referenced set of examinations. Award degrees on the basis of successful performance on such exams. Certify knowledge and competency, not seat time.

- In order to meet the accreditation demands of outcomes-based assessment, abolish the classroom practice of grading on the curve and, in its place, institute a criterion-referenced grading system. This will require, of course, that faculty become proficient in instructional systems design and instructional assessment techniques—or to make use of the appropriate instructional and assessment support services noted earlier.

- In order to attract the growing numbers of survival learners, offer curricular modules that lead to specific knowledge or skill without necessary reference to a particular degree. The knowledge explosion's effect on the workplace has been to make continuous learning a necessity for continued employability. Institutions offering such modules would be seen as knowledge or skill "filling stations" to which the working population would return from time to time throughout their careers in order to maintain their employability.

- Establish a differentiated faculty staffing model for colleges and universities in which faculty may be hired *only* to teach, or *only* to conduct research and write grant proposals, or *only* to advise students, serve as program administrators, and so on.

- Redefine the teaching professoriate as a meta-profession—a profession that is recognized as building upon, and going significantly beyond, scholarship. Start requiring individuals hired to teach to meet a higher professional standard than those hired solely to conduct research. That is, require such faculty to *not only* have high levels of content expertise but to also demonstrate high levels of expertise in instructional design, instructional delivery, and instructional assessment (Theall & Arreola, 2001). Pay such individuals higher salaries than the base salaries of individuals hired solely to conduct research.

- Establish faculty evaluation/development systems that *both* adequately reward faculty for the performance of their specific professional duties (whether it be teaching, research, or service) *and* provide meaningful support designed to enable faculty to gain the knowledge and expertise needed to carry out their meta-professional responsibilities.

- Require teaching faculty to be personally responsible for the maintenance of their content expertise. Cut back on traditional faculty development programs designed to support them in their efforts to become more proficient in their content fields (the one area in which they are already most expert). Instead, institute *fully supported* in-house professional development programs designed to provide faculty with expertise in the meta-professional skills of instructional design, delivery, and assessment.

- Include as a core offering within any doctoral degree program a sequence on instructional design, delivery, and assessment. Although not all individuals getting a doctoral degree will go on to become college professors, it is from such programs that college faculty come. Therefore, it is imperative that we plant the seeds of the meta-professional skills in our doctoral degree programs.

- Abolish tenure (or at least let it die a quiet death) and replace it with a series of three-, five-, and seven-year contracts that call for the performance of specific professional duties that lead to specific, measurable outcomes.

- Stop accepting academic freedom as an excuse for instructional incompetence. The new marketplace paradigm does not encompass the concept of academic freedom. Rather, it rewards and supports those that can deliver an instructional experience that results in the learner acquiring (quickly and cost effectively) the knowledge or skill required.

These changes are simply my take on what the academy must do to survive and thrive in the new marketplace paradigm. Not everyone will agree with these suggestions. Regardless, the marketplace will continue to nourish those organizations that make the appropriate changes and simply starve out those that do not. In short, the academy must learn to ride the monster or risk being consumed by it.

## Note

I am indebted to my good friend and colleague, Raymond H. Colson, vice chancellor for administration at the University of Tennessee Health Science Center, whose expertise in economics and government funding of education has provided me with a perspective on the market forces impacting higher education that I might otherwise never have gained.

## References

Arreola, R. A., Aleamoni, L. M., & Theall, M. (2001). *College teaching as meta-profession: Reconceptualizing the scholarship of teaching and learning.* Paper presented at the 9th annual American Association for Higher Education Conference on Faculty Roles and Rewards, Tampa, FL.

Arreola, R. A., Theall, M., & Aleamoni, L. M. (2003). *Beyond scholarship: Recognizing the multiple roles of the professoriate.* Paper presented at the 83rd annual meeting of the American Educational Research Association, Chicago, IL.

Boyer, E. L. (1990). *Scholarship reconsidered: Priorities of the professoriate.* Princeton, NJ: Carnegie Foundation for the Advancement of Teaching.

Burd, S. (2005, January 7). Change in federal formula means thousands may lose student aid. *Chronicle of Higher Education*, p. A1.

Davis, S., & Botkin, J. (1994). *The monster under the bed: How business is mastering the opportunity of knowledge for profit.* New York, NY: Simon & Schuster.

Field, K. (2005, January 7). Pork crowds out the competition. *Chronicle of Higher Education,* p. A33.

Howard Hughes Medical Institute. (2004). *Making the right moves: A practical guide to scientific management for postdocs and new faculty.* Chevy Chase, MD: Author.

Kuhn, T. S. (1970). *The structure of scientific revolutions* (2nd ed.). Chicago, IL: University of Chicago Press.

Mangan, K. S. (2005, January 14). Berkeley law dean calls for partial privatization of his school. *Chronicle of Higher Education,* p. A25.

National Center for Higher Education Management Systems. (2000, August). *The competency standards project: Another approach to accreditation review.* Washington, DC: Council for Higher Education Accreditation.

Schmidt, P. (2003, December 19). Accept more state control or go private. *Chronicle of Higher Education,* p. A24.

Selingo, J. (2003, February 28). The disappearing state in public higher education. *Chronicle of Higher Education,* p. A22.

Theall, M., & Arreola, R. A. (2001). *Beyond the scholarship of teaching: Searching for a unifying metaphor for the college teaching profession.* Paper presented at the 81st annual meeting of the American Educational Research Association, Seattle, WA.

# 3

# The Advantages of a Reciprocal Relationship Between Faculty Development and Organizational Development in Higher Education

Leora Baron
University of Nevada Las Vegas

*No campus organization exists in a vacuum, nor can it afford to be an island unto itself. Thus, the functions of faculty development need to be viewed in the context of the entire institution. The effectiveness of faculty development, and sometimes its very survival, are dependent to a large extent on its ability to influence and participate in organizational development outside of its own confines. This chapter suggests practical ways in which faculty development can contribute to, and indeed benefit from, a reciprocal relationship with institutional organizational development.*

## Introduction

Too often, the functions of faculty development are confined to a narrowly defined area of the institution and viewed through a very limited prism. Its constituency, similarly, may be very narrowly identified, usually full-time faculty only. When faculty development moves away from this restrictive vision and encompasses other constituencies such as part-time faculty and graduate teaching assistants, it is usually due to some contingency or the expedient need to address a burning issue. Seldom is a broad, institution-wide vision applied to the structure, functions, and approaches of faculty development.

This chapter is based on several simple, straight-forward premises. First, teaching and learning are the core mission of higher education, whether an institution is small or large. Second, the importance of the teaching and learning mission places every related aspect, and especially faculty development, in the center of every hot button issue faced by colleges and universities such as student retention, the changing student population, and student preparation. Third, faculty development is a major key to the success of the teaching and learning mission. Fourth, no campus organization can alone support and fulfill the teaching and learning mission—it takes the vision, commitment, and involvement of academic leadership (from president down to department chairperson), student support services, and technology infrastructure, to name a few. Fifth, through deliberate approaches to marketing itself, involvement in campus-wide activities, and the credibility of its leadership, faculty development can be positioned in a way that allows it to become politically neutral.

This chapter details a variety of possible approaches that will provide faculty development practitioners, as well as academic administrators, with frameworks, specific guidelines, and examples that can be easily adapted, adjusted, and built upon to suit a broad array of environments.

## Faculty Development and Organizational Development Defined

The definitions for both *faculty development* and *organizational development* come mainly from the premier professional organizations associated with each. For the purposes of this discussion, the definitions suggested by the professional organizations should provide the most generic and neutral description possible, thereby providing for the most flexible and broad-based interpretation and adaptation of the suggestions made in this chapter.

*Faculty development* refers to programs and activities whose purpose is to enhance the quality of teaching and learning. There are some ambiguities involved, of course, as occasionally faculty development may also support scholarly activities or career development activities. Similarly, in many cases the "learning" part of the faculty development mission is a desired outcome of the focus on teaching activities, and the actual support of learning is undertaken by separate campus entities such as learning centers or academic support centers. The campus teaching community—full-time faculty, part-time faculty, and graduate teaching assistants—forms the largest faculty development constituency but may not be the only one. Furthermore, faculty development may or may not be operating under a single administrative umbrella or even have a formal operational structure. For instance, in small colleges, faculty development may be done on a part-time basis by a single faculty member who is released from some teaching commitments, while in some larger institutions faculty development may be done separately within each college or academic unit, creating a large variety of operational schemes within a single institution.

The Professional and Organizational Development Network in Higher Education (POD) defines faculty development as follows:

> *Faculty development* generally refers to those programs which focus on the individual faculty member. The most common focus for programs of this type is **the faculty member as a teacher.** Faculty development specialists provide consultation on teaching, including class organization, evaluation of students, in-class presentation skills, questioning and all aspects of design and presentation. They also advise faculty on the other aspects of teacher/student interaction, such as advising, tutoring, discipline policies and administration. (POD Network, 2002)

This very broad definition has allowed faculty development to expand in many diverse ways in various types of institutions. Since its formulation, however, many additional aspects have been added in practice to the ones enumerated under *consultation* and *advice.*

As new insights into teaching and learning have evolved, the scope of faculty development activities has expanded. POD itself embraces two additional categories of activities that in its view round out the broadest scope of faculty development.

> *Instructional development* usually takes a different approach for the improvement of the institution. These programs have as their focus **the course, the curriculum and student learning.** . . . The philosophy behind these programs is that members of the institution should work as teams to design the best possible courses within the restrictions of the resources available.

> *Organizational development* takes a third perspective on maximizing institutional effectiveness. The focus of these programs is **the organizational structure of the institution and its sub components.** The philosophy is that if one can build an organizational structure which will be efficient and effective in supporting the faculty and students, the teaching/learning process will naturally thrive. (POD Network, 2002)

This definition of organizational development is concerned more with structure than with process. For the purposes of this chapter, organizational development can be defined in a less limiting way: *Organizational development, in a most generic sense, refers to overall institutional activities that are aimed at promoting and expanding institutional effectiveness, changing institutional culture, or modifying structures or substructures to adjust to changing circumstances.* Philosophically and practically, organizational development encompasses a variety of approaches and subfields. The Organization Development Network (1998–2005) defines it as follows:

> Organization Development is a dynamic *values-based* approach to systems change in organizations and communities; it strives to build the capacity to achieve and sustain a new desired state that benefits the organization or community and the world around them.

An interesting and often referenced early definition by Richard Beckhard (1969) states,

> Organization development is an effort (1) *planned*, (2) *organization-wide*, and (3) *managed* from the top, to (4) increase *organization effectiveness* and *health* through (5) *planned interventions* in the organization's "processes," using *behavioral-science* knowledge. (p. 9)

In recent years, organizational development has referred to both the scope of an organization and to the process of change. Readers may be familiar, for instance, with the terms *learning organization,* coined and developed by Peter Senge (1990), *corporate culture,* a concept introduced by Edgar Schein (1992), and *appreciative inquiry,* developed by Suresh Srivastva and David Cooperrider (1990). All of these concepts and their attendant approaches are widely viewed as aspects of organizational behavior. For the purposes of this chapter, organizational development will be used to describe an institution-wide process that is both systemic and ongoing.

Another early description of organizational development specifically in the context of higher education makes observations that in many cases are still true today. Although the reference is mostly to individual faculty members and to academic departments, it clearly describes realities that are pervasive among all internal organizations.

> Institutions of higher education have other internal organizational properties which are different from industrial organizations. There is a low degree of task interdependence among groups and between individuals. Departments and colleges tend to go about their activities in

relative isolation from other units except on issues related to budget and schedule. Individual faculty design, conduct, and evaluate their teaching without extensive consultation with colleagues, fostering an organizational pattern which is more like a collection of individuals than an integrated team working toward a common set of educational goals. (Boyer & Crocket, 1973, p. 343)

## Two Types of Relationships Between Faculty Development and Organizational Development

There are two distinct approaches for effecting a reciprocal relationship between faculty development and organizational development, and they are not necessarily mutually exclusive—they can coexist, support each other, and even increase the other's viability. Furthermore, reciprocity can sometimes be intentional and at other times incidental. Examples given in this section should be viewed just as examples and not as exemplary practice. Their purpose is not to suggest emulation but to provide a context for the practices described.

### Faculty Development-Centered Approach

In the faculty development-centered approach, activities such as programming are focused on the organizational development of the faculty development organization itself. In other words, faculty development is "the organization," and therefore, its functioning over time is of central interest. For example, a midwestern research university has dispersed faculty development, in which each of the academic colleges has its own faculty development unit; some are single practitioner operations and others have small centers. The organizational development activities at this institution revolve around creating a common set of goals and assessments while allowing each unit to develop its own operating systems. This organizational development focus is very necessary because the regional accrediting organization is more interested in institution-wide performance than in individual college performance. The approach used is one of collaboration among the faculty developers through a variety of groups and task forces, each focusing on a single aspect of organizational development related to faculty development. After the small groups complete their assignments, an umbrella group made up of representatives from each of the faculty development units determines the overall set of goals and assessment criteria. Under this plan, each internal faculty development unit will continue to have its own way of operating.

In another example, a small liberal arts college has determined that faculty development is a good and necessary idea. After many years of department
chairpersons taking responsibility for working with their faculty members on
enhancing teaching skills, the president has determined that faculty development has to be more centralized. The motivation is largely economic in that
the school needs to position itself in a competitive posture in a geographical
area that has a number of similar colleges as well as a couple of regional community colleges. As a result of the president's decision, the chairpersons'
council will now be responsible for faculty development. The immediate
organizational development tasks at this college are to define and describe the
college-wide faculty development and to set up policies and procedures that
all can agree to follow. In this case, while each chairperson will continue to be
responsible for the faculty development in his or her department, there will
be common standards and practices developed to which all departments will
have to adhere.

## Institution-Centered Approach

The institution-centered approach to reciprocity between faculty development and organizational development will form the backdrop for much of
the rest of this chapter. While faculty development is still concerned with its
own mission, operating procedures, and standards, it is very much involved
in organizational development activities that are essentially campus or institution based. In this approach, the direct benefits to faculty development may
not always be immediately obvious or accrued in the short term; they are but
one part of the larger picture. Taking this approach does not in any way
detract from faculty development's need to engage in faculty development-
centered organizational activities. What it does provide is a much larger context and tableau against which faculty development's needs, activities, and
accomplishments can be positively measured. Reciprocity is very evident
here; the engagement with institution-wide organizational development
activities can have a direct effect on the success of faculty development.

For example, at a large metropolitan commuter state university, faculty
development is a stand-alone unit under the vice president for academic
affairs. It has had its own staff and operating budget, and it has offered a wide
array of workshops and individual consultations. It has been noticed, though,
that the pool of faculty members taking advantage of the faculty development services and programs has become fixed over the past couple of years.
The same individuals and departments are involved, and it is very rare that a
faculty member who has not previously participated becomes involved in

faculty development. In a somewhat parallel fashion, the library has reached a point of frustration in trying to engage faculty in its very effective and necessary training programs in information literacy. An academic department, for instance, would sign up for a customized workshop in which databases and other resources from the specific discipline would be used as content and context. Of the 25 faculty members in the department, only five will actually show up for the workshop. It is quite clear that faculty development and the library share a common problem.

A joint organizational development approach can provide a more than satisfactory solution for each of the organizations. Only a semester ago the faculty senate adopted a resolution that identified information literacy as an institution-wide initiative. The reasons for the adoption of the initiative were numerous, not the least of which was the realization that no matter what discipline a student, undergraduate or graduate, pursues, one of the ultimate tests for the success of the academic program will be the ability to navigate the ever-expanding world of information. A great deal of motivation for the adoption has also come from new standards set by the regional accrediting agency. Therefore, the Information Literacy Initiative has become part of the university's overall organizational development process. Realizing the potential for successful collaboration, faculty development and the library have joined forces to modify and combine several of their existing programs into a new, joint program. The response from the faculty has been overwhelming as members recognized that the information gained through the new program would be important not only to their students' success, but also to the success of their own scholarly activities. In this case, without any new resources being tapped, two key university organizational development objectives—future employers' expectations and accreditation standards—are being met, while at the same time faculty development is able to greatly expand its sphere of activity, reach a much larger segment of the faculty than before, and establish credibility as being on top of important pedagogical issues.

In another example, at a 2,000-student rural community college, frustration has been mounting as incoming freshmen, both traditional and nontraditional, have been found to possess less than adequate basic skills in language and math. A few years ago, remedial courses were developed that are required of all students who do not meet admission standards in order for them to enroll in the regular program. It was obvious that the hot button issue of student underpreparation was not being adequately addressed. Enter faculty development. In the past, at the request of many faculty members, faculty development programs were implemented that addressed the issues inherent in large enrollments of underprepared students in nonremedial courses. Techniques and approaches were described and practiced that could alleviate some of the problems.

To the campus-wide curriculum committee it was obvious, however, that faculty development could take a leadership role in this area by engaging in an institution-centered organizational development activity that would address the core problem. A task force made up of representatives from faculty development, the student enrichment program, and college admissions recommended that a new faculty development initiative be implemented. In this new program, coordinated by faculty development, regular faculty from a variety of disciplines, mainly from those most directly affected, learn to teach remedial courses. A stipend provided by the administration allows each of the participants to devote time during the spring semester and the early part of summer to redesign remedial courses and eventually teach them during the latter part of the summer. The success rate of participating students has increased, and faculty's challenges in the mainline courses have decreased. In this case, too, the needs of faculty development are met through an initiative that addresses larger institutional needs.

## Catalyst Versus Participant

There are two distinct ways by which faculty development can become engaged in institution-centered organizational development: as a catalyst or as a participant. To be a catalyst, faculty development is aware of institutional hot button issues and is continuously engaged in institution-wide activities and conversations through membership on committees and other means. This ongoing involvement places faculty development in a good position to observe hot button issues and subissues in order to assess what the teaching/learning angles may be and how pedagogically oriented interventions or solutions may move the institutional agenda forward. Once such an opportunity has been identified, faculty development can proceed in a variety of ways, either by designing (or redesigning) segments of its own programming, or by suggesting collaborative programming with other units (e.g., the information literacy project described earlier). In either case, the impetus for change and development for an institutional need comes directly from faculty development.

As a participant, aside from programming initiated by itself, faculty development is looking for opportunities to join existing programs and initiatives across the institution. Programs of interest in this approach are ones that could benefit from faculty development's expertise, its credibility with faculty, and its (usually) apolitical nature (e.g., the remedial course redesign described earlier).

To be successful and ongoing, the catalyst and participant approaches are based on an entrepreneurial approach and on an ability to work collaboratively with a variety of campus organizations. In their discussion of lessons learned about academic affairs and student affairs partnerships, Martin and Samels (2001) suggest the following steps for building and rebuilding successful partnerships:

> (1) be opportunistic, (2) control the budget, (3) capitalize on turnover, (4) avoid collisions of culture, (5) design links to ongoing institutional assessment initiatives, (6) get press, and then get more press, (7) develop board awareness and support, and (8) don't become attached. (p. 89)

In the case of faculty development, because the focus is better and more narrowly defined than the generic "academic affairs," Martin and Samels' steps (1), (4), and (6) are the most important to remember. Finding the right opportunities for collaboration, creating a cultural synergy for the particular purpose or project, and letting the campus community know about the effort are keys to making an organizational development involvement successful and thereby paying off dividends for faculty development.

## Hot Button Issues

Hot button issues are the key to a successful faculty development and organizational development reciprocity. So what are hot button issues? While specific issues vary from one institution to another as to their relative importance, their timeliness, or their formal designation as core issues, they share several features in common. First, their life span is rather long—at least several years—and they are not issues that can be resolved quickly or that go away once they have been addressed. Second, to be addressed effectively, they require institution-wide involvement. Third, they are complex and multilayered. Fourth, they tend to create controversy because different constituencies have very different opinions as to the priorities, the approaches to be taken, and the significance of the outcomes.

The following hot button issues are meant to be representative, not exhaustive. Their purpose here is to suggest some key areas in which faculty development may have both a stake and an opportunity for organizational development contribution. Such involvement will be described through a possible program or initiative. The order of issues should not be taken to suggest relative importance. Some of the functions and units identified are mentioned generically for inclusiveness purposes.

## Accreditation

Regional and discipline-specific accreditation is an ongoing, usually stress-producing process. As accrediting organizations are focusing increasing attention on student-centered and/or learning-centered programming issues, opportunities exist for faculty development participation in all its phases: preparation, site visit, and follow-up. Examples:

- Faculty development assists units through customized programming to develop a unified format for faculty teaching or course portfolios.

- A visit with faculty development personnel or to the faculty development location is part of the site visit agenda.

- In response to any feedback requiring revisions related to faculty development areas of expertise, faculty development teams up with the affected unit (or in the case of regional accreditation, with affected campus groups) to address the issues raised and report back to the accrediting agency.

## Student Retention and Graduation Timelines

Retention in this category refers both to retention of enrolled students in individual programs and courses and the retention of students at the institution. Graduation timelines refer to the amount of time it takes students to graduate. The two issues are joined here because they tend to have some similar causes, and so the possible solutions are similar. Since student retention is often directly linked to the academic program, faculty development's possible connections are clear and they provide opportunities for involvement. Examples:

- A frequent, at least partial, solution is improved academic advisement. A collaborative program by faculty development, the advising council, and student academic support services is developed to focus academic advisors' and professional advisors' attention on learning advisement (i.e., study skills, academic discipline differentiation, etc.) as a companion piece to standard administrative advising (i.e., courses to take, scheduling, requirements, etc.).

- Faculty development either initiates or joins planning activities for programs that have shown a positive effect on retention and achievement levels. These may include learning communities, expanded freshmen orientation, or peer (upper level) student mentoring, all of which require and involve varying degrees of faculty development activities.

## Learning Technologies Integration

The push to integrate learning technologies into the teaching/learning matrix is growing, and its motivation is frequently other than pedagogical. In many cases, the move to use learning technologies can be described as an ongoing wild dance in which the institution knows that it has to keep up due to a variety of pressures. Therefore, the financial and political realities as well as the ever-changing nature of the technologies themselves keep getting in the way of a smooth integration. Few institutions have the learning technologies functions integrated into faculty development, a situation that creates a dual (and often competing) track for faculty development activities and which does not address the need for pedagogy to lead technology. Faculty development, as the "expert" unit on pedagogical matters, can play an important role in making the learning technologies' integration into the teaching/learning environment more rational and productive. Examples:

- Faculty development can initiate conversations with administrators and the technology unit(s) about moving the teaching/learning/technology (TLT) faculty development functions to faculty development.

- Faculty development can offer to add pedagogical components and materials to the faculty training in TLT wherever it is housed.

- Faculty development can initiate conversations among the appropriate stakeholders—information technology, student academic support services, academic units—about the desirability of establishing an institution-wide TLT roundtable that will discuss all technology matters that affect teaching and learning, such as classroom configuration, software priorities, technical support for faculty and students, and more.

## Diversity

This complex area includes but is not limited to issues of student diversity, faculty diversity, and curricular content. All of these issues are institution-wide and touch on so many areas of campus life that faculty development's approach may be both faculty development centered and institution centered. Examples:

- Faculty development creates sample materials that demonstrate the integration of diversity into the curriculum in different disciplinary areas, and such materials are made available through the faculty development's web site as well as through customized workshops for academic units.

- Faculty development and student life create a joint program to identify and address for faculty, advisors, and other academic support personnel the diversity issues that impact students' abilities to learn and to succeed in their college studies.

### Community Engagement

In addition to traditional outreach activities, community engagement may include student preparation for college learning, recruitment of nontraditional faculty, or repositioning the institution to become a central entity in the community. Faculty development may be instrumental in this area in several ways, all of which also directly impact its ability to perform well its standard tasks. Examples:

- Faculty development establishes collaborative programming with the K–12 educational system to provide continuing professional development to its teachers, especially those in grades 6–12, in the area of college preparation in both content and skills.

- Faculty development spearheads the integration of a service-learning program.

- Working with individual colleges or departments, faculty development facilitates an ongoing structured dialogue between the colleges and employer segments that leads to curricular adjustments and assessment activities to ensure students' preparation for the world of work.

## Faculty Development Characteristics That Support Organizational Reciprocity

There are many more roles that faculty development can play in institutional organizational development, and their success depends greatly on faculty development's ability to demonstrate specific traits and use deliberate approaches that may be advantageous to any campus organization.

- *Entrepreneurship.* The ability to seek and identify opportunities for expanding the boundaries of programs, relationships, and possibilities

- *Risk-taking.* A willingness to experiment with new alliances, cede some turf for the sake of successful collaborations, and the courage to know up front that not all efforts will yield the desired results

- *Collaboration.* A deliberate effort to work with other organizations on and off campus, realizing that pooled resources, human and material, can bring about enhanced results; offer programmatic support to other units

- *Neutrality.* Being able to work equally well with faculty, administrators, and campus organizations in other divisions by keeping a focus on the collective desired outcomes and avoiding turf issues

- *Strategic planning.* A constant recalibrating of short- and long-term goals, alignment of faculty development and institutional visions and missions, and the ability to keep the big picture in focus while concentrating on the details

- *Initiative.* A willingness to take a leadership role in all matters of teaching and learning and use proactive rather than reactive approaches to problem solving

- *Creativity.* Seeking new solutions to old problems

## Summary and Statement of Benefits

Faculty development is in a unique position to help affect institutional development while making progress on its own agenda. Consciously or otherwise, in many instances faculty development is well positioned to play this dual role because its mission is directly tied to the core mission of the institution— teaching and learning. While playing the institutional role, it is also strengthening itself in significant ways.

- *Longevity.* The more involved faculty development is with key institutional activities and the more it is seen as contributing to the betterment of the institution, the more likely it is to survive hard times or administrative whim.

- *Economy of resources.* Collaboration expands the scope of possibilities as shared activities also mean shared resources.

- *Advocacy.* Faculty members realize that faculty development serves as an informal advocate for their ability to perform teaching and other functions well.

- *Modeling.* Faculty development is able to model many of the practices it advocates for faculty such as entrepreneurial thinking, creativity, consistency, good communication, interactivity, and so on.

Nancy Chism (1998) has suggested that faculty development ". . . can develop a good track record for being helpful and knowledgeable. We can cultivate channels of communication, and by the usefulness of the information, ideas, and process facilitation we provide, improve our access, authority, and resources" (p. 148). Additionally, Mary Deane Sorcinelli (2002) discussed the various locations within an institution in which faculty development can be based.

> . . . a number of successful programs place the director of the teaching center in a direct reporting line to the top. . . . This reporting structure lets faculty know that the staff of the center have a direct line to the administration. In addition, proximity to the provost and other academic leaders . . . can allow the office to consult readily with and apprise key administrators about development. Finally, this reporting line can help facilitate the kind of faculty and administrative connections that the program needs to advance the institutional teaching mission. (pp. 16–17)

In other words, faculty development has to be able to serve its direct constituency, the teaching community, while at the same time working to address institutional priorities. "Trust," says Warren Bennis (1973), "is gained over time through repeated interactions. . . . Consensus is the end of OD [organizational development], a consensus based on trust, openness, confrontation, and feedback" (p. 391). Faculty development, as a campus entity that has the trust of faculty—a huge attribute for its own success—can build upon this trust and contribute significantly to the larger organization.

## References

Beckhard, R. (1969). *Organization development: Strategies and models.* Reading, MA: Addison-Wesley.

Bennis, W. (1973). An O.D. expert in the cat bird's seat. *Journal of Higher Education, 44*(5), 389–398.

Boyer, R. K., & Crocket, C. (1973). Organizational development in higher education: Introduction. *Journal of Higher Education, 44*(5), 339–351.

Chism, N. V. N. (1998). The role of educational developers in institutional change: From the basement office to the front office. In M. Kaplan & D. Lieberman (Eds.), *To improve the academy: Vol. 17. Resources for faculty, instructional, and organizational development* (pp. 141–153). Stillwater, OK: New Forums Press.

Martin, J., & Samels, J. E. (2001). Lessons learned: Eight best practices for new partnerships. In A. Kezar, D. J. Hirsch, & C. Burack (Eds.), *New directions for higher education: No. 116. Understanding the role of academic and student affairs collaboration in creating a successful learning environment* (pp. 89–100). San Francisco, CA: Jossey-Bass.

Organization Development Network. (1998–2005). *Principles of practice.* Retrieved May 10, 2005, from http://www.odnetwork.org/principlesofpractice.html

Professional and Organizational Development Network in Higher Education. (2002). *What is faculty development?* Retrieved May 10, 2005, from http://www.podweb.org/development/definitions.htm

Schein, E. H. (1992). *Organizational culture and leadership* (2nd ed.). San Francisco, CA: Jossey-Bass.

Senge, P. M. (1990). *The fifth discipline: The art and practice of the learning organization.* New York, NY: Currency Doubleday.

Sorcinelli, M. D. (2002). Ten principles of good practice in creating and sustaining teaching and learning centers. In K. H. Gillespie, L. R. Hilsen, & E. C. Wadsworth (Eds.), *A guide to faculty development: Practical advice, examples, and resources* (pp. 9–23). Bolton, MA: Anker.

Srivastva, S., & Cooperrider, D. (1990). *Appreciative management and leadership: The power of positive thought and action in organizations.* San Francisco, CA: Jossey-Bass.

# 4

# A Different Way to Approach the Future: Using Chaos Theory to Improve Planning

Marc Cutright
Ohio University

*Strategic planning is a good idea that gets a bad name from dubious efforts carry-ing the title. Much of this rap comes from half-hearted exercises, but some of it comes from efforts that founder due to faulty or limited conceptions of how the future "works." Chaos theory is an alternative approach and metaphor with po-tential to let us see the future and its dynamics in new ways. Cognizance of chaos's nature and underlying structure might help us do planning in new, non-intuitive, and more successful ways.*

## Introduction

Proponents of strategic planning in higher education were perhaps disheart-ened to see the process included among the management and leadership tools discounted and even ridiculed by noted scholar Robert Birnbaum in his 2001 book, *Management Fads in Higher Education: Where They Came From, What They Do, Why They Fail*. The approach to active leadership in shaping an institution's future was considered just another suit borrowed from the world of business, fit poorly to the world of academic endeavor.

Those of us with some years of experience in higher education, either in administration or faculty life, have no doubt seen the concept poorly executed, the description *strategic* attached to ideas of suspect merit. The word carries connotations of cunning, vision, lean-and-meanness, a crystalline contrast to the classic "organized anarchy" and "ambiguity of purpose" (Cohen & March, 1974) that so often seem to be conditions of our daily lives and interactions on campus. *Strategic* is a term that we've allowed self-appointed change agents to seize and attach to their efforts without challenge, as if they were granted authorization to self-declare their work "excellent."

Indeed, I came to the study of strategic planning not out of positive, revelational experience that I felt compelled to share with the world, but from discomfort with and vexation about the strategic planning processes into which I'd been drawn or had witnessed at close range at a number of institutions. I recall one university system "strategic" planning process that involved only a few trustees and high-level administrators, and no faculty representation. The group delivered their final product in a short series of closed-circuit video presentations from a central location, open locally to anyone on campus who wanted to have "input." The meetings were poorly attended, and at least at my location, no one offered reaction or questions. Perhaps the plan was perfectly conceived and delivered. Perhaps people felt no connection between it and their lives. I can't recall that it was ever again referenced to support the deployment of resources or the pursuit of goals.

In another instance, I was involved with a small group of administrators in updating a five-year strategic plan for the campus. In the plan's fourth year, it was dusted off and examined point by point. It seemed a bit distant from the realities of its conception, but we used it as the template to conceptualize our future. When it came to the issue of percentage of minority enrollment for the campus, we noted that the plan called for us to be at 13% African-American representation in the plan's fifth year, the one coming up. A new and high-ranking administrator felt that such a figure was unambitious, and was successful in setting a goal for the upcoming year of 15%. That we were then at 11% African-American enrollment, and that the target year of enrollment increase would welcome the incoming class in six weeks from the date of the meeting, was of little concern or worry. We were, after all, writing poetry, not policy that would affect daily lives and actions.

Yet there are shining examples of strategic planning well executed, instances of colleges seizing and directing their futures, cases that lead us to believe that our institutions need not be corked bottles bobbing on the sea, but that they can be fairly sleek ships capable of direction and purpose. George Keller (2004) describes Elon University's emergence, through strategic planning and execution, from middling reputation and precarious finances to preeminence as a liberal arts institution. I researched and described, with several others, 13 institutions, from community colleges to research universities, that have established preeminent programs for the first year of college, primarily through deliberate institutional will, planning, follow-through, and continuous improvement (Barefoot et al., 2005).

## Two Divergent Approaches

Strategic planning efforts can range from the superficial and ineffective, to the substantial and transformative. I have come to believe that these extremes might be characterized as the "Theory X" and the "Theory Y" of strategic planning, after and with apologies to McGregor's (1960) description of oppositional approaches to and theories of human motivation in organizations. Theory X of strategic planning might be characterized as follows:

- Planning is mandated by, and executed to meet at a minimal level, the policies of external agencies such as governing boards, state legislatures, or accrediting agencies.

- Planning is periodic, episodic, and discontinuous.

- Plans are crafted from sketchy and limited information, almost all of it statistical. Only persons of a certain status have meaningful opportunities for input, and information is gathered along conventional chains of command.

- The planning process avoids conflict, particularly as it might question the institution's core purposes and reasons to exist.

- Planning is directed and controlled to a very high degree by the institution's chief executive officer.

- Planning assumes that a sufficient amount of information on current circumstances will yield an accurate prediction of the future.

- Plans are highly detailed, project far into the future, and depend on a deliberate sequence of events.

- Budgets and plans are linked in one of two ways: not in the least, or in rigid lock, with no room for contingencies.

Theory Y, in contrast, might have these characteristics:

- Planning is driven by the institution's desire to identify and develop its potential.

- Planning is continuous.

- Planning is open to a broad range of opinion, information, aspiration, and argument throughout the broadly defined constituency of the institution.

- Planning is focused on the priority of articulating the institution's core purposes and priorities.

- Planning is energized and legitimized, but only generally directed, by the chief executive officer.

- Planning points a direction, but is not overly detailed and hard to remember.

- Planning allows for the pursuit of opportunities that may arise in the future but are not currently foreseen.

Theory Y has consistency with some of the most current, progressive, and successful practices of higher education planning. These would include Peterson's (1997) idea of contextual planning, which he proposes as more proactive and holistic than conventional planning in higher education; Neumann and Larson's (1997) emphasis on widely distributed leadership that rejects conventional linear leadership and instead draws upon existing institutional patterns and values; and Chaffee and Jacobson's (1997) foci on the criticality of identifying subtle organizational imperatives, of building a shared vision through trust and mutual understanding, and of opening the planning process to seeming, initial disorder.

Some of the differences between Theory X and Theory Y are rooted in sincerity in the planning process. Minimal compliance with external mandates, for example, is a practice that even its practitioners will concede is not a reasonable route to transformative change. Many of the differences are due, however, to very different world views, very contrasting preconceptions about the nature of our organizations, the means by which things are accomplished, and how the future unfolds. Theory X can come, in very large part, from the conception of organizations, including colleges and universities, as mechanical in nature.

The position espoused in this chapter is that metaphor, our borrowed constructs of sense-making in our organizations, is essential to how we view, explicitly and implicitly, our roles in these organizations and how things get done. Further, an argument is put forth that our dominant metaphor, that of our organizations as mechanical devices—machines—must be explicitly recognized and rather forcefully displaced if we are to be liberated from its limitations. Finally, an extended metaphor for organizations based on chaos theory is put forward, in the hope that it both provides a different way to conceptualize strategic change in the college or university and creates a "tent" under which some progressive and realistic planning concepts can be gathered.

## Why Metaphor?

A distant relative by marriage some years ago suffered a massive and cata-strophic stroke. His chances of surviving the night, let alone beyond, were put at 5%. But his resolve to live, the miracles of medical science, and perhaps miracles beyond human invention, brought him back from the brink of death. He began a slow and difficult recovery.

In the days and weeks of hospitalization to come, the victim would attempt to engage his visitors in "conversations" that seemed scattered and sometimes nonsensical. Eventually, in brief and tiring efforts, he tried to relate what had happened to him, what he had experienced. A description recurred: "Hard disk crash. Data lost. Can't reboot. Have to reboot."

Maybe that means nothing. I am neither psychologist nor neurologist, not that they have an uncontestable grasp on how the brain works. But it seems to me that while my relative had lost much of his ability to conceive and express what had happened to his mind and his efforts to heal it, the metaphor of his mind and its processes as a computer, a machine, was alive and explicit.

The importance of metaphor in our conceptions of our selves and our environments should not be underestimated or considered a mere poetic device. Since at least Plato's allegory of the cave, we have a record of the signif-icant role played by metaphor in our descriptions of the world around us. Linguist George Lakoff and philosopher Mark Johnson (1980), in their col-laborative *Metaphors We Live By*, assert that metaphor is inseparable from conceptualizations of the world and our organization of it:

> [M]etaphor is pervasive in everyday life, not just in language but in thought and action. Our ordinary conceptual system, in terms of which we both think and act, is fundamentally metaphorical in nature. (p. 1)

Further,

> We draw inferences, set goals, make commitments, and execute plans, all on the basis of how we in part structure our experience, consciously and unconsciously, by means of metaphor. (p. 158)

A metaphor for an organization and its processes, then, has utility for shaping our very conceptions of the organization. As Gareth Morgan (1986) wrote in the first edition of his book, *Images of Organization*,

> Metaphor is often just regarded as a device for embellishing discourse, but its significance is much greater than this. For the use of metaphor

implies a way of thinking and a way of seeing that pervade how we understand our world generally. . . . [M]etaphor exerts a formative influence on science, on our language and on how we think, as well as how we express ourselves on a day-to-day basis. (pp. 12–13)

## Metaphor and Organizational Life

Recent decades particularly have seen the emergence of key metaphors for organizational life in higher education. Among the most prominent of these are the *garbage can* and *organized anarchy* models of institutional choice and decision making (Cohen & March, 1974; Cohen, March, & Olsen, 1972). Weick (1976) described educational systems, including universities, as "loosely coupled systems," reminiscent of Cohen, March, and Olsen's "uncoupling of problems and choices." Orton and Weick (1990) would return to the idea that loose coupling "baffled and angered" (Weick, 1976) administrators in their efforts to plan and otherwise direct colleges and universities. Loose coupling, rather than being perceived as a means by which institutions could be more sensitive to environmental changes, was instead widely perceived as a diametrically oppositional concept to management, and a source of resistance to change (Orton & Weick, 1990). Indeed, George Keller (1983), the most prominent proponent of, and author on, strategic planning, considered both organized anarchy and loose couplings to be crises, not elements of flexibility and adaptability, in confronting a new era of harsh competition for resources.

If metaphor is central to our organization of the world, and if many in higher education would eschew metaphors such as those noted above, then what is, exactly, the operative metaphor, the implicit one, if not the explicit one?

Gareth Morgan (1997) is among those who say that the dominant organizational metaphor for our organizations is that of the machine. He notes that this metaphor can be useful, when the environment is stable, when the product is uniform, and when the "human 'machine' parts are compliant and behave as they have been designed to do" (p. 27). The description seems consistent with Frederick Taylor's (1911) scientific management of the early 20th century. The model has the characteristics of a machine, in that, consistent with Newtonian mechanics, there's a predictability and replicability to cause and effect; there's a hierarchy of actions and controls; and elements of the machine can be isolated and tinkered with.

Margaret Wheatley, in her 1992 book *Leadership and the New Science*, holds that we have focused our organizational energies on

Structure and organizational design, on gathering numerical data.
... We believed that we could study the parts ... to arrive at knowledge of the whole. We have reduced and described and separated
things into cause and effect, and drawn the world into lines and
boxes. (pp. 27–28)

Oxford physicist and philosopher of science Danah Zohar (1997) sees an
organizational world of "Newtonian organizations ... that thrive on certainty
and predictability.... Power emanates from the top.... [Such organizations]
are managed as though the part organizes the whole." The emphasis on control
and command "isolates these organizations from their environments" (p. 5).

Lincoln and Guba (1985) are among those who argue that such
metaphors extend to and dominate our views of educational organizations.
Higher education planners and authors Michael G. Dolence and Donald M.
Norris (1995) describe both the processes and organizations of higher education as being of "classic, late Industrial Age design," a "factory model" characterized by "insufficient flexibility" and a fixation on processes rather than
outcomes (p. 11).

## Why Chaos Theory, and What Is It?

A Virginia commission, charged in the late 1980s with the development of a
master plan or vision for higher education in that state, used chaos theory as
an analytical framework. The short definition of chaos theory given in that
report serves us well as a beginning point:

A mathematical concept called, somewhat misleadingly, "chaos,"
holds that at certain points small changes within systems will produce great and unpredictable results.... The mathematics created to
conceive ... "chaotic" situations is nonlinear: the future does not follow trends established in the past.... What [chaos theory] represents
to us is the probability that the future will not be simply a linear
extrapolation of the past, that small events happening today will
cause new patterns to emerge downstream. (Commission on the
University of the 21st Century, 1989, inside back cover)

Chaos, in the physical sciences, is not the random activity that the term's
common use suggests. Chaos theory instead holds that many seemingly random activities and systems in fact show complex, replicated patterns. The
behavior of these systems is nonlinear; that is, behavior feeds back upon itself

and modifies the patterns. Further, predictability of the system's behavior is restricted to a relatively short timeframe.

Chaos theory's roots in science go back more than a century (Ruelle, 1991), but ongoing attention to chaos theory is broadly considered to have begun with the work of meteorologist Edward Lorenz (1993). Working with early 1960s computers and a model of weather development, Lorenz sought to make his computations of prediction more efficient by rounding input conditions measurements, but to a very slight degree, after three decimal places. He expected only slight variations from more pinpoint inputs, but after only a short run of conditions, patterns began to vary substantially from earlier simulations and quickly bore no resemblance at all to earlier predictive calculations. Yet even with these variations, boundaries existed on the system's behaviors, and certain weather patterns recurred. These are conditions that characterize actual weather (Gleick, 1987).

A particularly key principle of chaos theory emerges from this work. Chaotic systems demonstrate extreme sensitivity to initial conditions and extreme sensitivity to influx. This notion is popularly called the *butterfly effect,* where the flapping of a butterfly's wings in Asia may eventually alter the course of a tornado in Texas (Lorenz, 1993).

The importance of small factors such as these comes through the circumstance that chaotic systems are dependent upon feedback. As opposed to Newtonian concepts that more clearly differentiate between cause and effect and their predictability, feedback is the notion that an effect becomes part of the cause in subsequent iterations of the pattern. Senge (1990) explored this concept as related to organizations in *The Fifth Discipline.*

What, then, allows chaotic systems to develop any sense of pattern, to stay within boundaries? It is the existence of attractors. Attractors are those elements in a system that have drawing or organizational power. Multiple attractors, even while establishing boundaries on a system, result in less stable, complex patterns, with the attractors acting upon one another. It is the presence of attractors that also gives chaotic systems the quality of self organization, the ability to recreate order and pattern, at least temporarily, despite continuous compensation for internal and external shocks to the system, or turbulence (Parker & Stacey, 1994).

Chaotic systems demonstrate self-similarity at their various levels. The pattern of the whole can be seen in the part. In natural systems, self-similar structuring, called fractals, is shown in cloud formation, plant structure, landscapes, circulatory systems, wherever chaotic organization appears.

To summarize, a chaotic system is one in which apparently random activity is in fact complexly patterned. Patterns, created by attractors, are disrupted and modified by the input of turbulence. Attractors work to keep systems within boundaries. Chaotic systems demonstrate self-similarity, or fractal structuring, at various levels of the system. The infinitely varied interaction of attractors and turbulence make pattern predictability difficult in the near term and impossible over the long term. Despite limited predictability, patterns do emerge and are substantially the creation of system conditions and inputs.

Some individuals working with metaphoric applications of these or similar principles use the term *complexity theory* rather than chaos theory. This body of work has yet to clearly distinguish itself from chaos theory, and the choice of complexity may be due in large part to the visceral reaction that the word *chaos* engenders when people fail to separate the theory from the conventional description of randomness. I find useful the distinction made by Edward Lorenz (1993) that complexity is "irregularity in space," and chaos is "irregularity in time" (p. 167). Planning, and organizational foci in general, are overwhelmingly concerned with time, and particularly the future, the single element of this dimension over which we have or seek control.

A word on the limitations of metaphor, including chaos theory, is in order. As Morgan (1997) and many others note, no single metaphor is universally useful or applicable to all circumstances. Metaphors can blind us to circumstances as well as give us new insights. The trick is to become facile in the consideration and application of multiple metaphors.

Metaphors appropriated from physical sciences to social circumstances can be particularly problematic. Social Darwinism comes to mind, with its rationalization of racism, colonialism, and robber-baron capitalism. A contemporary of Isaac Newton's sought to apply the theory of gravity to determination of the veracity of courtroom testimony (Cohen, 1994). Frederick Taylor (1911) and Henri Fayol (1984) were popularizing the application of physical science to social and business arrangements, just as Albert Einstein (1961) was undermining the universality of the Newtonian mechanics upon which scientific management was largely based.

Nonetheless, it is interesting to note that some of the most impassioned calls for the application of chaos theory to social systems have come from prominent scientists and mathematicians who have worked in chaos theory at developmental levels. See, for example, Gell-Mann's (1994) *The Quark and the Jaguar,* Ruelle's (1991) *Chance and Chaos,* and Prigogine and Stengers' (1984) *Order Out of Chaos.*

## Propositions for Strategic Planning

I put forth 10 propositions about strategic planning that are derived from a coincident consideration of chaos theory and classic and progressive ideas about strategic planning. Together, the propositions form an extended metaphor, a model, which provides a conceptual coherence for an overall approach to the endeavor. Some of the propositions are more obvious, while others might be counterintuitive. Some are bluntly stated; if a dominant metaphor, that of the machine, is to be displaced, it must be pushed aside, summarily if temporarily, to allow for the adequate consideration of this suggested alternative.

These propositions have been examined and largely affirmed against the planning practices and experiences of a number of institutions, particularly Carson-Newman College, a denominational college in Tennessee; the University of Calgary, an institution that would be considered a Carnegie Research University in the American context; Red Deer College, a public two-year college in Alberta; and Blue Ridge Community College in Virginia (Cutright, 1999). Among these four, only Blue Ridge Community College operated from an explicit metaphor of chaos theory (Levin, Lanigan, & Perkins, 1995; Perkins, Lanigan, Downey, & Levin, 2001).

Of course, the overwhelming limitation in going into an investigation with an *a priori* model is that the prejudice will be to confirm it; to a man with a hammer, every problem is a nail. In an effort to minimize this limitation, the preliminary model and draft propositions were made available to all individuals interviewed during the case studies, as were, for the more interested, prior papers and publications that I had produced on this general topic. The propositions were by this process refined for the better, but the overall model emerged largely intact.

Space limitations do not allow for a fuller detailing of these case studies or of the fuller literature foundations of the propositions, except in highlight.

### Proposition 1: *The ideal outcome of planning is planning, not a plan.*

Dwight Eisenhower was more direct: "Plans are nothing. Planning is everything" (Keller, 1983, p. 99). George Keller (1983) emphasizes the creation of a strategic direction over a fat, detailed document. Academic planners James Morrison, George Wilkinson, and L. Forbes (1999) affirm this viewpoint in their web-published book *Common Sense Management for Educational Leaders*: "Keep this in mind: *The product you are seeking at each step is not a written report. It is a strategic mind-set of the senior leadership, indeed the whole organization.*"

The tie to chaos theory is through the butterfly effect. Small, unforeseen changes in the environment mutate it in ways that are largely unpredictable at any level of likelihood. Higher education planning is often marked by plans issued on a time horizon of five, ten, or more years. They are highly sequential, with each step dependent upon the completion, within a specified timeframe, of precedent steps. The plan quickly breaks down. The approach is, one author suggests, somewhat like playing a game of pool by specifying, before the commencement of play, each and every shot through the sinking of the eight ball (Priesmeyer, 1992).

*Proposition 2: Planning begins with a distillation of the institution's key values and purposes. These elements are not dictated from above, but discovered from within.*

In the paradoxical context of chaos theory, these values and purposes provide a constant source of reference but are always open to challenge and modification. A chaos-theory corollary is that of attractors, those principles that bring order to a general direction for the future, despite turbulence.

The mission statement, so often a kitchen sink of disparate interests and topics, is rarely of much help. Nor is the mission or purpose statement imposed by executive fiat, which ignores the power and reality of existing conditions. As Chaffee and Jacobson (1997) noted, when vision and the institution's resident values go head to head, the result is almost always the same: "Culture 1, Planning 0" (p. 230).

*Proposition 3: The widest possible universe of information should be made available to all members of the institution. This universe of information includes ongoing, rich, and current feedback.*

Keller's (1983) advancement of the concept of environmental scanning and information gathering as critical to good planning has become widely accepted. Where chaos theory perhaps advances the concept of information gathering and sharing is an emphasis on the importance of feedback. The creation and discussion of plans are themselves a part of the changing environment. Not incorporating this feedback into the planning process separates planning from an evolving environment. While Keller (1983, 1988) initially supported the relatively secret Joint Big Decision Committee, he later revised his view to include more open communications to engender trust. Chaffee and Jacobson (1997) held that not only should communications be open and information transparent, but that a full gamut of communication means should be used to assure that all had the best opportunities for knowledge and input.

■Proposition 4: *Dissent and conflict are creative, healthy, and real. The absence of conflict is reductionist, illusory, and suspect.*

Chaos recognizes and respects the power of turbulence; it is the essence of creativity in chaotic systems. Yet how much of our planning is characterized by a desire to minimize conflict, to subtly suppress dissent, and to reach the earliest possible "consensus"? Premature closure of discussion and debate closes our fuller consideration of alternatives and leaves those of opposing opinion without input options and with an agenda that they will be able to execute, to some degree, in opposition to centrally settled directions. Holton (1995) suggested that conflict is not the problem, but the solution: Conflict "can be cathartic, providing opportunities for revitalization, energizing, and creativity by all in the academy" (p. 94).

■Proposition 5: *Linearity doesn't work in strategic planning. It doesn't work in dictation—planning and plans imposed from above—or in collation—planning and plans created solely by the collection of unit information.*

By this point in the argument, the reader may anticipate the argument from chaos theory against top-down, executive-committee-dictated planning: attractors are not identified, feedback is denied, faint recognition of the environment is inevitable, and implementation is crippled by a lack of fractal structure. But less obvious may be the limitations of the opposite impulse, collation. Collation is used here as the collection of individual "plans" by departments or other units, essentially only edited for presentation uniformity in a master document. Chaos theory suggests that this process lacks the connectivity between elements of an organization that would make it a system. Collation without feedback and discussion does not contribute to desirable self-organization that will guide the institution in coherent ways into the future.

■Proposition 6: *The institution should budget—fiscally and psychically—for failure. Pilots are alternate futures. Not all can be realized or succeed.*

Experimentation and striking out in new directions are often viewed heroically on the front end, but disparaged on the back side after less-than-favorable results. We should recognize that in planning, as in financial investment, higher returns are made possible by higher risk. The challenge is to improve—not assure—the chances of success. Dolence and Norris (1995) caution that if we wait until "the vision is perfectly clear and risks have vanished, the opportunities will have passed, as well" (p. 4). Morrison et al. (1999) encourage that "you and your [planning] colleagues must be imaginative, innovative, and willing to take risks," and "that means you are flexible, and not wedded to a set of strategies or action plans that you cannot change."

Chaos theory suggests that the predictive timeline is shorter than is likely the startup and testing times of complex projects. Even though strong data collection and ongoing feedback can result in what might be called wise piloting, some pilots will fail. If we subtly punish or isolate those whose pilots seemed reasonable and which were blessed, but fail, and we quickly distance ourselves from failure rather than examine it for lessons, we discourage the experimentation necessary to discover and create the future. Weick's (1976) articulation of loose coupling saw as one of its benefits the ability to test "mutations and novel solutions" through "many independent sensing mechanisms" (p. 7). Experimentation uses that loose coupling.

This is not to excuse or rationalize foolhardiness in the use of an institution's resources or the discharging of its responsibilities. Failures will be kept to a minimum by careful investigation of opportunities, and ongoing and transparent monitoring of their progress as implemented.

**Proposition 7**: *The considerable expense of time on the front end is an investment. It is recouped, with interest, in the future.*

Top-down, stripped-down, feedback-free planning is faster. The appearance of time saving is a false economy. Time and resources will subsequently be wasted trying to sell and implement a plan that is alien to a system's real dynamics. While directive "planning" may appear to be a manifestation of executive vision and an effort for higher education to appear more nimble-footed and businesslike, it is alien to the basic, underlying cultures of higher education and will heighten the chances of failure. In chaos terms, the fractal nature of the organization is ignored, rather than utilized.

Chaffee and Jacobson (1997) tie planning to institutional culture, and they note that changing or redirecting culture takes substantial time, but that the "payoff can be immeasurably large . . . in ways that the central administration could never have imagined or planned for" (p. 244). Conversely and "often, in the final analysis, [a] plan cannot be implemented, because key players have not agreed to it" (Innes, 1996, p. 470).

**Proposition 8**: *The executive is not demoted or minimized. The executive is the most critical shaper and champion of the process. Ultimately, the executive is empowered by the process.*

All of this may suggest, without intention, that the college president becomes a figurehead in a planning process informed by chaos theory. Descriptions of chaos-related metaphors and management viewpoints have perhaps reinforced this perception. Gareth Morgan (1997) writes, "In complex systems, no one is ever in a position to control or design system operations in a comprehensive way" (p. 272). James Fisher (1994), among the most visible of strong-presidency advocates and occasionally an acerbic commentator, has given voice to the feeling that constituent-involving processes are driven by a "misguided sense of democracy" (p. 62), result in an "unending and totally unproductive morass of committee meetings, faculty meetings, formal and informal dialogues" (p. 62), which leads to paralysis and undistinguished, lowest-common denominator compromise.

I would suggest that the president active in the promotion and advancement of strategic planning may be seen, in the language of chaos theory, as an attractor, a basic element in the formation of a system's patterns. He or she can speed or slow the process, give or deny it legitimacy, seek and celebrate small wins that encourage participation, and provide energy to the process when necessary. Too loose of a hand on the reins, and the president offers insufficient support and guidance. Too tight of a hand, and the process can focus on little else than the president's directives and opinions; think of a pendulum, originally lively, that comes to a stop when drawn to the force and a point of gravity.

Ultimately, the process enhances the president's power, when he or she can tie the widely supported strategic plan to personnel decisions, the allocation of resources, and the commencement or termination of programs.

### Proposition 9: *That which can be quantified is not to be overvalued, and that which cannot be quantified is not to be discounted.*

Much of the circumstance of unpredictability comes from our inability to discern which small factors in our environment, which butterfly wings, will be absorbed into the dynamics of the system and gain power far out of proportion with the seeming insignificance of their genesis. Originally thought to be most significant in its unemployment benefits, none of the G.I. Bill's massive effects on higher education were identified in advance; perhaps we discounted the power of hopes, dreams, and aspirations. On the other hand, the dominant "fact" of the planning future going into the 1980s was a declining pool of students, which would result in the closing of at least 10%, and perhaps as many as 25%, of American's colleges and universities in the decade then ahead (Keller, 1983). The realized future was an increase in enrollments, and the survival of most institutions on deathwatch.

Albert Einstein put over-reliance upon quantifiable data, and the concurrent under-consideration of such elements as opinion, desires, and ambitions into perspective: "Not everything that counts, can be counted; and not everything that can be counted, counts" (Marino, 1995, p. 218).

■Proposition 10: *The future is a creation, not a prediction.*

This power of agency is the distinguishing context of human chaotic systems. Despite the difficulties of prediction, the certainty of uncertainty, it would be a grave error to take from chaos theory the idea that planning is futile, because the future is unpredictable. Rather, the primary lesson is that the future can be created. Linear planning models stress trend lines and their potential for prediction of the future. Such approaches can project far into the future, but these futures are rarely realized in any recognizable form. Directors of linear planning attempt to execute the future less than they attempt to create it, and they are often wrong.

Peterson (1997) encouraged us to regard the future and the environment as "complex but malleable" (p. 134). But the ability to make long-term changes in the future is dependent upon our willingness, as actors within the university or social system, to make "long-term commitments" and to apply "consistent effort" toward desired ends (p. 153).

Participants in planning processes informed by chaos theory or similar approaches come to realize that the future is an invention; the external and internal environments are strong creative elements in the future, but so are dreams, values, and ambitions. Metaphorically, the flutter of a wing can move not only the breeze but also the system, the college or university, if applied with endurance and in partnership.

## Conclusion

While this chapter has sought to examine progressive and effective strategic planning through the lens of chaos theory, other authors have made provocative and persuasive use of the principles in other higher education contexts. For example, Kathleen E. Allen and Cynthia Cherrey's (2000) *Systemic Leadership* and Patrick G. Love and Sandra M. Estanek's (2004) *Rethinking Student Affairs Practice* both draw upon chaos theory and related concepts to advocate for more effective leadership mindsets and practices in student affairs. While these works are directed first and foremost to these practitioners, who often bemoan their lack of formal, directive power in higher education, both books are valuable to anyone in the enterprise who seeks models of leading from the middle and collaborative improvement.

## Note

Portions of this chapter have previously appeared in the chapters "Introduction: Metaphor, Chaos Theory, and This Book," and "A Chaos Theory Metaphor for Strategic Planning" in M. Cutright (Ed.), *Chaos Theory and Higher Education: Leadership, Planning, and Policy* (Peter Lang, 2001).

## References

Allen, K. E., & Cherrey, C. (2000). *Systemic leadership: Enriching the meaning of our work.* Lanham, MD: University Press of America.

Barefoot, B. O., Gardner, J. N., Cutright, M., Morris, L. V., Schroeder, C. C., Schwartz, S.W., et al. (2005). *Achieving and sustaining institutional excellence in the first year of college.* San Francisco, CA: Jossey-Bass.

Birnbaum, R. (2001). *Management fads in higher education: Where they come from, what they do, why they fail.* San Francisco, CA: Jossey-Bass.

Chaffee, E. E., & Jacobson, S. W. (1997). Creating and changing institutional cultures. In M. W. Peterson, D. D. Dill, & L. A. Mets (Eds.), *Planning and management for a changing environment: A handbook on redesigning postsecondary institutions* (pp. 230–245). San Francisco, CA: Jossey-Bass.

Cohen, I. B. (1994). *Interactions: Some contacts between the natural sciences and social sciences.* Cambridge, MA: MIT Press.

Cohen, M. D., & March, J. G. (1974). *Leadership and ambiguity: The American college president.* Boston, MA: Harvard Business School Press.

Cohen, M. D., March, J. G., & Olsen, J. P. (1972). A garbage can model of organizational choice. *Administrative Science Quarterly, 17*(1), 1–25.

Commission on the University of the 21st Century. (1989). *The case for change.* Richmond, VA: Commonwealth of Virginia.

Cutright, M. (1999). *A chaos-theory metaphor for strategic planning in higher education: An exploratory study.* Unpublished doctoral dissertation, the University of Tennessee, Knoxville. (ERIC Document Reproduction Service No. ED457931)

Cutright, M. (Ed.). (2001). *Chaos theory and higher education: Leadership, planning, and policy.* New York, NY: Peter Lang.

Dolence, M. G., & Norris, D. M. (1995). *Transforming higher education: A vision for learning in the 21st century.* Ann Arbor, MI: Society for College and University Planning.

Einstein, A. (1961). *Relativity: The special and general theory.* New York, NY: Crown Publishers.

Fayol, H. (1984). *Administration industrielle et générale.* Paris, France: Denod.

Fisher, J. L. (1994). Reflections on transformational leadership. *Educational Record, 75*(3), 54, 60–65.

Gell-Mann, M. (1994). *The quark and the jaguar: Adventures in the simple and the complex.* New York, NY: Henry Holt and Company.

Gleick, J. (1987). *Chaos: Making a new science.* New York, NY: Penguin.

Holton, S. A. (1995). Where do we go from here? *New Directions for Higher Education, 92,* 91–95.

Innes, J. (1996). Planning through consensus building: A new view of the comprehensive planning ideal. *Journal of the American Planning Association, 62*(4), 460–472.

Keller, G. (1983). *Academic strategy: The management revolution in American higher education.* Baltimore, MD: Johns Hopkins University Press.

Keller, G. (1988, February). Academic strategy: Five years later. *AAHE Bulletin,* 3–6.

Keller, G. (2004). *Transforming a college: The story of a little-known college's strategic climb to national distinction.* Baltimore, MD: Johns Hopkins University Press.

Lakoff, G., & Johnson, M. (1980). *Metaphors we live by.* Chicago, IL: University of Chicago Press.

Levin, B. H., Lanigan, J. B., & Perkins, J. R. (1995). *Strategic planning in a decentralized environment: The death of linearity.* Paper presented at the 24th annual Conference of the Southeastern Association for Community College Research, Asheville, NC.

Lincoln, Y. S., & Guba, E. G. (1985). *Naturalistic inquiry.* Newbury Park, CA: Sage.

Lorenz, E. N. (1993). *The essence of chaos.* Seattle, WA: University of Washington Press.

Love, P. G., & Estanek, S. M. (2004). *Rethinking student affairs practice.* San Francisco, CA: Jossey-Bass.

Marino, J. (1995). Clearcutting in the groves of academe. In G. Laxer & T. Harrison (Eds.), *The Trojan Horse: Alberta and the future of Canada* (pp. 209–222). Montreal, Canada: Black Rose Books.

McGregor, D. (1960). *The human side of enterprise.* New York, NY: McGraw-Hill.

Morgan, G. (1986). *Images of organization.* Newbury Park, CA: Sage.

Morgan, G. (1997). *Images of organization* (2nd ed.). Thousand Oaks, CA: Sage.

Morrison, J., Wilkinson, G., & Forbes, L. (1999). *Common sense management for educational leaders.* Retrieved May 13, 2005, from http://horizon.unc.edu/projects/CSM/

Neumann, A., & Larson, R. S. (1997). Enhancing the leadership factor in planning. In M. W. Peterson, D. D. Dill, & L. A. Mets (Eds.), *Planning and management for a changing environment: A handbook on redesigning postsecondary institutions* (pp. 191–203). San Francisco, CA: Jossey-Bass.

Orton, J. D., & Weick, K. E. (1990). Loosely coupled systems: A reconsideration. *Academy of Management Review, 15*(2), 203–223.

Parker, D., & Stacey, R. (1994). *Chaos, management and economics: The implications of non-linear thinking* (Hobart paper 125). London, England: The Institute of Economic Affairs.

Perkins, J. R., Lanigan, J. B., Downey, J. A., & Levin, B. H. (2001). Chaos theory applied to college planning: A case study in defense of ten propositions. In M. Cutright (Ed.), *Chaos theory and higher education: Leadership, planning, and policy* (pp. 79–112). New York, NY: Peter Lang.

Peterson, M. W. (1997). Using contextual planning to transform institutions. In M. W. Peterson, D. D. Dill, & L A. Mets (Eds.), *Planning and management for a changing environment: A handbook on redesigning postsecondary institutions* (pp. 127–157). San Francisco, CA: Jossey-Bass.

Priesmeyer, H. R. (1992). *Organizations and chaos: Defining the methods of nonlinear management.* Westport, CT: Quorum Books.

Prigogine, I., & Stengers, I. (1984). *Order out of chaos: Man's new dialogue with nature.* New York, NY: Bantam Books.

Ruelle, D. (1991). *Chance and chaos.* Princeton, NJ: Princeton University Press.

Senge, P. M. (1990). *The fifth discipline: The art and practice of the learning organization.* New York, NY: Currency Doubleday.

Taylor, F. W. (1911). *The principles of scientific management.* New York, NY: Harper & Row.

Weick, K. E. (1976). Educational organizations as loosely coupled systems. *Administrative Science Quarterly, 21,* 1–19.

Wheatley, M. J. (1992). *Leadership and the new science: Learning about organization from an orderly universe.* San Francisco, CA: Berrett-Koehler.

Zohar, D. (1997). *ReWiring the corporate brain: Using the new science to rethink how we structure and lead organizations.* San Francisco, CA: Berrett-Koehler.

**5**

# The New Demand for Heterogeneity in College Teaching

George Keller
Baltimore, Maryland

*The past half century has brought an astounding increase in U.S. college and university enrollments. The rapid rise of mass higher education has forced major changes at every institution and is reshaping the U.S. higher education enterprise. Each college needs to ask itself what the huge expansion means for future faculty hires, programs, and modes of teaching.*

## Introduction

Most persons in higher education are aware of the enormous enrollment growth at U.S. colleges and universities in the past half century. But relatively few have fully recognized the radical consequences of this evolution from elite higher education to mass higher education—for teaching, faculty hiring, and the structure of American higher education. Many persons, even scholars of higher learning, still write and speak of the enterprise of higher learning as if it were a unitary entity with only minor differences among the schools; or they advocate improvements in teaching or curriculum as if the improvements should be, or could be, fairly standardized across the nearly 4,000 nonprofit institutions.

But the American movement to make college available not just to a minority of the brightest, more affluent, and most ambitious youths, but to masses of youngsters—and adults—compels us to rethink some accepted postulates about tertiary education. We also need to become more knowledgeable about the numerous ways in which the nation's commitment to providing college education for all has been reshaping U.S. higher education.

We cannot improve the academy wisely unless we understand the consequences that mass higher education has brought to the campuses.

## The Dimensions of Enrollment Growth

It is difficult to comprehend the enormity of the growth of education in the United States during the past six decades. In 1940 only 25% of adult Americans had even a high school diploma. Twenty years later, in 1960, only 41% were high school graduates. Today 80% have completed high school. Similarly, in 1940 only a tiny minority went on to college, and in 1960 less than 8% of U.S. adults had college degrees. The now-huge University of California was then composed of only two major universities, a medical school and three undergraduate colleges. Today, however, America's 3,900 accredited colleges and universities enroll 15.3 million students. More than one-fourth of U.S. citizens 25 years or older now hold a college degree. The United States currently has double the college and university participation of most other countries, with only a few exceptions such as Norway.

Moreover, the composition of the students has changed. Since 1975 the number of students older than 35 has doubled, and the number of foreign students has quadrupled to roughly 580,000. There are many more women, African-Americans, Asians, and Latinos. Three in eight students now attend two-year colleges, where the learning tends to be largely vocational. More than 450,000 students, including many adults, are now enrolled in the newer for-profit colleges (National Center for Education Statistics, 2003). The overwhelming majority of the 15.3 million students are attending universities to prepare to become accountants, nurses, computer engineers, teachers, artists, technicians, and a host of other professions, semi-professions, and lines of work. Most of these persons are not bookish, deeply curious young intellectuals.

A great number of undergraduates, even some without talent, discipline, or ambition, are enrolled today because they are pushed and pulled to attend college, so they tend to be time-servers. Nearly half of all undergraduates drop out before completing their work for a degree. A growing number of students see little use in the liberal arts and are hostile to required courses in these subjects. They want courses that are "relevant," not those that explore Aristotle's philosophy, Giotto's or Rembrandt's paintings, plays by Shakespeare or books by Jane Austen or Alice Munro, poems by Keats or Yeats, texts by Adam Smith, Sigmund Freud, Reinhold Niebuhr, or Isaiah Berlin. A large number do not subscribe to the traditional values and purposes of higher education and demand instead that the professors teach to meet their needs and interests rather than teaching what the scholars think is best.

The first person to notice the radical implications of mass higher education was Berkeley sociologist Martin Trow, who, in two brilliant articles in the early 1970s, predicted that admitting millions of additional young persons with varying degrees of preparation and ambition would necessitate a restructuring of higher learning in America.

> There is a fraction of youth that can achieve its adult roles and intrinsic satisfactions through prolonged formal study. That proportion may be 10, 15, or even 20 percent of the age-grade. But I am sure it is not 50 or 60 or 70 percent of the age-grade. That reason is enough to believe that the future of higher education cannot be an extrapolation of past tendencies. (Trow, 1971, p. 45)

The United States has proudly moved from a relatively limited and elite higher education to a hugely enlarged system which enrolls unprecedented masses of young people and a rapidly growing number of working adults. The vast and far more heterogeneous cohort of college and university students has forced dozens of changes and innovations and several major transformations.

## The New Topography of Higher Education

The offerings at our colleges have had to expand in variety as the enlarged number of students come with a broader array of interests. Dozens of new majors and degrees have been added in fields as diverse as communications, physical therapy, black studies, public relations, and art therapy. Sports have ballooned on campus, along with new majors in sports administration and leisure studies. The core curriculum has eroded and been replaced usually by a Chinese-menu list of courses to fulfill a diluted set of liberal arts requirements. Undergraduate programs have become less research oriented and study has become more experiential, with increased time away from the professors through travel abroad, internships, and cooperative programs with employers. Discourse on campus has changed and is sprinkled as never before with vilification, harassment charges, and political attacks. At some campuses, speech codes have been installed to curtail increasing obscenities and gross insults.

A consensus about the values, behavior, and functions of university life has melted. A growing number of faculty are children of the rebellious 1960s, 1970s, and 1980s, and see as their primary mission the transformation of society rather than the advance of knowledge and introduction of students to the complexities, tradeoffs, wonders, and mysteries of life and the physical world. So-called political correctness is reported to be rife among the faculty at numerous institutions. Like the students, the composition of professors has become more diverse. As one trio of scholars writes, "The extent to which the faculty's demographic profile has changed in very recent years is unprecedented" (Finkelstein, Seal, & Schuster, 1998, p. xi).

To accommodate the increased breadth of courses and variety of students, the structure of academic appointments is being radically altered. As one of the leading experts on America's faculty recently noted,

> In the year 2001, only about one-quarter of new faculty appointments were to full-time tenure track positions (i.e., half were part-time and more than half of the remaining full-time positions were "off" the tenure track). . . . Less obvious (but no less widespread) have been attempts to re-specialize the full-time faculty role: that is, to create full-time positions that do not require the "integrated" (and costly) Humboldtian model, to a more functionally specialized model wherein full-time faculty are now hired as teaching-only or even lower division/introductory courses only; or in the natural sciences and the professions, research-or-clinical only . . . (Finkelstein, 2003, pp. 8, 12).

But perhaps the most significant result of the move into mass higher education has been the differentiation both within and among colleges and universities. Within and among the institutions, faculty and administrative leaders have introduced several structural elements to cope with the greater variety, backgrounds, levels of ability, and interests of the admitted students.

## Segmenting the Enterprise

Within colleges and universities, the schools have had to stretch the range of their teaching and programs of learning. To cope with the less prepared and dedicated entrants, many universities have introduced front-end remedial (or developmental) programs—22% of all freshmen in public colleges in 1995—and ESL (English as a Second Language) courses for the tidal wave of immigrant youths. At the other end, many colleges and universities have opened honors programs for the best prepared and more ambitious students. Most institutions have also abandoned the common core curriculum and increased the number of undergraduate semi-professional and vocational programs and the kinds of master's degrees. Such changes allow the colleges to serve the greatly expanded gamut of student abilities, interests, and needs.

Among the American institutions of higher learning, the advance of mass higher education has pressed into being a new, four-tier order. There are now four basic kinds of colleges and universities, each with its own collection of students, faculty, curriculum, and function for society. The most frequently cited and most prestigious stratum is that of the several dozen research universities. These have become primarily research factories, the principal source of new ideas, scientific findings, and discoveries. It may be hard to believe, but in 1952 the mean SAT-Verbal score at Harvard was only 583. The so-called Ivy League universities, Stanford, and similar schools, had enrollments only slightly above those of other good colleges in academic ability. But beginning in the late 1950s and 1960s they transformed themselves into meritocratic institutions. By 1990 just 10 universities—the Ivies plus Stanford and Berkeley—gathered in 31% of the country's students who scored in the 700s in their SAT-Verbal test (Cook & Frank, 1993; Herrnstein & Murray, 1994). The top 50 research universities, along with a dozen or so of the finest liberal arts colleges, now attract a huge share of the nation's most gifted and studious youth. These same institutions also recruit the most diligent and creative—and expensive—research scholars, and soak up a giant proportion of the federal and corporate research grants. With only a few exceptions, such as Columbia University, the undergraduate curriculum at these places has no core of required learning; methodology and theory are central concerns. Perhaps a third of the teaching of undergraduates at these prestigious houses of intellect is left to graduate students, adjunct instructors, and part-time academics. This tier often has excellent graduate programs and professional schools.

The second tier is that of the small liberal arts colleges, most of them private schools. These schools are often the snug "academical villages" that Thomas Jefferson envisioned, and they are the mainstays of liberal arts learning, exceptional teaching, and what is left of character development. Few have graduate programs of renown, although most of these 100 or so institutions have recently added master's programs and professional schools (Breneman, 1994). At several of the best endowed colleges, such as Amherst, Carleton, Pomona, Swarthmore, and Williams, the quality of student preparation and SAT test scores is on a par with those of the best research universities; but others mainly attract students who are reasonably strong, talented, and moderately affluent.

The third tier, and by far the largest in enrollments, prepares students largely for the world of work. In this layer is a polyglot array of state universities and colleges, regional private colleges and universities, and the specialized colleges of technology, art, education, and business. This tier skillfully turns out accountants, nurses, school teachers, farm managers, electronics experts, and engineers, as well as future lawyers, business executives, and doctors. Athletics is a major activity at many of the larger public and private schools. The faculty is usually a mix of research scholars, good teachers, specialists in some area of work, and many part-time instructors.

The fourth kind is composed of the 1,800 public and private two-year colleges and the less well endowed private four-year colleges. These schools take in more than 90% of their applicants, including some who are woefully underprepared, and they enroll a large percentage of adults in both degree programs and continuing education courses. The faculty tend to be more practically oriented and are called to be instructors that can motivate students (Grubb & Associates, 1999). At many places there is a faculty union. The curriculum is heavily vocational and frequently remedial, and many classes are held in the evenings and on Saturdays. The new for-profit colleges, which often use online delivery of courses to serve busy adults, also concentrate on training for work rather than the education of persons. Thus, as one leading economist of higher education, Duke University's Charles Clotfelter (1999), has observed, "As in other markets where large differences of quality exist, the market for U.S. college education is segmented, with students who are seeking admission to elite institutions, for example, rarely applying simultaneously to community colleges" (p. 5).

## Looking at Teaching With Fresh Eyes

If this brief analysis of the new world of mass higher education is close to reality, I believe that academics and administrators need to adopt a far more differentiated view of effective teaching and learning. We cannot alter the scale and breadth of America's higher education services in such a massive way without altering our outlook, structures, and modes of teaching. Effective teaching at the large research universities will differ from that at the state colleges and from that of the premier liberal arts colleges with their smaller classes and seminars, their stress on the accomplishments of civilization over the centuries, and their preparation for life and leadership rather than education for academic posts or professional or career distinction. Mass higher education decreases the worth of general, across-the-field prescriptions. The variety of students attending colleges and universities is different from that of several decades ago. The faculty seem in considerable part more active and opinionated politically, and their hiring and roles on campus have changed. The curricula of yesteryear have mostly dissolved and new majors have blossomed. The structure of higher education, with its increasingly segmented tiers, has become more hierarchical, with more distinct national missions for each tier. Teaching and learning should therefore become more clientele-specific, more institution-specific.

To me, a major need is for the faculty, administrators, and trustees at each institution to undertake a deep and frank assessment of its tradition and culture, the nature of its students, the quality, style, and teaching skill of the faculty, and the programs of learning the institution offers. They need to ask: How has the college been changing in the face of the greater heterogeneity of today's students, the new generation of faculty members, and the expanded range of academic fields of inquiry, from molecular genetics and software engineering to Chicano and Muslim studies? How should it change? How should your professors teach now that computers, young people from other ethnicities and cultures, and a wider range of student preparations and ambitions are present?

I have recently written about one college that did look into its soul and transformed itself for the coming decades (Keller, 2004). The scrutiny seems to have paid off. In the mid-1990s, Elon University had the usual three-times-a-week meetings for courses, with instruction offered heavily through lectures and reading assignments. There were roughly 300 courses in the catalog, and the faculty members each taught four or five courses a semester, which the academic vice president keenly wished to reduce. Earlier, a faculty member, who was also the director of advising, had begun giving each entering student a Myers-Briggs Type Indicator test. She found that most of the students were not heavily studious and introverted but for the most part, energetic, extroverted, and interested in learning. Elon's clientele were middle-of-the-graduating-class persons who loved to do things rather than read about what others have done.

So, the academic vice president decided to institute *engaged learning,* with students actively researching, creating, traveling, and building in their studies and extracurricular activities. He cut nearly 150 courses and stretched the class meetings to four times a week, with the extra hour devoted to active learning projects. The faculty's teaching load was reduced to three courses a semester, and their salaries were increased. A cocurricular program that encouraged students to do community service, travel and study abroad, work as interns in national businesses, run campus programs and help make policy, and conduct undergraduate research was installed. Thus, the teaching at this college became more interactive and problem oriented, and more learning was done through hands-on work outside of classes and active engagement with real-life situations. The teaching matched the kind of students that the institution was attracting instead of trying to force them to adhere to an older liberal arts pattern of instruction that is more appropriate for the elite colleges.

Given the new size and scope of American higher education, the leaders of every campus really should reappraise the operation of their houses of intellect. And each college and university should tailor its strategies, admits, and hiring to the specific role it plays, or intends to play, in advanced education in America.

## References

Breneman, D. W. (1994). *Liberal arts colleges: Thriving, surviving, or endangered?* Washington, DC: The Brookings Institution.

Clotfelter, C. T. (1999). The familiar but curious economics of higher education. *Journal of Economic Perspectives, 13*(1), 3–12.

Cook, P. J., & Frank, R. H. (1993). The growing concentration of top students at elite schools. In C. T. Clotfelter & M. Rothschild (Eds.), *Studies of supply and demand in higher education* (pp. 121–144). Chicago, IL: University of Chicago Press.

Finkelstein, M. J. (2003). The morphing of the American academic profession. *Liberal Education, 89*(4), 6–15.

Finkelstein, M. J., Seal, R. K., & Schuster, J. H. (1998). *The new academic generation: A profession in transition.* Baltimore, MD: Johns Hopkins University Press.

Grubb, W. N., & Associates. (1999). *Honored but invisible: An inside look at teaching in community colleges.* New York, NY: Routledge.

Herrnstein, R. J., & Murray, C. (1994). *The bell curve: Intelligence and class structure in American life.* New York, NY: Free Press.

Keller, G. (2004). *Transforming a college: The story of a little-known college's strategic climb to national distinction.* Baltimore, MD: Johns Hopkins University Press.

National Center for Education Statistics. (2003). *Digest of education statistics, 2002.* Retrieved May 13, 2005, from http://nces.ed.gov/pubsearch/pubsinfo.asp ?pubid=2003060

Trow, M. (1970). Reflections on the transition from mass to universal higher education. *Daedalus, 99,* 1–42.

Trow, M. (1971). Admissions and the crisis in American higher education. In W. T. Furniss (Ed.), *Higher education for everybody? Issues and implications* (pp. 26–52). Washington, DC: American Council on Education.

6

# Not Making or Shaping: Finding Authenticity in Faculty Development

Patricia Cranton
Penn State Harrisburg

*Authenticity is defined as a multifaceted concept that includes self-awareness, awareness of others, genuine relationships, awareness of contextual constraints, and living a critical life. Authenticity develops over time and with experience; a developmental continuum for authenticity is discussed. Drawing on a three-year research project on authenticity in teaching in higher education, this chapter suggests ways in which faculty developers can help foster authentic practice.*

## Introduction

I began my practice as a faculty developer in 1976, nearly 30 years ago. At that time, one of our primary concerns was how to increase faculty participation in our various programs, primarily workshops and individual or departmental consultations. The underlying implication was that we needed to get faculty members to change their practice. In 2004, at the 29th annual Conference of the Professional and Organizational Development Network in Higher Education (POD), I noticed that the same kinds of questions are still being asked. How can we "make" people come to faculty development sessions? How can we reach those people who "most need" faculty development? How can we "shape" people's attitudes?

I propose that attempting to "make" and "shape" denies the authenticity of the faculty member. My research on authenticity in teaching in higher education reveals that educators, through experience, find a variety of ways of becoming authentic and effective in their practice (Cranton & Carusetta, 2004). At the 2004 POD conference, I also heard a participant say, "If we praise one person, we leave out those we didn't praise." It is a fallacy of democracy that if we do not treat everyone equally, we discriminate against some. By attempting to treat everyone equally, by attempting to make everyone into our own version of what a good teacher should be, we renounce their uniqueness and their authenticity. If we presume to tell people what to do, we place ourselves above them—superior creatures who know the answers and hold the key to good teaching.

In this chapter, I first define authenticity, based both on the literature and on how the concept emerged from my research. I then describe a developmental perspective of authenticity that I constructed from interviews with new and experienced faculty members over a three-year time span. From this foundation, I suggest faculty development strategies that take into account the uniqueness of individuals and their journey to authentic teaching.

## What Is Authenticity?

Authenticity is a multifaceted concept that includes being genuine, showing consistency between values and actions, relating to others in such a way as to encourage their authenticity, and living a critical life. Authenticity is most often mentioned in passing in the literature rather than treated as a central idea. Brookfield (1995), for example, advises us of the importance of being authentic in our role as an educator, and Scott (1998) lists freedom, democracy, and authenticity as the goals of transformative learning. Freire (1984) refers to authentic witness based on a critical knowledge of the context of practice. Cranton (2001) suggests that authenticity is at the core of meaningful teaching and contributes to the spiral-like journey of individuation and transformative learning. Perhaps it is Palmer (1998) who has brought authenticity most vividly to our attention in higher education through his notion that good teaching comes from the identity and integrity of the teacher.

### Being Genuine

Cranton (2001) defines authenticity as the expression of the genuine self in the community and presents a process by which educators come to know themselves and their preferences within the social context of their work. She describes teaching as a specialized form of communication which has learning as its goal and points out that meaningful communication rests on the premise that those involved are speaking genuinely and honestly rather than with an intent to manipulate or deceive. Brookfield (1990) suggests that educators reveal personal aspects of themselves and their experiences, insofar as they are comfortable doing that, as a part of being genuine.

However, it is important to go beyond a definition of authenticity that focuses only on the self. Authenticity develops in relationships, through dialogue, and in a social and political context. Educators communicate with learners as a way of fostering their development, and this is done within a framework of the social responsibilities of the educator.

## Showing Consistency Between Values and Actions

Brookfield (1993) proposes that being an authentic teacher includes making sure our behaviors are congruent with our words and admitting we do not have all the answers and can make mistakes. He balances credibility and authenticity; educators should practice what they preach and be sure not to espouse one way of working then behave in a different way in their own teaching. Similarly, in discussing personal authenticity, Ray and Anderson (2000) emphasize that actions need to be consistent with beliefs. They see reliance on personal experience rather than "meaningless hype" (p. 8) and falsely objective journalism as the way to develop authenticity.

## Relating to Others

Jarvis (1992) sees people as being authentic when they choose to act so as to "foster the growth and development of each other's being" (p. 113). Jarvis sees this as an experimental and creative act where educators consciously have the goal of helping another person develop. In other words, teachers and students learn together through dialogue as Freire (1984) advocates, and the result of authentic teaching is that "teachers learn and grow together with their students" (Jarvis, 1992, p. 114). As we know from Buber's (1961) work, it is only through relationships with others that authenticity can be fostered. Brookfield (1990) also emphasizes building trust with students and respecting students as people. He provides educators with a practical focus—what we can *do* in the classroom to be authentic.

Freire (1984) outlines six attitudes that need to be present for meaningful and authentic dialogue (dialogue which is not oppressive) to occur: 1) love for the world and human beings, 2) humility, 3) faith in people and their power to create and recreate, 4) trust, 5) hope that the dialogue will lead to meaning, and 6) critical thinking and the continuing transformation of reality. Authenticity develops in relationships among people and is expressed in dialogue.

Hollis (1998), a Jungian, helps integrate an understanding of persona (the masks we wear) with the importance of relationships in authenticity. To enter into an authentic relationship requires self-understanding. "The quality of all our relationships is a direct function of our relationship to ourselves. . . . The best thing we can do for our relationships with others, and with the transcendent, then, is to render our relationship to ourselves more conscious" (Hollis, p. 13). The quality of relationships depends on how well we know ourselves and how authentically we bring ourselves to the relationship.

Although Jung (1921/1971) does not write directly about authenticity, the notion of persona plays a vital role in his understanding of human psychology. The persona is that aspect of an individual's psyche that lives up to what is expected and proper. We cover up our inferiorities with a persona; we are vulnerable without it. As Sharp (1998) says, "Civilized society depends on interactions between people through the persona" (p. 27). It becomes unhealthy when a person believes he or she is nothing but a persona or mask—no more than what is shown to others. This is inauthentic.

## Leading a Critical Life

Jarvis (1992) suggests that authenticity is linked with reflective learning. People need to develop as autonomous and rational individuals within their social context. When people's actions are "controlled by others and their performance is repetitive and ritualistic" (pp. 115–116), they are inauthentic. Heidegger (1962) sees authenticity as involving critical participation in life. By critical participation, he means we question how we are different from the community and live accordingly; we do not do something just because it is done that way by others or believe what others believe without considering whether it is true for us. This is a good way of understanding authenticity because we need to know who we are and what we believe and then act on that. However, this does not mean that we make such decisions in isolation. Authenticity involves knowing and understanding the collective and carefully and critically determining how we are different from and the same as that collective. Sharp (1995) suggests the first fruit of consciously developing as an authentic person is the "segregation of the individual from the undifferentiated and unconscious herd" (p. 48). In Jungian terms, this is individuation, and it includes not only separation from the herd, but also a simultaneous rejoining in a more meaningful way with the collective of humanity.

Thinking along parallel lines, Freire (1984) argues that authenticity comes through having a critical knowledge of the context within which we work and seeing the principal contradictions of that society. To be authentic, the educator is bold, dares to take risks, and recognizes that he or she will not always win over the people.

In order to create a genuine self, we need to critically participate in life rather than run with the unconscious herd. Part of this journey is understanding how others are different from us without attempting to make them into our own image; that is, we help others discover their authenticity as a way of fostering our own authenticity.

## Research on Authenticity

Using a grounded theory methodology (Glaser & Strauss, 1967), my colleagues and I interviewed and observed 22 faculty members from three university campuses over the course of three years. Participants came from the following disciplines: administration (business), philosophy, computer science, education, forestry, kinesiology, nursing, English, biology, psychology, botany, classics, and economics. There were 13 women and 9 men. Seven participants were new faculty in their first or second year of full-time teaching, and 15 were experienced teachers. We report on the full details of the methodology elsewhere (Cranton & Carusetta, 2004).

In order to search for developmental trends, we followed the transcripts of individuals over the three years of the project and also looked at differences between new and experienced participants. The conceptualization of authenticity that emerged from the research included five interrelated categories: self, other, relationship, context, and critical reflection.

### Self

Faculty spoke about their awareness of themselves as people and as teachers, how they came to be a teacher, what that meant for them, their values, their passions, the conflicts they experienced between the realities of teaching and their values, and the ways in which they brought themselves as people into their practice. They spoke of teaching as a calling or a vocation, as something that gave meaning to their lives. Most faculty spoke about the importance of bringing their sense of self into the classroom, though the degree to which people felt comfortable with revealing aspects of their personal lives varied. Everyone had stories to tell about how they became who they are as teachers, including stories about individuals who helped shape their perspectives.

### Other

Faculty recognized the importance of understanding others, especially their students. They showed a strong interest in and awareness of their students' characteristics, needs, and learning styles. Some participants also were aware of and concerned with students' personal problems and lives outside of the classroom, but others preferred to stay more distant.

## Relationship

The most commonly discussed facet of authenticity was the relationship between teacher and student. This was broadly defined to include helping students learn, caring for students, engaging in dialogue, and being aware of exercising power. Faculty talked about the nature of their relationships with students, and many struggled with where the boundary of their relationships should be, especially in light of their responsibilities for evaluation and grading. Underlying many of our conversations was an intense and powerful sense of caring about students and their learning. We also found a variety of perceptions of how power contributed to or inhibited relationships between educators and students.

## Context

The context within which faculty work influences their perceptions of themselves, their students, and their relationships with students. Context consists of several levels:

- The content of the teaching

- The discipline or subject area

- The physical classroom, including the size of the class and the room arrangement

- The psychological environment within the learning group

- The department in which people work and its norms and expectations

- Institutional norms and policies

- The general community or culture and the roles people expect faculty to maintain

Typically, faculty worked to create a comfortable atmosphere. They tended to speak positively about their departmental contexts in terms of the support they felt for being who they were and teaching in a way that suited their preferences. At the broader institutional level, people expressed some of the usual conflict between teaching and research responsibilities.

## Critical Reflection

Critical reflection was a strong theme throughout our conversations with faculty. Participants in the project questioned their teacher roles, the effectiveness of the methods they used, their ability to promote student learning, and evaluation and grading issues. Critical self-reflection and critical reflection on faculty relationships with students were the most common, but participants also reflected on student characteristics and the context of their teaching. Newer faculty were more interested in learning about and conforming to the social expectations of their role; more experienced faculty were more likely to differentiate themselves from collective norms.

## The Development of Authenticity

For each of the five facets of authenticity, we found a developmental progression that tended to move from fragmented, authority-based perceptions to more integrated, constructed understandings.

In their perceptions of self and self as teacher, the less experienced teachers tend to separate who they are as a teacher from who they are outside of their practice. Their teaching self was often described as an authority figure. New faculty reported on teaching according to what they had read or learned in a faculty development workshop. Acquiring techniques and tips and developing a "toolkit" were mentioned as priorities. New faculty were less comfortable in telling personal anecdotes in class or letting students see who they are. More experienced participants did not make this separation, or if they did, they did so deliberately and after considerable reflection on where and how they saw their teaching-self as different from their personal-self. Mature authenticity also involved a deep and often intense questioning of self.

The spectrum of awareness of others (primarily students) ranged from specific, unquestioned perceptions where all students are seen to possess the same characteristic through to a complex, multifaceted awareness of the diversity of others and a concern for students' personal development. For example, a young social science professor perceived her students solely in relation to their year of study (first-year students are like this, but third-year students are like that), but a professor of English literature who had been teaching for more than 30 years was deeply concerned that students get to know each other as individuals. In between, we saw people with an understanding of individual differences in learning styles, usually related to the acquisition of knowledge, and a consciousness of students' level of development and their engagement in critical reflection.

Faculty in the beginning phases of authenticity described their relationships with students according to concrete rules. They saw themselves as maintaining a distance, staying on one side of a line that separated their educator role from their students or basing the nature of the relationships on their position as teacher. They did not raise power issues, and when asked, they said they were not aware of power differentials in the classroom or they did not have power, even though they also talked about maintaining control and authority. New faculty were often concerned about being in charge of the events in the classroom. Those participants who demonstrated a more mature authenticity tended to emphasize students' development through relationships. For example, a senior nursing faculty member saw her primary goal as helping students make fundamental shifts in perspective in collaborative working groups. Experienced faculty were conscious of how their own development was influenced by interactions with students, and they expressed complex and sometimes contradictory perceptions of their relationships with students. In between these two points of view, we found faculty who had thought about their relationships with students and had a rationale for the way they chose to establish connections and those who allowed for a variety of ways of relating to students in different contexts.

In their awareness of the influence of context on practice, faculty mentioned a diverse collection of factors, ranging from the subject area to departmental, institutional, and social norms. New faculty tended to develop rules about the context of teaching. Context was seen to be inflexible and unchangeable. A faculty member from a business program created and followed a rule that required him to explain new material to students. Although new faculty members were aware of the influence of context, they did not see that there would be anything they could do about it. In the next phase, the awareness was more complex, but still maintained a cause-and-effect influence on teaching. For example, if the class size was too large, then it was impossible to have students work in groups. At the more mature levels of authenticity, participants questioned the influence of context, struggled with it, and looked for ways to challenge it so that they could fully express their own values and beliefs. An experienced literature professor challenged and bypassed policies on dropping courses.

Everyone involved in the project engaged in critical reflection on practice, but the nature of the reflection varied. Faculty members in the beginning phases of authenticity tended to reflect on the use of specific techniques and strategies and to look for solutions to teaching problems: what is happening and what can I do about it? For example, a young humanities teacher was looking for practical solutions to the problem of disappointing term papers.

At the other end of the continuum, the focus was on questioning the premises underlying educators' conceptualization of themselves, their students, and the context within which they work. A senior scholar in the humanities demonstrated "premise reflection" in his struggle to question the meaning of "good teaching." In between, we found people paying attention to how they came to be the teacher they are and thinking more broadly about the techniques of teaching. These faculty members also reflected on institutional norms and others' expectations of what a good teacher should be like.

## Helping Authentic Teachers Develop

More and more, I find it presumptuous to say that I am a "faculty developer," which seems to imply that I can "develop" others. I deliberately chose a heading here that emphasizes helping teachers develop—it is they who develop; it is I who provide suggestions, resources, and activities for that journey. I argue that we often, in faculty development work, try to make faculty members teach according to our own perceptions of what is right and good or, less overtly, try to shape their attitudes and beliefs to be more in line with our own notion of best practices. As an alternative, it is my intent here to challenge faculty developers to work with faculty members to develop *their* authentic way of being a good teacher. I use the five facets of authenticity as a framework for this discussion.

### Development of Self and Teacher as Self

Elsewhere, I propose a variety of strategies for helping faculty members develop self-awareness as a way of becoming more authentic (Cranton, 2001). I draw on some of those ideas here. In order for educators to bring a genuine sense of self into their teaching, a good self-awareness is helpful. To this end, I suggest that faculty members engage in a variety of activities:

- List and reflect on nouns or noun phrases that define their self, and if it is comfortable, share and discuss that list with a friend or colleague.

- Complete a psychological type preference, learning style, or teaching style inventory and discuss the results with a friend or colleague.

- List and reflect on significant experiences that have changed the way they see themselves and their teaching.

- List and reflect on 10 personal and 10 professional values.

- Write an educational autobiography.

- Consider areas of discrepancy or fragmentation between personal and professional preferences, behaviors, and values.

If the educator is willing, it can be useful to discuss the results of such activities with the faculty developer or with colleagues in a workshop. The goal should be to increase self-awareness and especially to determine how a sense of self is brought into teaching.

## Development of Awareness of Students as People

In developing authenticity in teaching, the focus can not be only on the self. This path takes us into what Taylor (1991) calls narcissistic authenticity—the notion of self-determining freedom where individuals make judgments for themselves alone without external impositions and find a license to do their own thing and find self-fulfillment at the expense of others and society. At a broader social level, the purely personal understanding of self-fulfillment denies commitment to a community. Increasing awareness of others in the teaching and learning environment is part of being able to engage in authentic relationships, which form the basis of authentic teaching. In order to help faculty members develop an awareness of students as people, faculty developers could suggest some of the following:

- Arrange to have students complete a learning styles inventory or psychological type preference assessment and discuss those results in groups in the class.

- Encourage students to talk about their experiences as they relate to the course content.

- Take time to meet individually with students outside of the class to get to know them; have an open door.

- Chat with students informally in the hallways or cafeterias; join students during a break for a cup of tea.

- Collect frequent feedback from students about their reactions to the course, their feelings about how things are going, and their suggestions for changes.

- Set up a listserv or a web-based discussion forum for students to exchange and discuss ideas.

When faculty are encouraged to get to know their students as people, the focus of teaching moves away from the *performance* of the faculty member to the characteristics and desires of the students—a transition from teacher-centered to student-centered learning almost follows automatically. Teaching comes to be about relationship and communication, rather than the handing over of information to a relative stranger.

## Development of Relationships With Students

Whatever faculty do to develop an awareness of their students as people will feed into the development of a relationship. It is only when we objectify people—see them as objects or see them only in relation to their role—that we have no relationship. Relationships cannot develop between roles or personas. Students cannot make a connection with an educator who only plays the role of teacher, and teachers cannot make a connection with students when they see them as a generalized category. Awareness of the humanity of the other is the basis for relationship, and I argue that relationship is the foundation of authentic teaching. Palmer (1998) says that when he "asks teachers to name the biggest obstacle to good teaching, the answer [he] most often hears is 'my students'" (p. 40). They are unmotivated, illiterate, cannot engage in meaningful discussions, and on the list goes. When we stereotype students, Palmer suggests, we widen the disconnect between students and teachers.

What we cannot do is tell faculty members what kind of relationship they should have with students. This presumes that there is one good relationship, a sort of persona of a relationship. In our research, we met educators who had a variety of ways of relating with students, each of which was true to the person's values and preferences. They ranged from fairly close and personal relationships, which included inviting students to dinner or other social gatherings, to more distant collegial relationships where the connection was based on a common interest in the subject area. The tasks of the faculty developer might include:

- Helping faculty members determine what style of relationship with students is most congruent with their values and personal preferences.

- Engage in discussions and activities which tease out the assumptions people make about how teachers and students "should" relate to each other—what are the social norms related to student-teacher relationships? Critically question those norms.

- Use videos, films, or novels that depict different relationships between educators and students.

- Encourage faculty to discuss with colleagues how they establish good relationships with students—share stories and experiences, work toward an understanding of alternative ways of connecting with others so as to find the way that best suits the individual.

Palmer (1998) writes that when "authentic community emerges, false differences in power and status disappear" (p. 138). Much of academic life is based on autonomy. We may collaborate on research projects or writing articles, but in the end, we go up alone to have our publications counted and our reward given. When this sense of autonomy is taken into the classroom, as it often is, we set ourselves as independent from and apart from the students. But when we find a genuine and open way of relating to students so as to create an authentic sense of community, learning can occur at new and deeper levels. I propose that faculty developers can help faculty do this, and that it has nothing to do with technique and everything to do with being oneself.

## Development of Awareness of the Teaching Context

Teaching is a social process that takes place within a context. The discipline, the institution, the community, and state and society all form a context for teaching, though most of us are more aware of the immediate context than the larger one. Faculty developers can be helpful in increasing awareness of the influence of context on authenticity in teaching. Institutional policies and procedures can pose some serious constraints to authenticity, and when people are unaware of them, it can be hard to sort out what the problem is. I make a few suggestions for faculty developers here:

- Help faculty members find out about both the written and the unwritten policies of their institution—everything from attendance policies and syllabus requirements to rewards for good teaching and the budgetary and resource availability.

- Encourage faculty members to explore written and unwritten departmental policies as they may differ from the overall institutional norms.

- Help faculty members determine where they stand in relation to institutional policies (are there policies with which they disagree, are there policies which violate their values?) and act as an advocate for change for faculty.

- Plan cross-departmental and cross-institutional discussion groups where faculty can compare contexts.

- Encourage people to participate in conferences on teaching either in their discipline or more general meetings such as the Professional and Organizational Development Network where they can learn about a variety of teaching contexts.

- Explore with faculty the types of communities to which they belong— communities based on shared interests such as professional associations, communities based on shared experiences such as attending school together, and geographical communities.

- Engage in activities with faculty which define the educational values and social norms of relevant communities and discuss how those values and norms influence teaching.

- Collect information about broad social expectations of educators—news stories, teacher movies, government policies, and funding for higher education reflect attitudes toward teaching.

Oddly, teaching is often seen as a solitary activity. We are "alone" with our students in our classroom, and talking about teaching is not a priority in most departments. If faculty do not share experiences about teaching, especially across disciplines and institutions, it may be difficult to know how influential context actually is. Whatever faculty developers can do to encourage exchange of information and consciousness-raising in relation to educational social norms will be useful. The greatest constraints to authenticity that faculty experience come from their teaching context.

## Development of Criticality

There has been considerable attention paid to critical reflection on teaching, and most faculty developers encourage reflective practice. Brookfield (2005) outlines four traditions of criticality:

- Ideology critique (ways in which people recognize uncritically assimilated and unjust dominant ideologies or sociocultural distortions)

- The identification of psychocultural assumptions that constrain how we see ourselves and our relationships

- Analytic philosophy and logic through which we become more skillful in argument analysis

- Pragmatic constructivism by which people construct and deconstruct their experiences and meanings

Each of these traditions has its place in developing authenticity, but perhaps ideology critique, whereby faculty examine the context of their teaching, and the identification of psychocultural assumptions, whereby faculty question their self-awareness and their relationships with students, are most relevant here. Brookfield (1990, 1995) also provides practical strategies for becoming a reflective teacher, many of which will be familiar to faculty developers. I make some suggestions here:

- Build critical reflection activities into workshops and seminars; for example, have faculty complete critical incidents where they describe a best or worst teaching experience and analyze it for underlying assumptions about teaching.

- Encourage faculty to keep a journal or a shared journal (with a colleague or friend) in which they write about and consider assumptions underlying their practice.

- Help people write a philosophy of practice in which values and assumptions are articulated and critically questioned.

- Provide reading materials or videos in which alternative approaches to teaching are presented.

- Ask faculty to immerse themselves into an aesthetic or artistic experience as a way of imagining alternatives to their current practice; this type of experience can help people break away from linear problem-solving approaches to teaching.

- Provide the opportunity for role playing or critical debate in which faculty try on perspectives different from their own.

Mezirow's (1991) concepts of content, process, and premise reflection are helpful here as well. In content reflection, people ask, "What is the problem here?" and in process reflection, they consider, "How did this get to be the way it is?" Premise reflection leads to an exploration of the assumptions underlying the situation, as people ask, "Why is this important in the first place?" To translate this into an examination of teaching, the reflective process might look like this: "My students cannot write a coherent essay. What is going on here?" Process reflection could take the form: "My colleagues all say that students can't write anymore; they are practically illiterate. How did this situation come about? Is this true of all students? How could this be the case?" And finally, the premise reflection questions might include: "Why is writing important? Whose responsibility is this? Why am I accepting my colleague's point of view? What are some alternative ways of understanding this situation?"

Leading a critical life as an educator means separating out who we are from who others think we should be by critically questioning ourselves and our practice. Faculty developers have an important role to play in facilitating this aspect of becoming authentic.

## Conclusion

Several years ago, I worked with a colleague who, at the end of a class, was so stressed and exhausted that he had to lie on the floor of his office for a time. I knew him outside of the classroom, and I knew how he taught. In order to try to live up to what he thought were the expectations of a professor, he taught in ways that were completely incongruent with his nature. Stress is just one danger of inauthentic practice. Communication with students is put at risk; students may see the inauthentic teacher as a fraud; and it is quite possible that no one will appreciate the effort to follow social norms anyway.

In doing research on, writing about, and teaching courses related to authenticity, I am always struck by the powerful draw that this concept has for people. In three years, no one dropped out of our research project, even though folks were extremely busy with many other things. Some people came in for interviews, even though they were on sabbatical. My courses on authenticity are always oversubscribed and workshops well attended. I suspect that in a time where the academic culture encourages fragmentation of knowledge and disconnected lives, it just feels good to think about integration of facets of our self and authentic connections. I hope that this brief foray into authenticity will assist those who help faculty to develop.

## References

Brookfield, S. (1993). Through the lens of learning: How the visceral experience of learning reframes teaching. In D. Boud, R. Cohen, & D. Walker (Eds.), *Using experience for learning* (pp. 21–32). Buckingham, England: Society for Research into Higher Education and Open University Press.

Brookfield, S. D. (1990). *The skillful teacher: On technique, trust, and responsiveness in the classroom.* San Francisco, CA: Jossey-Bass.

Brookfield, S. D. (1995). *Becoming a critically reflective teacher.* San Francisco, CA: Jossey-Bass.

Brookfield, S. D. (2005). *The power of critical theory: Liberating adult learning and teaching.* San Francisco, CA: Jossey-Bass.

Buber, M. (1961). *Between man and man.* New York, NY: Routledge and Kegan Paul.

Cranton, P. (2001). *Becoming an authentic teacher in higher education.* Malabar, FL: Krieger.

Cranton, P., & Carusetta, E. (2004). Perspectives on authenticity in teaching. *Adult Education Quarterly, 55*(1), 5–22.

Freire, P. (1984). *Pedagogy of the oppressed.* New York, NY: Continuum.

Glaser, B. G., & Strauss, A. L. (1967). *The discovery of grounded theory: Strategies for qualitative research.* Chicago, IL: Aldine.

Heidegger, M. (1962). *Being and time* (J. Macquarrie & E. Robinson, Trans.). New York, NY: Harper & Row.

Hollis, J. (1998). *The Eden Project: In search of the magical other.* Toronto, Canada: Inner City Books.

Jarvis, P. (1992). *Paradoxes of learning: On becoming an individual in society.* San Francisco, CA: Jossey-Bass.

Jung, C. (1971). *Psychological types.* Princeton, NJ: Princeton University Press. (Original work published 1921)

Mezirow, J. (1991). *Transformative dimensions of adult learning.* San Francisco, CA: Jossey-Bass.

Palmer, P. J. (1998). *The courage to teach: Exploring the inner landscape of a teacher's life.* San Francisco, CA: Jossey-Bass.

Ray, P. H., & Anderson, S. R. (2000). *The cultural creatives: How 50 million people are changing the world.* New York, NY: Three Rivers Press.

Scott, S. (1998). An overview of transformation theory in adult education. In S. Scott, B. Spencer, & A. Thomas (Eds.), *Learning for life: Canadian readings in adult education* (pp. 178–187). Toronto, Canada: Thompson Educational Publishing.

Sharp, D. (1995). *Who am I really? Personality, soul and individuation.* Toronto, Canada: Inner City Books.

Sharp, D. (1998). *Jungian psychology unplugged: My life as an elephant.* Toronto, Canada: Inner City Books.

Taylor, C. (1991). *The malaise of modernity.* Toronto, Canada: House of Anansi Press.

# 7

# A Theory-Based Integrative Model for Learning and Motivation in Higher Education

Chantal S. Levesque, G. Roger Sell, James A. Zimmerman
Missouri State University

*The shared mission of higher education institutions is to develop educated persons who are able to make connections and build on knowledge acquired across disciplines and fields and through various life experiences. This chapter offers a theory-based model that can be used by researchers and practitioners to enhance academic learning and motivation. Educators can create learning environments that move students from external regulation to self-determined forms of motivation. This model is used to describe conditions that enhance/restrict learning. It also has the potential to be used to interpret research on teaching and learning in higher education.*

## Introduction

The central purpose of colleges and universities is to develop educated persons who experience fulfillment as competent, caring, and free human beings. Toward this end, educators can design and implement engaging environments that move students from states of amotivation (without a desire or purpose) and behaviors dependent on external regulation to more self-determined and intrinsic forms of motivation. Highly engaging environments promote effective learning that satisfies basic psychological needs such as competence, relatedness, and autonomy.

In the field of college teaching and learning, theory tends to be dissociated from practice. In addition, researchers interested in learning principles tend to study the mechanics of *how* people learn. A crucially important aspect of learning that is often ignored is *why* people learn. The reasons behind peoples' learning—the motivation for learning—should receive greater attention by education researchers and practitioners.

Svinicki (2004) summarizes speculation about what motivation does for learning: it directs the learners' attention to the task at hand and makes them less distractible; it changes what learners pay attention to; it helps learners persist when they encounter obstacles; and it serves, in the form of goals, as benchmarks that the learners can use to monitor their own learning. Taking the position that "there is no grand or unifying theory of motivation in the psychological literature," she goes on to offer an amalgamated theory of extant "bits and pieces of a theory accumulated over the years" (p. 142) and suggests strategies for enhancing student motivation.

We agree with Svinicki that education can be improved with "good practice" based on research and theory. We also can endorse strategies that Svinicki recommends for enhancing motivation such as being a good role model of appropriate motivation, basing evaluation on progress or absolute level achieved, and providing learners with choice and/or control over goals or strategies.

However, because any eclectic theory attempts to amalgamate or synthesize disparate "bits and pieces" of extant theories, that themselves may be fragmented and have fundamental incompatibilities with other theories, we have taken a different approach to offer another option. We begin with an intact macro or comprehensive theory of motivation that has been elaborated with more than 25 years of sustained empirical research. Using that theory as a foundation, we have created an integrative model to specify and clarify the connections between learning and motivation and to offer a framework that can be used by researchers and practitioners to enhance academic learning and motivation. We use the term *integrative* in the title to mean three things: conceptualization of learning and motivation into a holistic perspective; use of a model to examine and synthesize research findings focused on learning and/or motivation; and combining of research and practice, the joining of theory with application.

As a springboard for this work, we draw on self-determination theory (SDT) to help interpret and synthesize research on teaching and learning and to describe conditions that enhance and restrict learning. We also link motivation to other key factors in learning such as students' active engagement, prior knowledge and beliefs, information processing approaches to learning, reflection, and self-regulation for learning. We believe that much of what is presented in this chapter can be useful for education from early childhood through adulthood, but our focus is particularly on formal learning experiences in higher education.

## Learning and Motivation Factors in Higher Education

In this chapter we argue that *educators contribute to, but cannot directly cause, student learning*. It is for this explicit reason, also aptly expressed by Knapper (2004), that we chose to situate learning strategies and outcomes at the center of our model (see Figure 7.1). Briefly, and to be discussed more fully, the major influences of the educator on learning are through the *design* of learning environments (considering social-cultural aspects as well as physical setting) in which students interact with content, the educator, peers, and others, and the *implementation* of strategies that help guide the student toward realizing the intended learning outcomes. Within this model, learning activities occur in the immediate academic environment of the classroom (including laboratories, studios, etc.) as well as in settings beyond the classroom and campus.

FIGURE 7.1

A Visual Representation of an Integrative Model for
Learning and Motivation

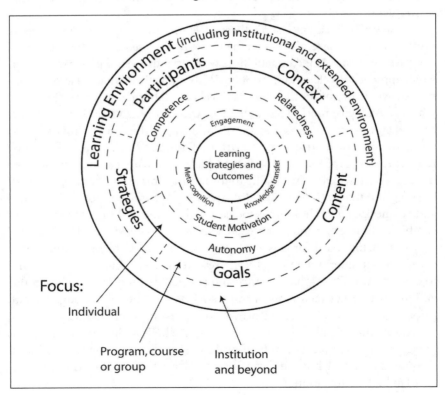

A major premise for our model is that the overarching goals of the educator and the institution should be to create learning environments that enhance students' satisfaction of basic psychological needs and to positively affect student motivation that increases the quality of the students' learning experiences and the outcomes attributed to those experiences.

We contend that effective learning is a self-regulated process. It is internal to the person and thus cannot be caused by an external source. Because learning involves changes that occur within the person, effective learning that is useful and long-lasting engages individuals in a process characterized by self-determination (volition) and meaningfulness.

With these premises, definitions, and assumptions, one of the most important questions is: How do we create learning environments that fulfill basic psychological needs and facilitate effective learning?

We propose that effective educators are those able to create learning environments which draw upon and lead to the satisfaction of needs for competence, relatedness, and autonomy. As portrayed in Figure 7.1, educators make decisions and carry out activities that influence five important facets of the learning environment: participants (educators and students), context (immediate setting), content (subject matter), goals (objectives and tasks), and strategies (methods and technologies). Although conceptually distinguishable from one another, these five facets of the learning environment are deeply intertwined, each one affecting and interacting with the others.

## Participants

Participants are the individuals directly involved in learning activities aimed at explicit goals and objectives. The central participants in the formal learning environment of a college or university are students and educators. At times, and depending on the course or program of study, others within the institution (e.g., staff and administrators) and practitioners beyond the institution (e.g., in community service-learning) also may be included as participants. Critical to the definition of participants are characteristics that affect their abilities and actions in the learning environment. Some key individual characteristics include prior knowledge, beliefs, self-regulatory skills, and emotional states. For example, students' prior knowledge and experiences affect how they perceive, understand, and integrate novel information. Similarly, an educator's epistemological beliefs regarding the nature of knowledge and intelligence subsequently affect his or her teaching approach as well as the extent of the help he or she is willing to provide to students.

## Context

Within this model, context is defined as the immediate learning milieu both within and outside the classroom in which the participant functions on a day-to-day basis. In contrast to the internal focus in the definition of participant, the definition of context has a decidedly external focus. For example, an individual's emotional state is internal to the person and in the domain of the participant, while the immediate learning environment that affects a participant's current emotional state is external to the person and in the domain of what we define as a participant's context.

## Content

Content refers to the subject matter and topics that are part of the learning environment. Content is the substance or the "what" that educators teach and students learn and, therefore, influences both the objectives and strategies for learning activities. Content includes the declarative, procedural, and conditional knowledge of a discipline or field of study. Learning objectives in our integrative model are addressed within the goals facet of the learning environment.

## Goals

Our definition of goals is not limited to educator-defined course or program goals, but also includes student-defined goals as well as the personal learning aspirations of the educator and students. Goals are the aims or intended outcomes of one or more learning experiences. Educator-defined and student-defined goals and learning objectives affect the strategies that both the educator and students select and adopt in order to achieve those goals.

## Strategies

Within our model, we define strategies as the ways in which students and educators proceed in order to attain their goals. Strategies include teaching and learning approaches, work habits, time management, and goal-setting, as well as cognitive and metacognitive activities used to direct learning and classroom behavior. The characteristics of participants, context, content, and goals interact with the strategies that students and educators use in their learning and teaching activities.

## Institutional and Extended Environments

In our integrative model the broader learning environment includes the institution and its culture, as well as the extended external environment (i.e., the world outside the institution). In Figure 7.1, the relationship between the larger learning environment and the five facets of the more immediate learning environment is shown as porous and interactive. For example, the larger, more extended learning environment includes features such as the institutional setting and culture, as well as its mission and goals. Because the institutional environment interacts with and influences the more immediate learning environment, the alignment of institutional purpose, mission, and priorities with course offerings, curriculum design, student expectations, and faculty incentives and rewards is crucially important.

## Summary

The five facets of the immediate learning environment are deeply intertwined. Educators both design and implement interconnections among these different facets of the learning environment that influence whether and to what extent the three basic psychological needs of participants are met. Educators act on their perceptions of how, for instance, student personal characteristics, preferences, and beliefs affect the content and learning objectives emphasized in a course. From the student perspective, we can examine how prior knowledge and experiences affect the adoption of learning objectives and strategies to reach those goals and, particularly, different motivational states for learning. A major issue that presents itself for empirical investigation is not which one of the facets of the learning environment is most important but rather how the various facets interact with one another to affect motivation and learning. Another major issue is how the larger institutional and external environment influences the more immediate learning environment. This includes opportunities and constraints educators encounter in attempting to create powerful learning environments that fulfill the three basic psychological needs of participants by drawing upon strategies that integrate the five components of the immediate learning environment proposed in our model.

## Self-Determination Theory

Self-determination theory (Deci & Ryan, 1985, 2000) is a humanistic, person-centered motivational theory that can help interpret and integrate different research findings and to understand and enhance student learning. As discussed in this chapter, research-based learning principles have been uncovered through empirical methods mostly conducted in disparate studies. Extant studies tend to be informed by mini-theories but without an overarching theoretical framework to help guide research and the application of research findings to teaching and learning practices. A theory such as SDT can help specify conditions under which learning will flourish, leading to positive learning outcomes. In short, SDT provides a comprehensive theoretical path from motivational *antecedents,* to motivational *processes* for learning, to learning and psychological *outcomes.*

## Overview

Self-determination theory helps specify and explain ways in which the learning environment can be designed to fulfill fundamental human needs and increase motivation for positive learning outcomes. With reference to Figure 7.1, SDT thus serves to interpret the movement from the outer to the inner circles of our integrative model for learning and motivation in higher education.

SDT postulates three basic psychological needs and proposes that the extent to which these needs are satisfied depends on the degree of self-determination as perceived by the individual. SDT also identifies a continuum of motivational states—from amotivation to extrinsic motivation to intrinsic motivation—and hypothesizes that the degree of self-determination and satisfaction of basic psychological needs varies from low to high across the motivational states.

## Basic Psychological Needs

Self-determination theory proposes three basic psychological needs that are generalizable across individuals and cultures: autonomy, competence, and relatedness.

*Autonomy* refers to the volitional endorsement of the reasons behind one's behaviors and actions. Autonomy involves volition (choice) and the desire to organize and behave in a way that is consistent with one's sense of self. Researchers and scholars have often confused the need for autonomy with the concept of independence, which is considered a Western construct. Autonomy signifies choice, and the consequences of choices, not independence. An individual could choose to be interdependent or to do something for someone else, or in contrast could feel pressured to act independently.

*Competence* refers to the ability to interact effectively with one's environment. Competence is similar to self-efficacy which is the central construct in self-efficacy theory (Bandura, 1997) and Bandura's conceptualization of motivation. It is the belief that one is able to effectively accomplish tasks or perform certain behaviors.

*Relatedness* refers to connections to and attachments with other people. Relatedness signifies a sense of belonging or affiliation with others. It involves secure relationships necessary for autonomy and competence needs to be fully satisfied.

Deci and Ryan (1985, 2000) make a clear distinction between needs and motives. Psychological *needs* are in a way similar to physiological needs insofar as they require satisfaction for individuals to be healthy. Deci and Ryan (1985, 2000) argue that, for people to develop, grow, and experience well-being, psychological needs are to be satisfied on a daily basis. Within SDT, psychological *motives* are not considered inherent characteristics of individuals but rather function more as wants than as needs. Motives are certainly powerful in their influence on behavior, but SDT contends they are not essential for psychological well-being when compared to the needs for autonomy, competence, and relatedness.

Deci and Ryan (2000) do not propose that SDT covers all human needs. They acknowledge that physiological needs (e.g., food, shelter, clothing, and sex) and acquired psychological motives (e.g., abasement, achievement, and dominance) are not included in the three innate psychological needs (Deci & Ryan, 2000).

Although all three basic psychological needs are important for well-being and effective behavior, SDT seems to hold, at least implicitly, that the need for autonomy may be the most central. Research has shown that increased competence in an environment that does not support the need for autonomy will not result in higher levels of self-determination, increased performance, or greater transfer of learning in real-life situations (Deci & Ryan, 2000; Levesque, Zuehlke, Stanek, & Ryan, 2004). Positive feedback and increased competence are more likely to result in effective learning and performance when abilities—knowledge, skills, and sensitivities—are developed in an autonomy supportive context. For example, even if an educator is very good at communicating content to students and increasing their subject matter knowledge, the learning may not be translated into improved retention of content or in real-life situations unless the learning occurs in an autonomy supportive educational environment.

## Role of the Environment

According to self-determination theory, optimal development and well-being will be fostered under environmental conditions that promote competence, relatedness, and autonomy and hindered in environmental contexts that do not satisfy the three basic needs. More than 25 years of research has uncovered key situational factors that either hinder or enhance the satisfaction of these basic psychological needs and self-determination.

Generally, satisfaction of basic needs will be undermined in situations in which rewards, threats, evaluations, and deadlines are salient (Amabile, DeJong, & Lepper, 1976; Harackiewicz, Manderlink, & Sansone, 1984). Those situations are not perceived as autonomy supportive. This is because external incentives, such as rewards, are usually perceived by the target recipient as an attempt to control her or his behavior. Early research examining the use of rewards to coerce performance of an intrinsically motivating activity tended to demonstrate an undermining of intrinsic motivation. Further research showed that this undermining effect is not limited to intrinsic motivation but also extends to self-determined motivation more generally. For example, at the elementary education level, tokens, gold star awards, and standardized tests tend to decrease intrinsic motivation for learning (see Amabile et al., 1976; Deci, Koestner, & Ryan, 1999, for a review; Deci & Ryan, 2000; Grolnick & Ryan, 1987). Similarly, at the college level, frequent evaluations, standardized tests, rewards, threats, and deadlines also tend to undermine intrinsic motivation for learning and self-determination (Deci et al., 1999). External motivators not only can undermine intrinsic motivation but also can stifle creativity, cognitive flexibility, conceptual learning, and complex problem solving (Amabile, 1982; Deci et al., 1999; Grolnick & Ryan, 1987; McGraw & McCullers, 1979), characteristics valued in lifelong learners.

Alternatively, contexts in which people are provided with choice and options can lead to enhanced feelings of autonomy and, consequently, higher levels of self-determined motivation and better performance (Black & Deci, 2000; Deci et al., 1999; Deci & Ryan, 2000). Even in situations where choice is not possible (e.g., taking the GRE in order to apply to graduate school), providing a rationale for doing what is required and acknowledging the individual's perspective and feelings often lead to a greater satisfaction of basic psychological needs and, consequently, to better learning outcomes.

Practically, what does it mean to create a positive learning environment that will satisfy students' basic psychological needs? When educators do something as simple as take into consideration what students bring to a learning situation—prior abilities, experience, knowledge, beliefs, and information processing approaches to learning—this can demonstrate to students that their perspective has been acknowledged. These kinds of educator behaviors are perceived as autonomy supportive and enhance a student's sense of self in a learning environment. Educators who use strategies that foster students' active engagement through experiential activities such as service-learning, problem-based learning, and collaborative learning also contribute to the enhancement of the learning environment (Baxter Magolda, 2000; Knapper, 2004). They create an autonomy supportive environment where competence and skills can be developed. The use of ConcepTests has been shown to substantially enhance the comprehension of introductory physics concepts (Mazur, 1997). Concept testing involves questions that are posed in the classroom setting along with a few possible answers soon after the educator presents a concept for the first time. Students vote on the possible answers individually, and then are given an opportunity to discuss their answers with other students. Students are encouraged to persuade their fellow students that they are correct. After these discussions subside, the students are asked to individually vote again. In terms of SDT, concept testing contributes to increased feelings of competence by allowing students to test their knowledge on a regular basis in a nonthreatening environment (i.e., outside of a formal testing situation). Students are encouraged to reflect on their own learning and the process by which they gain new knowledge and understand new concepts. Similarly, when students are asked to keep a journal or reflect on their performance on a test, they can develop skills that allow them to take ownership and feel autonomous about their own learning.

## Summary

We have defined learning as both process and outcome. As a *process*, learning is internal to the individual and thus cannot be forced or caused. As an *outcome*, learning is a change that happens within the individual. Significant learning that persists and transfers is substantially self-determined.

The motivation to learn is present in every human being at birth. Naturally, toddlers explore their environment out of interest and curiosity. As educators, we are drawn into a profession that is called upon to foster this natural tendency to learn and to grow, to seek fulfillment of basic psychological needs (autonomy, competence, relatedness), and to seek self-actualization.

In its purest form, learning is intrinsically motivated. It is primarily through intrinsic motivation (as well as curiosity and challenge) that individuals reach deeper levels of self-fulfillment (or, in Maslowian terms, higher levels of self-actualization). However, formal education necessarily involves extrinsic motivation that can limit and redirect intrinsic motivation.

That learning is not something *done* to students is of great importance in the development of our thinking and our integrative model. Because learning as a process happens within (not outside) the student, the student needs to feel a sense of ownership in her or his learning efforts. If students do not feel responsible (and influential) for their own learning and do not see the importance and value of what they are learning, their learning outcomes never will be internalized or accessible for transfer to other situations. This is because the "agent" of the learning would lie outside the self as opposed to within.

As we argued previously, the educator's primary responsibility is to create and implement environments that foster student learning. The key message here for educators is that learning needs to be sustained not forced, it needs to be fostered not produced. It is not the educator's role to *make* students learn. It is the educator's role and responsibility to create environments that will *help* students learn and with increasing responsibility for shaping their own learning. Because learning is a discovery process, educators are there to create environments for this natural process to take place, not to make the discoveries for the students. The educator's role is to create and implement environments that engage students' natural propensity to develop, grow, and learn—and to model learning processes by making them public and available to students.

## States of Motivation and Behavior for Effective Learning Derived From Self-Determination Theory

Motivation means to move or to bring into action. All intentional human behavior, including learning, involves motivation. The study of motivation addresses issues of *what* (needs and motives) and *how* (processes) purposive activities are initiated and sustained over time. The study of motivation also is concerned with *why* (reasons) individuals are moved to act, the time and effort (resources) invested in a goal-directed activity, the characteristics of environments, contexts, and situations (where) that influence motivation, and the learning, performance, satisfaction, and well-being (outcomes) associated with an intentional activity. Simply stated, within our model we treat motivation similar to the concept of learning, as both process and outcome.

When basic psychological needs are met, individuals' self-regulation of behavior becomes more internalized; individuals identify with the reasons for behaving and endorse the behaviors performed. That is, they begin to develop a sense of ownership in their own learning. Various frameworks and theories try to explain motivation relevant to learning and teaching in higher education (e.g., see Svinicki, 2004). One of the major dichotomies and essential distinctions discussed in the motivational literature is between intrinsic and extrinsic motivation.

### Intrinsic and Extrinsic Motivation

*Intrinsic motivation* refers to purposive behavior (including learning) wherein the goal (intention) is the action itself (Deci, 1975). Some examples of intrinsically motivated actions are pursuing curiosity, seeking meaning, developing competence, making choices autonomously, and serving others without the promise of external rewards or the threat of punishment. For intrinsically motivated behaviors, satisfaction is inherent in being fully engaged in the activity; the activity is both the means and end for involvement.

In the academic environment, it is worthwhile to try to foster intrinsic motivation, which has been associated with a host of positive outcomes (see Deci et al., 1999 and Pintrich, 2003, for reviews). However, even when learning activities are intrinsically motivating, other forms of motivation that involve instrumental behaviors are salient in a formal education setting. In this chapter we not only emphasize intrinsic motivation but also the experience of self-determination—doing something out of choice as opposed to coercion or obligation. As described below, some forms of extrinsic motivation also can be self-determined. Although intrinsic motivation is the prototype of self-determined behavior, people can act volitionally in responding to externally initiated requirements, not only the self-initiated activities that are personally interesting and enjoyable.

*Extrinsic motivation* refers to purposive behavior (including learning) wherein the activity is instrumental for reaching a goal that goes beyond the activity itself. Some examples of extrinsically motivated actions are studying to get a good grade (reward), completing a project in order to get a salary increase, participating on a committee to gain status or recognition, and obtaining an advanced degree to get a better job or earn more money. For extrinsically motivated behavior, satisfaction can result from the instrumental outcomes of an activity but not necessarily from engaging in the activity per se.

It is important to reiterate that an activity can be both intrinsically and extrinsically motivated, but the consequences of negative extrinsic motivators may undermine intrinsic motivation and self-determination. That is, when people feel coerced or obligated to engage in a certain behavior or to do a certain task or activity that they find interesting, a decrease in intrinsic motivation is generally observed. People tend to lose interest in an intrinsically motivated activity when they feel pressured to complete it. Similarly, when people feel coerced or obligated to behave in a certain way, they become less self-determined toward the activity.

One important contribution of SDT is the multidimensional conceptualization of extrinsic motivation along a continuum of self-determination. Specifically, SDT proposes and empirically supports four different forms of extrinsic motivation in addition to intrinsic motivation and amotivation. Figure 7.2 presents these six kinds of motivation along a continuum of increasing self-determination. The following discussion elaborates on

Figure 7.2 and on conditions under which learning is affected by different forms of regulated motivation.

FIGURE 7.2

Types of Motivation Along a Continuum of Self-Determination

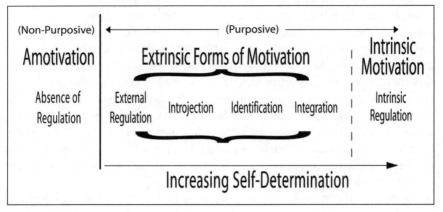

*Note.* Adapted from Ryan & Deci, 2000, p. 72.

## ▪Amotivation

For a particular learning situation or course, according to self-determination theory, amotivation is an absence of motivation. This does not mean that the student lacks motivation in general, but rather that the student lacks motivation for a particular learning task. The student could be highly motivated for learning tasks in other courses, for the social life of college, for sports, and so on. This is another way of saying that individuals always have multiple goals, and individuals may have different reasons for pursuing the same goal.

Amotivated students, however, are unable to see the connections between their behaviors and the consequences of those behaviors. This absence of motivation means that engagement in a purposeful activity is not initiated, or that once initiated the activity is disengaged. Amotivated students are not compelled by a reason for their learning or for a particular kind of learning (e.g., they may resist taking a general studies course because they do not perceive the value of taking the course with regard to a job or career).

Externally regulated behaviors are more advanced than amotivated behaviors on the continuum of self-determination. In the context of self-determination, it is better to be motivated by rewards and external contingencies than to not be motivated at all.

## Extrinsic Motivation and Regulated Behavior

Many of the behaviors people perform, particularly in an academic setting, are extrinsically motivated. For example, studying for a final examination tends to be extrinsically motivated. However, SDT argues that individuals are naturally motivated to internalize extrinsic motivators when they understand the reasons for their actions. The internalization process also is facilitated by environments that contribute to the satisfaction of the needs for autonomy, competence, and relatedness.

*External regulation* is the form of motivation commonly understood as extrinsic motivation in the education literature. It is the classic case in which the individual's behavior is controlled by specific external contingencies, such as rewards and punishments. When external regulation is emphasized, individuals do not understand or internalize the values associated with the required behaviors. For example, a student motivated by external regulation would study hard for a major test in order to get an A, or to make sure that his parents keep paying for college, or to impress his educators. External regulation is the least self-determined form of extrinsic motivation.

*Introjection* is an extrinsic form of motivation in which the external incentives administered by others (i.e., tangible rewards) are partially internalized by the individual. For example, a college student might study hard for an important test to prove to herself that she can do it, or because her sense of self-worth is dependent on the grades she gets, or to avoid feeling guilty or ashamed. This form of extrinsic motivation is interesting because, although it is external to the self, it is partially regulated by the individual himself or herself.

*Identification* is the process by which individuals begin to internalize the value of their behaviors and to accept them as their own. Identification is more advanced than introjection on the continuum of self-determination because, when behaving out of identification, individuals feel volitional while performing the behaviors. Identification represents an early stage of self-determined extrinsic motivation. For example, a student might study hard for a test because she feels it is important to learn the material covered in class, or because she understands that it is important to get a good grade in this class in order to get the job she wants. Inherent in identification is the sense of choice while doing what one is supposed to do. Identification has been consistently associated with positive outcomes such as better conceptual learning and increased creativity.

*Integration* is the most self-determined form of extrinsic motivation. It not only involves identifying with the behaviors performed and fully endorsing them, but also integrating those behaviors with other aspects of the self.

For example, a student might choose to study hard on an important test because the act of studying is part of the student's choice to be a responsible student and a lifelong learner.

## The Self-Determination Index

As shown in Figure 7.2, the various forms of motivation can be ordered on a continuum of self-determination. Amotivation is the absence of regulation and self-determination. Considering different forms of extrinsic motivation, external regulation involves the least amount of self-determination and integration the most, with introjection and identification between these two extremes. Intrinsic regulation represents the prototype (or ideal) of self-determination.

Any given activity can be performed for a variety of reasons by a single individual. For example, a student might work hard in a class in order to please the educator (introjection), but also because the student enjoys learning the material (intrinsic motivation) and because this class is covering important information that the student perceives as useful for a future career (identification). To assess the extent to which a student is self-determined toward a particular course or learning experience, we need to pay attention to the student's "relative autonomy" with regard to the type of regulation that occurs with the motivated behavior. For example, a student will experience more positive motivation and learning outcomes for a course if he endorses the self-determined reasons for taking the course to a relatively greater degree than reasons that are not self-determined for taking the course.

Researchers working with SDT have created a Self-Determination Index (SDI) to assess the relative level of autonomy or self-determination for performing any given activity. The SDI is computed by assigning weights to the different forms of motivation as a function of their underlying level of self-determination. Since intrinsic motivation, integration, and identification are considered self-determined forms of motivation, they each get a positive weight in the equation. Because amotivation, external regulation, and introjection are considered non-self-determined forms of motivation, they each receive negative weights in the equation. Specifically, the SDI is calculated in the following way:

$$\text{SDI} = 3^*(\text{intrinsic}) + 2^*(\text{integ.}) + (\text{iden.}) - (\text{intro.}) - 2^*(\text{external reg.}) - 3^*(\text{amotivation})$$

In this calculation, specific weights (from +3 to -3) are assigned to the different forms of motivation according to their relative position on the continuum of self-determination. Since intrinsic motivation is the most self-determined form of motivation, it receives the highest positive weight. Similarly, since amotivation represents an absence of regulation, it receives the highest negative weight in the equation. The validity and utility of the SDI has been established in studies both within and outside the field of education (see Vallerand, 1997, for a review).

## Summary

The most desirable learning experiences—that is, the ones that fulfill basic psychological needs and have the most positive long-term benefits—involve learning as a discovery process and as a self-determined activity. In the formal context of higher education, not all learning experiences are intrinsically motivated. Learning does not need to be intrinsically motivated to lead to positive outcomes. Environments that help satisfy students' needs for autonomy, competence, and relatedness facilitate the movement of students' motivation from amotivation and externally regulated behaviors toward more self-determined forms of extrinsic motivation. By creating learning environments that satisfy students' basic psychological needs, educators can facilitate students' natural propensity to integrate their reasons for behaving and move toward more self-determined forms of motivation. Through this internalization process, externally regulated behaviors become identified and even possibly integrated within the individual, which in turn leads to a host of positive learning outcomes—increased creativity, cognitive flexibility, conceptual learning, and better performance on complex problem solving (Deci & Ryan, 1991; Deci, Vallerand, Pelletier, & Ryan, 1991). Therefore, when a behavior is not predominantly intrinsically motivated, which is frequently the case in a formal educational setting, the goal of higher education should be to create environments that facilitate the internalization of extrinsically motivated behaviors instrumental for satisfying the basic psychological needs of autonomy, competence, relatedness. Those positive forms of motivation would in turn foster engagement, knowledge transfer, and the development of metacognition in students, which would then lead to positive learning outcomes.

### Concluding Comments

This chapter discussed essential building blocks of a theory (and philosophy) of learning and motivation in higher education. Our focus has been on formal education and planned learning, which we realize is only part of the larger learning enterprise that can be informal and spontaneous. The work represented in this chapter is a formative attempt to create a conceptual framework (model) useful for both research and application that can improve educational systems. Although our focus here has been on students in a formal educational setting, we believe that the principles outlined in this chapter also are applicable to every participant in a learning process (e.g., students, parents, faculty, staff, and administrators). The factors that contribute to the creation of positive learning environments can positively affect individuals at every level of the academic institution.

## References

Amabile, T. M. (1982). Social psychology of creativity: A consensual assessment technique. *Journal of Personality and Social Psychology, 43*, 997–1013.

Amabile, T. M., DeJong, W., & Lepper, M. R. (1976). Effects of externally imposed deadlines on subsequent intrinsic motivation. *Journal of Personality and Social Psychology, 34*, 92–98.

Bandura, A. (1997). *Self-efficacy: The exercise of control.* New York, NY: W. H. Freeman and Company.

Baxter Magolda, M. B. (2000). Teaching to promote holistic learning and development. In M. B. Baxter Magolda (Ed.), *New directions for teaching and learning: No. 82. Teaching to promote intellectual and personal maturity: Incorporating students' worldviews and identities into the learning process* (pp. 88–98). San Francisco, CA: Jossey-Bass.

Black, A. E., & Deci, E. L. (2000). The effects of instructors' autonomy support and students' autonomous motivation on learning organic chemistry: A self-determination theory perspective. *Science Education, 84,* 740–756.

Deci, E. L. (1975). *Intrinsic motivation.* New York, NY: Plenum.

Deci, E. L., Koestner, R., & Ryan, R. M. (1999). A meta-analytic review of experiments examining the effects of extrinsic rewards on intrinsic motivation. *Psychological Bulletin, 125*(6), 627–668.

Deci, E. L., & Ryan, R. M. (1985). *Intrinsic motivation and self-determination in human behavior.* New York, NY: Plenum.

Deci, E. L., & Ryan, R. M. (1991). A motivational approach to self: Integration in personality. In R. A. Dienstbier (Ed.), *Perspectives on motivation* (pp. 237–288). Lincoln, NE: University of Nebraska Press.

Deci, E. L., & Ryan, R. M. (2000). The "what" and "why" of goal pursuits: Human needs and the self-determination of behavior. *Psychological Inquiry, 11,* 227–268.

Deci, E. L., Vallerand, R. J., Pelletier, L. G., & Ryan, R. M. (1991). Motivation and education: The self-determination perspective. *Educational Psychologist, 26,* 325–346.

Grolnick, W. S., & Ryan, R. M. (1987). Autonomy in children's learning: An experimental and individual difference investigation. *Journal of Personality and Social Psychology, 52,* 890–898.

Harackiewicz, J. M., Manderlink, G., & Sansone, C. (1984). Rewarding pinball wizardry: The effects of evaluation on intrinsic interest. *Journal of Personality and Social Psychology, 47,* 287–300.

Knapper, C. (2004). *Research on college teaching and learning: Applying what we know.* Paper prepared for the Teaching Professor Conference, Philadelphia, PA. Retrieved May 17, 2005, from http://teachingprofessor.com/conference/sunday paper.html

Levesque, C., Zuehlke, A. N., Stanek, L. R., & Ryan, R. M. (2004). Autonomy and competence in German and American university students: A comparative study based on self-determination theory. *Journal of Educational Psychology, 96*(1), 68–84.

Mazur, E. (1997). *Peer instruction: A user's manual.* Upper Saddle River, NJ: Prentice Hall.

McGraw, K. O., & McCullers, J. C. (1979). Evidence of a detrimental effect of extrinsic incentives on breaking a mental set. *Journal of Experimental Social Psychology, 15,* 285–294.

Pintrich, P. R. (2003). A motivational science perspective on the role of student motivation in learning and teaching contexts. *Journal of Educational Psychology, 95,* 667–686.

Ryan, R. M., & Deci, E. L. (2000). Self-determination theory and the facilitation of intrinsic motivation, social development, and well-being. *American Psychologist, 55*(1), 68–78.

Svinicki, M. D. (2004). *Learning and motivation in the postsecondary classroom.* Bolton, MA: Anker.

Vallerand, R. J. (1997). Toward a hierarchical model of intrinsic and extrinsic motivation. In M. P. Zanna (Ed.), *Advances in experimental social psychology* (Vol. 29, pp. 271–360). San Diego, CA: Academic Press.

# 8

# Perceptions of Faculty Developers About the Present and Future of Faculty Development at Historically Black Colleges and Universities

Phyllis Worthy Dawkins
Johnson C. Smith University

Andrea L. Beach
Western Michigan University

Stephen L. Rozman
Tougaloo College

The Historically Black Colleges and Universities Faculty Development Network

*The development of faculty at Historically Black Colleges and Universities (HBCUs) has been a challenge and commitment since their inception before and after the civil war. Historically, faculty have assumed many roles, but they primarily sought to address the needs of black students. The HBCU Faculty Development Network, founded in 1994, has been instrumental in providing a platform to showcase accomplishments and challenges in education at this unique group of colleges and universities. To address future needs, we surveyed the membership to explore current program goals and influences, practices, and new directions. The results are compared with data for the Professional and Organizational Development Network in Higher Education, with some significant differences discovered.*

## Introduction

Historically Black Colleges and Universities (HBCUs) have a unique history and set of challenges on the American higher education landscape. But, just like other institutions of higher education, they are experiencing internal and external needs and pressure to change. The challenges of creating and promoting change are generally based on the needs of students, faculty, and the institution. Faculty development has increasingly played an important part in change at HBCUs. However, no research has yet focused on the unique development needs of faculty at HBCUs and the ways that faculty development programs can meet those needs. The purpose of this study is to explore the perceptions of faculty developers at HBCUs regarding the issues their faculty and institutions face, and their ability to address the issues they identify. Results of a survey of HBCU faculty developers will be presented and compared to a national survey of faculty developers at a wide range of colleges and universities. We wanted to know what is currently important to them and how the HBCU Faculty Development Network and other agencies such as The Professional and Organizational Development Network in Higher Education (POD) and The Collaboration for the Advancement of College Teaching and Learning can provide the tools for meeting their faculty development challenges. This chapter will begin with a short history of HBCUs and the challenges they have faced and continue to work with today. We will then outline the history of faculty development in HBCUs and the progress made by the HBCU Faculty Development Network. Finally, we will look at the perceptions of faculty developers at HBCUs regarding current and future practices and challenges.

## The History and Challenges of HBCUs in Higher Education

The Higher Education Act of 1965 defines an Historically Black College and University as: ". . . any black college or university that was established prior to 1964." The majority of the 105 HBCUs are located in the southeastern states, the District of Columbia, and the Virgin Islands (U.S. Department of Education, 2004b). They consist of 40 public four-year, 11 public two-year, 49 private four-year, and 5 private two-year institutions. Most are more than 100 years old, with Cheyney University of Pennsylvania, founded in 1837, being the oldest of these institutions. Nineteen of the HBCUs are land-grant institutions founded as agricultural, mechanical, and industrial schools as a result of the Morrill Act of 1862 and the second Morrill Act of 1890 (U. S. Department of Education, 2004b).

Prior to the 1860s, very few blacks received any form of educational training. By law and according to social customs in the south, it was forbidden to teach blacks to read or write (Browning & Williams, 1978). Northern missionaries and ex-slaves established schools and colleges for blacks from 1861–1880. A challenge after emancipation was to educate freed slaves and to obtain a squadron of people to educate them. To their rescue came the American Missionary Association, the Freedmen's Bureau, and other ex-slaves. The challenge to black colleges was to take former slaves, or the children of former slaves, educate them for survival, and mold them into people with self-respect and dignity (Thompson, 1978).

The Morrill Act of 1862 allocated funds for the provision of land-grant colleges to foster educational opportunities for all students, especially newly freed blacks. Before the extended Morrill Act of 1890, the primary goal of black colleges was to produce educated leaders for black people (Browning & Williams, 1978). Black colleges were established to train teachers, preachers, and other key community figures equipped to remedy the despair arising from slavery. But how to educate blacks during this time became a heated debate between Booker T. Washington, a graduate of Hampton Institute, and W.E.B. DuBois, a graduate of Fisk University. Hampton Institute, founded in 1868, led the development of industrial education, followed by Tuskegee Institute. Washington advocated vocational training appropriate for the masses. He believed that since most black people depended upon agriculture for their living, they should be educated in keeping with the requirements of an agriculture society (Washington, 1974). In contrast, DuBois advocated the development of an elite group, "a talented tenth" to teach and lead other blacks. DuBois argued that a liberal arts education provided blacks with the resources for attaining intellectual, social, and political equality (DuBois, 1961).

During the 1890s to the early 1900s, a series of laws were established to limit the education of blacks and to promote industrial training. The extended Morrill Act of 1890 led newly founded land-grant colleges to base their training on the industrial model of education for blacks and whites in southern states. In spite of the debate between DuBois and Washington, early curriculum in black colleges included character building, personal cleanliness, and instruction in both liberal and industrial subjects (Browning & Williams, 1978). The *Plessy v. Ferguson* decision of the Supreme Court in 1896 established by law the right to set up separate public institutions for blacks and whites. Black colleges, therefore, were the critical access points to higher education for blacks and crucibles for the development of the black elite and educated working-class alike.

McKinney (1932) reported that between 1907 and 1932, many black colleges had unparalleled growth. One growth area was graduate school opportunities. As more blacks earned an undergraduate degree, the challenge for many became obtaining a graduate degree. In the early part of the 20th century, graduate training was only available to blacks at a few northern universities or at some privately supported black institutions, such as Fisk University, Howard University, and Atlanta University (Franklin & Moss, 1994). Eager and ambitious black youths began to prepare themselves for the pursuit of medicine, teaching, engineering, and business. Furthermore, the vocational idea appeared to be dominant in all of these pursuits. However, during that time, black colleges faced challenges in meeting standards of regional and accrediting boards, professionalizing college teaching, updating the liberal arts colleges, raising general intellectual development, and promoting self-reliance and self-education (Florence, 1932). Also, as blacks became more educated and were able to articulate their views on how to educate blacks, they began to publish numerous books and articles in white and black journals (Franklin & Moss, 1994).

From the 1950s to the 1970s, black colleges were impacted by a series of events. The 1954 Supreme Court decision in *Brown v. Board of Education* declared that racial segregation in public schools deprives black students of equal protection of the law under the 14th Amendment of the Constitution. Title V of the Civil Rights Act of 1964 prohibited institutions that received federal funds from discriminating on the basis of race in hiring, promotion, and admission policies (Browning & Williams, 1978). This led to social and educational legislation that would change the face of colleges and universities across the country, ensuring black students access to and choices in higher education that had never before been available. It would also change the status and stability of black colleges.

A 2003 report from the U.S. Department of Education included the following statistics about the status of black students in HBCUs:

- Nearly one-quarter of all bachelor's degrees earned by blacks in 1999–2000 were earned at HBCUs.

- Fourteen percent of all blacks enrolled in postsecondary institutions were enrolled in HBCUs in fall 1999.

- Thirteen percent of black, non-Hispanic students were enrolled in HBCUs compared to the total enrollment of all blacks in all colleges and universities in fall 2000.

Despite recruiting challenges from predominantly white institutions, HBCUs continue today to be critical to the higher education of black students.

## The Challenges of Faculty at HBCUs

The challenges of faculty in HBCUs have evolved over time and have therefore impacted their growth and development. The educational preparation of black teachers after emancipation was a challenge because they first had to be educated before they could be recruited to teach. Many of the teachers were not educated beyond the seventh grade when they began to teach (Litwack, 1998). Litwack also reports that what a teacher could teach was limited by textbooks that were carefully selected by school boards to reflect a white southern point of view.

During emancipation, black teachers played numerous roles apart from instruction. Since they were among the initially educated leaders, they assisted freedmen in contract disputes, engaged in church work, and drafted petitions to the Freedmen's Bureau, state officials, and Congress (Foner, 1989). In 1978, Thompson reported that some black teachers were expected to provide tutorial counseling sessions and serve as sponsors of student organizations. More importantly, Thompson asserts that black faculty saw their role as preparing disadvantaged black youth for making it in a white-dominated middle-class environment. Today, faculty in black colleges continue to serve in multiple roles that include mentors, advisors, tutors, and administrators.

The quantity and quality of black college faculties have been challenges for a number of years, especially since predominantly white colleges began actively recruiting black faculty in the 1970s. At one time, black colleges had a faculty that was predominantly black. They were able to recruit and retain outstanding teachers, despite low salaries and poor working conditions (Thompson, 1978). Today, many black teachers have attractive opportunities to join white-college faculties. The number of black teachers at white colleges and universities has steadily increased due to the growing demand for teachers of black studies, the demand for a black presence among teaching personnel at institutions where the number of black students has increased, and affirmative action programs connected to hiring practices (Franklin & Moss, 1994). However, because of the efforts of many black colleges to also recruit and retain faculty who are black, the U.S. Department of Education (2004a) reports that blacks constitute 60% of the full-time faculty at HBCUs and whites constitute 27%.

In spite of the opportunity to go to other colleges, many black faculty remain in black colleges because they are dedicated to black youth. The same is true for white faculty who are in black colleges. Carrell P. Horton of Fisk University summarized the challenges facing faculty with black students in black colleges as the necessity for student enrollment in remedial courses, dropping of standardized test scores for admission, and perceptions of the student mix, as well as below average faculty salaries and the decline in institutional funds for faculty development (in Drewry & Doermann, 2001). Ben E. Bailey of Tougaloo College also reported that some students were not prepared for college study (in Drewry & Doermann, 2001).

## The History of Faculty Development at HBCUs

Faculty have responded to these challenges in a number of ways. In 1932, Florence described the training of black college teachers by universities as providing in-service training consisting of extension courses, correspondence courses, study clubs, professionalized faculty meetings, syllabus preparation, research and investigation, and leaves of absence.

Horton reported that Fisk University streamlined all curricula, dropped some majors, developed cooperative and dual degree programs, offered limited programs for adult learners, added business and computer science, addressed criteria for and expectations of new hires, and strengthened commitment to faculty development (Drewry & Doermann, 2001). Tougaloo College instituted a writing across the curriculum program, addressed learning styles, utilized case studies, added community service as a degree requirement, and offered a pre-freshman summer program (Drewry & Doermann, 2001). Many of these reform efforts were supported through a variety of faculty development programs.

The faculty development movement in private black colleges really did not occur until the 1980s (Drewry & Doermann, 2001). Many of these programs were funded by Title III, private grants, and foundation grants such as those from the Andrew Mellon Foundation and the Bush-Hewlett Foundation. In 1994, Dean Whitla of Harvard University and Asa Grant Hilliard evaluated the faculty development programs of 23 private colleges for the Bush Foundation and the William and Flora Hewlett Foundation (Bush-Hewlett Grants). They found that the Bush-Hewlett Grants touched the professional lives of many of the faculty in the participating colleges, that project activities helped to improve the quality of teaching, and that virtually all projects concentrated on meeting the needs of students rather than focusing on research or faculty sabbaticals (Drewry & Doermann, 2001). Selected projects Whitla and Hilliard listed as responding to the needs of the students included computer skills of faculty, writing across the curriculum, faculty travel to conferences on teaching critical thinking, general education development, new course development, and learning communities (Drewry & Doermann, 2001).

## The HBCU Faculty Development Network

The HBCU Faculty Development Network was created in 1994 with a grant from the Bush Foundation to Tougaloo College. The network was founded by Stephen Rozman, a faculty member and the director of the Tougaloo College faculty development grants since 1989, who continues to serve as the network's co-director. The grant coordinating team at Tougaloo worked with Rozman, Bush Foundation officers, and faculty development leaders at various private HBCUs to put an initial conference together. Phyllis Worthy Dawkins, the other co-director from Johnson C. Smith University, Carrell Horton from Fisk University, Barbara Frankle from LeMoyne-Owen College, Argiro Morgan from Xavier University, and Jesse Silverglate from Florida Memorial College became members of the steering committee that founded the network. As the network grew, faculty from public HBCUs were added to the committee, most notably Cecilia Steppe-Jones from North Carolina Central University, J. Jonathan Lewis from Texas Southern University, and M. Shelly Hunter from Norfolk State University.

The Bush Foundation is an important supporter of faculty development efforts at HBCUs that are members of the United Negro College Fund (UNCF), and has also funded The Collaboration for the Advancement of College Teaching and Learning (The Collaboration). The Collaboration has been giving travel grants to faculty from UNCF-affiliated HBCUs to attend their semi-annual faculty development conferences since the 1980s. The experience of attending The Collaboration conferences gave us the idea of creating our own network.

More than 100 people—nearly all serving as presenters—attended the first HBCU Faculty Development Symposium in 1994, which featured presentations in a variety of areas related to faculty development. The response to the initial call for proposals was very positive, and submissions were received by faculty from a wide variety of HBCUs—and a few non-HBCUs. It became clear to all that this effort was filling an important gap by holding a faculty development conference for historically black institutions. In 1994, when there was far less focus on faculty development at minority serving institutions, it was hard to imagine that a startup organization on a shoestring budget could become successfully established. With the success of the initial conference, the steering committee was committed to making the symposium an annual event and moving it around to other cities in the Southeast, given the location of most HBCUs.

The mission of the HBCU Faculty Development Network is derived from the rich legacy of HBCUs in providing educational opportunities for underrepresented students. Building on this heritage, the network is committed to promoting effective teaching and student learning through a variety of collaborative activities that focus on faculty enhancement. These collaborative activities are designed to make a connection among teaching, research, and service. The network also facilitates collaboration between faculty and administrators to share individual achievements for collective success in meeting student needs.

The vision of the HBCU Faculty Development Network is to empower faculty to promote effective teaching and learning practices that will enable students to become engaged lifelong learners in an ever-changing society. The network aims to be recognized as the main organization among the 105 HBCUs for advancing the following strands to encourage the delivery of effective teaching and learning: collaborative models, teaching and learning styles/instructional strategies and techniques, curriculum design and revision, diversity and globalization, learning across the curriculum, educational technology, evaluation of assessment and learning, and community service/service learning. The goals of the network are to enhance the teaching and learning process based on the collective experience of HBCUs and to provide leadership and coordination efforts among HBCUs.

The HBCU Faculty Development Symposium has been attracting between 175 and 200 participants every year. Faculty representing the majority of the HBCUs have attended the symposium over the past 11 years, as have some chief academic officers of these institutions. As the network matures, the steering committee wants to understand the unique needs, influences, practices, and challenges of HBCU faculty developers. This understanding can help the network serve the unique needs of HBCUs in the future.

## Design, Methods, and Results

The data reported here is from a survey developed by Mary Deane Sorcinelli of the University of Massachusetts Amherst, and Ann Austin, Pamela Eddy, and Andrea Beach of Michigan State University. During the 2002 POD Conference in Atlanta, Georgia, Sorcinelli and Austin presented the results of the survey—"Understanding Our Present and Future: A Study of POD Professionals." Phyllis Worthy Dawkins, a co-director of the HBCU

Faculty Development Network, attended their session and met with them to discuss the possibility of administering the survey to our membership. As a result of this and follow-up conversations, all colleagues from the University of Massachusetts Amherst and Michigan State University and members of the HBCU Faculty Development Network agreed to work on the project. Andrea Beach, now of Western Michigan University, took the lead on survey administration and data analysis.

After the Human Welfare Committee at Johnson C. Smith University approved the administration of the survey, it was sent to faculty on the mailing list of the HBCU Faculty Development Network during the spring semester of 2004. Of the 105 surveys sent to faculty representing each institution that was involved in some form of faculty development, 49 responded after a first or second mailing, resulting in a response rate of 47%.

The survey is composed of 18 questions with some sub- or follow-up questions, using Likert-type scales, rankings, and open-ended questions. The data were statistically analyzed using frequencies, means, and analysis of variance. After reporting the results of the demographic data, we will focus on the results of three major questions. The questions address program goals and purposes, current practices, and new directions for faculty development.

## Demographics

In terms of demographics, the titles given by respondents included senior-level administrator (35%), director or program coordinator (45%), and faculty member (51%). Most (69%) reported two or more titles, often an administrative title first and faculty or some other role second or third, hence the percentages that add to greater than 100% (see Table 8.1). The mean of their years in faculty development was 7.5, with a mean of 10 years at their institutions. Forty-six percent of respondents worked in liberal arts colleges, 32% in comprehensive universities, and the rest in community colleges, research/doctoral institutions, and others. Forty-nine percent of the respondents were from public universities and 51% were from private institutions, exactly mirroring the number of public and private HBCUs in the country.

The structure of faculty development programs at the institutions included a centralized unit with dedicated staff offering a range of programming and services (31%); a "clearinghouse" for programs and offerings that are sponsored across the institution, but offering few programs itself (11%); a committee charged with supporting faculty development (17%); an individual faculty member or administrator charged with supporting faculty development (31%); and some other kind of structure (10%). These structures

TABLE 8.1

Titles Given by Survey Respondents

| Title | First Response | Second Response | Third Response | Total and % of respondents (N = 49) |
|---|---|---|---|---|
| Director or program coordinator | 21 | 0 | 1 | 22–45% |
| Senior administrator | 14 | 3 | 0 | 17–35% |
| Faculty member | 8 | 16 | 1 | 25–51% |
| Midlevel administrator | 3 | 9 | 3 | 15–31% |

differed somewhat from the structures found in the national sample of POD respondents, in that there were fewer centralized units (national: 59%), and more individuals charged with responsibility for faculty development (national: 15%). However, they match more closely the national liberal arts college structures (central unit: 24%; individual: 30%). Overall, there are a variety of structures for faculty development at HBCUs, and for a movement that started only in the 1980s, these structures are evidence of the swift growth and development of faculty development on these campuses.

## Goals and Purposes

Developers were asked to respond to 10 statements of goals and purposes that may guide faculty development programs. They rated the degree to which each goal guides their program or unit (1 = not at all, 2 = to a slight degree, 3 = to a moderate degree, 4 = to a great degree), and they indicated the three primary purposes that guide their programs. The rankings of primary purposes were converted into percentages of respondents indicating a goal in their "top three" and are reported as such. Developers at HBCUs across all institutional types perceived the top three goals guiding their programs as:

- Creating or sustaining a culture of teaching excellence (mean = 3.4, 75%)

- Responding to and supporting individual faculty members (mean = 3.3, 58%)

- Advancing new initiatives in teaching and learning (mean = 3.3, 43%)

In a comparable fashion, developers from the national sample of POD members (Austin, Sorcinelli, Eddy, & Beach, 2003) (n = 499) across all institutional types perceived the same top three goals guiding their faculty development programs:

- Creating or sustaining a culture of teaching excellence (mean = 3.7, 73%)

- Responding to and supporting individual faculty members (mean = 3.5, 56%)

- Advancing new initiatives in teaching and learning (mean = 3.6, 49%)

Austin et al. state that these top goals reflect the longstanding interest of faculty development programs in teaching and learning issues and in strategies to support individual faculty members. In addition, advancing new initiatives in teaching and learning among HBCUs supports their history and mission to advance the education of black students according to the demands of society and the need to be unique in their educational approaches. This statement is further supported by the following secondary goals for HBCUs:

- Acting as a change agent within the institution (mean = 2.9, 23%)

- Supporting departmental goals, planning, and development (mean = 2.8, 20%)

- Responding to the critical needs of the institution (mean = 3.1, 18%)

These secondary goals support the unique perspective and mission of HBCUs, and it appears that faculty development in HBCUs is more attuned to the need for the institutions to demonstrate their uniqueness. Therefore, faculty developers see responding to the critical needs of the institution as much more within their realm of responsibility. In contrast, the database for POD (Austin et al., 2003) showed the following as secondary goals:

- Acting as a change agent within the institution (mean = 3.2, 26%)

- Fostering collegiality within and among faculty and departments (mean = 3.1, 26%)

- Providing support for faculty members having difficulty (mean = 2.9, 17%)

The goals developers at HBCUs consider less influential on their programming consisted of:

- Providing recognition and reward for excellence in teaching (mean = 2.8, 18%)

- Fostering collegiality within and among faculty and departments (mean = 2.8, 15%)

- Providing support for faculty members having difficulty with their teaching (mean = 2.9, 13%)

- Positioning the institution at the forefront of educational innovation (mean = 2.8, 10%)

In contrast, the POD sample showed the following as the least influential goals:

- Responding to critical needs as defined by the institution (mean = 2.9, 15%)

- Providing recognition and reward for excellence in teaching (mean = 2.5, 13%)

- Positioning the institution at the forefront of educational innovation (mean = 2.6, 7%)

- Supporting departmental goals and development (mean = 2.5, 7%)

Clearly, although the HBCUs share primary faculty development goals with the larger national field, their secondary driving purposes are somewhat more institutionally oriented.

## Current Practices

The survey also sought to determine the extent to which faculty development programs are currently offering services pertaining to 21 different issues that potentially affect faculty. Respondents were asked to indicate the extent to which they believe it is important for their programs to offer services pertaining to those issues (1 = not at all, 2 = to a slight extent, 3 = to a moderate extent, 4 = to a great extent). They also reported on the same scale the extent to which their faculty development programs offer services to address those issues. Table 8.2 compares the ratings of HBCU faculty developers with the responses of the national group. ANOVAs were run comparing the HBCU responses to the responses from the national sample as well as from different types of institutions. Significant differences are reported for the comparisons.

TABLE 8.2

Current Issues for Faculty Development

| Current Issues | HBCUs | | POD | |
| --- | --- | --- | --- | --- |
| | Important | Offer | Important | Offer |
| Assessment of student learning outcomes | 3.66 | 3.00* | 3.43 | 2.57 |
| Teaching underprepared students | 3.32** | 2.63** | 2.75 | 1.98 |
| The shifting characteristics/demographics of students | 3.21* | 2.32 | 2.85 | 2.24 |
| Integrating technology into traditional teaching and learning settings | 3.61 | 3.55 | 3.51 | 3.28 |
| Teaching in online and distance environments | 3.05 | 2.53 | 2.96 | 2.63 |
| Multiculturalism and diversity related to teaching | 3.43 | 2.74 | 3.36 | 2.75 |
| Teaching for student-centered learning | 3.58 | 2.89 | 3.69 | 3.25* |
| Teaching adult learners | 3.05* | 2.39 | 2.63 | 2.08 |
| Active, inquiry-based, or problem-based learning | 3.37 | 2.84 | 3.51 | 3.00 |
| Writing across the curriculum/writing to learn | 3.53** | 2.89* | 3.06 | 2.46 |
| Team teaching | 3.00** | 2.13 | 2.49 | 1.91 |
| Scholarship of teaching | 3.26 | 2.58 | 3.28 | 2.57 |
| New faculty development (e.g., mentoring) | 3.45 | 2.82 | 3.60 | 3.03 |
| Mentoring faculty from underrepresented populations | 3.00 | 1.92 | 2.86 | 1.90 |
| Course/teaching portfolios | 3.16 | 2.37 | 2.97 | 2.46 |
| Peer review | 2.95 | 2.13 | 2.93 | 2.26 |
| Post-tenure review | 2.89** | 1.92 | 2.33 | 1.62 |
| Graduate student teaching development | 2.11 | 1.47 | 2.46 | 2.07** |
| Course and curriculum reform | 3.37* | 2.45 | 2.98 | 2.40 |
| General education reform | 3.16** | 2.51** | 2.60 | 1.98 |
| Community service learning | 3.26** | 2.47* | 2.67 | 2.08 |

*p = .05
**p = .01

As shown in Table 8.2, the three most important issues to HBCU faculty developers—assessment of student learning outcomes, integrating technology into traditional teaching and learning settings, and teaching for student-centered learning—are the same as those for the POD faculty developers.

HBCU faculty developers reported offering services to address assessment more than the POD group, and the POD group reported addressing teaching for student-centered learning to a greater extent. New faculty development, active or inquiry-based teaching and learning, and the scholarship of teaching were also equally important to the two groups. Interestingly, both judged addressing multiculturalism and diversity as important to offer, but were equal in their assessment that services to address the issue were far below the perceived need for them.

The next most important issues for HBCUs diverge strongly from the POD respondents' priorities and are also addressed by HBCU faculty development programming to a greater extent. These include writing across the curriculum, teaching underprepared students, addressing the changing characteristics and demographics of students, community service learning, course and curriculum reform, general education reform, and teaching adult learners. These issues closely match the strands developed by the network to improve teaching and learning at HBCUs.

## Perceptions of Important Future Directions

HBCU Network developers were asked to respond to a number of new challenges and pressures on institutions which affect faculty work, both in terms of how important they think it is to address those issues through faculty development and the extent to which their institutions are already responding (1 = not at all, 2 = to a slight extent, 3 = to a moderate extent, 4 = to a great extent). Table 8.3 contains a comparison of HBCU developer responses with those of the POD respondents. Again, ANOVAs were run to assess the difference between HBCU and POD responses.

For both groups, the training and support of adjunct and part-time faculty, the changing roles and rewards for faculty, and balancing multiple faculty roles were important. For HBCUs, however, other issues were of equal or greater importance. Unit and program evaluation and assessment, departmental leadership and management, the ethical conduct of faculty work, and supporting institutional change priorities were all rated significantly higher by HBCU respondents than by POD respondents. Further, HBCUs appear to be addressing those pressing new challenges to a much greater degree than their national counterparts. HBCU respondents rated preparing the future professoriate as a greater concern than did POD respondents, but the national sample indicated that their campuses are addressing this issue to a greater extent than the HBCU developers.

TABLE 8.3

## New Challenges and Pressures for Faculty Development

| New Challenges and Pressures | HBCUs | | POD | |
|---|---|---|---|---|
| | Important | Offer | Important | Offer |
| Departmental leadership and management | 3.47* | 2.17 | 3.10 | 1.94 |
| Changing faculty roles and rewards | 3.30 | 2.17 | 3.18 | 2.12 |
| Training and support for part-time/adjunct faculty | 3.38 | 1.88 | 3.26 | 2.11 |
| Ethical conduct of faculty work | 3.38** | 2.17* | 2.81 | 1.84 |
| Preparing the future professoriate | 3.26* | 2.11 | 2.87 | 2.20 |
| Support of institutional change priorities | 3.26* | 2.46 | 2.89 | 2.34 |
| Balancing multiple faculty roles | 3.33 | 2.28 | 3.08 | 2.12 |
| Community-based research | 2.89** | 1.91 | 2.18 | 1.64 |
| Outreach/service activities | 3.22** | 2.45** | 2.37 | 1.99 |
| Faculty and departmental entrepreneurship (e.g., consulting on behalf of the institution) | 2.59** | 1.64 | 1.75 | 1.44 |
| Unit/program evaluation | 3.54** | 2.58* | 2.70 | 2.20 |
| Program assessment (e.g., accreditation) | 3.50** | 3.09** | 2.76 | 2.47 |
| Collaborative departmental work teams | 3.11** | 2.30** | 2.60 | 1.76 |
| Interdisciplinary collaborations | 3.20 | 2.37 | 3.05 | 2.24 |
| Commitment to civic life/the public good | 3.06* | 2.42** | 2.60 | 1.97 |
| Post-tenure review | 3.02* | 1.98 | 2.37 | 1.69 |
| Faculty roles in learning communities | 3.15 | 2.21 | 2.83 | 1.95 |

* $p = .05$

** $p = .01$

## Discussion and Conclusion

HBCUs have had unique cultures, missions, and challenges throughout their more than 100 years of existence. In recent decades HBCUs have had to become very creative in supporting themselves and their missions as changes in society have threatened their survival. Faculty development has become a key ingredient in the ability of HBCUs to survive and thrive serving a student population that is disproportionately disadvantaged and underprepared. The HBCU Faculty Development Network serves as a consortium within which HBCU faculty developers can support each other, share ideas, and plan for change.

The program structures reported by HBCUs depict movement toward institutionalization of faculty development. More than two-thirds of respondents are part of a centralized unit with dedicated staff who are responsible for faculty development programming, and the involvement of senior-level administrators and directors indicates the centrality of faculty development on these campuses.

The program influences, current issues, and new challenges reported here highlight the unique missions and strengths of HBCUs and reinforce the idea that different types of institutions have different needs in terms of faculty development (Austin, Sorcinelli, Eddy, & Beach, 2003). HBCU faculty developers indicated a number of areas of concern and services that were not high priorities for the national sample, in particular, issues of program and institutional assessment and support, community service learning, outreach, commitment to civic life, and writing across the curriculum.

The HBCU Faculty Development Network has always been responsive to the needs of faculty in our institutions. The results of the survey can be used to share with the membership in planning future activities, including the annual symposium and the summer institute, and with administrators and faculty to assist them with their own institutional planning.

# References

Austin, A. E., Sorcinelli, M. D., Eddy, P. L., & Beach, A. L. (2003). *Envisioning responsive faculty development: Perceptions of faculty developers about the present and future of faculty development.* Paper presented at the 83rd annual meeting of the American Educational Research Association, Chicago, IL.

Browning, J. E. S., & Williams, J. B. (1978). History and goals of black institutions of higher learning. In C. V. Willie & R. R. Edmonds (Eds.), *Black colleges in America* (pp. 68–93). New York, NY: Teachers College Press.

Drewry, H. N., & Doermann, H. (2001). *Stand and prosper: Private black colleges and their students.* Princeton, NJ: Princeton University Press.

DuBois, W. E . B. (1961). *The souls of black folks.* Greenwich, CT: Fawcett.

Florence, C. W. (1932). Critical evaluation of present policies and practices of Negro institutions of higher education. In T. E. McKinney, *Higher education among Negroes* (pp. 39–58). Charlotte, NC: Johnson C. Smith University.

Foner, E. (1989). *Reconstruction: America's unfinished revolution, 1863–1877.* New York, NY: Perennial.

Franklin, J. H., & Moss, A. A., Jr. (1994). *From slavery to freedom: A history of African Americans* (7th ed.). New York, NY: Alfred A. Knopf.

Litwack, L. F. (1998). *Trouble in mind: Black southerners in the age of Jim Crow.* New York, NY: Alfred A. Knopf.

McKinney, T. E. (1932). *Higher education among Negroes.* Charlotte, NC: Johnson C. Smith University.

Thompson, D. C. (1978). Black college faculty and students: The nature of their interaction. In C. V. Willie & R. R. Edmonds (Eds.), *Black colleges in America* (pp. 180–194). New York, NY: Teachers College Press.

U.S. Department of Education. (2003). *Status and trends in the education of blacks* (NCES 2003–034). Retrieved May 15, 2005, from http://nces.ed.gov/pubs2003/2003034.pdf

U.S. Department of Education. (2004a). *Historically Black Colleges and Universities, 1976 to 2001* (NCES 2004–062). Washington, DC: Government Printing Office.

U. S. Department of Education. (2004b). *White house initiative on Historically Black Colleges and Universities.* Retrieved May 15, 2005, from http://www.ed.gov/about/inits/list/whhbcu/edlite-index.html

Washington, B. T. (1974). *Up from slavery.* New York, NY: Dell.

# Preparing Faculty for Pedagogical Change: Helping Faculty Deal With Fear

Linda C. Hodges
Princeton University

*How receptive faculty are to changing their pedagogical approach is a complex issue, but one factor that impedes change is the fear of taking a risk. Underlying this fear may be the fear of loss, fear of embarrassment, or fear of failure. Addressing these issues can empower faculty to be more innovative in their teaching. Drawing on research literature, personal teaching narratives, and my own work in faculty development, I discuss some of these underlying fears. I then offer concrete strategies for working with faculty to enable them to overcome these emotional barriers and embrace change.*

## Introduction

One way to ensure a lively, even heated, debate among college and university faculty is to turn the conversation to the newest pedagogical strategies. Teaching approaches such as collaborative learning and problem-based learning have been extolled by some as ways to develop students' critical thinking and problem-solving abilities and to increase students' engagement in their learning. But these techniques have also been seen by some as trendy, resulting in little more than an increase in the students' "feel good" factor and a decrease in content covered and knowledge retained by students. These concerns may be countered by those who adopt the constructivist's view that knowledge cannot be transferred intact from lecturer to listener but must be actively created in part through interactions with others. Other educators point out challenges in some of these student-centered approaches, however, such as the danger of misconceptions promoted by group work and the difficulties in transferring content learned in highly contextualized formats such as problem-based learning. Often the difficulty of assessing the effectiveness of various teaching methods punctuates these discussions.

If we start probing in these conversations, we may find that skepticism is expressed not only about those strategies that may be considered most non-traditional, such as problem-based learning, but also for more conventional teaching formats such as class discussions or student-led problem sessions. And, conversely, proponents of highly interactive formats may devalue any form of lecturing. How receptive faculty are to the perceived value of pedagogical strategies is a complex issue that depends less on how compelling the data are in support of these approaches and more on what teachers believe about teaching. Teachers' beliefs is an important topic in educational research, as are studies on how these beliefs may affect practice (Hativa & Goodyear, 2002). These beliefs need not be static but evolve over a teacher's career depending on experiences and the ability of the teacher to reflect on those experiences. Even then, the impetus to change one's teaching practices based on experience and reflection is affected by both intrinsic and extrinsic motivations. For example, an intrinsic motivation may be how much teaching generates a personal sense of satisfaction and an extrinsic motivation may be how teaching is rewarded in our professional career.

Although certain critical impediments to faculty undertaking new pedagogical approaches are institutional and thus extrinsic, those that are most readily addressed are personal. A prerequisite step to the willingness to teach differently is the reflection on practice. Yet reflective teachers may not change the approach they take in the classroom, even though they themselves perceive a need for change based on student feedback, student performance, or their own sense of dissatisfaction with the status quo. As we work with these faculty to improve their teaching, we may face resistance that is hard to decipher. We cannot begin to uncover the range of experiences that faculty have that shape their beliefs about teaching, nor to understand each teacher's psychological, philosophical, and emotional underpinnings for their practice. Yet one factor that has been shown to stand in the way of teachers changing their practice is the fear of taking a risk (McAlpine & Weston, 2002). Addressing this fear can help faculty become more receptive to introducing innovation and flexibility in their teaching. In this chapter I outline some possible reasons for this fear, and I offer suggestions that can help them push past this emotional barrier.

## Underlying Fears

Several eloquent personal narratives of teaching exist that highlight a professor's fears and how they have shaped life and career. Elaine Showalter (2003) in her memoir-handbook, *Teaching Literature,* devotes an entire chapter to teaching anxiety and categorizes it into seven types depending on its source: lack of training, feelings of isolation, tension between teaching and research, coverage demands, performance issues, grading challenges, and student and peer evaluation. She highlights fears involved in teaching literature, pointing out that "we believe that what we say in the classroom reveals the deepest aspects of ourselves" (p. 3). This fear of exposure may take many forms and may be more acute in the classroom than in other public arenas because instructors face this audience day after day. Perceptions of mistakes, inadequacies, even character flaws, reenter the classroom daily with one's students, to be compounded by each new infraction.

In his insightful and moving account, *The Courage to Teach,* Parker Palmer (1998) echoes what research and our own experiences tell us:

> In unguarded moments with close friends, we who teach will acknowledge a variety of fears: having our work go unappreciated, being inadequately rewarded, discovering one fine morning that we chose the wrong profession, spending our lives on trivia, ending up feeling like frauds. But many of us have another fear that we rarely name: our fear of the judgment of the young. (pp. 47–48)

Palmer notes how these fears can lead eventually to stagnation and cynicism if faculty fail to interpret their experiences accurately or, we might say, fail to reflect productively on those experiences.

Unlike Palmer and Showalter and a few other narrators, to many faculty *fear* is indeed a four-letter word, one not to be spoken in polite society. As faculty talk to us about their teaching, it is up to us to recognize the various fears that underlie apparent resistance, frustration, or complacency. We may then respond more effectively with strategies that allow them to push past their fears and give them new hope to re-reinvigorate their teaching.

### Fear of Loss

In 2002, Daniel Kahneman won the Nobel Prize in Economics for applying insights from psychological research to economic science. Specifically, he and his colleagues studied how human judgment affects decision-making under uncertainty or risk. This work was based on an area of cognitive science that deals with the concept of *cognitive bias*. Cognitive bias arises when we are faced with complex problems that have no simple solution and our intuitive thinking resorts to heuristics (i.e., general guidelines) to tackle the issue quickly. Unfortunately, in some cases these simple procedures produce erroneous conclusions, especially when our decision depends on a good understanding of the probability of certain events. Kahneman and Tversky (1979) found that people would pass up the possibility of great financial gains in order to avoid a loss—the idea of loss aversion. When making a decision that involves risk, many of us do not base our choices on rational arguments. A person who is loss averse dislikes symmetric 50–50 bets, and the dislike increases with the absolute size of the stakes. This observation relates this work to a behavioral concept dealing with preferences (p. 279).

We humans do not consider gains and losses rationally—our first priority is not to lose. Even though this conclusion was drawn from work with people faced with financial decisions, we may speculate that other apparent high-stakes situations in which we stand to lose something of value might evoke similar responses. Reflecting on this idea, we can see that change of any kind is fraught with possibilities of loss. When applied to changing our teaching, these potential losses can seem to be monumental. What do we fear losing?

We fear losing content "coverage." This principle is usually cited first and foremost when faculty confront nontraditional pedagogical choices. The tyranny of content coverage is especially acute in certain disciplines that have a recognized body of information on which subsequent courses build, for example, the sciences and engineering. Our illusion is that if we tell students the information that we want them to know, students who are motivated will absorb it, and our obligation to the discipline has been met. Thus, the most readily recognized and accepted pedagogical choice is lecture. It's hard to argue with this premise head-on because most professors themselves learned very well by the lecture method, and it does have its place as one option in our set of pedagogical tools.

We fear losing control. What do the more student-centered strategies all have in common? They all represent shifts in the nature of authority in the classroom. They require us to move away from the idea that information may be transferred intact from expert to novice. Instead, they ask us to move toward the model of the student as self-teacher, recognizing that knowledge is of necessity constructed in the mind of the learners as they seek to reconcile new knowledge with mental models they've built based on former experience.

Research in cognitive science may currently be interpreted as validating the view that knowledge is constructed, not simply absorbed, yet for many of us this theory is not necessarily readily accepted. We need to believe that we can control the development of students' ideas through our eloquent prose and detailed explanations; otherwise, it's hard to know our role in the classroom. Interestingly, research in cognitive science also shows us how important the fear of loss of control is to human thinking (LeDoux, 1996). Our students may struggle against learning in our disciplines because they perceive that we are imposing our control over them (Zull, 2002). How much more then may we as instructors resist handing over our hard-earned position of authority to students? And we may even perceive those who encourage the use of alternate pedagogies to be someone else seeking to tell us what to do.

Proposing that we change our preferred way of teaching seems to assault us on two levels. First, the classroom has usually been an arena in which faculty work in isolation and in absolute control. We do not typically engage in collegial discussion about teaching, so raising questions about our choice of techniques may seem to be an unexpected and inhospitable attack on our professional expertise. Add to this the fact that the pedagogical methods being touted often ask the teacher to relinquish authority in the classroom to novices, and we have added insult to injury.

## Fear of Embarrassment

Necessary for academic success is the ability to pose intellectual questions and to generate recognizably valid arguments to answer them. In general, most of us didn't need to be highly adept in social situations to get where we are in academia. Yet many of the teaching modes other than lecture require us to navigate and direct human interactions, a somewhat daunting task. When working with students in groups or even facilitating a meaningful discussion, we are in danger not only of losing content coverage and control, but also of embarrassing ourselves—we fear being seen as incompetent, less smart, perhaps even just silly. As Palmer (1998) said, we fear students' judgment of us. We fear losing respect. Most of us have spent a great deal of time honing our lecture skills in order to avoid being embarrassed in public. Asking us to step into another area of perceived performance for which we have limited training is asking a lot.

## Fear of Failure

Finally, and not least importantly, we fear failure—failure to transmit critical concepts in our discipline, failure to resonate with students, failure to be perceived as experts in our field. Whatever mode of teaching we have been using represents the known. Any failures we noted in the past using these strategies have been rationalized and dealt with. To change means to bring the effects of our teaching under close scrutiny again. We may need to find different explanations for student failures and put our own performance under review and judgment again.

## How Prevalent Are These Fears?

A number of anecdotal accounts document a teacher's fears, but what does the research literature say about this phenomenon? Several studies exist on math anxiety, test anxiety, even computer anxiety, but very little on teaching anxiety—unless we lump it under the very broad category of performance or speech anxiety. Two studies dealing specifically with teaching anxiety, one among psychology professors (Gardner & Leak, 1994) and one among accounting professors (Ameen, Guffey, & Jackson, 2002), found that a large majority of faculty (78%–87%) had experienced some form of teaching anxiety, broadly defined as "distress that comes from either the anticipation of teaching, the preparation for teaching, or the experiences that occur while teaching" (Gardner & Leak, 1994, p. 29). In the majority of cases this anxiety was described by faculty as arising from external events, not existing as a part of the professor's self-described personality, and presenting an ongoing challenge.

In these studies, teaching anxiety was associated with some activities that involve talking to any group, such as standing before the class before speaking, but other triggers were not so related: class preparation, students' questions, negative feedback or disruptions from students during class, and end-of-term evaluations. As one might expect, in both studies anxiety felt while teaching diminished in a statistically significant way in teachers with more experience and higher rank. The amount of teaching experience, however, did not correlate with reducing the other potential triggers of anxiety; that is, student questions and evaluations or class preparation activities, at least in the study of psychology professors (Gardner & Leak, 1994). Instructors did not significantly associate anxiety with a class format, such as discussion versus lecture, but more with lack of familiarity with course material as noted in the study of accounting professors (Ameen, Guffey, & Jackson, 2002).

Neither of these studies asked specific questions about anxiety when using alternate teaching strategies such as group work, but certainly we could speculate that the unfamiliarity with this style of teaching and the perceived loss of control could act as an anxiety trigger, perhaps in a similar way as does lack of familiarity with course material. The student-centered formats are more likely to expose professors to possible negative responses from students, an identified trigger in both studies. Both class preparation activities and student evaluations were noted sources of anxiety in these studies, and one can imagine that changing one's teaching to include flexibility in class format and more student interaction could elicit these fears as well.

## Addressing These Fears and Encouraging Change

Keeping these fears in mind as we consult with faculty about their teaching, we may find it helpful to draw on a model of how beliefs about teaching change with experience and reflection. Douglas Robertson (1999) presents a three-stage developmental model of professors' perspectives on teaching. In his model, what teachers perceive as shaping the teaching and learning process moves through the following progression:

- The teacher controlling the dynamic

- The learner and his or her needs directing the dynamic

- The interconnectedness of teacher and learner as integral to the dynamic

Each of these stages encompasses and expands upon the previous, and the transition between each view may be fraught with some discomfort, anxiety, and feelings of loss. Each transition requires instructors to renegotiate the idea of control in the classroom, to recreate the vision of what the classroom dynamic entails, and to reevaluate the ultimate goals of teaching. Robertson's work shows that instructors deal with the discomfort of these transitions either by reverting back to comfortable though unsatisfying prior practices or by changing direction.

When faculty have reached a stage in their experience and reflection in which they feel a need to try something new in their teaching, we need to support them in taking what they probably perceive as a risk. We need to decrease their sense of perceived losses and recognize that their anxiety might be particularly acute when thinking about class preparation, class dynamic, and student response to the strategy. What approaches we suggest for them have to fit within their comfort zone based on disciplinary traditions, past practices, and overall teaching experience. In this regard we may find useful ideas in the classic work of Everett Rogers (1962), *Diffusion of Innovations*. To be appealing, an innovation must:

- Confer a relative advantage

- Be compatible with existing values, past experiences, and needs of potential adopters

- Be relatively simple to implement

- Be doable as a trial sample

- Have positive results that are observable

These ideas offer us ways to help faculty allay their fears. For example, fear of loss may be offset by emphasizing the relative advantage of a pedagogical innovation. Does an instructor's current mode of teaching best help reach his or her goals based on what we know about student learning? Or would another pedagogical approach actually confer an advantage for the class? Is the strategy simple to try in a limited way that does not detract too much from traditional content coverage? May this strategy be planned in such a way that the risk of embarrassment and failure is minimized?

If faculty attempt such a trial, then it is imperative that the strategy be one that has a good chance of producing a quick, modest success, again in terms of some instructional goal. That success is crucial to building an instructor's confidence and spurring additional ventures, perhaps even those that seem to be riskier. In helping faculty think through these strategies, however, we must keep in mind the values and experiences of the instructor as well as his or her pedagogical or curricular needs. Strategies that seem appropriate in the format of a history class may seem alien and off-putting to a chemistry instructor. The incorporation of this strategy in a professor's course planning should seem natural and not too intrusive, so that preparation is not too anxiety-producing. And the strategy should not require the instructor to navigate a radical shift in class dynamic. Likewise, the strategy should not dramatically deviate from what students' might expect, so that student response could be expected to be at least neutral to this change.

These ideas are best illustrated by posing some hypothetical examples of our work with faculty. Let's first examine the case of Professor Williams, an instructor of a large lecture class. She is a fairly new instructor who attends a book group session in your teaching and learning center. After one session she makes a casual comment that she'd really like to have more class interaction but she is concerned that introducing discussions or group work will mean loss of content coverage and control of the class dynamic. She also says that she feels awkward moderating such activities. Taking this opportunity, you suggest a simple, no-risk strategy such as a "one-minute paper" (Angelo & Cross, 1993). In this classroom assessment technique, instructors ask students at the end of the class to write down a key point they remember from the session or a question they still have. Between that class and the next the instructor peruses these comments, and then takes a small amount of time in the following class to address students' concerns or misconceptions. Very little time is required either during the class lecture time or by the professor afterwards, yet this simple technique can quickly provide Professor Williams with a great deal of information about her students' progress and help her students feel that she is indeed interested in their learning. This strategy can be a successful first venture into adding more communication between her and her students in the class. As we think again of Robertson's faculty development model, the one-minute paper begins to build a bridge from the teacher-centered approach to a more student-sensitive mode of class dynamic.

You follow up with Professor Williams a week or so later, asking how she found the use of the one-minute paper and offering further resources. She mentions that students have begun using the course management software to send her these comments. From the tenor of your conversation, you discern that she found this strategy very helpful and is open to further ideas. Because Professor Williams has access to and is apparently comfortable with technology, a number of low-risk options are available for increasing student interaction. Perhaps the technological intervention that poses the least risk is the use of course management systems to facilitate student online discussions, either with or without the instructor's participation. She can pose questions to the class to help prepare students for class lecture or direct their reading more productively, or students can be asked to generate questions based on readings or lectures.

Professor Williams indicates that she has been using the course management software in this way, and she would really like to bring something like this into the classroom. An interesting and potentially powerful use of technology to increase student interaction during class is the use of personal response systems. These devices can be fairly inexpensive and allow faculty to pose questions and poll student response in real time. In this case, Professor Williams poses a question with numbered possible answers, and students click on the number of their response which is recorded electronically using the same kind of technology as a television remote control. A graphical summary of responses can be generated via computer connection and projected to the class or to Professor Williams alone. This process encourages student involvement while maintaining student anonymity. Again, the cost in terms of content coverage is small, Professor Williams maintains control of the class dynamic in the broadest sense, and the risk of embarrassment to her is minimized. And this technique provides her with immediate feedback on her students' understanding of key concepts. She should also perceive positive effects from this in terms of an increased energy level in the class and improved student interest.

This particular strategy has an advantage in that instructors who become satisfied with its use in more simple applications may be willing to use it to experiment with peer learning techniques. For example, Professor Williams can pose a conceptually complex question, have students post responses, and review the class summary. But before disclosing the best answer, she can ask students to pair up and discuss the questions with a classmate for a specified amount of time and then reenter a response. Professor Williams may then provide needed commentary or facilitate student discussion. This technique is a powerful way to promote conceptual change, and Professor Williams can see the immediate effect of student interaction on student learning.

The sequencing involved in the progression of suggestions made to Professor Williams is an important element in the process. Without Professor Williams having had a positive experience with other less intrusive class exercises, the use of peer learning activities in class might appear too risky. What if students don't talk? Preparing the perfect question and eliciting student answers might be anxiety-producing in this case. What if students perceive her as making busy work for them, or worse still, as shirking her responsibility? In this case, the students' potentially negative response is an anxiety trigger and a probable deterrent to her willingness to try this approach. Technology can provide a crutch in the sense that it allows the professor to transfer some of the weight of responsibility in capturing student interest and stimulating student interaction to the equipment. It provides a way to communicate and connect in a meaningful way that still allows a comfortable distance between instructor and student, or between implementation of pedagogical strategy and student response.

A second case is posed in Professor Adler, a senior professor who is teaching a small seminar class. You meet Professor Adler when he asks for a consultation because his teaching evaluations are not what he (and his department) expect. He tells you that he has been teaching the same course for years. He used to lecture to the 12 or so students, and he often spent hours in preparation. He says that the students didn't appreciate his efforts, and he thinks that lectures are a "bad" pedagogical choice. He thinks that the students should be doing the work, and he now asks students to do all the class presentations and he uses videos to supplement. He says that his low evaluations are a consequence of student passivity.

One interpretation of Professor Adler's choices is that he has willingly embraced the more student-centered pedagogies but lacks the skill to help students navigate this dynamic effectively. And this idea may explain part of the issue. But during this conversation you sense that Professor Adler was discouraged by student reaction to his lecture performance and has tried to relieve this stress by transferring responsibility for the class dynamic to students. His pedagogical choice may have been driven by fear rather than by understanding his goals for student learning and developing strategies to help students reach them. He has traversed Robertson's first stage of teacher development, but was impelled to do so by a desire to avoid student judgment.

Professor Adler's is a complex case that is too often seen on campuses. The challenges for us as consultants are to help him find a way to reengage with his class that relieves some of his apprehension and invigorates him, yet at the same time minimizes the chance for negative student response or other anxiety triggers. In order for Professor Adler to see an advantage to any change you suggest, he needs to be clearer on his goals for the class. He may have leaped to an alternate pedagogical strategy out of fear and without adequate reflection. Thus, your first task is to help him reflect more productively. And, in general, he may find that students respond more positively if he shares with them his goals for their learning, how these goals inform his teaching choices, and what he expects from them. As he outlines those with you, he may become clearer himself on what he really hopes to accomplish in the class. What does he perceive as students' responsibilities? How may he as professor help students successfully assume those responsibilities?

Once he is clearer on his goals for the class, we need to offer suggestions of approaches that provide an advantage, are not too far from his experience and comfort level, and are doable on a small scale with good chance of success. We also need to remember that he may feel more anxious when preparing for a new pedagogical approach and when thinking about dealing with student response to it. If one of his goals is to have students become more independent learners, as suggested by the approach he has taken, you may initially suggest that he provide some guidance for students on their presentations based on his expectations and the learning goals for the exercise. He might talk a bit with them about the structure of the presentations and provide a sheet that outlines the key expectations, thus illustrating for them his own thinking process. Afterwards he could provide written feedback to the student presenter noting strengths of the presentation and suggestions for improving the next one. He might consider having the first presentation by a student be evaluated formatively, not for a grade, or for a lesser percentage of the grade than later attempts. This approach allows students to take risks without the threat of dire consequences. Professor Adler may also benefit from using one-minute papers to solicit students' concerns and questions about the presentations before unspoken ill feelings begin to erode the class dynamic. These interventions should cause him little concern during his preparation for class, and the increased communication in the class can help ease his anxiety about student response to his teaching.

At a follow-up meeting Professor Adler tells you that he has implemented these ideas, and he notes that the students seem more receptive to the class format. You discern that he may be relaxing a bit more with the class as well. You then propose to him what may seem a riskier strategy—that of adding some group presentations/projects to the class. Because he wants students to become more independent learners, having students work together in groups may seem counterintuitive. What advantages does this strategy offer him? It allows him to challenge students beyond their own individual limitations while providing them with some support for that challenge, and studies suggests that this strategy promotes students' critical thinking skills and increases their engagement and satisfaction with the class (Johnson, Johnson, & Smith, 1991; Springer, Stanne, & Donovan, 1999). Group work may raise his concerns about ensuring individual accountability and monitoring group process, as well as anxiety about student response and fears about losing control of the classroom dynamic. Giving him ideas on how to structure the group process and evaluate student group work can ease his discomfort in preparing for this unfamiliar strategy. There is the risk that students will be ill at ease with group work as well, so providing structure, such as assigning roles in the group, may help everyone's comfort level. Allowing students some choice of topic, role in the group, and style of presentations may motivate them and ease their apprehension. He may want to talk with the class about the benefits of this format and solicit their concerns. Helping Professor Adler and his students think about teaching and learning as process and not performance should lessen the fear in the classroom environment. And along the way, Professor Adler may recognize the interconnectedness of the teacher and learner in the classroom dynamic, the final stage in Robertson's development model.

You encounter Professor Adler on campus near the beginning of the next term, and he tells you that his evaluations for the seminar course improved and he felt more positive about the class than he had in some time. When you query him about his use of groups, he sheepishly admits that he never tried using them. You can tell that his concerns about navigating group dynamics and generating negative student reactions were too great. But he points out that he enjoyed his conversations with his students and that he might consider the use of groups next time. His example illustrates that even with our best efforts, faculty fears will sometimes win out. But we also see that succeeding with small steps can reenergize faculty and pave the way for future attempts with new, riskier strategies.

## Conclusions

In *A Life in School*, Jane Tompkins (1996) recounts her re-envisioning of her teaching after years of soul-searching in various aspects of her life:

> Whereas for my entire teaching life I had always thought that what I was doing was helping my students to understand the material we were studying . . . that moment I realized that what I had actually been concerned with was showing the students how smart I was,

how knowledgeable I was, and how well-prepared I was for class. I had been putting on a performance whose true goal was not to help the students learn, as I had thought, but to perform before them in such a way that they would have a good opinion of me. I realized that my fear of being found wanting, of being shown up as a fraud, must have transmitted itself to [my students]. Insofar as I was afraid of being exposed, they too would be afraid. (p. 119)

This cycle in which our fears feed those of our students is also recounted by Palmer (1998). The more we fear student disapproval, for example, the more we may tend to act in ways that evoke student negativity. We may distance ourselves from students, thus cutting ourselves off from the type of communication that undergirds all successful teaching. Bernstein (1983) speculated that anxiety associated with teaching could lead to teaching behaviors that were detrimental to the class, such as avoiding answering students' questions or relying too much on student presentations or videos. Thus, helping faculty overcome these fears that stand in the way of productive reflection and openness to change can lead to a more positive class experience, regardless of the pedagogical strategies that the professor chooses to use.

In all our work with faculty, being aware of the implicit fears that may underlie an instructor's interest or disinterest in certain pedagogical approaches can inform our work in powerful ways. This awareness can help us realize what is apparently at stake when faculty respond emotionally to suggestions for pedagogical change, can help us form an understanding connection and find common ground with them, and can ultimately help us suggest strategies that resonate with the faculty member's experience while avoiding specific anxiety-producing triggers.

## References

Ameen, E. C., Guffey, D. M., & Jackson, C. (2002). Evidence of teaching anxiety among accounting educators. *Journal of Education for Business, 78*(1), 16–22.

Angelo, T. A., & Cross, K. P. (1993). *Classroom assessment techniques: A handbook for college teachers* (2nd ed.). San Francisco, CA: Jossey-Bass.

Bernstein, D. A. (1983). Dealing with teaching anxiety: A personal view. *Journal of the National Association of Colleges and Teachers of Agriculture, 27,* 181–185.

Gardner, L. E., & Leak, G. K. (1994). Characteristics and correlates of teaching anxiety among college psychology teachers. *Teaching of Psychology, 21,* 28–32.

Hativa, N., & Goodyear, P. (2002). *Teacher thinking, beliefs and knowledge in higher education.* New York, NY: Springer.

Johnson, D. W., Johnson, R. T., & Smith, K. A. (1991). *Cooperative learning: Increasing college faculty instructional productivity* (ASHE-ERIC Higher Education Report No. 4). Washington, DC: George Washington University, School of Education and Human Development.

Kahneman, D., & Tversky, A. (1979). Prospect theory: An analysis of decision under risk. *Econometrica, 47*(2), 263–291.

LeDoux, J. (1996). *The emotional brain: The mysterious underpinnings of emotional life.* New York, NY: Putnam.

McAlpine, L., & Weston, C. (2002). Reflection: Issues related to improving professors' teaching and students' learning. In N. Hativa & P. Goodyear (Eds.), *Teacher thinking, beliefs and knowledge in higher education* (pp. 59–78). New York, NY: Springer.

Palmer, P. J. (1998). *The courage to teach: Exploring the inner landscape of a teacher's life.* San Francisco, CA: Jossey-Bass.

Robertson, D. L. (1999). Professors' perspectives on their teaching: A new construct and developmental model. *Innovative Higher Education, 23*(4), 271–294.

Rogers, E. M. (1962). *Diffusion of innovations.* New York, NY: Free Press.

Showalter, E. (2003). *Teaching literature.* Malden, MA: Blackwell.

Springer, L., Stanne, M. E., & Donovan, S. S. (1999). Effects of small-group learning on undergraduates in science, mathematics, engineering, and technology: A meta-analysis. *Review of Educational Research, 69*(1), 21–51.

Tompkins, J. (1996). *A life in school: What the teacher learned.* New York, NY: Perseus.

Zull, J. E. (2002). *The art of changing the brain: Enriching the practice of teaching by exploring the biology of learning.* Sterling, VA: Stylus.

# Section II

# Innovations and Outcomes

# 10

# Tailoring Faculty Development Programs to Faculty Career Stages

Peter Seldin
Pace University

*College faculty progress through a series of sequential career stages. Each is characterized by different motivations and professional development needs. Yet, too often, faculty developers rely on hunches rather than empirical data to guide programming decisions. This chapter describes the important research findings of a just completed national study to determine the different programming interests and needs of more than 500 beginning, mid-career, and senior-level faculty in the United States.*

## Introduction

At the 2003 POD (Professional and Organizational Development Network in Higher Education) Conference, six friends—all long-term members of POD—had dinner together. During the course of the evening, our wide-ranging conversation eventually narrowed, and we began to focus on our own aging. We discussed our changing professional needs and personal interests and agreed that they were quite different now from what they were years earlier. We felt certain that the evolution in *our* needs and interests were likely similar to changing needs and interests of faculty at our institutions as they experienced their own aging.

After the POD conference ended, I returned to my own university and read some of the literature on the topic of faculty career stages. Particularly helpful was the work of Austin (2002); Baldwin (1985); Bland and Bergquist (1997); DeZure (2002); Kalivoda, Sorrell, and Simpson (1994); Karpiak (2001); Rice, Sorcinelli, and Austin (2000); Robertson (1999); Robertson

(2000); and Sandberg (2003). All wrote that faculty careers evolve over time as professors mature, gain experience, and revise their interests and professional objectives. They said that professors progress through a series of sequential career stages and that each is characterized by different demands, different motivations, and different professional development needs.

That conclusion seemed logical and reasonable to me. After all, the findings were consistent with widely accepted theories of human development, aging, and developmental psychology. But I wanted to go beyond the theories and directly ask faculty at different career stages about their specific developmental needs. My goal was to match career stages to specific professional development needs.

## The Study

Three broad career stages were used: beginning faculty (1–5 years in the classroom), mid-career faculty (10–20 years in the classroom), and senior faculty (30 or more years in the classroom). A one-page questionnaire listing an array of possible professional development activities was developed and field tested at my own university. It asked participants to indicate the number of years they had been teaching, and identify the development activities on the list in the questionnaire that were most relevant to them at this point in their careers.

After a small number of adjustments for clarity, in spring 2004 the revised questionnaire (see Appendix 10.1) was distributed to the academic deans of 30 colleges and universities across a range of Carnegie classifications. Also included was a cover letter that explained the purpose of the study and asked for the deans' help in forwarding the questionnaire to a sampling of beginning, mid-career, and senior faculty at their institutions. A total of 618 questionnaires were distributed, and 508 were returned to the author with usable data. The overall response rate of 82% was virtually the same across the three faculty career stages. It is an unusually high rate of return for social science research, but it is consistent with the rate of return I have obtained in 10 previous national studies.

## Results

### Beginning College Faculty (1–5 Years in the Classroom)

Beginning teachers are at a transition point in their careers. They have left the friendly comfort zone of graduate school where they knew the major players, the daily routine, what to do, and what not to do. Now they have begun their professional careers in a new and unfamiliar environment and many are learning to perform their duties in the classroom by trial and error. To their dismay, beginning faculty have learned that earning their doctorate does not mean that they have complete knowledge of their discipline and that they may well be assigned to teach courses that are outside their narrow field of specialization. At the same time, many are struggling to find an appropriate balance between teaching and scholarship and between their personal and professional lives.

This is the context within which beginning professors work. The development activities they selected in the survey as most relevant to them follow. The headings in italics that precede the developmental activities are my suggestions of umbrella topics under which the activities can be grouped.

*Opportunities to acquire new knowledge in their academic field of specialization.* Beginning faculty may be newly minted doctorates but they still have a strong need to expand their knowledge base in their chosen discipline. Participants in the study said that this need can be meet effectively if an institution:

- Provides modest financial grant support to enable them to initiate new discipline-specific scholarly research

- Provides resource help—financial and otherwise—to attend discipline-specific programs and conferences

- Provides support for the purchase of discipline-specific readings, reports, CDs, and periodicals

- Offers faculty development programs that address the value and usefulness of collaborative discipline-specific scholarly work

*Programs to develop their skill in the classroom.* Unless beginning faculty members took part in a strong TA training program on teaching during graduate school, they have an urgent need to enhance their skill in the classroom. This can be met through well-designed, campus workshops on such topics as:

- Teaching techniques

- Testing student knowledge

- Use of educational technology

- Course design

- Leading classroom discussions or lecturing

*Programs on time management and balance between professional and personal lives.* Beginning faculty are typically swamped by an array of time-consuming tasks. They need to learn how to manage their limited time and how to create balance in their lives. These needs can be met by well-developed workshops as well as occasional programs to orient them to their new professional home.

## Mid-Career College Faculty (10–20 Years in the Classroom)

In most cases, mid-career faculty are recognized as reasonably competent in their disciplines and in the classroom. But they are confronted with a dilemma in their careers: As they anticipate another 25–30 years in the academic profession, do they maintain the same career path they have traveled to this point? Or do they take on new professional activities and new roles? For many, mid-career is a turning point in their academic lifecycle.

This is the context within which mid-career faculty work. The development activities that they selected in the survey as most relevant to them follow. The heading in italics reflects my suggestion of an umbrella topic for the chosen activities.

*Opportunities to redefine and enlarge the scope of their professional careers.* Participants in the study said that this important need can be met if an institution provides such professional development opportunities as:

- A weekend career assessment and planning workshop to help them focus systematically on the future. The workshop encourages faculty to explore new areas and new avenues for broadening their perspectives, deepening them, and maybe even changing them.

- Rotation of administrative positions or other short-term non-teaching assignments. A year or two as an assistant dean or director of institutional assessment gives a mid-career faculty member a break from the routine of teaching and, at the same time, enables the institution to take advantage of the faculty member's talents. Similarly, chairing a major institutional task force at one's institution provides healthy variety in an academic career.

- Faculty exchanges, such as a year as a visiting professor at another institution, provide an opportunity for faculty to engage with new colleagues and experience new perspectives on teaching strategies, disciplinary issues, and maybe even institutional policies.

- Summer internships in a corporation or government agency offer opportunities for mid-career faculty members to learn new skills and acquire new knowledge in their academic disciplines.

- Opportunities to lead a group of students on a trip abroad for a two- or three-week academic experience. Leading such trips permits faculty to interact with their students in a refreshingly new way in a different venue and further develops faculty organizational and leadership skills.

## Senior Faculty (30 or More Years in the Classroom)

Senior faculty are the elder statespersons at their institutions. Most are between the ages of 55 and 65 and have worked at their institutions for many years. They have risen through the academic ranks to a senior position and many have held short-term administrative positions within their college or university, such as assistant dean, special assistant to the provost, or chair of an institutional self-study committee.

But at this point in their careers, they may find their influence diminishing as many of their long-term colleagues retire and as younger colleagues assume the important departmental roles that they held previously. At the same time, senior faculty may experience a disturbing sense of disquiet as the age gap between themselves and their students widens and they realize that some of their students are young enough to be their grandchildren.

This is the context in which senior faculty work. The development activities they selected as most relevant to them follow. The headings in italics reflect my suggestion of umbrella topics for the chosen activities.

*The need to leave behind a meaningful and lasting legacy.* This is consistent with the idea that a principle task of adult life is the quest for a sense of generativity—a need to produce something that will outlive oneself, to leave a legacy in some way. Participants in the study said that this need can be effectively met if an institution:

- Provides an opportunity for senior faculty to mentor young colleagues, either junior faculty or graduate students. Those with decades of experience in the higher education trenches can serve as master teacher, research design specialist, or career counselor to their younger colleagues. They can assist them in knowing the vital ropes to climb and the less important ropes to skip.

- Offers a convenient way for senior faculty to give something back to the community, both within and outside the institution. Senior faculty can volunteer time and expertise to assist their institution with a major project—for example, serving on a fundraising or athletic department task force or directing new faculty orientation. They can also contribute time and expertise to the outside community—for example, serving on a town beautification committee or a task force to enhance the quality of education in the local high school.

*Preparation for retirement.* Senior faculty who are about to retire are entering unchartered waters. They have no experiential background to fall back on. Too often, institutions fail to recognize the crucial need of senior faculty for information and guidance as they approach the tail end of their academic careers and prepare for retirement. This important need can be met if an institution:

- Provides an opportunity for senior faculty to get together for dialogue about the *financial* aspects of retirement. Institutions can offer programs presented by TIAA-CREF that address this vital aspect of retirement. The focus would be on examining one's financial assets, typical monthly expenses, and expected monthly payout from TIAA-CREF.

- Provides an opportunity for senior faculty to address the important *psychological* aspects of retirement. Consider the new life of just-retired senior faculty members: No longer do they prepare for classes. No longer do they have faculty colleagues to talk with. No longer do they have a place to go each morning. The loss of these things has a powerful impact on a person's sense of self. That's why veteran faculty can benefit from programs that provide psychological support as well as those that offer financial support.

- Facilitates structured meetings between those who will retire shortly and those who have already retired, especially those who retired within the last few years. The goal is for those who are about to retire to learn from academic colleagues who have already done so such things as what to expect, how to productively use their time, things to do, pitfalls to avoid, important things they wish they had known before they retired.

## Additional Finding

The study also found that faculty at *all* career points can benefit from certain opportunities to enhance their professional performance. Participants at all three career stages—beginning, mid-career, and senior level—said they could benefit from developing and annually updating a teaching portfolio and attending brown-bag lunches with faculty colleagues to share research, common readings, or teaching strategies. This result will not be surprising to faculty developers who have noted that faculty at all three career stages typically take part in programs focused on preparing and updating teaching portfolios as well as brown-bag lunches that are structured to encourage informal faculty discussion at their colleges or universities.

## Implications for Faculty Developers

In this era of scarce resources, few institutions can afford to offer a large number of programs that are geared only to faculty at a particular career stage. It is just too costly. But too often institutions offer *no* such programs. The rationalization is that many faculty will get something out of broad-based programs, even if they are not geared to the needs of their individual career stages. There is probably some truth to that perspective, but I would argue that faculty development programs would better serve their constituents by finding a middle ground and offering at least some programs geared to faculty at specific career stages. How might this be done?

At a minimum, institutions could offer an occasional program or two—on a rotating semester or annual basis—geared to faculty at a specific career stage. For example, a program of special interest to beginning faculty could be offered one year, the next year, a program of special interest to mid-career faculty, and the following year, a program geared to senior faculty.

This would be an important first step in recognizing that while faculty at all career stages can benefit from certain opportunities, other programs and activities are better suited to the professional development needs of faculty at specific career stages.

## References

Austin, A. E. (2002). Preparing the next generation of faculty: Graduate school as socialization to the academic career. *Journal of Higher Education, 73*(1), 94–122.

Baldwin, R. G. (Ed.). (1985). *New directions for higher education: No. 51. Incentives for faculty vitality.* San Francisco, CA: Jossey-Bass.

Bland, C. J., & Bergquist, W. H. (1997). *The vitality of senior faculty members: Snow on the roof–fire in the furnace* (ASHE-ERIC Higher Education Report, 25[7]), Washington, DC: George Washington University.

DeZure, D. (2002). *Priorities/concerns of faculty at several career stages.* Paper presented at a University of Michigan Faculty Seminar, Ann Arbor, MI.

Kalivoda, P., Sorrell, G. R., & Simpson, R. D. (1994). Nurturing faculty vitality by matching institutional interventions with career-stage needs. *Innovative Higher Education, 18*(4), 255–272.

Karpiak, I. E. (2001). Midlife: The "second call" for faculty renewal. *The Department Chair, 11*(4), 11–12.

Rice, R. E., Sorcinelli, M. D., & Austin, A. E. (2000). *Heeding new voices: Academic careers for a new generation* (New Pathways Working Paper Series No. 7). Washington, DC: American Association for Higher Education.

Robertson, D. L. (1999). Professors' perspectives on their teaching: A new construct and developmental model. *Innovative Higher Education, 23*(4), 271–294.

Robertson, D. R. (2000). Professors in space and time: Four utilities of a new metaphor and developmental model for professors-as-teachers. *Journal on Excellence in College Teaching, 11*(1), 117–132.

Sandberg, K. (2003). Senior professors, too, sometimes need a helping hand. *The Department Chair, 14*(1), 26–27.

## Appendix 10.1

## Faculty Survey

What is your teaching career stage? (If you are between stages, check the stage that you are closest to at the end of this academic year.)

_____ Beginning faculty (1–5 years)

_____ Mid-career faculty (10–20 years)

_____ Senior faculty (30 or more years)

*Instructions:* Please rate the level of relevance that you assign to each of the following professional development activities. Place a checkmark at the appropriate response level for each item.

| Development Activities | Most relevant | | Least relevant | |
|---|---|---|---|---|
| | 1 | 2 | 3 | 4 |
| Attending a workshop on time management | \_\_\_\_ | \_\_\_\_ | \_\_\_\_ | \_\_\_\_ |
| Holding a rotating administrative position | \_\_\_\_ | \_\_\_\_ | \_\_\_\_ | \_\_\_\_ |
| Taking part in faculty exchanges | \_\_\_\_ | \_\_\_\_ | \_\_\_\_ | \_\_\_\_ |
| Attending brown-bag lunches to share research, common readings, or teaching strategies | \_\_\_\_ | \_\_\_\_ | \_\_\_\_ | \_\_\_\_ |
| Taking part in workshops on leading classroom discussion or lecturing | \_\_\_\_ | \_\_\_\_ | \_\_\_\_ | \_\_\_\_ |
| Obtaining a small-grant financial support | \_\_\_\_ | \_\_\_\_ | \_\_\_\_ | \_\_\_\_ |
| Being given teaching release time to take on special assignments | \_\_\_\_ | \_\_\_\_ | \_\_\_\_ | \_\_\_\_ |
| Attending a career assessment workshop | \_\_\_\_ | \_\_\_\_ | \_\_\_\_ | \_\_\_\_ |
| Learning about the psychological aspects of retirement | \_\_\_\_ | \_\_\_\_ | \_\_\_\_ | \_\_\_\_ |
| Chairing an important institutional task force | \_\_\_\_ | \_\_\_\_ | \_\_\_\_ | \_\_\_\_ |
| Acquiring new knowledge in one's discipline | \_\_\_\_ | \_\_\_\_ | \_\_\_\_ | \_\_\_\_ |
| Developing and annually updating a teaching portfolio | \_\_\_\_ | \_\_\_\_ | \_\_\_\_ | \_\_\_\_ |
| Mentoring other faculty | \_\_\_\_ | \_\_\_\_ | \_\_\_\_ | \_\_\_\_ |
| Learning about collaborative scholarly work | \_\_\_\_ | \_\_\_\_ | \_\_\_\_ | \_\_\_\_ |
| Taking part in programs that address course design or educational technology | \_\_\_\_ | \_\_\_\_ | \_\_\_\_ | \_\_\_\_ |

| Development Activities | Most relevant | | Least relevant | |
|---|---|---|---|---|
| | 1 | 2 | 3 | 4 |
| Taking part in a summer internship | ____ | ____ | ____ | ____ |
| Leading a group of college students on a trip abroad | ____ | ____ | ____ | ____ |
| Giving something back to the community (within and outside the institution) | ____ | ____ | ____ | ____ |
| Learning about the financial aspects of retirement | ____ | ____ | ____ | ____ |

# 11

# Creating Engaged Departments: A Program for Organizational and Faculty Development

Kevin J. Kecskes, Sherril B. Gelmon, Amy Spring
Portland State University

*Portland State University encourages faculty participation in service-learning by providing faculty with individual incentives to support and reward them. Now, in recognition of this central role of the department in higher education, administrators interested in creating sustained civic engagement initiatives on campus are looking to the department as a strategic leverage point for change. This chapter investigates a yearlong engaged department initiative and finds that a collective approach can (re)connect individual faculty to their initial motivations for engaging in the profession, to a community of scholars, to their students, and also to their surrounding community.*

## Introduction

Higher education faculty members find their intellectual and professional home in their discipline. At the institutional level, the disciplines are organized as departments or similar academic units. Departments house faculty with similar scholarly interests, where the chair and other leaders set policies in accord with disciplinary expectations, and faculty generally support and review each other's work as well as look to each other for collaboration and collegiality. These administrative units of discipline-related faculty provide a structure to recruit and select new faculty, negotiate research agendas, develop reward systems, establish curriculum, and respond to disciplinary and student priorities (Leaming, 1998). In recognition of this centrality of the department, administrators interested in effecting lasting change on campus are looking to the department as a strategic leverage point for change.

Portland State University (PSU) encourages faculty participation in service-learning in part by providing faculty with individual incentives to support and reward them. One of the incentives, administered by PSU's Center for Academic Excellence (CAE), has been a competitive, peer reviewed, service-learning, small grant program. Since 1997, more than 200 faculty have received these grants for service-learning course development or enhancement. This individual-level strategy has significantly facilitated the expansion of service-learning at PSU. However, faculty have reported frustration with the lack of *department* resources to support their service-learning and civic engagement work. They have also expressed concern that the existing practice of providing grants to support individuals required them to be in direct competition with their department colleagues. Shifting to a department incentive strategy would encourage individual faculty within department units to work together and provide funds to help support the development of a sustainable department infrastructure for ongoing engagement.

## The Engaged Department Concept

There have been many discussions about *engaged* universities, departments, and disciplines at various national meetings and in multiple publications. Initiatives related to service-learning and civic engagement were initially perceived as *institutional* activities, with considerable support from senior administration. As campuses gained increased experience in civic engagement, the faculty value of conceptual, disciplinary frameworks was acknowledged, and new initiatives began within the disciplines (e.g., the Campus Compact Engaged Disciplines Project) to provide faculty with peer review and recognition. This led to further consideration of the department (i.e., a cluster of disciplinary related individuals who work together and are rewarded through this unit) as a key unit for institutional transformation.

Since 2000, Campus Compact has taken the lead in department engagement by offering the Institute on the Engaged Department. The institute helps academic departments think about the department as a unit of engagement and change (see the Campus Compact web site for more information on the institute: http://www.compact.org/faculty/engageddept.html). PSU has participated in this initiative by forming department teams consisting of faculty, the chair, and a community partner, who work together for three intense days to develop action strategies for engagement within the department context.

These institutes have proven to be a valuable tool for launching department plans (Battistoni, Gelmon, Saltmarsh, Wergin, & Zlotkowski, 2003).

This national effort to encourage increased and enhanced community-university partnerships by focusing resources on academic departments provided the impetus for the CAE staff to rethink our individual faculty incentive strategy. In 2001, we decided to build upon the experiences of Campus Compact to develop and pilot a similar campus-wide program, the Engaged Department Initiative. In our initiative, we use *department* as a general term for a variety of academic units that have equivalent functions to a department. For example, one unit was a major component of an academic program, and two other units are called *schools* but function as departments.

Our program was designed to involve a select number of departments in a yearlong planning and development process to create action strategies relevant to their context with respect to engagement. Each department would receive various resources (human, fiscal, printed, and consultative) to assist in this work. The aim was for faculty and departments to become more engaged in mission-related activities relevant to civic engagement and related teaching and research strategies.

## Research Questions

We wanted to develop evidence to answer the following questions:

- What can departments accomplish through a one-year program with respect to developing civic engagement activities?

- What opportunities exist to support departments in this work, and how can they take advantage of them?

- What challenges exist, and how might they be overcome?

- What central institutional capacity is needed to help departments become engaged departments?

Our intent was to learn as much as we could through this initial one-year project in order to inform future development activities sponsored by the university and to provide a basis for dissemination to a larger audience. Given the interest in department engagement at many institutions in the United States and our impression that during the 2001–2002 academic year no other campus had pursued a similar formal program to build institutional capacity around department engagement, we believed there was much to learn that would have local relevance and broad applicability.

## Methods

Portland State University has invited participation in various developmental programs sponsored by CAE through a request-for-proposal (RFP) process. An RFP is created and mailed in hardcopy and electronic formats to all faculty and academic leaders in the university. We determined that an RFP process was appropriate for the Engaged Department Initiative in order to make the invitation open to all departments on campus. We identified departments we believed already had an interest in this area, and we gave them additional encouragement to consider the RFP and determine whether they could assemble a team to apply for participation. The RFP invited departments (programs, units, etc.) to "participate in an in-depth process to become an engaged department." Given that this work was funded in part by a grant from the Corporation for National and Community Service, we defined an *engaged* department in keeping with the corporation's goals as one that does the following:

- Uses community-based (or service) learning to help students integrate community work and reflection into their academic studies

- Encourages the scholarship of engagement where community-based action research is pursued that addresses issues defined by community participants

- Provides support to other activities prominent on the department agenda in which the department responds to the community through the activities that fulfill the university's mission

One of our strategies for inviting departments to apply to participate in this project was to offer department grants to support their work. The RFP specified options regarding the use of the grants, with an emphasis on grants that would accomplish one or more of the following: purposefully integrate community-based work into teaching and scholarship; develop community-based learning as a regular part of the academic content and expectations of a curriculum; and/or develop and implement plans for department coherence for engagement in scholarly and service activities. The RFP included guidelines regarding the use of funds, and it specified expectations of participating departments to include designation of a three- to five-person leadership team, a commitment to participate in an internal planning and development process, and a commitment to participate in monthly cross-campus discussions of initiative participants to build collective knowledge and learning.

Proposals were reviewed by a team assembled by the Center for Academic Excellence, who independently ranked each proposal against nine primary criteria derived from the RFP content and three other criteria related to institutional goals (in order to gain leverage across campus initiatives). Reviewers met, discussed their rankings, and identified seven departments to invite to participate: Department of English, Department of Mathematical Sciences, Department of Psychology, School of Business (management grouping), School of Community Health, School of Urban Studies and Planning (community development grouping), and University Studies (freshman inquiry grouping). Each team identified at least three faculty participants, and some teams included a graduate student. Although teams were also invited to include a community partner on their team, none elected to do so.

## Program Process and Content

Upon acceptance of participation in the Engaged Department Initiative, each team was sent a planning document to complete. We modified the planning document used by Campus Compact for the national institute (Campus Compact, 2001). This document asked departments to reflect on the question "Where are you now?" They did this by:

- Articulating mission

- Describing strengths, weaknesses, challenges, and opportunities

- Offering their own definition of civic engagement

- Assessing the extent of engagement within the department

- Identifying core communities and constituencies

Departments then addressed the question "Where do you want to be?" This led to articulating goals for the project, projecting accomplishments, and anticipating impact(s) of the project. These documents provided a useful basis for helping departments begin their work and for assisting program leaders in gaining a better understanding of the assets and challenges of the participating departments.

There were three major components of the work of this project: individual department activities, facilitated learning/networking sessions of the seven departments and program leaders, and individual monthly consultations with each department. The common theme for all participating departments was the opportunity to learn together through the monthly sessions and to identify challenges and possible solutions. Of the seven sessions that were held, six were content based and addressed topics that included strategizing barriers and facilitators, curricular change, engaging the rest of the department, and related scholarship. The final session was a public poster session at which each department presented a poster summarizing its work. The campus community and others interested in civic engagement were invited to view the posters and discuss the content and experiences with the department representatives.

Our assessment of this project is based on six primary sources of evidence: the initial project proposals, the planning documents submitted at the beginning of the process, observations throughout the monthly learning sessions, observations from the monthly consultations, final project reports (including posters), and a final interview conducted by the CAE staff with each team. We conducted content analyses of each of the documents and collectively analyzed our individual and group reflections and observations.

## Findings

Findings are based on a review of the various sources of evidence. We have synthesized these according to the four research questions that address accomplishments, opportunities and facilitators of department engagement, challenges and strategies, and necessary central institutional capacity.

### Accomplishments

What can departments accomplish through a program lasting one academic year with respect to developing civic engagement activities? The seven departments proposed projects that varied tremendously. Notwithstanding these differences, similarities do appear among them. In terms of accomplishments, we have organized the projects into three broad categories: creating initial course offerings, fostering broad-scale engagement, and refining engagement activities. In all cases it should be noted that the project period of this initial study was approximately seven months. This abbreviated time period affected the scope and depth of what the departments were able to accomplish.

*Creating initial course offerings.* Two departments focused their efforts on developing and offering a service-learning course as a strategy to build civic engagement within their units. Both departments strategically determined the critical place within the curriculum where a service-learning course would best serve student learning and recognized that students within their academic programs could benefit from discipline-related service-learning courses. Each department had limited previous experience offering service-learning courses; therefore, the focus for these two teams was to develop discipline-based service-learning expertise among a small group of department faculty. By offering these initial service-learning courses, the departments were able to develop their comfort and skills with service-learning pedagogies, confirm the need for discipline-based service-learning (as expressed by their students), and explore ways to expand their efforts to include additional service-learning courses in subsequent academic terms. The two departments were also able to assess the impact their service-learning courses had on student learning, particularly as it relates to the students' understanding of themselves in discipline-based professional settings. Now both departments are exploring ways to make the service-learning experiences a sustained part of their curricula.

*Fostering broad-scale engagement.* Three departments proposed projects to expand and enhance the level of engagement the departments' faculty and students have with the surrounding community. Two of the three departments proposed a department-focused faculty discussion series to increase understanding of how and why to integrate service-learning into course curricula. The third department proposed a project centered on a community-identified concern. The focus of this department's work was to create department enthusiasm to integrate this community-identified concern into a department-wide teaching and research agenda.

These three departments hosted a series of events designed to encourage department-wide discussions about integrating community-based projects into teaching and research. Some of these events were held during regularly scheduled department meetings. Others were brown-bag meetings meant to provide faculty with specific service-learning skills. Still others were student-organized department events meant to highlight and encourage participation in a specific community-identified concern. Finally, some were events where nationally recognized speakers were invited to discuss their community-based work. Although these events took many different forms, the overall goal for these units was to encourage department-wide discussions about why and how to engage with the Portland metropolitan community.

As a result of these events, the three departments that employed this department-wide change strategy have been able to document an increased interest among their faculty colleagues to integrate community-based engagement into their teaching and research. In each department, four new service-learning courses will be offered during the next academic year. Additionally, an increased number of internships for graduate students were created, a new web site that identifies community projects now proclaims success, and at least three community-based research publications are in press. In the ideal state, community-building efforts can (re)invigorate deep interest in and (re)connect individual faculty members to their initial motivations for engaging in the profession, to a community of scholars, to their students, and to their surrounding community.

*Refining engagement activities.* Although all of the departments involved assessed their engagement activities, two departments used this initiative to more comprehensively assess the current level and quality of the engagement activities taking place across their departments. Both have a long tradition of community engagement, and they saw this initiative as a means to more fully understand what they were currently doing and to inform their practice to enhance department work with their community partners.

They used different processes to assess their current engagement activities. One department took a highly formal approach which included using facilitated focus groups with students and a survey of students, faculty, and community partners. This data was used to determine their current level of engagement and strategies that would enhance community-department partnerships. The other department utilized a broad-scale engagement approach. A graduate student interviewed each of the faculty members within in the department to determine the extent and nature of existing community-based teaching and research. This approach allowed the graduate student to gain a deep and highly specific understanding of the types of projects faculty were pursuing with the community and a good sense of the resources they need to enhance their work with the community.

As a result of these efforts, the two departments are now able to articulate with increased clarity the level at which their departments are engaged in community-based teaching and research. Also, they are able to structure department resources to strengthen their engagement efforts. In the next academic year, both departments will put structures in place to enhance the quality of community-based engagement for their students, faculty, and community partners.

## Opportunities and Facilitators of Department Engagement

Moving from a model of support of individual faculty to a model where support is provided to groups of faculty within a department substantially changes the way in which community-based teaching and research is understood and advanced within the university. The facilitators for increasing and enhancing community-based work when departments are the strategic point for resource allocation are significantly different. The department is the community in a sense. Using the department as the unit of focus models local community development. Motivation for community engagement does not come primarily from a centralized service-learning center. Instead, it emanates from the department team members involved in the project. There are several facilitating elements that assisted the seven engaged department teams in their work.

*Opportunities for faculty to work together.* Establishing programmatic structures to facilitate teams of faculty to work together was one of the initial motivators to shift from a program model that encourages individual faculty to integrate community engagement into their teaching and research to one that encourages department teams to integrate engagement into the collective work of the department. The faculty teams involved in this initiative found that the support facilitated the development of useful and important actions that would not have occurred if they had not been encouraged to work as a team. One team utilized the initiative as a means to educate colleagues about the theoretical and scholarly foundations of community engagement. They had a modest goal to encourage their colleagues to integrate community engagement into their own work but, more importantly, they sought to provide information so that those colleagues would be more effective at evaluating promotion and tenure portfolios that have documented community engagement activities.

Several of the teams described their work together as offering critical opportunities to think about their departments' complete curriculum and how community engagement can be woven throughout with developmentally appropriate projects that would match students' theoretical understanding and skills. The department teams were made up of individual faculty, some with many years of community-based project experience and some with relatively little previous experience. The teams provided an infrastructure to have faculty with more experience mentor and assist those with less experience. Faculty from each team reported they were able to accomplish much more because of the synergy created through their work together on this project. Without the luxury of being able to provide funding and programmatic support to promote this collective work among faculty, the level of attention and focus dedicated to department engagement would have been minimal.

*Discipline-focused resources.* Development of discipline-specific resources to assist faculty and students in their community-based engagement was an important facilitator of the departments' work. The Engaged Department Initiative was created in part to respond to faculty requests for assistance with the development of department infrastructure to support community engagement. Most of the departments used a portion of their funds to develop a discipline-specific library of electronic and material items that would assist them in effective community-based teaching and research. Department teams collected sample syllabi, course assignments, examples of structured reflection strategies, publication and presentation outlets for community-based research and scholarship, and student learning assessment techniques, as well as lists of community partners with whom the department could effectively work. Once assembled, the department teams made these materials accessible to the entire department by creating an electronic link to the departments' web pages, locating the materials in the departments' libraries, or developing copies of the materials and distributing them to each department faculty member. Many of these items already exist in the campus faculty development center, but having access to them at the department level and having them specifically tailored to the discipline helped faculty and students in their engagement initiatives.

In addition to these print and electronic resources, most of the teams utilized a portion of their funds to hire a student to assist them with their engagement projects. The students were identified and selected by the department teams, and in almost every case, the students were majors from the department with whom they were working. Faculty teams uniformly recognized that student involvement with this initiative was an essential facilitator of the project. Students attended to many of the logistical elements that moved the projects through their various implementation stages, such as organizing guest speakers for department workshops, identifying community partners with whom faculty and students could work, organizing department library resources, helping service-learning students get to their service sites, and helping to organize various elements of assessment. In addition to these varied and essential logistical support roles, the students provided the faculty teams with a student voice and perspective. Those departments that did not utilize students as facilitators of their department engagement projects reported that they would incorporate students as a resource to advance their work if they were to propose a project of this type again.

We have identified two primary reasons why these student, electronic, and material resources served as important facilitators to the work of the departments: most of the resources were identified by the department teams involved in the initiative, and most of the resources were specifically tailored to the teams' disciplines. Both of these factors contribute to the usability of the resources. They were selected and organized by the people who will access them and were based on a theoretical framework familiar to the departments.

*Individual and organizational commitment.* Organizational and individual leadership on behalf of community engagement facilitated the effectiveness of the Engaged Department Initiative. For those departments in which civic engagement and applied learning experiences reflected a long tradition and articulation in the department mission, the ability to mobilize department resources to increase and enhance engagement within the department came with relative ease. Teams cited their department mission and academic tradition as recognition that engagement in the community is a viable and expected activity of the department. Many faculty accepted that community-based teaching and research is a legitimate and expected means to contribute specifically to the department and generally to the disciplinary field.

For those teams where the department's chair expressed a high level of leadership and commitment to the Engaged Department Initiative, the efforts of the faculty team were tremendously enhanced. The chair's commitment helped the department team tie the initiative to other department initiatives. They were also able to garner additional resources to support the initiative, mobilize increased faculty support and participation across the department, and use department meetings to discuss the Engaged Department Initiative.

Those departments without such organizational and individual leadership were able to make advances with respect to department engagement; however, they did not engage the entire department in conversations about integration of engagement throughout the curriculum. These departments took initial steps by offering a limited number of service-learning courses and utilizing them to understand and promote how student learning is affected by the applied experiences service-learning offers. As faculty develop expertise with respect to service-learning pedagogies, the conversation and application of engagement strategies within the department is expected to increase. Faculty will likely expand their notion of engagement beyond service-learning and begin to explore expanded ways to incorporate engagement into the work of the department.

*Broad understanding of community engagement.* To the extent that the Engaged Department Initiative encouraged departments to think broadly about community engagement (including service-learning courses, internships, practica, field study, community-based scholarship, and action research), the level of department engagement and interest increased. Several teams proposed engagement projects that primarily focused on expanding and enhancing service-learning activities within the department. This singular goal allowed them to collect focused department resources and craft specific language that was inviting to their faculty colleagues concerning the development of service-learning in their disciplinary work. Although effective in facilitating the accomplishment of some targeted outcomes, the narrow focus of their engagement efforts limited the number of people within the department who thought of their work and interests in engagement terms. With a broader exploration and articulation of engagement, these departments would likely have been able to attract the interest of more department colleagues.

## Challenges and Strategies

Department reports, faculty interviews, and observations have helped us to identify programmatic and institutional structural challenges, as well as conceptual challenges to supporting the development of engaged departments.

Predictably, perceived shortages of resources, specifically time and money, surfaced as recurring challenges to department teams. In particular, the short timeframe of the initiative was a clear source of concern. To partially mitigate this concern, the second year of the program ran the full academic year (September to June).

A second concern related to the size and scope of the grants. Total resources available to support this initiative are dependent primarily upon external grant support with limited internal allocations of funds. An approach to address minimal funds is to limit the number of department teams selected and provide each team with additional resources. While this may help the individual team(s), it limits the diffusion of the initiative across multiple departments. A second approach is to mandate that each department team provide matching funds toward the effort. This requirement could raise the total amount of resources available for the team and the profile of the initiative, potentially leveraging additional commitments from the department chair. An issue underlying this challenge is the perception that engagement requires new funds as compared to a reallocation of existing resources and effort. The feasibility of providing multiyear grant support to participating teams will depend on the availability of external funding.

Another challenge was the perceived utility of the monthly cross-department learning sessions. Most participants appreciated the opportunity to regularly discuss progress, voice concerns to an interdisciplinary cohort, and brainstorm potential solutions to specific department issues. However, these sessions lacked coherence as an integrated program due to the diversity of interests, needs, and availability of team members, which raised further challenges of developing common foundational knowledge across the participating teams. Team members provided many suggestions and insights regarding how to increase the value this programmatic component might add. The suggestions for enhancement ranged from stylistic to substantive, including frequency of meetings, balance of efforts to share individual experiences versus work on group learning on a new theme, requirements of attendance, provision of focused professional development seminars on key engagement topics (such as syllabus conceptualization, partnership development, facilitating reflection, planning strategies), and the most effective strategies for teaching and learning with an interdisciplinary faculty group.

A recurring challenge for many program participants was indifference or resistance of faculty. Some questions surfaced toward the end of the initiative, including:

- "Does everyone in my department need to be involved for us to be an engaged department? What percentage of involvement will make us engaged?"

- "To determine our overall level of department engagement, should we consider only our tenure-track faculty, or should we consider the views and activities of adjuncts associated with the department as well?"

Participants observed that community-based engagement activities were not necessarily suitable for all individuals. As well, most agreed that increasing the quality and quantity of department-level engagement activities was a worthy pursuit, independent of an arbitrary determination of critical mass. Many participants agreed that student and community member participation in department dialogue and decisions would, over time, help determine which departments were perceived as engaged. However, this position does not account for perceptions of the rest of the institution as a whole, other departments within the institution, or the field at large. Concerns about levels and determination of engagement appeared somewhat counterproductive.

A final challenge dealt with goal accomplishment. In the initial planning document, departments articulated their own specific goals based upon their knowledge of themselves, the institution, and their disciplines. Emphasis should be placed upon each team assessing their progress with respect to these individualized goals throughout the initiative rather than trying to compare performance to some artificial generalized norm. Teams should periodically revisit their goals, assess their interim progress, and reflect on how to accelerate their progress.

## ∎Necessary Central Institutional Capacity

What central institutional capacity is needed to help departments become engaged departments? Four elements emerged from the work of the engaged department initiative.

*Central support office.* The presence of a central administrative office with dedicated staff charged with faculty development and support of service-learning is a key factor for increasing department engagement. Staff are available to secure and disseminate funding and provide grant program structure and technical assistance. The presence of a centralized office (especially one reporting to academic affairs) provides legitimacy to community-based, civically motivated professional faculty activities. The role and scope of the centralized office needs to be determined in alignment with the particular campus climate and culture.

At PSU, the provision of civic engagement opportunities is centralized generally, while the design and activity parameters, as well as the responsibility and ownership of the activities, are decentralized. The central office (CAE) provides overarching direction and associated funding and support for initiatives, while the actual programs grow out of department or individual faculty interests and commitments.

This structural arrangement makes sense for several reasons. The central office monitors trends and allocates resources to ensure that campus engagement activities align with the best practices in the field. Meanwhile, departments and individual faculty translate broad visions and trends into scholarly work that makes the most sense in the contexts of their disciplinary foci. This arrangement strategically leverages resources, providing opportunities for individuals most appropriately positioned on campus to maximize their efforts and avoid unnecessary duplication. Furthermore, the overarching view of CAE facilitates cross-institutional programming and communication. For example, in the case of the Engaged Department Initiative, a key program design parameter was the development of a cross-disciplinary learning collaborative which, in the best-case scenario, may evolve into a learning community. The center can generate economies of scale in terms of university-wide programmatic activities. In turn, this creates organizational capacity that is both operationally effective and externally attractive to funding agencies.

*Leadership and commitment.* Departments that were able to make substantial progress intentionally included the department chair in program activities. Ideally, the chair articulates a compelling department purpose and facilitates connections between core department activities and faculty agendas on one hand, and between the school and university core purposes on the other. Not unlike the presence of a respected centralized office, a strong and supportive chair legitimizes community-based, civically motivated scholarly activities. This manifests itself in myriad ways, including internal resource allocation, recognition of faculty activities, and support in the promotion and tenure process (a well-established faculty motivator).

*Recognition.* A supportive campus culture that includes formalized structures to recognize and reward community-based efforts significantly facilitates and legitimizes a department engagement initiative. At PSU, supportive promotion and tenure policies, annual awards, travel grants, and university communication vehicles actively encourage civic engagement efforts. In the mid-1990s, PSU revised its promotion and tenure policies to expand the definition of scholarship and to recognize and reward the scholarship of engagement as well as other community-based activities (Portland State University, 1996). CAE hosts an annual campus-wide Civic Engagement Awards Ceremony where specific departments, community-based organizations, and individual faculty are formally recognized. The Office of Academic Affairs provides professional development travel grants; often, priority is given to individuals pursuing scholarly venues for their civic engagement activities. And monthly and quarterly university publications recognize and provide a regular dissemination venue for the scholarly civic engagement activities of faculty. These efforts contribute to high visibility and recognition of PSU's civic engagement efforts.

*Promotion of mission and vision.* PSU is an urban, public institution nationally recognized for its innovative curricular approaches and commitment to community engagement. The university motto, "Let Knowledge Serve the City," is well known and internalized by a majority of the faculty and student body; externally, the motto is also well recognized. This campus history and culture support a collaborative community-university environment—one that facilitates the creation of, and regularly reinforces the operations of, the necessary central institutional structures mentioned earlier. Thus, where there is obvious community-focused alignment between department and university missions and vision such as at PSU, department and campus-wide engagement activities are more easily created and sustained. In institutional cases where the civic purposes of higher education are defined in less active terms or are deemphasized, encouraging department engagement initiatives would be significantly more challenging to support.

## An Integrated Model for Department Engagement

Throughout this process, we have learned that an effective place to start with departments is to encourage the chair and supportive senior faculty to do an organizational scan of current activities. Departments can then develop a picture of their current and recent scholarly work, with a particular focus on community-based activities. This can be accomplished in a variety of ways over the course of a couple of months and then brought to the attention of the full department faculty during one or two unit meetings. We have found that faculty appreciate this activity; indeed, in many cases, it energizes them. A starting place might be to identify all the courses taught by department faculty, highlighting those that are required for the major and for various minors supported by the unit. Simultaneously, unit faculty could be invited to provide a list of all publications that are works in progress or that they have completed in the last three years. Finally, a list of the community partners (very broadly defined) that faculty are working with could be initiated. These partners may include private enterprises, not-for-profit organizations, and neighborhood, political, student, and other advocacy groups both on and off campus. The simple gathering of this information can be quite illuminating for everyone involved. It is very important to keep a broad definition of *community engagement*. Inviting faculty to share their accomplishments and works in progress with colleagues and aggregating the data in a low-tech, transparent manner can be very energizing for most, if not all, members of the department.

Next, any one of several things may take place, depending on the climate and context of the department. Some units have intentionally chosen short articles to read and discuss together—focusing on core disciplinary values or on the integration of civic learning into core curricula, for example. Other units have chosen to revisit their department mission or, in some cases, to rewrite it completely. Many advanced departments have found it useful to reanalyze their overall curriculum to identify where (in which specific courses, for example) key civic or other applied learning outcomes emerge. Once collective thinking amid the faculty takes place, a developmental approach to student learning within the major can emerge and, in many cases, erstwhile individualistic faculty orientations can give way to a sense of collectivity. Where the community is involved, commitments by one faculty member to a key community partner may transform into a deep department commitment. Over the course of years within the major, students from a variety of classes may engage in community placements that connect to and build upon each other. Relationships between faculty, students, and community members become durable, learning can deepen, and applied disciplinary research can have greater impact. Figure 11.1 shows one way to delineate some of the relationships in an engaged department.

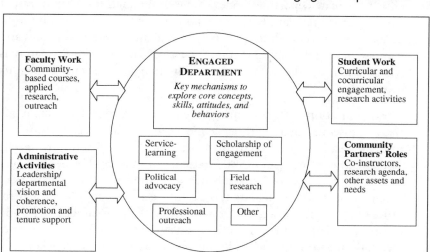

FIGURE 11.1

Model of Some of the Relationships in an Engaged Department

## Conclusions and Recommendations

This experience and analysis leads us to four primary recommendations that supplement the many observations contained throughout this chapter.

- The role of leadership at all administrative levels is essential in supporting and fostering work on civic engagement. In a department initiative, the chair or director is a vital player in assisting faculty to begin this work and in providing validation to other faculty members of the centrality of this work to the department mission. Deans, provosts, and presidents all play additional roles in promoting civic engagement. Their specific roles are beyond the scope of this chapter, but their presence and support in reinforcing work at the department level is an important accelerator toward becoming an engaged institution.

- Relevance is key to success with respect to department engagement activities. Department conversations and discussion around core department mission(s) can be a way to (re)invigorate and (re)connect faculty to the core meaning and purpose(s) of their work. Seeking linkages to civic engagement is the next step if work such as that described here is to be accomplished in order to identify those relevant connections of department missions to teaching, scholarship, and service. An important part of efforts to create department relevance is to find definitions and frameworks that are relevant to the department's own work—terminology, inventories, assessment tools, expected student learning outcomes and competencies, relevant scholarship. These discipline-specific materials will greatly foster the department's ability to make civic engagement its own work.

• The organizational structure and process of an engaged department initiative is essential for a multi-department initiative to succeed. The initiative can best be organized by presenting it as a continuum from self-assessment (planning and initial status), through development, implementation, rewards, further assessment, and dissemination. The work of engagement is not an isolated, time-limited activity. When a central office facilitates the process, it is essential that there be sufficient staff and resources to support the initiative. Staff time is vital for organization, facilitation, and consultation. Resources are needed to provide key relevant documentation to each team, as well as whatever fiscal support is feasible for graduate assistants, travel, or other professional development needed to pursue engagement efforts. The development of Campus Compact's Engaged Department Toolkit (Battistoni et al., 2003) will greatly help institutions to conduct their own yearlong initiatives.

• Clarity of expectations for learning and accountability must be stated at the beginning so that departments know what they can expect of themselves and so that they understand what the institution expects them to do (and hopes they will accomplish). This might include steps we have described here, such as preparation of an initial self-assessment planning document, participation in learning sessions, use of consultation, and preparation of a final report/poster for dissemination. Teams need clarity from the beginning of the performance expectations so that they can plan appropriately—both to generate sufficient support within their own departments and so that they can have dedicated time to participate in a learning community with others from the institution.

The department (or equivalent academic unit) is a key organizational structure within higher education institutions and can be viewed as an important leverage point for developing and accelerating civic engagement efforts, as illustrated by the work described in this chapter.

## Acknowledgments

We gratefully acknowledge the fiscal support of the Corporation for National and Community Service and Portland State University. We also are indebted to the PSU participants in the Engaged Department Initiative, including: Department of English, Department of Mathematical Sciences, Department of Psychology, School of Business (management grouping), School of Community Health, School of Urban Studies and Planning (community development grouping), and University Studies (freshman inquiry grouping).

## References

Battistoni, R., Gelmon, S. B., Saltmarsh, J., Wergin, J., & Zlotkowski, E. (2003). *The engaged department toolkit.* Providence, RI: Campus Compact.

Campus Compact. (2001). *Planning document for the engaged department institute.* Providence, RI: Author.

Campus Compact. (2002). *Intermediate institutes on the engaged department.* Providence, RI: Author.

Leaming, D. R. (1998). *Academic leadership: A practical guide to chairing the department.* Bolton, MA: Anker.

Portland State University. (1996). *Policies and procedures for the evaluation of faculty for tenure, promotion, and merit increase.* Retrieved May 17, 2005, from www.oaa.pdx.edu/documents/pt.doc

# 12

# Promoting Intellectual Community and Professional Growth for a Diverse Faculty

Dorothe J. Bach, Marva A. Barnett,
José D. Fuentes, Sherwood C. Frey
University of Virginia

*Minority faculty retention is key to increasing faculty diversity at most colleges and universities. Because retention depends on individual faculty choice and administrative tenure decisions, institutions need to help junior faculty develop a tenurable profile and enhance their desire to remain at their institution. This chapter examines a fellows program that supports beginning faculty in developing successful long-term careers, taking into account research on helping diverse faculty members thrive. It also presents strategies for establishing viable peer support networks and partnerships with senior consultants and for creating programming that ensures new faculty successfully transition into teaching, research, and the university community.*

## Introduction

> Women and minorities who make unadaptive starts in the professoriate evidence a series of reliable turning points early in their career, typically within their first few semesters on campus. . . . The simple nature of these turning points also implies strategies for preventing or reversing the disappointing and marginalizing beginnings so common for nontraditional hires. (Boice, 1993a, p. 71)

The new perspectives and approaches (often interdisciplinary) brought by faculty from diverse backgrounds help invigorate and stimulate the intellectual environment. If institutions of higher education are to provide students from increasingly diverse backgrounds with diverse faculty role models, they need to improve their hiring practices and their strategies for retaining new hires. Although sometimes successful retention depends on factors outside university administrators' immediate control, research by Austin (1990), Boice (1993a, 1993b), Fink (1992), Olsen and Sorcinelli (1992), Sorcinelli (1992), and others shows that institutional support early in professors' professional lives has a significant impact on their decision to stay at or leave their institutions when new opportunities arise. A close look at crucial career turning points suggests that specific interventions can help prevent the all-too-common frustrations and early disillusionment experienced by nontraditional faculty. Faculty developers are often in a position to facilitate appropriate interventions. In designing the Excellence in Diversity Fellows Program for incoming and second-year faculty at the University of Virginia, steering committee members kept clearly before them the importance of the early turning points for women and minority faculty members that Boice (1993a) identified in his research: collegial isolation, rejection by students, and stresses of marginalization.

The University of Virginia and the University of Colorado (Alire, 2002) are two of the few state universities where retention programs have been implemented. Since U.Va. adopted diversity as a core value in 2002, members of the Teaching Resource Center have worked closely with administrators and senior faculty to develop the Excellence in Diversity Fellows Program with one main goal: that new faculty members remain at the university as productive scholars. The assumption is that the University of Virginia hires excellent faculty members; it is in the interest of the university to support their successful professional development. In addition, of course, by diversifying the faculty, the university can provide better role models to our diverse undergraduate student body (25% are students of color and international students; 54% are women).

## Faculty Diversity as a National Issue

African Americans, Hispanic Americans, other people of color, and women continue to be woefully underrepresented in a number of academic disciplines (particularly in science and engineering) and in the professoriate (National Science Foundation, 2000b), as well as at institutions of higher education in general. Thus the wider academic community is not taking advantage of the talents and skills of an increasingly large segment of society. Underutilizing talent in this way has clearly detrimental societal consequences: an educated workforce representing all segments of society is crucial for social well-being and essential for competing in the current and future global economy. In fact, "the recent U.S. census showed the changing demographics of the country. The data make it clear that the underrepresented minority is becoming the underrepresented majority" (Morrissey, 2002, p. 24). Academic institutions, professional societies, and federal government agencies all need to take leadership in developing and coordinating innovative strategies to meet the challenges of this major culture change.

The Excellence in Diversity Fellows (EDF) Program is rooted in the tenet that university faculty members in the United States play a fundamental role in preparing and shaping future generations of those who contribute to society at all levels. Faculty members serve as professional and citizen role models and thus influence young people's career expectations. At a time when our student bodies are becoming more diverse, the lack of role models is felt acutely. Sadly, the relatively few diverse faculty members who pursue academic options are often dissatisfied with their initial experiences and leave their universities in search of a more welcoming institution, or they abandon academia completely in favor of a career in business or industry.

The EDF Program explicitly targets this failure to retain promising individuals by directly responding to the challenges these junior colleagues face at the beginning of their careers. Since research has shown that networks of mentors and peers are often not as accessible to nontraditional faculty as they are to majority groups, the program proactively alleviates collegial isolation by ensuring prearranged networks of support (Boice, 1993a). Committed mentoring and strong peer and extended networks provide incoming colleagues with opportunities for greater intellectual discourse among junior faculty members and between junior and senior faculty members who act as mentors. Through such a mentoring program and by offering incoming faculty key information about strategies for success, we aim to assure them that they can develop successful and rewarding academic careers. An additional assumption underlying the EDF Program is that nontraditional faculty members are motivated to remain in academe when they develop a sense of belonging to an institution and feel wanted for their academic contributions (Boice, 1993b; Hale, 2004; Sorcinelli, 1992).

Certainly, programs such as EDF should be viewed as part of a broader, national effort. In the recent past, federal government agencies and professional societies funded strategies to improve the representation of minority groups such as African Americans, Hispanic Americans, and women in the professional ranks and in all levels of the education spectrum, ranging from K–12 education to the doctoral level (National Science Foundation, 2000a).

Today, in a climate where national funding for minority programs is being eliminated, programs such as EDF can make a significant difference in realizing the goal of universities to offer an inclusive liberal education and serve all members of society.

## Faculty Diversity at the University of Virginia

The current situation regarding diversity at the University of Virginia (U.Va.) is unique only insofar as the university's particular history has amplified some of the challenges that research institutions in general face as they strive to diversify their campuses. As a state university, U.Va. was one of the last to lift its restrictions regarding the admission of African American and women students. Although the first black student was admitted to the School of Law in 1950—after attorneys of the National Association for the Advancement of Colored People sued the university— it was another 20 years before the university's containment policy was finally abandoned in 1969 in the face of protests of a coalition of radical, liberal, and moderate students. Because U.Va. has a longer history of race- and gender-based exclusion than most other institutions, it offers a good test case to assess the effectiveness of administrative interventions designed to remedy persistent inequalities.

Over the past 30 years, the U.Va. has continually increased on-campus representation of women and minority students. Women now comprise 54% and African Americans 8.8% of the undergraduate student population. The percentage for African Americans compares relatively well with that of peer institutions. For example, the University of North Carolina–Chapel Hill enrolls 11.1% African American undergraduate students, the University of Michigan enrolls 7.8%, and University of California–Berkeley enrolls 3.8%.

In addition, for the past 10 years, the University of Virginia posted the nation's highest African American graduation rates among major public institutions (Cross, 2003). With a graduation rate of 85%, U.Va. takes a clear lead among state-chartered institutions in the nation, followed by the University of New Hampshire and the University of North Carolina–Chapel Hill at 66%, and the University of California–Berkeley and the University of Delaware at 64%. This success is a result of administrative commitment and progressive programs such as the Office of African-American Affairs Advising Program, which matches black upperclassmen with black freshmen to make both academic and social transitions easier.

Although the University of Virginia has made considerable progress in helping African American students feel welcome and supported academically, it has not so successfully hired and retained minority faculty. According to the report of the U.Va. President's Commission on Diversity and Equity, the upper echelons of the university's faculty and administration are still overwhelmingly white and male, while females and minorities are aggregated in lower-paid areas such as clerical and custodial positions: women represent only 13% of full professors, and African Americans only 2% (Davis & Smith, 2004). Both groups are overrepresented in lower-level and in nontenure-track faculty positions. The numbers have stayed relatively flat since 1998, despite the increasing attention that has been given to matters of diversity (Davis & Smith, 2004).

U.Va.'s situation is indicative of a crisis facing most research institutions in the nation.

> While the nation is doing a good job of turning out women with research doctorates, the top 50 institutions in research spending are not doing such a good job of hiring them. Other recent research shows that women at doctorate-granting universities advance more slowly on the tenure track than men do, are paid less than their male counterparts, and are more apt to be dissatisfied with their jobs. (Wilson, 2004, p. A8)

The U.Va. President's Commission on Diversity and Equity worked to determine the status quo in regard to diversity at the university and to coordinate the change initiatives created when diversity was first adopted as a core value in 2002. The Excellence in Diversity Fellows Program is one such initiative. It is currently funded by the provost and by the deans of arts and sciences, engineering, and medicine. It has been cited by the co-chairs of the President's Commission on Diversity and Equity as a "best practice" and a "vital component of our collective efforts to attract and retain faculty from underrepresented populations" (Michael Smith, personal communication, October 31, 2004). It is an example of the work that can be achieved with support from an institution's leadership.

## Program Goals and Assumptions

In an effort to help new faculty navigate early career challenges and promote their long-term development as productive scholars, the Excellence in Diversity Fellows Program cultivates these colleagues' connection to the university. It thereby supports the university's larger vision of invigorating the institution's intellectual climate by improving the retention rate of diverse faculty members, particularly those dedicated to working with our increasingly diverse student body. The program's mission statement stresses that learning and understanding others' values and ways of thinking is integral to the educational process in an increasingly heterogeneous society. We believe that the intellectual vitality and well-being of our students depends in great measure on having a faculty whose perspectives span and envelop the cultural, ethnic, and scholarly traditions and interests of the entire "academical village." Our particular assumptions about faculty retention that underlie the Excellence in Diversity Fellows Program come from a variety of sources: our personal experiences (both as diverse faculty members and as colleagues of diverse faculty, some of whom have left the university and told us why); research on faculty retention; and knowledge derived from a previous, related endeavor, the University Teaching Fellows Program. The Excellence in Diversity Fellows Program is based on the following key assumptions:

- Faculty are more likely to find their place within the university when they feel broadly valued and appreciated in ways such as these:

  ~ They believe they contribute.

  ~ They feel successful and valued in their research and teaching.

  ~ They have effective mentors and confidants.

  ~ They see progress in their careers.

  ~ They interact positively with senior colleagues.

  ~ They feel recognized for their contributions.

- Committed mentoring and strong peer and extended professional connections are essential to the professional success of faculty. Research has shown that networks may not be as accessible to nontraditional new faculty as they are to those from majority groups. Such collegial isolation, one of the main reasons for early career disillusionment, can best be avoided by ensuring prearranged networks of support and mentoring (Boice, 1993a).

- Because retention depends on individual faculty choice and administrative tenure decisions, this program helps junior faculty develop a tenurable profile and enhances their desire to remain at U.Va.

- As a result of recommendations from the U.Va. President's Commission on Diversity and Equity, we expect that administrators and senior faculty will work increasingly with diverse faculty and will benefit from direct and constructive interaction with those colleagues. In addition, junior faculty will gain insights into policies and procedures and will develop greater confidence and comfort in communicating with their senior colleagues.

Since the main goal of the EDF Program is to improve retention of faculty members who contribute to the overall diversity of our faculty, the program's activities aim to address the challenges identified in the research. Ensuring prearranged networks of support and mentoring has had a strong impact on the following program objectives:

- Offer new junior faculty direct, early insights into how to succeed in the academic world, including engaging them in defining their teaching and research agendas

- Promote a peer-level support network and serious intellectual discourse among a diverse group of faculty members

- Initiate and support productive interactions between fellows and the senior faculty (senior consultants) who serve as knowledgeable, generous mentors, thus deepening and broadening their connections to colleagues and to the institution

- Offer senior faculty opportunities to share and develop their mentoring skills

- Foster improved interactions among junior and senior faculty members and academic administrators

- Support faculty in teaching students from diverse backgrounds and in creating inclusive learning environments

- Establish and maintain an environment in which junior faculty, particularly those from diverse backgrounds, develop a sense of belonging to a community, not only within individual academic units but also to the university as a whole

- Offer senior faculty and administrators insights into perspectives and concerns of diverse faculty members

## Application Process

We encourage applications from all junior faculty who will begin their first or second year as tenure-track assistant professors at U.Va. during the fellowship period and who are interested in connecting with both university colleagues and our increasingly diverse student body. We particularly solicit applications from faculty from underrepresented groups (including but not limited to first-generation college graduates, women faculty, faculty of color, and international faculty) and from faculty whose research interests may not fit traditional organizational frameworks. Senior faculty and chairs are urged to encourage candidates to apply and to utilize this program as part of their junior faculty development initiatives.

To solicit applications from as many interested faculty as possible, we keep the application form simple and short. Besides basic information, we ask applicants to answer multiple-choice questions regarding their research and teaching interests as well as what they seek in a mentor in order to better match them with their mentoring consultants. Other questions include: What are your short-term scholarly goals (for the next two to three years) related to teaching and research? What do you see as the benefits of being on the U.Va. faculty and a participant in the EDF Program? What are your plans for and concerns about a successful career, including strategies for connecting your teaching and research to U.Va.'s diverse student body? What benefits would you like to gain from working with one or more mentors, colleagues with more experience at U.Va.? (A complete application form can be found at http://trc.virginia.edu/Programs/EDF/EDF.htm.) In 2003, we received 19 applications for eight fellowships. In 2004, we were able to expand the program and offer 14 fellowships, for which we received 26 applications from a pool of 60 invited new faculty members.

In reviewing applications, the EDF steering committee considers each application carefully and makes individualized decisions based on a broad range of criteria that include the following:

- Applicants' diverse backgrounds including, but not limited, to academic disciplines, research and teaching interests, personal achievement, leadership, socioeconomic background, minority identification, special skills and talents, and unique experiences

- Date of terminal degree and any previous years of experience as assistant professor

- Potential for serving as a teacher and mentor as well as interest in and capacity for connecting their teaching and research to diverse students at the university

- Level of complexity and interdisciplinarity of applicant's research and teaching interests and goals

- Commitment to fully participate in an academically and culturally diverse peer group

- Plans for developing a productive long-term career at U.Va.

- Acknowledgement of challenges and concerns regarding early career development

- Potential benefit to each candidate from participation in the EDF Program

In addition, to the extent possible we take into account *shared* as well as diverse backgrounds, plans, and concerns when composing the groups of fellows; that is, we look for ways to create a connected group of fellows. For example, all other things being equal, we might select two candidates from different backgrounds and disciplines who both have research interests in the impact of violence. We have found that such commonalities help the group bond.

## Program Activities

Each year, steering committee members work to tailor the monthly events to fellows' specific needs, while consistently offering them the information and mentoring research has shown to be helpful (Boice, 1993b). During their year in the EDF Program, fellows gain insights into their roles as professors and learn about the university both through group activities (including a retreat followed by seminars, workshops, and discussions) and through individual consultations and conversations with their senior consultants. They may also each apply for up to $1,000 funding for at least one professional development opportunity (e.g., travel to professional conferences, seminars, or workshops; curriculum development projects; student assistant support).

### Retreat

Early in the semester, fellows accompany members of the program steering committee on a day-long retreat away from the university, preferably in a rural setting conducive to relaxation. There, the fellows from a wide variety of academic disciplines—most of them new to the university—get to know each other, each one introducing another in terms of educational background, research and teaching interests, and interests/life beyond the academy. Since Boice (1993a) has found that events very early in assistant professors' careers can color their feeling about the institution and affect their sense of belonging, we offer a positive, connecting experience as quickly as possible. One goal of the retreat is to reduce the feeling of isolation so common to new faculty, especially those who find themselves to be unique in their departments or schools.

For much of the morning, fellows interview each other to discover their ideas about challenges of doing research and teaching as well as of being a minority faculty member. Using the Jigsaw cooperative learning technique, they share the results of their interviews, creating a summary of key challenges for new faculty in each of these areas. In discussing these challenges— and in individually choosing their top three issues—they come to see that they have several common concerns across disciplines; they also begin to develop a peer-level support network and consider various ways in which the program can address their needs. After discussing readings relevant to academic success (e.g., Boice, 1991, 1993a; Felder, 1994; Martini, 1999a, 1999b; Moody, 2004), they refine their personal research and teaching agendas and define career-development strategies that will work in their individual circumstances.

## Workshops and Seminars

Fellows' monthly workshops, panels, and meetings thus grow out of the retreat conversation and respond directly to the concerns and challenges the fellows identified. We choose workshop leaders from among the most respected, knowledgeable senior faculty and administrators, and involve former fellows as panelists in ways that require little time commitment from them. In conversation with invited speakers, panelists, and senior administrators, the fellows explore strategies for key career development issues such as:

- Building a support network across the university and broadening their connections

- Developing their research agendas and scholarly productivity

- Developing a high level of comfort in the classroom, including discussions of teaching about diversity and teaching diverse student groups

- Balancing teaching and research efficiently

- Nurturing constructive professional relationships, including strategies for broad professional recognition both nationally and internationally

- Blending university service with career progression

- Considering strategies proven successful for junior faculty and helpful to diverse faculty

When appropriate, consultants, deans, associate deans, and department chairs are invited to participate, enabling all to learn more directly about each others' perspectives and concerns. Since most of the challenges anticipated by the first fellows fall into categories which coincide closely with those identified by the research literature, we hope that we can cultivate a pool of speakers over the years.

Some examples from the pilot year's program may help illustrate these interventions. High on the list of challenges noted at the first retreat were concerns about interdisciplinary collaborations. Since many fellows work across disciplines or have dual appointments across departments, they were interested in learning more about how to successfully negotiate multidisciplinary engagements. In a discussion with panelists from the humanities, science, and medicine, the fellows explored strategies for earning recognition of their interdisciplinary work in an environment that is still largely shaped by disciplinary paradigms.

The dinner conversation with senior administrators was one of the most highly praised meetings of the year. The vice president and provost, the vice provost for academic programs, and the co-chairs of the U.Va. President's Commission on Diversity and Equity answered the fellows' questions regarding university policies and promotion and tenure procedures. One fellow commented in his final report on the value of the exchange: "Very effective, hands down the highlight of this year's agenda. The insight and enthusiasm of the participants was special. This meeting brought much needed clarity on promotion and tenure issues." Another fellow found the meeting useful "not only because of what was discussed, but because it gave me the feeling that I could e-mail or walk up to any of these people in the future and raise concerns or questions I might have." Reactions from senior administrators strongly suggest that they in return make use of the opportunity to learn about the concerns of diverse junior faculty. One senior administrator reported in an email following the discussion that he found the meeting valuable because "it helps us to identify where we need to clear up some things."

At the fellows' request we also organized a family potluck for both EDF fellows and the university teaching fellows (junior faculty who have slightly more university experience). The potluck was one of the ways we addressed the issue of isolation that junior faculty, particularly women and minority faculty, often report (Boice, 1993a; Wilson, 2004). Almost all of the fellows had small children and welcomed the opportunity to expand their social and professional peer networks.

Other activities included an information exchange about publishing and research resources with the associate vice president for research enhancement and the University of Virginia Press acquisitions editor, as well as an afternoon tea following a university-wide teaching workshop. With a reception at the provost's pavilion, the fellows concluded the year in the company of deans, associate deans, department chairs, consultants, and program speakers and supporters.

## Connections With Senior Consultants

Through thoughtfully designed partnerships, fellows learn the ropes from senior consultants much more quickly than they would on their own. Research repeatedly shows the value of good and early mentoring (Boice, 1993a, 1993b; Moody, 2004). To choose appropriate mentors, faculty developers on the steering committee use their knowledge of the teaching and research interests, as well as the mentoring potential, of faculty volunteers. Whenever possible, we try to match fellows with one or two consultants from different departments and avoid replicating any mentoring that individual departments offer to their new hires. Combining that information with details supplied by consultants and fellows (information forms can be found at http://trc.virginia.edu/Programs/EDF/EDF.htm), we match each fellow with one or more senior colleagues who serve as teaching coach, research counsel, or university confidant for a fellow, depending on their experiences and interests.

- *Research counsels* help fellows develop promising and coherent research agendas and a strong professional standing in their field. We match research counsels to fellows based on parallels between their research interests and types of research experience and plans. Research counsels are thus more likely than other consultants to be matched with fellows from related disciplines.

- *Teaching coaches* help fellows develop their teaching skills and manage their courses efficiently and productively. The best teaching coaches are thoughtful about how and why they teach as they do, regularly analyze their teaching, undertake teaching innovations, and like to share ideas about teaching. We expect that teaching coaches and fellows will visit each others' classes and compare notes on teaching approaches and philosophies. Normally, teaching coaches work with fellows outside their own departments.

- *University confidants* help fellows get to know and feel comfortable within the university, outside their own departments. The best university confidants have had experiences (e.g., faculty senate, dean's or provost's promotion and tenure committee, department chair) through which they learned how their schools (or the college) and the entire university operates. They are willing to share insights gained from those experiences and help fellows understand and feel connected to the university beyond their departments. University confidants typically work with fellows outside their own departments.

Because new women and minority faculty in particular often hesitate to ask senior colleagues for their time (Moody, 2004), we strongly encourage consultants to initiate the first meeting and take the lead in setting up a regular monthly schedule. To help the consultants hit the ground running, the steering committee members meet with them as a group. In this setting, we give them information about the needs of incoming faculty, particularly of diverse faculty members, and share with them comments from former fellows about ways in which their consultants helped them. We discuss a short excerpt from Moody (2004) on good mentoring strategies; fellows read it as well. Finally, we encourage those consultants with successful previous mentoring experience to share what worked for them and those whom they mentored.

Admittedly, there is a great of deal luck involved in making good matches, even for someone who is very familiar with the volunteering senior colleagues. And we encourage both fellows and consultants to ask us for new arrangements if the initial pairing does not work. Judging from the final reports, however, both fellows and consultants found the relationships productive and rewarding. As one fellow describes her experience,

- "My consultants were wonderful! [My university confidant] made me aware of university politics and how to avoid unnecessary road blocks. . . . Most of all, she helped me think through my role as a wife, mother and professor. The juggling that this requires is exhausting, but so very rewarding. The key is not to keep all the balls in the air at all times, but to pick them up when they fall."

## Program Evaluation

The steering committee evaluates the program in an ongoing manner in order to improve pilot activities and, eventually, to learn how the program influences faculty members' future professional success and tenured retention at U.Va. We are collecting evaluation data such as the following:

- After workshops, fellows respond to open-ended questions, noting what was effective and recommending changes to better meet the program objectives.

- Presenters in workshops and seminars are asked for suggestions for future programs.

- At midyear, fellows and consultants complete a brief questionnaire asking them about the number and quality of their encounters and the usefulness of the workshops they attended and their recommendations for improvements.

- At the end of each academic year, both fellows and consultants summarize their experiences, highlighting program initiatives and discussion topics that proved especially beneficial and noting activities that could be improved.

## Pilot Program Assessment

It is difficult to evaluate the ultimate success of a three-year pilot program within its lifetime because the principal goal of diverse faculty retention can be measured only over a longer time period (the six years necessary to a normal promotion and tenure decision). Nevertheless, at the end of the third year we will seek feedback on the value and future direction of the pilot program from colleagues at peer institutions who have significant experience regarding diverse faculty retention.

In 2003, six of the eight fellows reported that the EDF Program had a very significant impact on their sense of connection to the university community. (The other two found the impact to be significant and rated it a 4 on a 5-point scale, with 5 being "very significant" and 1 "none.") The fellows valued the time and attention they received from consultants, panelists, and senior administrators, as well as their connection to peers in other disciplines. One of the fellows put it this way: "The EDF Program reinforced my sense of being welcomed and valued; it broadened my awareness of the university outside my own and related disciplines; and it put faces to the names of high-up people in the administration."

## Long-Term Assessment

The long-term assessment project (2009–2010) will study the program's impact on the retention of fellows by surveying former fellows and a control group of faculty who did not participate in the program. We will collect data about these colleagues' interest in remaining at the University of Virginia, their sense of connection and collegial support, and their overall level of satisfaction with their career at the university. We will also ask for feedback on ways to improve the program.

## Questions to Consider in Setting up a Similar Program

Before setting up a program such as this one, you may want to consider the following situational factors specific to your particular institutional structure and culture:

- How supportive are your upper-level administrators? How committed is the institution as a whole?

- What are the specific shortcomings that cause minority faculty members to leave? Exit interviews as well as interviews with faculty who remain may help you to assess the particular challenges of your institution.

- Who are the key supporters, and how can they be involved in shaping the program to address specific institutional needs?

- How can your institution convince new faculty that they are valued?

- What are the roles of mentors?

- How are they selected, involved, and trained?

- How are senior faculty and administrators best educated about the experiences of faculty from underrepresented groups?

- What are funding sources?

(For additional considerations regarding timing, content, and target audience of new faculty programs in general, see Fink, 1992.)

## Conclusion

The ultimate goal of the Excellence in Diversity Fellows Program is that the university be so successful at retaining a diverse faculty population that critical mass is attained. At that point, we hope that the size of the program can be expanded to serve all interested incoming faculty, since all new tenure-track faculty face significant obstacles to success on various professional fronts (Sorcinelli, 1992). Fellows from the program's first year voiced enthusiasm about continuing the connections and about helping future fellows. We are including them in events and in planning as their time allows. Since we are in the second year of a three-year funding cycle, we are currently seeking future funding through the university's Office of Development and looking into grant possibilities.

It is very heartening and encouraging to witness the generous and enthusiastic support the Excellence in Diversity Fellows Program receives from the provost's office and our senior colleagues who serve as consultants and program speakers. Judging from the fellows' final reports, the pilot program was a great success in terms of the immediate impact on the fellows' sense of belonging and the meaningful connection to colleagues both junior and senior. It is our hope that these first positive experiences will translate into successful long-term careers at the University of Virginia.

## References

Alire, C. A. (2002). The new beginnings program: A retention program for junior faculty of color. In T. Y. Neely & K.-H. Lee-Smeltzer (Eds.), *Diversity now: People, collections, and services in academic libraries* (pp. 21–30). Binghamton, NY: Haworth.

Austin, A. (1990). *To leave an indelible mark: Encouraging good teaching in research universities through faculty development.* Nashville, TN: Peabody College of Vanderbilt University.

Boice, R. (1991). Quick starters: New faculty who succeed. In M. Theall & J. Franklin (Eds.), *New directions for teaching and learning: No. 48. Effective practices for improving teaching* (pp. 111–121). San Francisco, CA: Jossey-Bass.

Boice, R. (1993a). Early turning points in professorial careers of women and minorities. In J. Gainen & R. Boice (Eds.), *New directions for teaching and learning: No. 53. Building a diverse faculty* (pp. 71–80). San Francisco, CA: Jossey-Bass.

Boice, R. (1993b). New faculty involvement for women and minorities. *Research in Higher Education, 34*(3), 291–341.

Cross, T. (2003). The nation's colleges show a modest improvement in African-American graduation rates, but a huge racial gap remains. *Journal of Blacks in Higher Education, 41,* 109.

Davis, A. M., & Smith, M. J. (2004). Embracing diversity in pursuit of excellence. *Report of the President's Commission on Diversity and Equity.* Retrieved May 20, 2005, from the University of Virginia, Voices of Diversity web site: http://www.virginia.edu/uvadiversity/embracing_report04.html

Felder, R. M. (1994). Things I wish they had told me. *Chemical Engineering Education, 28*(2), 108–109.

Fink, L. D. (1992). Orientation programs for new faculty. In M. D. Sorcinelli & A. E. Austin (Eds.), *New directions for teaching and learning: No. 50. Developing new and junior faculty* (pp. 39–50). San Francisco, CA: Jossey-Bass.

Hale, F. W., Jr. (Ed.). (2004). *What makes racial diversity work in higher education: Academic leaders present successful policies and strategies.* Sterling, VA: Stylus.

Martini, K. (1999a). *Making service count (a little): Guiding principles for junior faculty.* Retrieved May 20, 2005, from the University of Virginia web site: http://www.people.virginia.edu/~km6e/Papers/service-essay-99.html

Martini, K. (1999b). *Making your case: Strategies for an effective tenure package.* Retrieved May 20, 2005, from the University of Virginia web site: http://www.people .virginia.edu/~km6e/Papers/make-case/

Moody, J. (2004). *Faculty diversity: Problems and solutions.* New York, NY: Falmer.

Morrissey, S. (2002). Academic diversity. *Chemical and Engineering News, 81*(34), 24.

National Science Foundation. (2000a). *GEO 2000 full report (NSF 00–27).* Retrieved May 20, 2005, from http://www.nsf.gov/geo/adgeo/geo2000/geo_2000_full_report.jsp

National Science Foundation. (2000b). *Women, minorities, and persons with disabilities in science and engineering: 2000.* Retrieved May 20, 2005, from http://www.nsf.gov/sbe/srs/nsf00327/start.htm

Olsen, D., & Sorcinelli, M. D. (1992). The pretenure years: A longitudinal perspective. In M. D. Sorcinelli & A. E. Austin (Eds.), *New directions for teaching and learning: No. 50. Developing new and junior faculty* (pp. 15–25). San Francisco, CA: Jossey-Bass.

Sorcinelli, M. D. (1992). New and junior faculty stress: Research and responses. In M. D. Sorcinelli & A. E. Austin (Eds.), *New directions for teaching and learning: No. 50. Developing new and junior faculty* (pp. 27–39). San Francisco, CA: Jossey-Bass.

Wilson, R. (2004, December 3). Where the elite teach, it's still a man's world. *Chronicle of Higher Education,* p. A8.

# 13

# Building It for Them: Faculty-Centered Program Development and eManagement

Bonnie B. Mullinix
Monmouth University

*This chapter documents the effectiveness of a responsive, multilevel, web-based system for identifying and responding to faculty interest and needs for training and development. A case-based description illustrates the advantages of using a web-facilitated approach to schedule sessions according to faculty interest and availability. From needs assessment survey, to session design and scheduling, to registration, communication, and monitoring of participation, to evaluation and feedback, this integrated system has proven effective in engaging faculty. Data collected over two years of program implementation is shared and implications for the design, facilitation, and evaluation of such approaches are considered.*

## Vision, Direction, and Theoretical Foundations

If you build it, will they come? Well, perhaps the answer is to build it for them, with each individual in mind, according to their wants, needs, and availability. This is what we did at Monmouth University as we designed and established the Instructional Technology Services' Faculty Resource Center in fall 2002. By taking advantage of the technological capabilities at hand, we created a system that allowed us to gather information and maintain both an individualized and collective vision of faculty needs and interests. This is what guides us as we continue forward. It is our touchstone and a practical and philosophical antidote to administrative tendencies to project faculty needs and sidetrack effective faculty development designs. Constructed to be locally responsive, our approach was informed by and built directly out of the collected knowledge base and experience of faculty developers and adult learning theorists and practitioners.

One of the greatest challenges for faculty development efforts has been ensuring faculty participation in workshops and other development offerings. Faculty development professionals regularly comment on the importance of building programs based on strategies of faculty engagement and a solid understanding of faculty needs (Fink, 1988; Hilsen & Wadsworth, 1988; Sorcinelli, 1988). Adult learning theorists have long spoken to the fact that learner participation is enhanced by learning activities that address the interests and needs of adult learners in ways that highlight the relevance and immediate usefulness of information and skills (Brookfield, 1986, 1987; Knowles, 1970). By collecting data on interests and needs from faculty and constructing offerings that directly respond to these needs and interests, we address such concerns. By coordinating this information with data on faculty availability and cyclical instructional needs that emerge over the course of a semester we engage in a sophisticated scheduling process that enhances faculty participation and programmatic responsiveness. Through such strategies we take our process a step farther than Farr's (1988) recommendation for creating faculty development centers as resource centers that through a variety of resources might draw faculty into "what should be purely voluntary participation" (p. 35). Beyond providing an instructionally oriented structure and clear communication strategies, we work to design sessions that actively engage faculty in relevant and reflective activities, allowing them to critically situate new information within their own understanding, relationships, and teaching/learning approaches. In doing so, we draw on philosophical and practical advice from key educators over the past century (Dewey, 1916, 1938; Freire, 1984; Kolb, 1976, 1984). Further, our sessions are designed to model participatory instructional and learning methodologies and to create a safe, nurturing, and connected environment where action, risk, and challenge promotes learning (Meyers & Jones, 1993; Silberman, 1998). Recognizing that our growth as scholar/practitioners is facilitated by reflective participation and immersion in learning experiences and communities of practice (Abdal-Haqq, 1998; Freire, 1982, 1984; Knowles, 1970; Kolb, 1984; Merriam & Caffarella, 1999), we attempt to facilitate such experiences and networks. We actively promote training series and follow-on sessions and as faculty networks and interest grows, we nurture emergent working groups that connect cohorts of faculty in continuing, reflective learning.

## Origins and Context of the Case

Recognizing that the ability of faculty developers to appreciate and ultimately replicate and adapt strategies requires knowledge of the grounded context of a case. The following narrative provides this vision and weaves a holistic view of how the center's faculty-centered approach unfolded.

Monmouth University is a midsize, comprehensive private university of approximately 6,000 students. The Faculty Resource Center (FRC), established in October 2002, represents Monmouth University's primary faculty training and support initiative on campus. In two years since the FRC began, the faculty has grown from 220 to 275 full-time faculty and from nearly 250 to more than 300 part-time/adjunct faculty. The full-time faculty complement had expanded by more than 34% in the previous five years, with 75% of the entire faculty having joined the university during the preceding eight years. The need for faculty support and development was (and remains) keen. The university confirmed this through a survey of faculty in 2001 as they began to explore the development of a Center for Excellence in Teaching and Learning (CETL).

In early 2002, faculty development existed on campus in a decentralized fashion as documented in an institutional assessment and preceding the initial design of CETL (Mullinix & Sarsar, 2002). Beyond the traditional support of faculty scholarship, the strongest component of faculty development existed in Instructional Technology Services (ITS), which supported faculty through facilitation of online and web-enhanced Course Management Software, web design and classroom media, and computer lab and office desktop support services. To relate this to the broader historical context of faculty development, Sorcinelli, Austin, Eddy, and Beach (2006) might situate Monmouth in the Age of the Scholar and, with the emergence of the Faculty Resource Center, move it into the Age of the Teacher. While the current focus on outcomes assessment in higher education pushes the university quickly toward a focus on the learner, it may well be important for Monmouth, as for any university growing its faculty development program, to move progressively, if quickly, through each of the "Ages" of faculty development.

The key individuals responsible for the design of the FRC were the director of Instructional Technology (IT) and the newly appointed instructional design specialist. Their perspectives and complementary skills turned out to be critical resources in the design of the center. The IT director offered a strong background in education, a master's in instructional technology, and two years facilitating and building the Course Management System support on campus. With strengths in web design, presentation software, and multimedia, his technical knowledge and human resource management skills served to promote a creative, collaborative, and enabling environment within the IT unit. In addition, training as a K–12 teacher and teaching courses in information technology and computer art at the university kept him keenly connected to the instructional realities on campus. While new to the ITS department, the instructional design specialist spent four years as faculty at the university, teaching fourteen courses in four departments across two schools, serving two years as a research chair, initiating faculty peer mentoring programs, supporting multiple grant and program initiatives, and promoting a campus-wide learning community for global understanding. With a doctorate in adult learning and education and 25 years experience as an educator and international educational consultant, the instructional design specialist brought a wealth of ideas for responsive, participatory, and collaborative program design as well as a well-grounded faculty perspective. Her focus at Monmouth became faculty development and support. Her close collaboration with the university's Office of Academic Program Initiatives and its associate vice president to survey faculty and design CETL further informed her knowledge of faculty needs and the institutional context.

This team began by acknowledging the needs and constraints of the environment and resources, recognizing the need for gathering more information directly from faculty that would guide their efforts. In their first month together, they took stock and shared their thoughts on potential, needs, and possibilities. Faculty were increasingly asking for orientation to technology and assistance integrating technology into their teaching. It was also clear that support for instructional design and improving the teaching and learning environment was, by in large, not available on campus. So they challenged themselves to create such a support structure, building on their knowledge of best practices in adult learning and faculty development, tapping integrative technology potential, and working within the contextual realities and existing institutional constraints and resources. With the approval of the ITS department leadership and the provost, they moved forward to create a Faculty Resource Center within ITS, all the while keeping their design focus learning-driven, needs-based, and faculty-centered.

These design goals inspired and required that they begin with a survey of faculty needs, interests, and availability—the core information needed to design responsive offerings that can be scheduled at convenient times. Realizing that their base within IT made it both convenient and appropriate to leverage the talent and ability of their Web Factory and IT unit colleagues, they created an online survey. This served as the beginning of a web-based management system encouraging the collection and swift analysis of key data. The original survey solicited faculty needs and interests regarding instructional design and technology (across eight faculty role-focused categories), personal availability, and expertise. Once posted to the web, faculty were informed via email of the survey's availability and encouraged to complete either the hyperlinked online form or an attached copy. While hardcopies were not distributed, the accommodation for the less technologically savvy was to allow the attached copies to be printed, completed, and returned by mail or email. Faculty were promised that if survey responses were received within a week and a half, their input and information would guide the design of the Faculty Resource Center and be used to prioritize the first round of FRC offerings.

The web-based survey proved extremely powerful and inspiring, and the survey information compiled clearly indicated priority topics for faculty. Those topics receiving the highest scores became the FRC offerings that were created and offered first. Sessions with less of an interest/need were slated to be offered later in the semester or academic year (see Table 13.1).

TABLE 13.1

### Distribution of Needs/Interest Survey Across FRC Training Series Categories

| # Responses | Survey Categories (FRC Training Series) | # Sessions/ Items |
|---|---|---|
| 198 | Organizing, managing, and communicating | 6 |
| 217 | Preparing for class—designing courses and sessions | 5 |
| 179 | Designing class materials and multimedia presentations | 4–7 |
| 111 | In the classroom | 3 |
| 287 | Class on the web | 9 |
| 169 | Evaluation and assessment | 4 |
| 190 | Web design and publishing | 4–5 |
| 87 | Beyond the classroom—peer support for research and scholarship supporting teaching and learning | 4 |
| 1,438 | Total responses from 149 respondents to faculty needs/interest survey | 39–43 |

A second scheduling criterion, which helped to determine the approximate order of offerings, was the immediacy of need extrapolated from the common instructional cycle within a semester (e.g., sessions on generating course lists in support of organization or active-learning techniques were generally scheduled before sessions oriented toward evaluation). With the support of the IT Web Factory, a schedule overlay applet was developed to take the survey data and display all individuals interested in a topic across a week-block schedule. Precise scheduling of day and hour for priority sessions could then be determined by identifying the schedule blocks where the largest numbers of faculty were available. Once scheduled, these same individuals received priority registration in the sessions that had been developed with them in mind. This proactive outreach helped to ensure a base participation for each session planned that maximized the small physical space of the FRC (accommodating only 6–12 participants, depending on the need for wireless laptop access).

The developing web-based management system included automated communications that sent messages confirming registration into the system and registration into sessions as well as messages when sessions were rescheduled or canceled. The full complement of offerings was then shared with full- and part-time faculty through email and posted to the FRC web site, at which point all faculty were invited to register themselves for sessions through the web-based system. The web site was established to share current offerings categorized by faculty role-oriented series. It helped to document the FRC's activities, listing dates and times and offering descriptions and a growing complement of handouts and session guides.

Following sessions, participants' status was updated to "attended" (or "cancelled" or "no show") in the system and each received a thank-you email soliciting feedback on the session, what was learned/what was useful, how they planned to use/apply what they learned, and how the session could be improved.

It was clear that this approach to developing a faculty-oriented FRC was well received. The reward was steady participation and clearly articulated appreciation. Seventy-two faculty (approximately 13% of the entire faculty population) completed the online survey during the first year. This moved up to 128 responses by the second year of the FRC (representing a 22% response/participation rate for the overall faculty and a 49% response rate for faculty participating in the FRC offerings). By December 2004, the number of responses on the survey was 149. By the end of our first semester (lasting approximately two months), the FRC had offered 27 sessions covering 17 unique topics. By the end of its inaugural year, the FRC had offered 82 sessions to more than 400 faculty participants. By the end of the second year, this expanded to 115 events for approximately 408 attendees. By December 2004, the total cumulative offerings of the FRC's two and a half years was 240 events covering 43 unique topics for more than 850 faculty participants and reaching 46% of the total faculty at Monmouth (for greater detail on events and participation rates, see Figures 13.1 and 13.2; for detail on the representative distribution across positions, see Table 13.2, shown later).

At the end of the first academic year, the FRC coordinators created another web-based applet that allowed them to use the data in the FRC management system to display individual participation and create letters of acknowledgement for each of the faculty participants, documenting sessions attended as well as officially noting the faculty member's commitment to improving their facilitation of learning. These letters are signed by the FRC coordinator-facilitators and distributed directly to faculty members at the beginning of each academic year so they may share them with colleagues, chairs, or deans, and/or include them in their promotion and tenure dossiers. This approach to sharing FRC-witnessed documentation of their participation directly with faculty is in keeping with a process that encourages faculty control and empowerment in professional development and respects the need for confidentiality in faculty development. Participant names are not shared with the administration by the FRC; rather descriptive and comparative statistics (as embedded herein) are tracked and shared on a semiannual basis and as requested.

## Approach, Components, and Processes

The FRC team keeps its focus on faculty by directly and regularly referencing faculty data, maintaining proactive and supportive communication strategies, and offering hands-on sessions that situate skills, information, and technologies firmly within the teaching and learning arena and clearly associated with faculty roles and responsibilities. The following sections describe how and why we do what we do and how we see each of our efforts as faculty-centered. It touches on the following:

- Faculty needs and interest assessment
- Design of offerings
- Prioritization of offerings
- Scheduling of offerings
- Communication of offerings
- Participant registration

- Communication with registered FRC participants
- Recognition and utilization of faculty expertise
- Monitoring, evaluation, and reporting
- Acknowledging faculty participation

At the core of this approach is a responsive, technology-facilitated, multi-level, web-based system that includes a faculty interest/needs assessment survey with a dynamic analysis interface and a registration system with automated communication that helps monitor participation and solicits evaluation and feedback. This approach has helped to underscore in the minds of faculty the direct relationship between their needs and the center's offerings. We have found that coordinating data on faculty needs with availability and cyclical instructional needs that emerge over a semester results in a sophisticated scheduling process that enhances faculty participation. While we are still working on improving our web-based system, it has drawn on our collective creativity and shows great promise as a management tool. Indeed, we have received a POD (Professional and Organizational Development Network in Higher Education) grant to allow us to enhance it to a point where we can share it with other faculty developers. While any information-based system takes time to manage (Plank, Kalish, Rohdieck, & Harper, 2005), there is no doubt that the web-based nature and automated features of this system results in an ultimate effectiveness in both time and cost.

The following provides a description of each web-based component of our e-management system and a link to the associated tool.

## Faculty Needs and Interest Assessment

This is the foundation of our faculty-centered approach and accomplished through an online survey that gathers information about individual faculty interests, needs and availability (following the initial generic survey, the questions were updated to reflect actual offerings and serve as a preview of the full range of FRC sessions/series). *Tool:* Faculty Interest and Needs Assessment Survey (http://its.monmouth.edu/OnlineSurvey/ its/faculty_needs/).

## Design of Offerings

Responding to recognizable roles and responsibilities of faculty, offerings include instructionally oriented and learning-centered session series that focus on design in support of learning and technology use and are developed to fit faculty timeframes and desires. Offerings fit within eight robust and inclusive categories: organizing, managing, and communicating; preparing for class—designing courses and sessions; designing class materials and multimedia presentations; in the classroom; class on the web; evaluation and assessment; web design and publishing; beyond the classroom—peer support for research and scholarship supporting teaching and learning. *Tool:* List of offerings (http://its.monmouth.edu/FacultyResourceCenter/FRC-Training SeriesList.htm).

### Prioritization of Offerings

Offerings are prioritized by viewing faculty survey responses through a web-based dynamic interface that displays numbers of responses with links to actual respondent availability distributed across a schedule of session time blocks in a week (we encourage faculty to update their availability each semester and whenever their schedules change). *Tool:* See a sample display page at http://its.monmouth.edu/trainingGuest/survey/results/answertable.asp.

### Scheduling of Offerings

By overlaying the prioritized offerings onto semester instructional cycles and reviewing faculty availability, we are able to schedule sessions for a cohort of participants, registering individuals who expressed interest in a specific topic and availability at a common time. *Tool:* See the FRC home page (http://www.monmouth.edu/frc) and the FRC registration page (http://its.monmouth.edu/training/trainingForm.asp).

### Communication of Offerings

The schedule of offerings is communicated through multiple mechanisms. It is posted online at the Faculty Resource Center home page and email communications summarizing current offerings are sent to all faculty with links to this page and the online registration system. *Tool:* FRC home page (http://www.monmouth.edu/frc).

### Participant Registration

An online registration system that allows faculty to directly register for (and cancel out from) sessions of interest and FRC administrators to facilitate the same. *Tool:* FRC registration page (http://its.monmouth.edu/training/training Form.asp).

### Communication With Registered FRC Participants

The registration system's automated communication seamlessly informs participants of sessions when they register. Once marked as attended, the system acknowledges their participation and solicits feedback. *Tool:* See sample emails at http://its.monmouth.edu/trainingGuest/frc-sicem.html.

### Recognition and Utilization of Faculty Expertise

An important part of faculty-centered development, we strive to identify and utilize faculty expertise. We begin by soliciting faculty interest in sharing their skills in the FRC survey, encouraging faculty to facilitate FRC sessions, and sponsoring events to highlight faculty innovations in teaching and learning. *Tool:* Homegrown Innovations in Teaching and Learning (http://its.monmouth .edu/facultyresourcecenter/HomegrownShowcase2004-Program.htm).

### Monitoring and Reporting

We maintain a tracking system to monitor and record faculty participation levels to facilitate planning, research, evaluation, and reporting. *Tool:* FRC resigtration systems reports page (http://its.monmouth.edu/training Guest/admin.asp [login: guest; password: guest]).

### Acknowledging Faculty Participation

We have developed an applet that allows us to produce personalized letters of recognition/acknowledgement for participants through a merged narrative that draws directly from our management database and is linked off of a web-based listing of participant attendance. Sensitive to the delicate balance between faculty confidentiality concerns and public acknowledgment of faculty development, we have opted to send these letters directly to faculty at the end of the academic year and allow/encourage them to disseminate and use them as they feel appropriate (with chairs, deans, for tenure and promotion reviews, etc.). *Tool:* See a sample page and letter at http://its.monmouth .edu/trainingGuest/frc-sicem.html.

## Data Analysis Strategies Informing Reflective Practice

Faculty needs and interests drove not only the FRC and participation in its offerings but also the survey response and participation rates. Descriptive statistical analysis of both datasets were used to confirm that this faculty self-selection mechanism produced a remarkably representative sample of the university faculty complement with respect to both survey respondents and FRC event participants. In analyzing faculty feedback on the importance, impact, and design of the FRC and its offerings, grounded theory informed an analysis strategy that relied on capturing emergent themes from written feedback on sessions and allowing for their growth and ongoing validation (Strauss & Corbin, 1998). Periodic informal and formal discussions served as an inductive base from which to identify effective and ineffective practice, and themes of topic impact were then further expanded and identified through document analysis (of email, online surveys, and handwritten evaluation forms). Data analysis was further enhanced and influenced by use of NVivo Qualitative Software . Joint and cross-coding approaches were utilized by the researchers to increase validity (Richards, 1999) and generate multiple free- and tree-noded categories supported by quotations and emergent analysis. While results from the qualitative analysis of narrative evaluation and feedback findings is not explicitly illustrated here, it has proven an important source of formative and inspirational guidance.

## Patterns of Participation, Findings, and Considerations

It has been important to build in time for analysis, documentation, and dissemination of the statistical participation patterns, particularly to ensure their inclusion in formative development of the FRC. Visual and tabular data had been prepared and shared both with university administrators through regular reporting and through professional presentations to colleagues regionally and nationally (Mullinix, 2004; Mullinix & Harr, 2003, 2004; Mullinix & Savoth, 2004). Figures 13.1 and 13.2 show, respectively, the relationship between total and unique sessions and events offered over time and the distribution of faculty in terms of cumulative and unique attendees.

In the first year, participation encompassed approximately 43% of the university's full-time faculty and more than 18% of part-time faculty from a full cross-section of departments and schools. By the end of the second year, the FRC was able to increase this participation rate to 46% and 26%, respectively, even in the face of decreasing human, physical, and financial resources. The breakdown of faculty participation among those actively engaged in FRC sessions by the end of 2004 was distributed as follows: 63% full-time faculty (with 40% tenure-track faculty) and 30% part-time faculty. The percentage representation of FRC participants across faculty categories is remarkably representative of the percentage representation of Monmouth University faculty overall (see Table 13.2).

FIGURE 13.1

FRC Events and Topics
Fall 2002 – Fall 2004

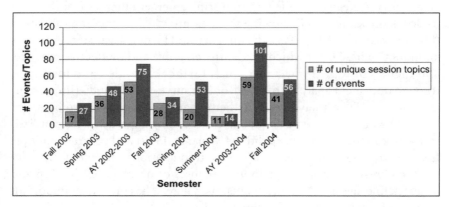

FIGURE 13.2

FRC Event/Session Participation
Fall 2002 – Fall 2004

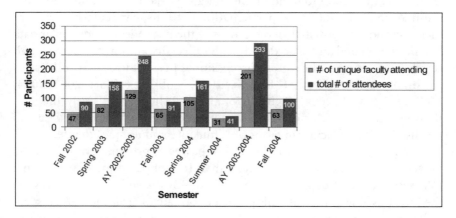

## Limitations of the Approach and System

As with every initiative, there exist limitations to be acknowledged and addressed. For each limitation identified, an attempt was made to shift focus and utilize it as an advantage. Utilization of the dynamic web-based data to schedule FRC sessions was sufficiently effective to produce a profile of FRC offerings that mirrored closely the training needs profile resulting from the

TABLE 13.2

Faculty Participation Distributions

| | FRC Participants | Percentage of FRC Participants | Percentage of MU Faculty | Total MU Faculty |
|---|---|---|---|---|
| *Part-Time Faculty* | 79 | 30% | 26% | 306 |
| Part-time/adjunct | 60 | 22% | | 300 |
| Faculty (P-T)/admin. | 19 | 7% | | 6 |
| *Full-Time Faculty* | 188 | 63% | 61% | 274 |
| Full-time instructor | 44 | 16% | | 72 |
| Visiting assistant professor | 13 | 5% | | 3 |
| Specialist professor* | 4 | 1% | | 12 |
| *Tenure-Track Faculty* | 127 | 40% | 57% | 187 |
| Assistant professor | 47 | 18% | | 58 |
| Associate professor | 43 | 16% | | 86 |
| Professor | 17 | 6% | | 43 |
| *Guest/Admin.* | 20 | 7% | | |
| *Totals* | 267 | — | 46% | 580 |
| *Inclusive of:* | | | | |
| Chairs | 14 | 5% | 61% | 23 |
| Deans/associate, assistant deans | 5 | 2% | 26% | 19 |
| Directors | 3 | 1% | — | — |

*Specialist professors are faculty hired with unique qualifications and specific experience for five-year periods.

faculty needs and interest survey. While some may consider the subjective self-analysis and reporting approach of a needs assessment survey an inferior baseline data source, as an initial catalyst to encourage participation we found it to be a strength. Another potential limitation of the survey could be its online and email delivery, which may have limited response from certain quarters. However, the fact that the FRC was situated within the Instructional Technology Services department of the university justified and supported this strategy as did the intended dynamic use of the information (and interest in limiting costs associated with ongoing implementation of the system overall). Online results and the creation of the dynamic web-based analysis interface allowed for the easy, ongoing integration of data as new faculty complete the survey over time. Posting survey access on the FRC web page and presenting it as an integrated component of participating in FRC sessions helps to encourage continued submissions.

A limitation of this system may well be the importance of its proactive engagement of faculty and continuing focus on faculty-identified topics. Contextual constraints placed on the FRC during academic year 2003–2004 have resulted in lower participation rates among faculty. Early in the year, an increasing number of sessions driven by administrator recommendation rather than faculty request have inflated the number of sessions offered in certain categories that were neither priority response items nor integral to the FRC (i.e., they were focused on technical training on generic computer use rather than being instructionally oriented). Though offered, few faculty attended these sessions. In addition, decreased opportunities for active outreach to faculty—the loss of high-level web page links, a buried web site, fewer public outreach opportunities, a decreasing focus on FRC team priority registration of faculty into sessions, and less personal encouragement of faculty to participate—have also impacted participation.

## Impact, Advantages, and Contributions

Ultimately, this approach is nothing more than good learning facilitation practice grounded in learning theory and research. By clearly and strategically embedding these elements in our practice we create an effective program and model effective practice with the intent that faculty may replicate and integrate the following as they work to enhance their facilitation of learning:

- Base their curriculum on participant interests and needs

- Design sessions that actively engage participants in learning

- Gather feedback and suggestions for improvement

- Modify their approach and techniques appropriately and continue to monitor and improve their practice

Using faculty interests, needs, and availability to directly design events and sessions, prioritize offerings, and determine appropriate schedules allows for an increased sense of ownership as well as increased participation levels among faculty. This approach has helped to underscore in the minds of faculty the direct relationship between their needs and the center's offerings. We have found that coordinating data on faculty needs with availability and cyclical instructional needs that emerge over the course of a semester results in a sophisticated scheduling process that enhances faculty participation.

Each element of this system offers its own acknowledgement of and contribution to faculty development strategies. The needs-based survey tool was compiled through a review of offerings by centers for teaching and learning across the nation and based on an extensive, categorized list of training topics. These overarching categories were then woven into the FRC's structure and have proven robust over two years of use. They may well prove useful for others who wish to establish new faculty support programs or evaluate existing centers for teaching and learning. Such responsive faculty development designs hold promise for encouraging meaningful participation by clearly highlighting and acknowledging the faculty-driven nature of the program and its offerings. In addition, they offer a structure that directly addresses and counteracts the longstanding problem of low-level participation by faculty by tailoring offerings directly to needs, interests, and time constraints. Our experience has shown that when you build it for them, faculty will come.

## Implications for Growth and Future Practice

POD has proven a nurturing and enabling scholarly environment for the growth and innovative expansion of a place such as the FRC and such a web-based system. Indeed, this chapter has grown from and built on several presentations, workshops, and/or papers presented at POD conferences (Mullinix & Harr, 2003; Mullinix & Savoth, 2004) and POD's sister association, the Faculty Training, Evaluation, and Development Special Interest Group of the American Educational Research Association (Mullinix & Harr, 2004).

While presenting and receiving their Bright Idea Award from POD, Mullinix and Harr noted significant interest in their approach and received encouragement to develop the web-based management system so that faculty developers at other institutions might make use of it. A grant was submitted to POD with the support of key POD members who saw promise in the system. Mary Deane Sorcinelli and Barbara Millis offered up their institutions' Centers for Teaching and Learning as collaborating partners. While the instructional technology area of Monmouth University underwent substantial reorganizations from May through early 2005, the grant was accepted in October 2004. Interest has continued to grow and several regional community colleges have expressed interest in participating in the early testing of the system. Work has begun on developing the web-based e-management system into a more modifiable and user-friendly version that can be shared with interested POD member institutions in higher education.

PIECES, as we have named our next-generation system, embeds the key components within its name: Participant Information, Event, and Communication E-Management System. It also represents the vision that we have for the flexible implementation of this system, as we hope to allow faculty developers to pick and choose the "pieces" of PIECES that best fit their needs and contexts. The ultimate goal will be to build on the strengths of this system and encourage data-referenced design and evaluation of faculty development in higher education.

Evaluation is a broad umbrella that easily spans the distance from needs assessment to formative, summative, and impact evaluation. The needs assessment and formative evaluation pieces provide us with the information needed to build a responsive program that can increasingly and appropriately meet specific faculty needs. Summative and impact evaluation provide us with the information we need to chart outcomes and progress, remain on track, and help everyone involved to understand how we are making a difference.

Ultimately, we believe that the power of this faculty needs and interest-centered approach lies in its ability to help individual faculty members identify and act on their desire for skills and knowledge development, directly informing their abilities as learning facilitators and designers. As initial findings indicate, when self-motivated and institutionally supported, faculty feel empowered to take risks in instructional design and practice. One of the best ways to support faculty on this journey is to design learning opportunities directly based on their needs and interests. Our integrated system provides the tools to do this and takes the next step toward providing the summative and impact data that can help document and ensure sustainability of faculty development efforts.

# References

Abdal-Haqq, I. (1998). *Professional development schools: Weighing the evidence.* Thousand Oaks, CA: Corwin Press.

Brookfield, S. D. (1986). *Understanding and facilitating adult learning.* San Francisco, CA: Jossey-Bass.

Brookfield, S. D. (1987). *Developing critical thinkers.* San Francisco, CA: Jossey-Bass.

Dewey, J. (1916). *Democracy and education: An introduction to the philosophy of education.* New York, NY: Macmillan.

Dewey, J. (1938). *Experience and education.* New York, NY: Touchstone.

Farr, G. (1988). Faculty development centers as resource centers. In E. C. Wadsworth (Ed.), *A handbook for new practitioners* (pp. 35–38). Stillwater, OK: New Forums Press and Professional and Organizational Development Network in Higher Education.

Fink, L. D. (1988). Establishing an instructional development program. In E. C. Wadsworth (Ed.), *A handbook for new practitioners* (pp. 21–25). Stillwater, OK: New Forums Press and Professional and Organizational Development Network in Higher Education.

Freire, P. (1982). Creating alternative research methods: Learning it by doing it. In B. Hall, A. Gillette, & R. Tandon (Eds.), *Creating knowledge: A monopoly* (pp. 29–37). New Delhi, India: Society for Participatory Research in Asia.

Freire, P. (1984). *Pedagogy of the oppressed.* New York, NY: Continuum.

Hilsen, L., & Wadsworth, E. C. (1988). Staging successful workshops. In E. C. Wadsworth (Ed.), *A handbook for new practitioners* (pp. 45–52). Stillwater, OK: New Forums Press and Professional and Organizational Development Network in Higher Education.

Knowles, M. S. (1970). *The modern practice of adult education: Andragogy versus pedagogy.* New York, NY: Associated Press.

Kolb, D. A. (1976). *The learning style inventory: Technical manual.* Boston, MA: McBer.

Kolb, D. A. (1984). *Experiential learning: Experience as the source of learning and development.* Englewood Cliffs, NJ: Prentice-Hall.

Merriam, S. B., & Caffarella, R. S. (1999). *Learning in adulthood: A comprehensive guide* (2nd ed.). San Francisco, CA: Jossey-Bass.

Meyers, C., & Jones, T. B. (1993). *Promoting active learning: Strategies for the college classroom.* San Francisco, CA: Jossey-Bass.

Mullinix, B. B. (2004). *Tapping technology to facilitate a faculty-centered approach to faculty development.* Paper presented at the 2nd annual Technology in Education Conference, Plainsboro, NJ.

Mullinix, B. B., & Harr, C. (2003). *Faculty-centered program development.* Paper presented as Bright Idea Award Winner at the 28th annual meeting of the Professional and Organizational Development Network in Higher Education, Denver, CO.

Mullinix, B. B., & Harr, C. (2004). *Build it for them, they will come: Interest-based and scheduled faculty development.* Paper presented at the 84th annual meeting of the American Educational Research Association, San Diego, CA.

Mullinix, B. B., & Sarsar, S. (2002). *Institutional proposal for establishing a center for excellence in teaching and learning at Monmouth University* [Internal report]. West Long Branch, NJ: Monmouth University, Office of Academic Program Initiatives.

Mullinix, B. B., & Savoth, W. (2004). *Technological tools of our trade: Managing and assessing faculty development.* Pre-conference workshop at the 29th annual meeting of the Professional and Organizational Development Network in Higher Education, Montreal, Canada.

Plank, K. M., Kalish, A., Rohdieck, S. V., & Harper, K. A. (2005). A vision beyond measurement: Creating an integrated data system for teaching centers. In S. Chadwick-Blossey & D. R. Robertson (Eds.), *To improve the academy: Vol. 23. Resources for faculty, instructional, and organizational development* (pp. 173–190). Bolton, MA: Anker.

Richards, L. (1999). *Using NVivo in qualitative research.* Thousand Oaks, CA: Sage.

Silberman, M. (1998). *Active training: A handbook of techniques, designs, case examples, and tips* (2nd ed.). New York, NY: Wiley.

Sorcinelli, M. D. (1988). Encouraging excellence: Long-range planning for faculty development. In E. C. Wadsworth (Ed.), *A handbook for new practitioners* (pp. 27–31). Stillwater, OK: New Forums Press and Professional and Organizational Development Network in Higher Education.

Sorcinelli, M. D., Austin, A. E., Eddy, P. L., & Beach, A. L. (2006). *Creating the future of faculty development: Learning from the past, understanding the present.* Bolton, MA: Anker.

Strauss, A., & Corbin, J. (1998). *Basics of qualitative research: Techniques and procedures for developing grounded theory* (2nd ed.). Thousand Oaks, CA: Sage.

# 14

# An Electronic Advice Column to Foster Teaching Culture Change

Donna M. Qualters , Thomas C. Sheahan, Jacqueline A. Isaacs
Northeastern University

*First-year engineering students receive most of their teaching from instructors outside of engineering. As a result, these instructors are typically not a teaching community with a shared commitment to engineering student learning. Retention of engineering students is strongly tied to the quality of teaching, thus addressing collective teaching quality is important. This chapter describes the development of a carefully crafted, electronically distributed advice column on teaching developed by an interdisciplinary editorial team, written under the pseudonym* Jonas Chalk. *Surveys of* Chalk Talk *readers indicate that this is an effective means to promote teaching culture change.*

## Introduction

First year engineering students (FYES) face a variety of challenges as they adapt to college life. Perhaps the most problematic involves the first-year curriculum in which the majority of their coursework is outside of engineering, primarily in chemistry, math, and physics. These courses provide the necessary knowledge base that every engineer needs but are taught primarily by math and science faculty. Thus, the community of instructors who teach these students at this initial, critical point in their engineering curriculum are typically drawn from different departments, each with its own level of emphasis on teaching (versus scholarship and research activities) as a component of its identity. Faculty from math and the sciences often view teaching engineering students as more of a service activity and feel that their teaching energies need to be devoted to students in their own majors. In other words, the instructors of our FYES are too often not a community of instructors at all, lacking a shared sense of purpose, mission, and commitment to prepare engineering students for succeeding courses.

This issue of a shared teaching mission by instructors of FYES is important when one considers the number of engineering students who leave engineering after the freshman year. The well-known study by Seymour and Hewitt (1997) examined concerns among two groups of undergraduate science, technology, engineering, and math (STEM) students: those who changed majors away from science, math, and engineering ("switchers"), and those who remained to complete their respective degrees ("non-switchers"). Poor teaching by science, math, and engineering faculty was cited as a concern by 93% of all students, including 98% of switchers and 86% of non-switchers.

To complement the Seymour and Hewitt (1997) data, Besterfield-Sacre, Atman, and Shuman (1997) developed an attrition model based on student attitudes, particularly their initial attitudes about engineering and their abilities to succeed. They surveyed engineering students at the end of the freshman year using both open-ended and numerical scale items. One item is particularly noteworthy. Using a rating scale of 1 ("does not strongly hold this belief or preference") to 5 ("strongly holds this belief or preference"), students were asked to rate "Preference for math and science courses over liberal arts courses." The non-switchers rated this at 4.19 while switchers gave this statement a 3.40. While this result could indicate attitudes developed prior to the first-year experience, it may also reflect the quality and culture of teaching during the first year, when so many of the required courses are in math and science.

Seymour (2002) also noted that there is a change in the STEM classroom activities from the traditional focus on teaching to a new focus on learning. Among a number of implications of this shift, she cited the rethinking of professional relationships among STEM faculty and the restructuring of professional development activities related to teaching, including training for new faculty and "reeducation" of mid-career faculty. Further, a report by the National Research Council (2003) noted the increased level of concern among senior faculty and administrators about improving undergraduate STEM education.

As part of a project to address these issues to promote an improved learning environment for FYES at Northeastern University (NU), methods were needed to build a community of reflective practitioners (Schön, 1983; Wenger, 1998); that is, teachers of FYES who discussed with each other, evolved, and adapted their teaching strategies to meet the needs of this particular group of students. By creating this community of practitioners and a climate of change in teaching practices, we hoped to improve the quality of the learning experience among our FYES. This chapter describes the development of a mechanism to achieve these objectives that took the form of an advice column, much like "Dear Abby." An editorial team was formed consisting of faculty from chemistry, math, physics, and engineering; members of Northeastern University's Center for Effective University Teaching (CEUT); and an educational technology specialist. Critical topic areas around the issue of teaching freshman engineering students were identified, and questions on those topics were formulated by the editorial team (as if "readers" had asked the questions). The experiences of the editorial team, as well as the teaching and learning literature, were integrated to compose "responses" to these questions, written under the pen name of *Jonas Chalk*. The development of the *Chalk Talk* column provided a means to form the teaching community and disseminate specialized teaching practices for a target population.

## Background

The College of Engineering at NU was faced with a number of significant obstacles in addressing communication and teaching among STEM faculty. Communication about teaching between the Colleges of Arts and Sciences and Engineering was limited, usually confined to deans, associate deans, and some course coordinators. Instructors' knowledge about learning theory and educational research was typically nonexistent except for those instructors who had been involved in education grants. Perhaps the biggest challenge is that, in general, change itself is difficult, and changing ingrained teaching practices is even more so. For the most part, many instructors are comfortable with their teaching. This level of comfort often leads to rote classroom practices with little questioning or reflection on teaching methods.

Our task became one of creating an awareness and mechanism for change in teaching practices with our instructors, some of whom were faculty with many years of teaching experience. The literature on change reveals that change often occurs in stages (Prochaska, DiClemente, & Norcross, 1992). Figure 14.1 shows a model of such change adapted to faculty development, where the center set of boxes indicates stages through which an instructor progresses as his or her teaching awareness and approaches evolve. As shown in the right-hand "Community" set of boxes, it is vitally important for the community in which the instructor works to provide necessary support to move through these various stages of change. A final component of this model is shown on the left—that an instructor is prone to so-called relapse at any stage. When this occurs, the instructor may stop pursuing teaching improvement and reflection on his or her practices. This relapse can result in

204 To Improve the Academy

a return to a so-called precontemplative stage, at which point the instructor will need to reinitiate the progression.

Depending on an instructor's place on the "Stages of Change" continuum shown in Figure 14.1, different interventions will be needed to facilitate further change. Many faculty, especially those who have not been reflective or are not invested in a course or major, fall into the precontemplative stage; that is, they see no reason to change and need mechanisms through which they can begin to explore their assumptions and beliefs around existing practices. Faculty at this stage are not likely to seek help with teaching or try classroom innovations unless they can be convinced otherwise. Precontemplative faculty usually do not come to workshops, brown-bag lunches, or join learning communities; they see no relevance of these activities to their teaching or their other responsibilities such as research and scholarship in their discipline area. Further, math and science instructors may be far less interested in teaching engineering students than their own majors or may not relate to engineering students' content needs and learning objectives as compared to those of their own students. Convincing precontemplative faculty to move to the contemplative stage necessitates an intervention that attracts their attention and then

FIGURE 14.1

## Stages of Change in Teaching Attitude

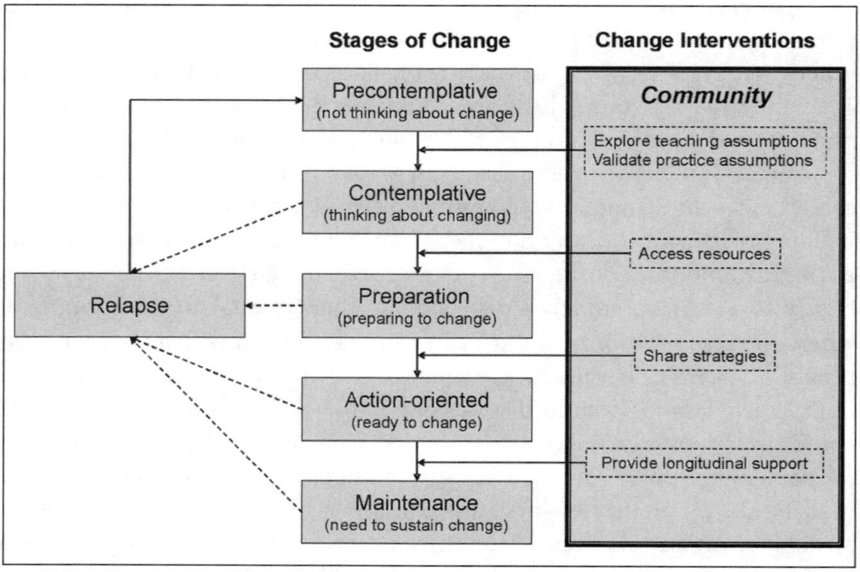

*Note.* Adapted from Prochaska, DiClemente, and Norcross, 1992.

simultaneously causes them to question and reflect on their teaching practices. This was the goal of the team that developed the *Chalk Talk* columns.

## Solution to Create Change

A significant constraint on the design of our method for promoting change was time and efficiency. An intervention had to be developed that would meet the needs of as many instructors as possible on the "Stages of Change" continuum with relatively little cost on their part in both time and energy. With this in mind, the idea of an electronic advice column emerged, which was named *Chalk Talk*. The editorial team consisted of an interdisciplinary group from chemistry, math, physics, and engineering, as well as from the Center for Effective University Teaching (CEUT) and the Educational Technology Center. These individuals met to exchange practical ideas and talk about different discipline models of teaching and learning (Donald, 2002). This created a forum for significant reflection and dialogue on teaching among these constituents. Next, the group (collectively calling themselves *Jonas Chalk*) investigated, read, and utilized the research on teaching and learning provided by the CEUT staff to inform the writing of the columns and combined this information with reflection and discussion on our own successful practices. This process allowed a wider variety of faculty to have access to the latest research on learning and teaching as well as the benefit of peer experience.

The method of delivery was in electronic format via weekly email, and columns were posted and remained available on the *Chalk Talk* web site (http://gemasterteachers.neu.edu/chalktalk.htm), which allowed easy access for faculty consultation. The titles of the columns were specifically designed to attract the faculty's attention so that they would open at least a few of them, particularly since the columns addressed very common teaching issues strategically placed at appropriate times in the semester. For example, during midterm exams, *Jonas* would run a column on cheating on tests or devising multiple-choice exams. These were issues that even the most seasoned practitioners usually struggled with at some point in their own classrooms. The use of an electronic dissemination tool provided the means to address significant faculty development issues while creating an interdisciplinary (albeit virtual) community of teachers. By sustaining this flow of information founded on the experience of the editorial team and current teaching and learning literature, we hoped to promote a culture of teaching excellence for FYES. Part of this process was helping FYES instructors understand the learning style for this student group as well as the needs of each discipline involved in the first-year engineering experience.

It was challenging for the team to "become Jonas," with a single coherent voice (Master Teaching Team, 2004). Each week, the editorial team met to discuss possible column ideas. A first-draft writer was usually assigned to compose the initial "question" and response that would address the particular issue that had been agreed upon. This initial draft was then passed electronically from one team member to the next, with each member editing by using the tracking function in Microsoft Word. At the end of this process, the draft writer typically sorted through the changes and made final edits. This final draft was discussed in great detail and with great passion at the following week's meeting. These intense conversations led to the development of another feature that was added to *Chalk Talk* to increase the likelihood that faculty would try something different. We added a postscript to all columns titled "Quick Tip." The team wanted to provide a tool/method that an instructor could try immediately at his or her next class, or a reference (usually a web site) that would provide further guidance on a topic. The Quick Tip was a means for *Jonas* to propel instructors into the action stage of Figure 14.1. A typical column is shown in Figure 14.2.

*Chalk Talk* was launched as a teaching advice column on February 13, 2001. The first column, "Lost Students," addressed the issue of engineering students who were "lost" in their math and science classes because of varied high school preparation. From this beginning, the *Chalk Talk* editorial team began producing a column every week for two academic years. These were sent to a freshmen instructor email list, which initially included about 35 instructors in chemistry, engineering, math, and physics. In year three, after two years of producing weekly columns, *Jonas* decided to run a new column every other week and reprint a relevant archived column on the alternate weeks. This was an effective strategy as *Chalk Talk* continually attracted new readership in successive years outside of the initial disciplines. These republished columns had a two-fold effect: they allowed new subscribers to read those columns directed toward recurring teaching challenges and, for existing subscribers, the archived columns provided reminders and reinforcement, important deterrents to relapse.

The creation of *Chalk Talk* provided a venue for regular, face-to-face communication among the chemistry, math, physics, and engineering faculty, many of whom are involved in teaching FYES. Often, problems that arose with teaching or other instructor-student interactions were resolved using the editorial team as a sort of mediation group. Discussions during *Chalk Talk* editorial meetings allowed teaching and related administrative issues to be addressed in a collaborative setting, often leading to genuine institutional change that benefited FYES. For example, while discussing a column on final exams, it became clear that the existing exam schedule was not acceptable to

FIGURE 14.2

## Sample *Jonas Chalk* Column

---

Dear Jonas:

Yesterday, I gave my class a test. At the end of the period, only about half the students had finished the exam. The students started getting very vocal, complaining about needing more time, asking whether they could do it over, claiming that the test wasn't fair, and so on. So I told them that for those who didn't finish, I would grade only the part they had completed. After class, the students who had finished the test came to me and were very angry. They said it wasn't fair: Since they had finished the test, why should these other students have less work graded? Now I've got everybody in the class mad at me. What should I do?

Tested Out

---

Dear Tested Out:

First, think about what you might have done to avoid this. For example, did you try the test yourself to see how long it took you to do it? Even though you're an expert, you often get a feel for how much time it might actually take if you try to answer your own questions. It's always best to try any assignments yourself beforehand so that you have a better understanding of what's involved in doing the work. If you have a TA or grad student working for you, you could ask him or her to take the test and note how long it took; you can then adjust the questions accordingly. If this happens again, you can try a couple of strategies. You could tell students that you're going to grade the entire test, but because so many students had problems with it, you're willing to drop one grade this quarter (assuming that you are sure your future tests can be done in the allotted time). If you believe in extra credit, you could give students an opportunity to make up points. With this class, you're already in a bind. It's best to be frank with the group and tell them you were really surprised that they couldn't finish the test in time. You might also consider telling them that those who want the test to count should let you know, and for the others, you'll disregard the test grade in the final grade calculations. You should then set the policy clearly with the class for future tests. They'll appreciate that you've heard their concerns and are planning to address them in the future.

Jonas

---

Quick Tip: To approximate whether an allotted exam time will be adequate for students, determine the time it takes you to complete the exam and multiply by three.

---

the teaching faculty in math, science, and engineering. Discussion of the column allowed this issue to surface and led to ongoing talks to create a compromise solution implemented by the registrar the following semester.

## The Impact of *JONAS*

Although attributing any one intervention to improved retention or culture change is difficult, data collected indicate that the freshman-to-sophomore retention for NU engineering students rose from 73% to 79% over the three-year period that the *Chalk Talk* column has run. We surveyed our targeted readership of faculty, instructors, and teaching assistants from math, science, and engineering after the columns had been published for five academic quarters. The survey, distributed in spring 2002, was intended to find out how many of our email list recipients were aware of *Chalk Talk* and, more importantly, how many of those were actually reading the column. The survey also asked about the usefulness of the column for changing classroom practices and getting precontemplative faculty to think about changing their practice, the first crucial step in the change continuum. Surveys were sent via email, as part of the *Chalk Talk* column, and paper versions were handed out at a luncheon to 50 science, math, and engineering instructors who teach FYES. Our survey generated 25 respondents for a 50% return rate from all the disciplines involved in the project. Respondents ranged from lecturers and teaching assistants with only limited classroom time to full professors with more than 20 years of teaching experience.

Of the respondents, 96% were familiar with the column, 92% had actually visited the *Chalk Talk* web site and found *Jonas* helpful, and 59% had spoken to another colleague about their teaching because of a *Chalk Talk* column. Perhaps the most impressive survey result was that 92% of survey takers had thought about their teaching practices and tried at least one new idea. In the portion of the survey where respondents could write comments, 10 faculty members responded. It was clear from their responses that *Jonas* had prompted these instructors to reflect (or contemplate) on their teaching methods. For example:

- "[*Jonas*] helped me recognize some of the philosophies I hold and the techniques I use."

- "[*Jonas*] helped me think about things [and] caused me to consider how I do things and possible techniques I can try."

- "[*Jonas* columns] cause one to reflect on one's own teaching and what one could do better to improve teaching, how to interact better with students and how to be more effective as a communicator and teacher."

These comments provided emerging evidence that the columns were prompting teachers of FYES to be contemplative or reflect on the assumptions underlying their teaching practice. For those in the action phase, the columns provided a variety of techniques from different disciplines that instructors could experiment with in their own classes. The action phase was also being reinforced by the Quick Tips provided as a postscript to each column.

There was further on-campus anecdotal evidence that *Jonas* was gaining some notoriety among the target audience. Teaching practitioners started to ask who Jonas Chalk is (when, in fact, "he" is really a product of 8 to 10 editorial team members). There were also unsolicited responses to columns from the readership, including comments on points of debate in the columns, suggestions about how to address a particular issue, and recommendations for future columns (which were welcome inputs to an editorial team that occasionally struggled with ideas for column topics).

As word of *Chalk Talk* has spread, we have added more than 200 faculty from five different colleges in our university to our email subscriber list. For example, the Bouvé College of Applied Health Sciences at NU, faced with similar issues teaching their first-year students, was so impressed with the results that the *Chalk Talk* column is now sent to faculty teaching their first-year students.

With increased readership we decided to send out a second survey in fall 2004 (see Figure 14.3). The purpose of this survey was to track the readership's progress along the change continuum. Our questions measured awareness and reflection (pre-contemplative to contemplative), implementation of new techniques (action to maintenance), and abandonment of techniques (relapse). We also asked opened-ended questions to see what effect, if any, reading *Chalk Talk* had on teaching. This survey was sent as an electronic survey embedded in a *Jonas* column to the 140 faculty then on the *Chalk Talk* email list. Along with two subsequent weekly columns, a reminder was posted at the beginning of each column prompting faculty to respond to the survey. The following week the survey was again sent electronically to the entire list. Twenty-seven readers responded for a 20% return rate. The respondents included eleven professors, four associate professors, two assistant professors, four academic specialists, one teaching assistant, and five who classified themselves as other. Results from this survey reinforced our intuitive belief that the columns were a useful mechanism to facilitate faculty movement through the stages of change. Table 14.1 shows the responses to the Lickert scale questions. Before reading the columns, faculty varied in their comfort with their current teaching practices (2.85), but identified the lack of knowledge of alternatives (3.35) and the concern over student reaction to change (3.42) as the two most important barriers to trying something new in the classroom. The questions referring to stages of change showed that after reading *Chalk Talk* respondents were more aware of teaching issues, learned new ideas/methods and techniques, and had tried new approaches. In other words, *Chalk Talk* appears to be supplying the necessary elements to overcome barriers to change.

FIGURE 14.3

## November 2004 Survey for *Chalk Talk* Readers

Thank you for taking the time to fill out this survey. This information is being collected to study the impact *Jonas Chalk* has had on teaching attitudes and practices of our readers. Your response is important and will be tabulated without attribution. If you have any question about the survey, please contact . . .

*JONAS CHALK* READER SURVEY

Position: ___Professor ___Associate Prof. ___Asst. Prof.
___Academic Specialist ___TA ___Other

How long you've been reading *Jonas Chalk* ___years ___months

**Please rate your agreement to the following statements** BEFORE **reading *Jonas Chalk***

1) I was comfortable with my teaching practice and didn't think about changing it.
___Strongly Agree ___Agree ___No Opinion/Not Applicable ___Disagree ___Strongly Disagree

2) I thought about trying new ideas/methodologies/techniques, but it/they seemed too time-consuming to actually implement.
___Strongly Agree ___Agree ___No Opinion/Not Applicable ___Disagree ___Strongly Disagree

3) I thought about trying new ideas/methodologies/techniques, but was unsure how to implement it/them.
___Strongly Agree ___Agree ___No Opinion/Not Applicable ___Disagree ___Strongly Disagree

4) I thought about trying new ideas/methodologies/techniques, but was concerned/uncertain about how my students would react.
___Strongly Agree ___Agree ___No Opinion/Not Applicable ___Disagree ___Strongly Disagree

**Please rate your agreement to the following statements** AFTER **reading *Jonas Chalk***

5) I became more aware of issues in teaching that I had not thought about before.
___Strongly Agree ___Agree ___No Opinion/Not Applicable ___Disagree ___Strongly Disagree

6) I learned new ideas/methods/techniques to enhance my teaching.
___Strongly Agree ___Agree ___No Opinion/Not Applicable ___Disagree ___Strongly Disagree

7) I tried some new approaches because of the *Jonas Chalk* column.
___Strongly Agree ___Agree ___No Opinion/Not Applicable ___Disagree ___Strongly Disagree

If so, which ones?

8) I tried one or more teaching approaches and abandoned it/them because it/they didn't work.
___Strongly Agree ___Agree ___No Opinion/Not Applicable ___Disagree ___Strongly Disagree

If so, which ones?

9) I tried one or more teaching approaches and abandoned it/them even though it/they *did* work.
___Strongly Agree ___Agree ___No Opinion/Not Applicable ___Disagree ___Strongly Disagree

If so, which ones?

10) How often do you now read *Chalk Talk*?

**Open-Ended Questions**

11) How has your reading of the *Chalk Talk* columns influenced your classroom teaching?

12) What parts of *Chalk Talk* did you find particularly helpful (e.g., multiple techniques, Quick Tips, new ideas, etc.)?

13) What would you change or add to the *Chalk Talk* columns to make them more useful?

TABLE 14.1

## Response Results From the November 2004 *Chalk Talk* Reader Survey

| Question | Strongly Disagree | Disagree | No Opinion | Agree | Strongly Agree | Mean |
|---|---|---|---|---|---|---|
| | Frequency of responses | | | | | |
| **Prior to reading *Jonas* . . .** | 1 | 2 | 3 | 4 | 5 | |
| 1) I was comfortable with my teaching practice and didn't think about changing it. | 4 | 8 | 3 | 11 | 1 | 2.89 |
| 2) I thought about trying new ideas/methodologies/ techniques, but it/they seemed too time-consuming to actually implement. | 1 | 10 | 5 | 11 | 0 | 2.96 |
| 3) I thought about trying new ideas/methodologies/techniques, but was unsure how to implement it/them. | 1 | 7 | 2 | 15 | 2 | 3.37 |
| 4) I thought about trying new ideas/methodologies/ techniques, but was concerned/uncertain about how my students would react. | 1 | 7 | 2 | 13 | 4 | 3.44 |
| **After reading *Jonas* . . .** | | | | | | |
| 5) I became more aware of issues in teaching that I had not thought about before. | 1 | 1 | 0 | 14 | 11 | 4.22 |
| 6) I learned new ideas/methods/techniques to enhance my teaching. | 1 | 0 | 0 | 11 | 15 | 4.44 |
| 7) I tried some new approaches because of the *Jonas Chalk* column. | 0 | 2 | 3 | 16 | 6 | 3.96 |
| 8) I tried one or more teaching approaches and abandoned it/them because it/they didn't work. | 1 | 11 | 9 | 6 | 0 | 2.74 |
| 9) I tried one or more teaching approaches and abandoned it/them even though it/they *did* work. | 3 | 12 | 10 | 1 | 1 | 2.44 |

*Note.* N = 27 for a 20% return rate from 17 tenure-track faculty, 4 academic specialists, 1 TA, and 5 others.

Perhaps more illuminating were the qualitative results. In answering the question regarding the influence of reading *Chalk Talk* on classroom teaching, analysis of the data using the check code methodology of Miles and Huberman (1994) revealed the following themes. These themes show emerging evidence that *Jonas* is providing a virtual community of learners for our readers. Respondents told us that *Jonas* decreased their isolation as teachers and validated their teaching practice, which made them more confident as teachers.

- "It is very nice to know that other instructors [are] faced with some of the exact same issues. As I read each issue, I either feel confident about how I have handled situations in the past or need to address in my teaching."

- "[The column helps m]ostly by giving me more confidence. Seeing discussions of various issues that have arisen with other teachers gave me support in my own responses to those issues."

A second theme that emerged was the increased awareness and reflection that reading *Chalk Talk* provided for these teachers. Readers told us that reading *Chalk Talk* provided them with the insight that, as one reader put it, "makes me think about and evaluate the effectiveness of my approach," or that "it is a constant reminder to assess my teaching." One reader summed it up this way:

- "[Reading *Chalk Talk*] heightened awareness that one size does not fit all and that effective teachers address the diverse learning styles of their students. I was one of the education reformers who was too quick to label some teaching techniques 'good' or 'bad.' After a more thoughtful review, it has become clear that there are many approaches to effective teaching. The key is to be constantly examining my practice, trying out new approaches, and fine tuning old ones."

*Jonas* also strongly addressed the lack of knowledge about teaching alternatives as the third theme. The most highly rated sections of *Jonas* were the Quick Tips and the editorial tone of the columns that emphasize multiple approaches and solutions to the initial question. One faculty member told us:

- "[The most helpful part is] multiple techniques, so that I can try a couple of approaches, if one doesn't work for me or the students."

A final unexpected and emergent finding was the ability of *Chalk Talk* to encourage instructors to consider students more consciously in the teaching and learning process. Respondents stated that they were "aware of students' needs as individuals," "provided me with a more sympathetic view of my students," and "I . . . more easily put myself in the shoes of my students to try to assess my effectiveness."

Lastly, *Jonas* provided inspiration to some and at least renewed faith in their university for others:

- "I have learned several classroom management techniques and some participation techniques. It is also inspiring to read the techniques of a master and try to bring the same attitude, if not actual techniques to my classes."

- "I can't say that Chalk Talk has had much of a direct influence. However, it is very important for me to be at an institution that cares enough about teaching innovation to sponsor something of this sort."

While the response rate was lower than hoped for, there is evidence that this format has provided the needed mechanism to begin to break down barriers to change and to create an electronic virtual community of teachers to provide the information, support, and confidence needed to change and sustain a new teaching culture.

## Conclusion

This chapter describes an electronic dissemination tool for improving teaching practices and changing teaching culture for instructors of first-year engineering students. The tool took the form of an "advice column" for instructors, and each column provides carefully crafted guidance on a particular teaching issue, written by an editorial team of eight to ten faculty and staff. The columns were distributed via email to instructors in chemistry, math, physics, and engineering. The goal was to build a community of reflective practitioners and effect teaching culture change with increased awareness of teaching beliefs and collegial interactions among faculty from different schools. The model for change was based on that of Prochaska, DiClemente, and Norcross (1992), with the objective to encourage a more action-oriented teaching culture—one in which instructors are inspired to try new methods and reflect on the results.

The results of the column, after three years of dissemination, have been significant. While the results cannot be attributed exclusively to the *Chalk Talk* initiative, freshman-to-sophomore engineering student retention at NU has increased from 73% prior to the start of the column to 79% in 2003.

The number of faculty enrolled in the email list has increased from about 35 at the column's inception to 140 in 2004 to 227 in 2005. In the first survey of target instructors, 96% were familiar with the column, and 92% had thought about their teaching practices and tried at least one new idea. The second survey showed strong evidence that readers of the column are supported as they proceed through the stages of change. Most particularly, the column has contributed to raising awareness of practice assumptions, the first critical step in moving from precontemplation to the beginning stages of change.

While *Jonas* may not have opened the classroom door (i.e., made teaching practices transparent to all [Shulman, 1993]), the *Chalk Talk* column has created an electronic teaching community among disparate disciplines. It has provided an inspiration to act and reflect on teaching practices and serves as a forum for continuing discussion.

## Acknowledgments

We wish to acknowledge the support of a grant from the General Electric Foundation, "GE Master Teachers for Freshman Engineering Students," which has partially supported the development and perpetuation of the *Chalk Talk* column. The efforts and congeniality of the members of the editorial team are also greatly valued. We appreciate the support of Allen L. Soyster and Richard J. Scranton, dean and associate dean of engineering, respectively, and James R. Stellar, dean of arts and sciences, for sustaining this ongoing initiative.

## References

Besterfield-Sacre, M. E., Atman, C. J., & Shuman, L. J. (1997). Characteristics of freshman engineering students: Models for determining student attrition in engineering. *Journal of Engineering Education, 86*(2), 139–149.

Donald, J. G. (2002). *Learning to think: Disciplinary perspectives.* San Francisco, CA: Jossey-Bass.

Master Teaching Team. (2004). Becoming Jonas: Reflections from the team. In D. M. Qualters & M. R. Diamond (Eds.), *Chalk talk: E-advice from Jonas Chalk, legendary college teacher* (pp. 11–20). Stillwater, OK: New Forums Press.

Miles, M. B., & Huberman, A. M. (1994). *Qualitative data analysis: An expanded sourcebook* (2nd ed.). Thousand Oaks, CA: Sage.

National Research Council. (2003). *Evaluating and improving undergraduate teaching in science, technology, engineering, and mathematics.* Washington, DC: National Academies Press.

Prochaska, J. O., DiClemente, C. C., & Norcross, J. C. (1992). In search of how people change: Applications to addictive behaviors. *American Psychologist, 47,* 1102–1114.

Schön, D. A. (1983). *The reflective practitioner: How professionals think in action.* New York, NY: Basic Books.

Seymour, E. (2002). Tracking the processes of change in U.S. undergraduate education in science, mathematics, engineering, and technology, *Science Education, 85*(6), 79–105.

Seymour, E., & Hewitt N. M. (1997). *Talking about leaving: Why undergraduates leave the sciences.* Boulder, CO: Westview Press.

Shulman, L. S. (1993). Teaching as community property. *Change, 25*(6), 6–8.

Wenger, E. (1998). *Communities of practice: Learning, meaning, and identity.* Cambridge, England: Cambridge University Press.

# 15

# Helping Faculty Learn to Teach Better and "Smarter" Through Sequenced Activities

Barbara J. Millis
University of Nevada Reno

*Faculty developers can help faculty learn to intentionally sequence assignments and activities to promote greater learning when they understand the convergent research—with its practical implications for teaching—on how people learn, on deep learning, and on cooperative learning. Such a sequence includes a motivating out-of-class assignment (homework), in-class "processing" that includes active learning and student interactions, and feedback and assessment, often given in multiple ways. This approach is modeled through two examples using graphic organizers.*

Faculty are always looking for ways to teach better and "smarter." They don't want gimmicks or quick fixes or even worse, they don't want to feel overloaded by trying to respond to simultaneous teaching demands, such as teaching for critical thinking, diversity, writing across the curriculum, and so on. They—and those of us in faculty development—know that simply splicing these new elements into existing courses without a clear sense of purpose, commitment, or competence will simply result in incoherence and a lack of alignment between goals, assessment, and activities (see Robertson, 2003).

Faculty members are more likely to be motivated to change their teaching practices when they have confidence in a research-based *integrated* approach to teaching and learning. Palmer (1997) reminds us that

Our challenge is not to reduce good teaching to a particular form, model, methodology, or technique, but to understand its dynamics at the deeper levels, the underpinnings, to understand the dynamics that make connectedness a powerful force for learning in whatever forms it takes. (p. 12)

Similarly, Leamnson (1999) emphasizes that "a good pedagogy *selects* what is appropriate and is not wedded to a method, no matter how innovative or popular" (p. 8).

This chapter therefore offers faculty developers—who can then share with faculty—an intentional approach to learning and course design that is based on integrated and synthesized research from three fields: the eclectic research on what is sometimes called "how people learn," the international research on deep learning, and the longstanding research on cooperative learning, which includes both pair work and small group work.

Faculty can be coached to sequence activities—both outside and inside the classroom, with implications, too, for distance education—in order to strengthen student learning and motivation to learn. They need to create motivating homework assignments—remembering that students are motivated by assignments with relevance to their own lives—to get students involved with the course content. They then need to use classroom or distance education interactions to reinforce that content. These reinforcing activities get students actively working together on academic tasks that build on the foundational homework. It is important, as Marton, Hounsell, and Entwistle (1997) point out, that we view

The teaching-learning process as a constellation of learning tasks, some of which take place in a classroom setting in the presence of a university teacher while others are pursued alone or in the company of peers in the university library, the study-bedroom, or even in the course of travelling [sic] to and from campus. (p. 247)

To bring research into practice, we will examine two specific examples from different disciplines with suggestions for further use in other contexts. First, to provide background information, we need to examine the research on how people learn, which leads us to a multilayered look—almost like hypertext—at deep learning, which in turn suggests that cooperative learning can provide a seamless approach to the active learning and student interactions needed for deep learning.

## The Research and Premises Behind How People Learn

Bransford, Brown, and Cocking (2000) have assembled a groundbreaking report that looks at how people learn through convergent research from a variety of fields including cognitive psychology, developmental research, social psychology, neuroscience, and technology. They note that "one of the hallmarks of the new science of learning is its emphasis on learning with understanding" (p. 8).

According to Bransford et al., three research-based findings have profound implications for how we structure learning with understanding. The first finding involves prior knowledge:

> . . . The contemporary view of learning is that people construct new knowledge and understandings based on what they already know and believe . . . [and thus] . . . teachers need to pay attention to the incomplete understandings, the false beliefs, and the naive renditions of concepts that learners bring with them to a given subject. (p. 10)

The second finding coalesces perfectly with the international research on deep learning. The finding is that to teach for understanding, not memorization—which these researchers identify with deeper learning—teachers must eschew breadth in coverage in favor of depth. Students need a deep foundational knowledge, but the knowledge base needs to be organized around conceptual frameworks to facilitate retrieval and application. The third finding, which is emphasized repeatedly in the book, is the value of metacognition—getting students to think about their thinking—a practice that makes them self-aware learners better able to solve problems and to transfer knowledge from one arena to another.

Because it is so critical, Bransford et al.'s second learning principle—deep, conceptual learning—deserves a closer look.

## The Research and Premises Behind Deep Learning

International research on deep learning has been ongoing in a number of countries including Britain, Sweden, Australia, and New Zealand. Four key components characterize a deep, rather than a surface, approach to learning. Rhem (1995) summarizes them as follows:

> **Motivational context:** We learn best what we feel a need to know. Intrinsic motivation remains inextricably bound to some level of choice and control. Courses that remove these take away the sense of ownership and kill one of the strongest elements in lasting learning.

**Learner activity:** Deep learning and "doing" travel together. Doing in itself isn't enough. Faculty must connect activity to the abstract conceptions that make sense of it, but passive mental postures lead to superficial learning.

**Interaction with others:** As Noel Entwistle put it in a recent email message, "The teacher is not the only source of instruction or inspiration." Peers working as groups enjoin dimensions of learning that lectures and readings by themselves cannot touch.

**A well-structured knowledge base:** This doesn't just mean presenting new material in an organized way. It also means engaging and reshaping the concepts students bring with them when they register. Deep approaches and learning for understanding are integrative processes. The more fully new concepts can be connected with students' prior experience and existing knowledge, the more it is they will be impatient with inert facts and eager to achieve their own synthesis. (p. 4)

This research strongly reinforces the need to think intentionally about how we structure and sequence assignments and activities so that we capitalize on motivating students to tackle our content as preparation for class and then reinforcing that preparation through meaningful social learning exchanges with peers. Another emphasis in Bransford et al.'s work is the importance of community in learning:

Teachers must attend to designing classroom activities and helping students organize their work in ways that promote the kind of intellectual camaraderie and the attitudes toward learning that build a sense of community. (p. 25)

Thus, the research on cooperative learning has enormous relevance as teachers sequence activities for deep learning. Cooperative learning—because of its structure and its emphasis on metacognition/monitoring—provides a valuable way to build in the peer interactions and active learning that are the heart of deep learning.

## The Research and Premises Behind Cooperative Learning

Cooperative learning, like collaborative learning, entails small groups working on specific tasks. It seeks to overcome some of the weaknesses of traditional small group approaches by structuring activities carefully. Cooper

(1990), in fact, regards the key to successful cooperative learning as "Structure! Structure! Structure!" (p. 1).

Two basic premises govern all cooperative classrooms. The first is positive interdependence. Students have vested reasons to work cooperatively together on tasks or problems too complex for one individual to complete. Through careful planning, teachers can establish positive interdependence by having students achieve mutual goals, such as reaching a consensus on specific solutions to problems or arriving at team-generated solutions; mutual rewards, such as individually assigned points counting toward a criterion-referenced final grade, points that only help, but never handicap; structured tasks, such as a report or complex problem with sections contributed by each team member; and interdependent roles, such as having group members serve as discussion leaders, organizers, recorders, and spokespersons.

The second premise is individual accountability. No matter how much mutual support, coaching, and encouragement they receive, students must be individually responsible for their own academic achievements. Teachers can grade quizzes, projects, and final exams just as they would in a class where group work is not the norm. When teachers assign group projects, they must avoid merely stamping a grade on the final product. Ethically, they must determine the contributions of each member and assign grades accordingly. Most teachers use a combination of peer, individual, and teacher assessments.

Additionally, some other premises, which lead to deliberate practice, can promote effective cooperative learning. Heterogeneity in teams or pairs helps build the skills needed for critical thinking. Brookfield (1987) and others have emphasized that critical thinking depends on identifying and challenging assumptions and subsequently exploring and conceptualizing alternatives. These challenges will not occur when students all think alike. Group heterogeneity also helps students build needed workforce and community skills by learning to value the contributions of others.

It is also important to build in group processing activities so that students acquire teamwork skills and the metacognitive skills advocated by Bransford et al. that help them become intentional learners. Cuseo (2003) notes:

> Such meta-cognitive processing involves student reflection on:
> (a) individual steps involved in their thinking or problem-solving,
> (b) specific strategies or approaches they used in the process of reaching problem solutions, and, (c) underlying rationales for their ideas. (p. 73)

Some good resources for cooperative learning are Cooper, Robinson, and Ball (2003); Johnson, Johnson, and Smith (1991); Millis (2002); and Millis and Cottell (1998).

## Sequencing Activities and Assignments

Bransford et al. conclude that "The emerging science of learning underscores the importance of rethinking what is taught, how it is taught, and how learning is assessed" (p. 13). Teachers who understand this emerging science of learning—including the premises behind the brain-based, deep learning, and cooperative learning research—are prepared to bring theory into practice through intentional sequencing. Walvoord (2004) suggests that faculty can teach well and save time by using in-class time for what she calls "process and response." When they deliberately sequence materials by assigning motivating homework that is then "processed" in class through active learning and peer interactions, students can learn at a deep level.

The two examples that follow illustrate the process of sequencing, both of them using graphic organizers. A graphic organizer can be defined as a diagram to organize information in a visual format that suggests relationships. Particularly common in science and engineering, graphic organizers are useful because they provide organizing principles or prompts that can focus homework assignments. Bransford et al. point out that novice learners do not have the "command of concepts" held by experts (p. 17) whose thinking is guided by "core concepts" and "big ideas" (p. 37). Thus, graphic organizers can help students, who are not experts, to see patterns and relationships. Marzano, Pickering, and Pollock (2001) recommend graphic organizers based on "six common patterns into which most information can be organized: descriptive patterns, time-sequence patterns, process/cause-effect patterns, episode patterns, generalization/principle patterns, and concept patterns" (p. 75).

## Example 1: Using a Graphic Organizer Called a Double Entry Journal

With a double entry journal (DEJ) students identify on the left side of a grid (a Word table template emailed or distributed to students) the key points of an article, chapter, or guest lecture. Just opposite the key point they respond, linking the point to other academic material, to current events, or even to their personal experiences and opinions (see Figure 15.1).

FIGURE 15.1

## Sample Double Entry Journal (Two Points Cited Only)

| Key Points | Responses |
|---|---|
| Mental health issues—including suicide and depression—are growing on campuses, requiring more resources to solve them. | I have been hearing this for years, particularly from teachers in schools with open enrollments. Resources are always an issue, it seems, no matter what the problem. As a faculty developer, I want to see—selfishly—more resources spent to bolster teaching. But, on the other hand, if the students we attempt to teach have barriers to learning that transcend the classroom, then more needs to be done. |
| Fortunately, most common problems, including eating disorders, substance abuse, and anxiety, are treatable but only if students recognize the symptoms and seek help. | I think faculty and teaching assistants can definitely help in this arena if they recognize key symptoms and steer students toward the appropriate resources. I am glad we are adding this semester a new mental health component to our three-day TA training. I will now be certain that we continue to offer workshops on "Distressed and Distressing Students." |

Name: Barbara J. Millis

Article: "The Mental Health Crisis: What Colleges Must Do" by Richard D. Kadison (2004)

To avoid overloading students, faculty members can limit either the length of the DEJ or the number of key points.

A DEJ prepared outside of class gets students into the knowledge base and motivates them. Motivation is heightened with a DEJ for two reasons. First, when students know their homework will be reviewed by peers, they are more likely to come to class prepared (Nelson, 2004). Second, students often become motivated when the material is relevant to their own lives and learning, as when they write reflective responses to the key points in an article. These reflective responses also promote learning because students who place content knowledge in a personal context are more likely to retain the information and be able to retrieve it—the "self-referral" effect—(Rogers, Kuiper, & Kirker, 1977). Similarly, Jensen (2000) advises faculty members to help students "discover their own connections . . . [and] use their own words with regard to new learning" (p. 282).

What becomes of the out-of-class homework assignment is critically important. Too often, teachers merely collect and grade homework, suggesting to students that their work is an artificial exercise intended for evaluation by a bored expert (the teacher). To avoid this perception and to build in the active learning and interaction with peers in the deep learning/cooperative learning models, teachers can pair students and have them read and comment on each other's DEJ. (Unprepared students do not pair, they work on their DEJ at the back of the room.) The paired conversations should lead to both learning and genuine exchanges. Intellectually, students should return to the original article or to their lecture notes to review the key points, particularly when there are dissimilarities. But the reflective responses, too, should prompt authentic connections. In a nursing class, for example, a student would react humanely when learning something personal about his partner: "Your Uncle Joe died of AIDS? I am so sorry."

The learning is further sequenced when the teacher provides feedback beyond the peer feedback offered through the paired discussion. Bransford et al. emphasize that "students need feedback about the degree to which they know when, where, and how to use the knowledge they are learning" (p. 59). Teachers can return DEJs with their own brief comments focused on the accuracy of the key points and the relevance and depth of the reflective responses. (Although marked, DEJs need not receive a labor-intensive letter grade: a pass/fail grade motivates students without adding significantly to the grading load. A "pass" counting 10 points toward a criterion referenced point-based final grade, for example, allows the teacher to comment quickly and personally, rather than justifying a grade based on the nuances between an A- and a B+.)

Feedback can also be provided through yet another stage in the sequence: whole-class feedback on DEJs. In this case, the teacher can share exemplary student DEJ examples or (my preferred practice) they can build a composite DEJ based on excerpts—key points and responses—from a variety of student examples. These exemplary DEJs are shared with the class ostensibly to coach students to write better DEJs in the future. But, as part of a sequence, this final stage also promotes learning through repetition without rote.

Two biologists help us understand the basics of learning and why sequencing is so important: Zull (2002) identifies the art of teaching as "creating conditions that lead to change in a learner's brain" (p. 5) and Leamnson (1999) defines learning as "stabilizing, through repeated use, certain appropriate and desirable synapses in the brain" (p. 5). Reading the assigned article or hearing the guest lecture is exposure one. Then, crafting the DEJ draws the student back into the material—with personally relevant responses—for repetition two. The paired discussion in class provides a third repetition. As a fourth repetition, students are likely to review their DEJ when the teacher returns them with comments. A fifth repetition occurs when teachers coach students on preparing an ideal DEJ by presenting exemplary examples as an in-class follow-up.

Because DEJs are based on assigned readings or guest lectures (the lecturer will gain insights into how well students understood their presentation), they are useful in virtually any discipline.

## Example 2: Using a Graphic Organizer With Jigsaw

Many courses involve demanding problem-solving skills that require students to confront complex, challenging topics involving multiple pieces of information necessary for final, overall mastery. Even if a definitive answer is neither possible nor desirable, students need to come to an understanding of in-depth issues. Cuseo (2003) suggests that if instructors seek to develop students' higher-order thinking skills, then the learning task should focus on "(a) ill-structured problems that may not be readily resolved, (b) issues to be discussed or debated, or (c) decision-making tasks that require exploration of, and determination from equally appealing alternatives" (p. 71). Such problems are ideally suited for the cooperative learning structure Jigsaw.

Jigsaw, like a DEJ, is carefully sequenced and monitored. Students prepare outside of class and bring their homework assignments to class where they work in a "home team" composed of students with various parts of the complex problem or issue. In a Jigsaw activity, students temporarily leave their home teams to form expert teams. In the expert teams students have two tasks: they must master the material, and they must also develop with other expert team members creative ways to teach the other members of their home teams the material they have mastered and respond knowledgeably and positively to questions raised by their teammates.

As an example, Jigsaw works well in literature classes where a key goal is to develop students' proficiency in close textual readings. After a mini-lecture on characterization that explains and models close textual analysis, the instructor assigns a literary work such as *Antigone* with four strong characters (Antigone, Creon, Haemon, and Ismene) and asks each student in a four-person home team to choose one character. (Teams can have more than four members; with five members, for example, two students can work with Creon, who is very complex.) To focus their reading, students receive a graphic organizer (McTighe, 1992) on which, as a homework assignment, they list each trait that describes their character on the extending arms. In the corner boxes they list (with page numbers) each episode or event that provides evidence for this trait (see Figure 15.2).

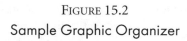

FIGURE 15.2
Sample Graphic Organizer

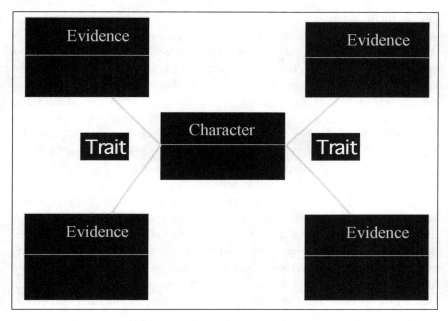

In the subsequent class meeting, all the students with the same character compare their graphic organizers in expert groups of three to five students. The team discusses the importance of the traits and the value of the supporting evidence and agrees on the best four traits and the best evidence to support them. Then, each member completes a second graphic organizer, using the best ideas of all members. Those familiar with the original Bloom's (1956) taxonomy will recognize that students are engaged in the highest levels of cognitive development because they are making judgments about the best traits (evaluation) and determining the most relevant evidence to create a new graphic organizer (synthesis). In a revised version of Bloom's taxonomy by Anderson and Krathwohl (2001), students still are working at the highest end of the cognitive process dimension because they are evaluating (making judgments based on criteria and standards) and creating (putting elements together to form a coherent or functional whole; reorganizing elements into a new pattern or structure).

At a signal, the expert members return to their home teams where they explain in depth their character's four key traits and the evidence in the text to support this interpretation. They are, in other words, teaching their team-mates their portion of the Jigsaw, a practice that capitalizes on the use of peer tutoring to enhance learning (Fantuzzo, Dimeff, & Fox, 1989; Fantuzzo, Riggio, Connelly, & Dimeff, 1989).

As with a DEJ, students get individually involved with the materials through a homework assignment. But what becomes of the homework assignment is the key. In the expert groups, students are making judgments about the value of the traits and the evidence to support them. In addition to challenging them to think at the highest levels on the cognitive domain, this practice also helps students learn to attend closely to textual clues. They learn from one another in the expert teams by comparing and contrasting their different approaches to the same homework assignment and by preparing to teach their home team members. Gartner, Kohler, and Riessman (1971) emphasize that various cognitive processes occur when someone prepares to teach effectively. First of all, teachers must review the material, resulting—one assumes—in a deeper understanding. Second, teachers must organize the material in order to present it to others unfamiliar with it. In this process, they will likely seek creative ways to get the points across. They may discover or design, for instance, relevant anecdotes, concrete examples, visual or oral illustrations, graphic organizers, charts, and classroom or homework activities. Third, teachers are also likely both to identify and subsequently to reorder or rearrange the salient facts, resulting in in-depth understanding and, sometimes, in a reconceptualization of the subject.

The clarification and amplification, including stretching to find clearer examples, helps co-peers, students who teach other students (Whitman, 1988), to enlarge their own understanding. Webb (1983, 1991) has found that giving detailed, elaborate explanations increases student achievement. Additional benefits of peer teaching and coaching have emerged. Working with peers can reduce the sense of working in an isolated vacuum for an artificial audience, usually the teacher. Gere (1987), in speaking of the power of writing groups, emphasizes that

> The peer who says "I don't understand" establishes—more powerfully than any theory, instructor's exhortation, or written comment can—the "otherness" of the audience and pushes writers to respond to this otherness by more effective ways to convey ideas. (p. 68)

Students receive pass/fail points for the individually prepared graphic organizer they brought to share in the expert team. It might be worth five points, for example, toward the final course point total. Even though the expert-team graphic organizer receives no additional points, it is collected with the individual ones to be used for further feedback, as in the DEJ sequence. Bransford et al. emphasize the value of feedback based on thinking that is "made visible." Such feedback must "focus on understanding, and not only on memory . . . and does not necessarily require elaborate or complicated assessment procedures" (p. 140). Thus graphic organizers, such as the DEJ and the trait diagram, submitted for pass/fail points can contribute to student learning when they are part of a carefully organized sequence.

Jigsaws can be used in virtually any complex discipline. In a psychology class, for example, students can first explore as homework some research-based questions on the underpinnings of childhood moral development. These assignments could point them to the particular areas in which they will become experts: cognition, social, emotional, and biological. Each home team has an expert assigned to the particular topic area. These students delve into their particular specialty initially through homework or research assignments. Then they meet in expert teams with other people assigned to the same specialty to review their findings and to prepare to teach their topics. In their home teams composed of three or four experts, these students then teach their home team members the essence of their expertise. Other jigsaw examples might be botany students who can learn and teach others about the major plant groups (nonvascular land plants, seedless vascular plants, vascular plants with "naked" seeds [gymnosperms], vascular plants with flowers and protected seeds [angiosperms]). In other jigsaw examples, history students can learn from one another about photographers at Gettysburg (Gardner and his men, Mathew Brady, the Tyson brothers, and miscellaneous photographers such as Frederick Gutekunst and Peter and Hanson Weaver); anthropology classes can explore the various branches of the discipline (cultural, linguistic, physical, and archeology). Jigsaws can contain up to five pieces (more makes the sequencing and monitoring harder to manage) or can have only three, such as biochemistry students teaching each other about polymers of carbon (carbohydrates, lipids, and proteins).

## Conclusion

Wiggins and McTighe (1998) discuss at length the importance of "sequence in the design of the curriculum" (p. 134). They argue for a "spiral" curriculum where "the same ideas and materials are revisited in more and more complex ways to arrive at sophisticated judgments and products" (p. 135). On the college level, ideas and materials can be sequenced through the intentional use of tools such as graphic organizers or carefully sequenced case studies, role plays, and debates. The challenge—one where faculty developers can play a crucial role—is designing the sequence itself to capitalize on how students learn, deep learning, and cooperative learning.

## References

Anderson, L. W., & Krathwohl, D. R. (Eds.). (2001). *A taxonomy for learning, teaching, and assessing: A revision of Bloom's taxonomy of educational objectives* (Abridged ed.). New York, NY: Longman.

Bloom, B. S. (Ed.). (1956). *Taxonomy of educational objectives: Book 1. Cognitive domain.* New York, NY: Longman.

Bransford, J. D., Brown, A. L., & Cocking, R. R. (Eds.). (2000). *How people learn: Brain, mind, experience, and school* (Expanded ed.). Washington, DC: National Academies Press.

Brookfield, S. D. (1987). *Developing critical thinkers.* San Francisco, CA: Jossey-Bass.

Cooper, J. (1990). Cooperative learning and college teaching: Tips from the trenches. *The Teaching Professor, 4,* 1–2.

Cooper, J. L., Robinson, P., & Ball, D. (Eds.). (2003). *Small group instruction in higher education: Lessons from the past, visions of the future.* Stillwater, OK: New Forums Press.

Cuseo, J. B. (2003). Critical thinking and cooperative learning: A natural marriage. In J. L. Cooper, P. Robinson, & D. Ball (Eds.), *Small group instruction in higher education: Lessons from the past, visions of the future* (pp. 63–74), Stillwater, OK: New Forums Press.

Fantuzzo, J. W., Dimeff, L. A., & Fox, S. L. (1989). Reciprocal peer tutoring: A multimodal assessment of effectiveness with college students. *Teaching of Psychology, 16*(3), 133–135.

Fantuzzo, J. W., Riggio, R. E., Connelly, S., & Dimeff, L. A. (1989). Effects of reciprocal peer tutoring on academic achievement and psychological adjustment: A component analysis. *Journal of Educational Psychology, 81*(2), 173–177.

Gartner, A., Kohler, M. C., & Riessman, F. (1971). *Children teach children: Learning by teaching.* New York, NY: Harper & Row.

Gere, A. R. (1987). *Writing groups: History, theory, and implications.* Carbondale, IL: Southern Illinois University Press.

Jensen, E. (2000). *Brain-based learning: The new science of teaching and training* (Rev. ed.). San Diego, CA: The Brain Store.

Johnson, D. W., Johnson, R. T., & Smith, K. A. (1991). *Cooperative learning: Increasing college faculty instructional productivity* (ASHE-ERIC Higher Education Report No. 4). Washington, DC: George Washington University, School of Education and Human Development.

Kadison, R. D. (2004, December 10). The mental-health crisis: What colleges must do. *Chronicle of Higher Education,* p. B20.

Leamnson, R. (1999). *Thinking about teaching and learning: Developing habits of learning with first year college and university students.* Sterling, VA: Stylus.

Marton, F., Hounsell, D., & Entwistle, N. (1997). *The experience of learning: Implications for teaching and studying in higher education* (2nd ed.). Edinburgh, Scotland: Scottish Academic Press.

Marzano, R. J., Pickering, D. J., & Pollock, J. E. (2001). *Classroom instruction that works: Research-based strategies for increasing student achievement.* Alexandria, VA: Association for Supervision and Curriculum Development.

McTighe, J. (1992). Graphic organizers: Collaborative links to better thinking. In N. Davidson & T. Worsham (Eds.), *Enhancing thinking through cooperative learning* (pp. 182–197). New York, NY: Teachers College Press.

Millis, B. J. (2002). *Enhancing learning—and more!—through cooperative learning* (IDEA Paper No. 38). Retrieved May 22, 2005, from the Kansas State University, IDEA Center web site: http://www.idea.ksu.edu/papers/Idea_Paper_38.pdf

Millis, B. J., & Cottell, P. G., Jr. (1998). *Cooperative learning for higher education faculty.* Phoenix, AZ: American Council on Education/Oryx Press.

Nelson, C. E. (2004). *Responding to diversity: Three pedagogical changes that can make a real difference in ANY college classroom.* Paper presented at the 24th annual Lilly Conference on College Teaching, Oxford, OH.

Palmer, P. J. (1997). The renewal of community in higher education. In W. E. Campbell & K. A. Smith (Eds.), *New paradigms for college teaching* (pp. 1–18). Edina, MN: Interaction Book Company.

Rhem, J. (1995). Close-up: Going deep. *The National Teaching and Learning Forum, 5*(1), 4.

Robertson, D. R. (2003). *Making time, making change: Avoiding overloads in college teaching.* Stillwater, OK: New Forums Press.

Rogers, T. B., Kuiper, N. A., & Kirker, W. S. (1977). Self-reference and the encoding of personal information. *Journal of Personality and Social Psychology, 35,* 677–688.

Walvoord, B. (2004). *Teaching well, saving time.* Keynote address presented at the 24th annual Lilly Conference on College Teaching, Oxford, OH.

Webb, N. (1983). Predicting learning from student interaction: Defining the interaction variable. *Educational Psychologist, 18*(1), 33–41.

Webb, N. (1991). Task-related verbal interaction and mathematics learning in small groups. *Journal of Research in Mathematics Education, 22,* 366–389.

Whitman, N. A. (1988). *Peer teaching: To teach is to learn twice* (ASHE-ERIC Higher Education Report No. 4). Washington, DC: Association for the Study of Higher Education.

Wiggins, G., & McTighe, J. (1998). *Understanding by design.* Alexandria, VA: Association for Supervision and Curriculum Development.

Zull, J. E. (2002). *The art of changing the brain: Enriching the practice of teaching by exploring the biology of learning.* Sterling, VA: Stylus.

# 16

# Practicing What We Preach: Transforming the TA Orientation

Patricia Armstrong, Peter Felten, Jeffrey Johnston, Allison Pingree
Vanderbilt University

*Brookfield (1995), Schön (1983), and others articulate the necessity and complexity of being critically reflective in our work. Indeed, the value of critical reflection is inherent to educational development as a field in that we frequently encourage such thinking in our consultations with instructors. But practicing what we preach can be difficult. This chapter reflects on an experiment in the transformation of a teaching assistant orientation, a central event of our teaching center. We not only describe and assess the process of revising this orientation, but we also reflect on the implications of this case for broader programming issues in faculty and teaching assistant development.*

## Introduction

Historically and currently, orienting and training new graduate teaching assistants (TAs) has been a fundamental, core offering by teaching centers and TA developers at doctoral institutions (Frantz, Beebe, Horvath, Canales, & Swee, 2005). For many programs and centers, these events mark the beginning of the academic year and serve as signature events, consuming significant amounts of money, time, and energy.

Our practice as educational developers at Vanderbilt University is no different. Started in 1986 as part of the College of Arts and Science, the Vanderbilt University Center for Teaching has placed a central focus on TAs from its inception. The first Teaching Assistant Orientation (TAO) was offered in the late 1980s. Typically attended by 150–200 new TAs, our orientation has traditionally included both plenary and breakout sessions, sorted by discipline and/or teaching duties, as well as additional sessions for international TAs, all spanning a three-day period prior to the beginning of the academic year. In preparation for this event, the staff of the Center for Teaching, which now includes graduate student teaching fellows, participates in a two-week training. In terms both of our labor and the monies budgeted for the event, TAO is far and away the most expensive event in our annual list of programs.

Given this local significance, along with the traditional importance of teaching orientations in the work of educational development as a field, the Center for Teaching professional staff has analyzed our TA orientation over the years in order to make it as effective and efficient as possible. In response to this regular evaluation, Vanderbilt's version of the teaching assistant orientation has changed notably over the past 15 years. But the changes have tended to be logistical rather than paradigmatic in nature. Indeed, even after a decision in 2003 to transform our teaching orientation by structuring it around a conceptual, research-based model, we seem only to have made further adaptations to a model that we fear may not be fully meeting our articulated goals for the orientation.

In this chapter, we will briefly describe the small, incremental changes made in the recent past (1998–2002) to Vanderbilt's Teaching Assistant Orientation, discuss the transformational shift we envisioned in 2003 and implemented for TAO 2004, analyze the successes and failures of the orientation in 2004 that resulted from that shift, and reflect on the implications of that analysis for future practice at the center and for educational developers in general. In so doing, we hope to answer three important questions about faculty/TA development programming: What goals are we hoping to achieve through planning and running specific programs? How do we know if these goals are being met? What do we do if (or when) we determine that these goals are not being met?

For us, the function of asking and answering such questions in a public forum is clear. As consultants, we work with clarity and persistence to encourage instructors to identify learning goals for their students and then design courses, assignments, and activities that will help students reach, if not exceed, those goals. We believe we should apply the same principles of alignment to our work, to inspect the process and results of doing so, and to share this reflection with our colleagues. By doing this, we embody the reflective practitioner (Brookfield, 1995; Schön, 1983), who looks thoughtfully at his or her practice and changes that practice—when warranted—on the basis of that inspection.

## Expansion and Adaptation: Vanderbilt's Teaching Assistant Orientation From 1998 to 2003

In 1997, Vanderbilt's Board of Trustees expanded the scope of the Center for Teaching to include all nine colleges and schools constituting Vanderbilt University. The scope of our teaching assistant orientation necessarily expanded along with that of the center and so, since 1998, has included sessions for students from all of Vanderbilt's schools in which graduate students routinely teach as part of their education: College of Arts and Science, Peabody College of Education and Human Development, Owen Graduate School of Management, School of Engineering, and the Divinity School.

In the wake of this expansion, the center faced a variety of opportunities and challenges associated with our orientation, many of them specific to Vanderbilt, with others resulting from its status as a research-extensive institution. Table 16.1 details some of these challenges as well as the manner in which the Center for Teaching staff addressed them during the initial phases of expansion from 1998–2003.

Strikingly, many of these changes were driven more by logistical and constituency concerns than by adherence to conceptual and theoretical frameworks. That is, they were shaped more in response to the implied question "What can we do to make people like the event better?" rather than by our learning goals ("What do TAs need to learn in order to be effective teachers?"). Even as we worked through the organization and logistics of our teaching assistant orientation to make it more learner-friendly, we were not necessarily looking at our goals for those learners or determining whether logistical changes might adversely affect our learning goals, let alone questioning at a deep level what our fundamental goals were and investigating whether a campus-wide teaching orientation could even bear the weight of those goals.

## Enduring Understandings and *How People Learn* as Paradigm Shifts for TAO 2004

After our teaching assistant orientation in 2003 we began to consider another revision to the orientation. Past changes had responded to a variety of institutional needs, but the impetus this time emerged from our own questions about the event's goals and purpose. Wiggins and McTighe's (1998) *Understanding by Design* prompted our original questions and shaped our approach to rethinking our teaching assistant orientation. Wiggins and

TABLE 16.1

## Challenges Addressed in Organizing TA Orientations (1998–2003)

| Challenge | Response |
|---|---|
| Departments want TAs trained with specific reference to the discipline and the teaching duties TAs assume in that discipline. | The Center for Teaching recruits teaching fellows from a variety of disciplines and works with them to develop breakout sessions by discipline and teaching type. |
| The need for teaching fellows from science and engineering disciplines grows, but the laboratory research demands in these disciplines make it difficult for the Center for Teaching to recruit from these fields. | The Center for Teaching creates half-time (academic year) and August-only teaching fellow positions as a more feasible option for science and engineering graduate students. |
| The teaching fellows' time and the Center for Teaching's funds (to pay the fellows) need to be used efficiently. | The Center for Teaching compresses training into the two to three weeks immediately prior to TAO; current fellows are encouraged to use plans of TAO sessions created by fellows in previous years. |
| Departments have many other tasks for graduate students in the days before classes begin; preparation for teaching is often seen as tangential or subservient to coursework and research programs. | The Center for Teaching holds TAO just before classes begin but varies the date/schedule configuration over the years to fit department needs: four half days, two full days, then two six-hour days. |
| Departments and schools want TAs to be made aware of policies and resources related to teaching (e.g., sexual harassment, privacy of student records, honor code, etc.). At the same time, TAs find plenary sessions devoted to these topics unengaging. | To move away from the talking heads approach, the Center for Teaching shifts discussion of policies and resources to breakout sessions. |
| Experienced TAs express an interest in teaching workshops aimed at their level of experience. | Teaching fellows develop concurrent sessions to address needs and interests of both first-time TAs and returning instructors. |

McTighe posit a "backward" approach to course and curricular design, similar to Fink's later "integrated course design" (Fink, 2003). The backward design process begins by identifying desired results, moves next to determining acceptable evidence of the achievement of those results, and concludes with developing plans for concrete learning experiences to enable students to generate evidence of their learning (Wiggins & McTighe, 1998).

To clarify goals in the first stage of backward design, Wiggins and McTighe suggest sorting priorities into three nested categories. We adapted this approach to create the categories for our teaching assistant orientation goals shown in Figure 16.1.

FIGURE 16.1

## Adaptation of Backward Design to Teaching Assistant Orientation Goals

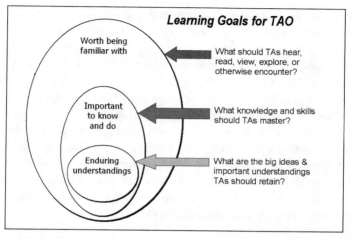

*Note.* Adapted from Wiggins, G., & McTighe, J. (1998). *Understanding by Design.* Alexandria, VA: Association for Supervision and Curriculum Development. Reprinted by permission. The Association for Supervision and Curriculum Development is a worldwide community of educators advocating sound policies and sharing best practices to achieve the success of each learner. To learn more, visit ASCD at www.ascd.org. Copyright laws prevent reproduction of this figure without express permission from the Association for Supervision and Curriculum Development.

This categorization helped us see a significant flaw in TAO's basic design. The orientation had evolved over the years to emphasize details that are "worth being familiar with," what Fink (2003) calls the "list of topics" approach (p. 61). It included sessions on institutional policies, grading, holding office hours, and a host of other relevant topics; however, even the Center for Teaching professional staff could not identify our orientation's "enduring understandings" among the mass of details covered. We realized that the orientation seemed to have no unified intellectual or pedagogical core.

In response to that realization, we used a series of brainstorming discussions to articulate four enduring understandings that would serve as the foundation for a reorganized orientation:

- Teaching, like all scholarly activity, is an evolving process of inquiry, experimentation, and reflection.

- The fundamental purpose of teaching is to promote student learning.

- Understanding how people learn can help one become a more effective teacher.

- Disciplinary differences are significant for both teaching and learning.

To be sure, fragments of these understandings had been present in past versions of our orientation, but none had played a central or shaping role. We wanted to change that in 2004.

As we pondered how we might implement that change, we recalled how the findings in *How People Learn*—a National Research Council publication tracking "the scientific literatures on cognition, learning, development, culture, and brain" (Bransford, Brown, & Cocking, 2000, p. 5)—had transformed our own teaching and educational development practice by providing us important insights into the complexities of the learning process. Thus, we decided to use the *How People Learn* framework as a central conceptual structure to reflect and enact our four enduring understandings for TAO.

The framework, as Figure 16.2 indicates, suggests that effective learning environments comprise four interrelated elements.

FIGURE 16.2

The *How People Learn* Framework

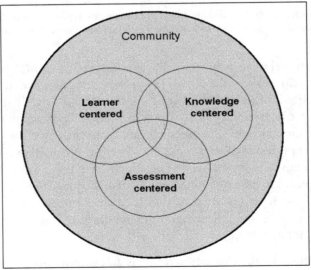

*Note.* Reprinted with permission from Bransford, Brown, and Cocking, *How People Learn: Brain, Mind, Experience, and School* (expanded edition). © 2000 by the National Academy of Sciences, courtesy of the National Academies Press, Washington, DC.

- *Learner centered* environments "pay careful attention to the knowledge, skills, attitudes, and beliefs that learners bring to the educational setting" (Bransford, Brown, & Cocking, 2000, p. 133). In other words, learner centered environments take into account the distinctive characteristics, abilities, and needs of the students who will be learning.

- *Knowledge centered* environments focus on the types of information, activities, and reasoning that help students to develop expertise in a particular discipline. Thus, what it means to be knowledge centered will vary from classroom to classroom depending on the structure and purpose of the discipline being learned.

- *Assessment centered* environments allow frequent opportunities for feedback and revision that directly align with the overall learning goals. Learners need regular opportunities to learn from mistakes and to develop their understanding over time.

- *Community centered* environments are characterized by "norms for people learning from one another and continually attempting to improve" (Bransford, Brown, & Cocking, 2000, p. 144). Learning, in short, is a social activity.

Learning might occur in an environment that has any combination of these characteristics, but the authors of *How People Learn* strongly suggest that deep learning is more likely to occur when these components are in relative balance with one another.

## Implementing the Changes in TAO 2004

For a variety of reasons, including personnel changes at the center and the long planning time required for such a large orientation, we retained the basic two-day structure of our teaching assistant orientation in 2004, even as we revised our core goals. Indeed, in many ways the orientation in 2004 appeared identical to the one held in 2003; we had roughly the same number of participants (243 in 2003, and 232 in 2004). The schedule of plenary, cluster, and concurrent sessions remained essentially the same (see Appendices 16.1 and 16.2). Additionally, participants in 2004 were grouped in discipline clusters identical to those used in 2003 (see Appendix 16.3).

Despite these similarities, we were aiming for a truly transformative change in 2004 by establishing our enduring understandings and the *How People Learn* framework as the foundation for each part of the orientation.

We introduced this framework during the initial plenary of the orientation, and then structured the disciplinary breakout sessions according to three of the four components of that framework: knowledge centered, learner centered, and assessment centered. While the fourth component, community centered, did not have a dedicated cluster session, we underscored this component by weaving it throughout TAO in two important ways: during the plenary we emphasized how new TAs were entering a community of teachers at Vanderbilt, and in every other orientation session our graduate teaching fellows were explicit about building a sense of community within the session that could be carried on after the session ended. Such changes, we hoped, would keep both us and the TAs focused on learning goals, rather than on logistical adaptations.

## Analysis

We went into TAO 2004 expecting a transformed event. However, when we assessed the orientation after the fact, we began to doubt our achievement. While we emphasized our enduring understandings and the *How People Learn* framework in the plenary, we did not consistently see major transformations of the disciplinary breakout sessions. But one teaching fellow who facilitated orientation sessions for the second time in 2004 did note a significant change: "I gave the same grading exercise at TAO in 2003 and 2004, but in 2003 it was more about how to grade fairly whereas this time the emphasis was on how we can grade to increase student learning." Despite this instance of transformation, our observation of TAO sessions indicated that more often than not TAO 2004 disciplinary breakouts simply reordered the material covered in 2003. In Table 16.2, we compare the learning goals of the TAO engineering sessions in 2003 and 2004.

This comparison highlights an all too common trend. While familiarity with the *How People Learn* framework was added to the list of learning goals, further use of the framework was limited mostly to the organization of the content of the sessions. Many sessions still focused more on a "list of topics" "worth being familiar with" than on enduring understanding.

So why did our transformative intentions not manifest themselves more fully and effectively? One factor derives from how we prepared teaching fellows to facilitate orientation sessions. Although the Center for Teaching professional staff planned and implemented the pre-orientation training for our 12 teaching fellows according to the *How People Learn* framework, we encouraged them to use session outlines and handouts from previous orientations.

TABLE 16.2

## Comparison of Learning Goals for Engineering Sessions in 2003 and 2004

| TAO 2003<br>Discipline: Engineering | TAO 2004<br>Discipline: Engineering |
|---|---|
| **Teaching Cluster I**—Getting Started: Expectations and Duties of TAs<br>*Learning Goals*<br>• Get to know other TAs<br>• Duties of TAs in School of Engineering departments<br>• What do students expect from TAs?<br>• What do professors expect from TAs? | **Teaching Cluster I**—Learner Centered Teaching<br>*Learning Goals*<br>• Get to know other TAs<br>• Become familiar with the overall content of the cluster sessions and the *How People Learn* framework<br>• Think about teaching and learning<br>• Who are the Vanderbilt students and why have they chosen Vanderbilt?<br>• Become familiar with Vanderbilt policies governing TA boundaries |
| **Teaching Cluster II**—Teaching at Vanderbilt: Students, Policies, and Resources<br>*Learning Goals*<br>• Become familiar with Vanderbilt policies on the honor code, sexual harassment, and disabilities<br>• Become more familiar with Vanderbilt students | **Teaching Cluster II**—Knowledge Centered Teaching<br>*Learning Goals*<br>• Discuss how the metaphor we relate to in our teaching shapes our perspective of teaching<br>• Discuss the novice to expert continuum<br>• The role of the TA in relation to students and faculty<br>• Discipline-specific teaching challenges:<br>  ~ Problem solving<br>  ~ Running a lab<br>  ~ Office hours |
| **Teaching Cluster III**—Giving Students Feedback, Assessing Student Work, and Grading<br>*Learning Goals*<br>• The importance of giving students feedback on their work<br>• Best practices and rules to establish early in the semester that can help avoid future problems<br>• Grading objectively | **Teaching Cluster III**—Assessment Centered Teaching<br>*Learning Goals*<br>• Introduce classroom assessment techniques and discuss why they are an important tool for teaching<br>• Formative assessment versus summative assessment<br>• Self-reflection on different types of grading<br>• Become familiar with relevant grading policies (e.g., the honor code and the Buckley Amendment)<br>• Discuss best practices for facilitating lab sessions |

Moreover, we failed to provide our teaching fellows with sufficient guidance on how to adapt old materials to the new framework and to the enduring understandings we hoped they and our orientation participants would develop through TAO. Additionally, for some of the pre-orientation training sessions, the professional staff itself relied upon materials from previous years rather than developing workshops based on the *How People Learn* framework. In other words, we gave our teaching fellows neither solid models nor effective scaffolding to adapt existing materials to the new paradigm. This lack of integration and coherence was exacerbated by way the Center for Teaching's professional staff members developed training sessions in isolation from one another; although we agreed on some broad overall goals, we did not make the time to plan or integrate our individual sessions together.

Post-training feedback from teaching fellows reveals the extent to which they noticed the mixed message of the pre-orientation training. While several fellows mentioned the value of using the *How People Learn* framework for the training, at least one noted that there was "too much coverage of material," a phrase that suggests that we as educational developers had failed to act upon the lessons learned from Bransford, Brown, and Cocking (2000), Wiggins and McTighe (1998), and Fink (2003), not to mention our own experience as teachers. Another fellow suggested that the training sessions model the TAO sessions more directly, a sentiment echoed by the fellow who wrote, "I would have liked more examples of how to connect activities to participant learning. Perhaps 'uncover' our own process?" The conclusion is clear: In order to *cover* important concepts such as backward design and enduring understanding, we lost sight of our goal to have our graduate student teaching fellows *discover* how to design an orientation workshop based on learning goals. We presented Wiggins and McTighe's important ideas to our fellows, but did not honor those ideas fully by putting them into practice.

As an overall result, while we conceptualized orientation sessions in 2004 much differently from how we had in the past, the content of and activities in these sessions only sometimes differed in significant ways from those of previous orientations. Additionally, roughly one-third of the orientation was devoted to concurrent sessions conceived outside of the *How People Learn* framework, so experienced TAs had little chance to encounter our enduring understandings or new framework since they did not attend the plenary for the orientation (see Appendix 16.4). Further, we distributed a book to all TAO participants, *From First Day to Final Grade* (Curzan & Damour, 2000), that had no direct connection to the *How People Learn* framework.

While none of these pieces—teaching fellow training, session preparation and delivery, and distributed reading—was deficient or unhelpful to the intended audience, we certainly did not achieve alignment among them or reach our ambitious goals for transforming TAO according to the *How People Learn* framework. Did this have an appreciable impact on the overall effectiveness of the orientation? Probably not, as 78% of those orientation participants returning feedback forms (n = 114) agreed or strongly agreed that they learned about a variety of teaching strategies useful to them as they assume teaching duties in the future. But the impact of the *How People Learn* framework on the effectiveness of the orientation remains doubtful. Only 2% of participants returning evaluation forms mentioned the framework (albeit positively), but many participants expressed a preference for the practical rather than the theoretical aspects of the orientation, the latter of which must necessarily include the *How People Learn* framework.

## Lessons Learned and Next Steps

The changes in our TAO over the past six years reveal several things. First, the event was created, and then altered over time, for very good reasons. But as incremental changes have crept in without our taking a look at the bigger questions of what the overall goals are and whether the structure of the orientation itself can even begin to bear them out, the result has been an event that increasingly seemed to strive to be everything to everyone.

In writing this chapter, we have seen a need to revise how we think about orienting and training TAs and to be even more intentional in how we put that thinking into action. We are actively considering a hybrid model and exploring this possibility with current and past teaching fellows. In this model, we would hold a one-day orientation before the semester begins in order to communicate basic information about teaching (topics "worth being familiar with") and to let new instructors practice through microteaching (thereby practicing what's "important to know"), followed by other sessions several weeks into the semester based in individual departments. It is in these follow-up sessions that we, our fellows, and department instructors would begin to explore the "enduring understandings" of teaching as scholarly practice. In this way, the Center for Teaching would encourage through planning *and* practice a belief that is at the heart of our profession: Teaching is best done as a scholarly venture, in community and with the support of peers and collegial resources. We hope that devoting the time, energy, and resources to buck the trend of the two-day, front-loaded orientation and disaggregating it into an ongoing series of events and programs—as well as using critical reflection on our changes and their results over time—will result in our practicing what we preach.

# References

Bransford, J. D., Brown, A. L., & Cocking, R. R. (Eds.). (2000). *How people learn: Brain, mind, experience, and school* (Expanded ed.). Washington, DC: National Academies Press.

Brookfield, S. D. (1995). *Becoming a critically reflective teacher.* San Francisco, CA: Jossey-Bass.

Curzan, A., & Damour, L. (2000). *First day to final grade: A graduate student's guide to teaching.* Ann Arbor, MI: University of Michigan.

Fink, L. D. (2003). *Creating significant learning experiences: An integrated approach to designing college courses.* San Francisco, CA: Jossey-Bass.

Frantz, A. C., Beebe, S. A., Horvath, V. S., Canales, J., & Swee, D. E. (2005). The roles of teaching and learning centers. In S. Chadwick-Blossey & D. R. Robertson (Eds.), *To improve the academy: Vol. 23. Resources for faculty, instructional, and organizational development* (pp. 72–90). Bolton, MA: Anker.

Schön, D. A. (1983). *The reflective practitioner: How professionals think in action.* New York, NY: Basic Books.

Wiggins, G., & McTighe, J. (1998). *Understanding by design.* Alexandria, VA: Association for Supervision and Curriculum Development.

Appendix 16.1

# 2003 Fall Teaching Assistant Orientation Workshop

**Tuesday, August 19, 2003**

8:30–9:00    Registration and Continental Breakfast

9:00–10:00   Plenary

- Welcome, Director, Center for Teaching
- Welcome, Associate Provost for Undergraduate Education
- Welcome, President of Graduate Student Council
- Center for Teaching Staff and Services
- A Panel of VU Undergrads Talk about Teaching
- F2P2: Future Faculty Preparation Program

10:15–11:30  Teaching Cluster I

Getting Started: Expectations and Duties of TAs

1:00–3:00    Teaching Cluster II

Teaching at Vanderbilt: Students, Policies, and Resources (Buckley Amendment, Honor Code, Sexual Harassment, Evaluations, Campus Resources)

**Wednesday, August 20, 2003**

8:30–9:00    Registration and Continental Breakfast

9:00–10:15   Teaching Cluster III

Giving Students Feedback, Assessing Student Work, and Grading: Grading with Fairness and Consistency, Avoiding Over-Grading and Under-Grading, Managing Grade Complaints

10:30–11:45  Concurrent Sessions I

1:15–2:30    Concurrent Sessions II

2:30–3:00    Social

## Appendix 16.2

# 2004 Fall Teaching Assistant Orientation Workshop

**Tuesday, August 17, 2004**

8:30–9:00      Registration and Continental Breakfast

9:00–10:00     Plenary

- Welcome, Associate Provost for Undergraduate Education
- Overview, Director, Center for Teaching
  - ~ TA Orientation Agenda
  - ~ *How People Learn* Framework
  - ~ Center for Teaching Staff and Services
- F2P2: Future Faculty Preparation Program
- VU Faculty Panel: How and Why Do TAs Matter?

10:15–11:30    Teaching Cluster I: Learner-Centered Teaching

- Who are the Vanderbilt students? What do they want and value most in a TA?
- How do you manage boundaries and authority? With your students? With your faculty?
- Relevant policies concerning sexual harassment, consensual sexual relations, and learning disabilities
- Introduction to relevant resources (e.g., the Opportunity Development Center, the Psychological and Counseling Center, and the Chaplain's Office)

1:00–3:00      Teaching Cluster II: Knowledge-Centered Teaching

- Who are you vis-à-vis your profession?
- Office hours
- Guiding problem solving
- Teaching in the lab setting
- Leading discussions
- Teaching critical thinking skills

**Wednesday, August 18, 2004**

9:00–10:15     Teaching Cluster III: Assessment-Centered Teaching

- How can grading be a form of teaching?
- Criterion-referenced grading
- Time management in grading

- Resources for grading
- Relevant policies and resources for grading, such as the honor code, the Buckley Amendment
- Grading problem sets, lab reports, papers, and essay exams

| | |
|---|---|
| 10:30–11:45 | Concurrent Sessions I |
| 1:15–2:30 | Concurrent Sessions II |
| 2:30–3:00 | Social |

## Appendix 16.3

# Disciplinary Clusters in TAO 2003 and 2004

| Teaching Types | Disciplines |
|---|---|
| Assisting Professors I | Anthropology, Art History, Economics, Psychology, Sociology |
| Assisting Professors II | School of Education, Graduate School of Management |
| Engineering I | Biomedical, Civil/Environmental, Management of Technology |
| Engineering II | Electrical Engineering and Computer Science |
| Engineering III | Chemical Engineering, Material Science, Mechanical Engineering |
| Labs I | Biological Sciences, Physics and Astronomy, Geology, Biomedical Science and Medicine |
| Labs II | Chemistry, Neuroscience |
| Leading Discussions/ | |
| Own Course | Comparative Literature, History, Philosophy, Political Science |
| Leading Discussions | Graduate Department of Religion |
| Own Course | English, Mathematics |
| Own Course | Classical Studies, French/Italian, Germanic/Slavic, Spanish/Portuguese |

## Appendix 16.4

# Concurrent Session Topics in TAO 2003 and TAO 2004

**TAO 2003**
**Concurrent Session Topics**

- Course design and syllabus construction
- Learning styles
- Writing exams and quizzes
- Managing difficult situations in class and office hours
- Time management/balancing workloads
- Technology overview
- Leading effective class discussions
- Daily lesson plans to engage students in lectures and discussions
- Effective lectures
- Engaging students in problem solving in economics, mathematics, engineering and sciences
- Working with students one-on-one in labs, office hours, and review sessions

**TAO 2004**
**Concurrent Session Topics**

- Course design and syllabus construction
- Learning styles and group dynamics in the classroom
- Writing exams and quizzes
- Managing difficult situations in class and office hours
- Time management/balancing workloads
- Establishing your teaching persona
- Engaging students/providing a positive atmosphere in the classroom
- Service-learning
- How to get the most out of your TA experience (geared toward those not excited about teaching)
- Fostering critical thinking
- Psychology of grading
- Differences in the classroom—race, class, gender

# 17

# Exploring the Application of Best Practices to TA Awards: One University's Approach

Laurel Willingham-McLain, Deborah L. Pollack
Duquesne University

*This chapter explores how to adapt best practices from the general literature on teaching awards in higher education to graduate student teaching assistant (TA) awards. Although most criteria apply, they must be fitted to the career stage and aspirations of TAs. The Duquesne University Graduate Student Award for Excellence in Teaching serves as a case study demonstrating how these practices can be modified to both recognize excellent teaching and promote the professional development of graduate student instructors.*

Several articles provide guidelines for faculty teaching awards. According to Menges (1995), for example, for a teaching award to be considered effective, it must pass the three tests of "selection validity," to address accurate selection and representativeness; "faculty motivation," to ensure an increase among the number of faculty striving to meet award criteria; and "public perception," whereby an external audience has noted the institution's dedication to rewarding exemplary teaching.

In their overview article, Svinicki and Menges (1995) put forth 10 guidelines. They propose that the program be aligned with the institution's mission and be based on "sound assessment practices" and "research-based teaching competencies" (p. 110) in order to minimize bias and the common objection that such awards are popularity contests. Svinicki and Menges also advise that the award not replace proper remuneration for teaching, that the winners contribute to faculty development on their campus, and that the program be flexible and open to change.

Carusetta (2001) reports that whereas 70% of two-year and liberal arts colleges and 96% of research institutions have teaching awards, empirical research on the effects of such awards on both the individual and institutional levels is sparse in the literature. Chism and Szabo (1997) provide a list of six areas for studying the impact of teaching awards, including whether the awards actually fulfill their most commonly stated goals of affirming good teachers, rewarding good teachers, improving teaching and learning, and improving the campus climate for both learning and teaching.

Unfortunately, although many institutions have TA awards, the literature on these is thin. Our review of the literature, as well as personal communications with Karron Lewis and Laura Border (December 3 and December 7, 2004), former and current editors of the *Journal of Graduate Teaching Assistant Development,* yielded only one brief article by Langford (1987). Many faculty award practices clearly apply to TA awards, but we conjecture that the goals and impact of TA awards differ sufficiently from typical faculty awards to merit their own study.

First, since most graduate students only teach at their universities for a few years, the institution will not have the long-term benefit of those particular individuals' teaching effectiveness. In fact, by the time they receive a teaching award many TAs have nearly completed their graduate studies. The projected outcome of the award thus shifts from promoting excellence in teaching at the home institution to a focus on supporting the professional development of TAs as they prepare to leave. TA awards might best serve, then, not only to recognize *symbolic* achievement, or a "job well done" (Chism, 2005, p. 320), but also to engage TAs in a *formative* process whereby nominees reflect on their teaching and prepare an evidence-based dossier.

Whereas faculty may decry the extensive effort it takes to develop a solid dossier (Menges, 1995), graduate students with teaching aspirations need to prepare a statement of teaching philosophy, and sometimes a teaching portfolio, for their academic job search. Indeed, the demand is increasing internationally for faculty to provide teaching portfolios for such reasons as applying for entry-level positions, awards, teaching grants, and promotion and tenure (Schonwetter, Sokal, Friesen, & Taylor, 2002). Moreover, even if a candidate is not asked to submit a teaching philosophy, the ability to articulate one's teaching practice is generally expected in the oral interview. Graduate students who are not preparing for academic careers can nonetheless benefit from the process of reflecting on their teaching experiences and learning to implement changes based on feedback.

Some faculty view teaching awards as "low stakes activities" (Chism, 2005, p. 320; Menges, 1995, p. 5), compared to the pressure to achieve more highly coveted honors such as publications and research grants. Whereas many faculty may perceive a teaching award to be a drop in the bucket, the stakes are often much greater for graduate students preparing to enter the competitive academic job market. TAs may be more motivated to prepare the submission hoping that the award will highlight their teaching abilities to prospective employers.

In addition to the formative emphasis we propose for TA awards, attention needs to be paid to establishing appropriate criteria and standards. For example, drawing from Schonwetter et al.'s (2002) "rubric for evaluating Teaching Philosophy Statements," Chism (2005) lists tentative standards for judging teaching effectiveness for faculty, whereby "good/excellent" evidence of participation in the scholarship of teaching and learning would include activities such as a "presentation of teaching work at conferences or workshops," and "exemplary" evidence would include the "above, plus at least one publication on the scholarship of teaching and learning" (p. 323). Although some graduate students achieve this, it should certainly not be expected of them at this career stage. The question then arises as to how to define evidence of excellence in teaching at the graduate student level.

Our investigation of about 20 TA teaching awards via the World Wide Web indicates wide variability in the evidence used to judge effective teaching. For example, although most of these require at least one faculty nomination or recommendation, additional materials include a CV, graduate transcripts, student evaluations, sample syllabi, peer or student evaluations, classroom observation data, an essay about a teaching challenge, a statement of teaching philosophy, and full teaching portfolios. Based on a review of 118 teaching awards in higher education, Chism (2005) suggests that

> the reliance by most awards programs on secondary forms of evidence (such as appraisals by others) rather than primary evidence (such as course materials, teaching philosophy statements, or samples of student work) indicates reluctance on the part of many committees to actually engage the evidence firsthand. (p. 320)

Although Chism includes several TA awards in her analysis (personal communication, December 1, 2004), she does not highlight the differences between TA and faculty awards. Preliminarily, we have found that many TA awards require both primary and secondary forms of evidence.

Finally, although they are not addressed in the literature, we would suggest the following benefits of TA awards. Possible advantages to *nominees* participating in the award process include guided reflection, career preparation, CV enhancement, and practice developing a sound statement of teaching philosophy and presenting teaching materials. Of course, *winners* have additional benefits such as university-wide recognition at a ceremony, letters, certificates, and monetary prizes. The institution profits from having TAs set the standard for their peers about what constitutes good teaching, and from their inspiring less experienced TAs to develop the habit of reflecting on and improving their teaching.

TA award programs should certainly be informed by the guidelines in the general literature on teaching awards in higher education. At the same time, we need to examine the potential uniqueness of their purpose, the level of motivation among nominees, the perceived importance of the award, the types of evidence (primary, secondary, or both), and the criteria and standards best used to judge nominees. In order to illustrate this process, we will discuss how we developed a TA award program at Duquesne University.

## Establishment of the Award

In 2001, we began exploring the possibility of a university-wide teaching award for TAs to recognize the major contribution they make to teaching and learning on our campus. We had been conferring a faculty teaching award for a decade, but TAs were not eligible nor was it fitted to their experiences. Only one school had a TA award, and it was based solely on faculty nomination.

A start-up committee consisting of TAs, faculty members, deans, and Center for Teaching Excellence (CTE) staff met the year prior to implementation. Based on the literature describing effective teaching awards as well as our understanding of the general career stage and aspirations of Duquesne University graduate students, we agreed upon the following statement to describe our Graduate Student Award for Excellence in Teaching:

> The purpose of the award is to promote and reward teaching effectiveness by current graduate students and to provide award nominees with training on how to present evidence of teaching excellence.

Knowing that many of our TAs are planning to pursue academic careers and that they are likely to be hired at teaching-oriented institutions, we chose a two-step process whereby faculty write nominations, and nominees then compile a teaching portfolio as the award dossier.

We chose a significantly more intensive formative component than we had seen at other institutions. Nominations are made in early October, and nominees then have three months to attend CTE sessions on portfolio development, write, reflect, have their courses observed by faculty, and meet with CTE staff for feedback on their portfolios.

We established three award criteria by integrating principles from two research domains: teaching awards and successful practices of junior faculty. Our purpose for the latter was to reward and encourage practices that are reported to enhance the transition to academic careers.

- Mastery of the basics of teaching (preparation, clear communication of course content, effective use of time, availability to students, feedback on learning, and fairness in grading)

- Professional interactions about teaching with faculty and graduate student colleagues

- Ability to reflect on teaching and apply what they learn from feedback

For the first criterion, the committee chose *basic* college teaching and articulated six indicators of mastery at this level. Note that we do not consider these to be sufficient indicators for faculty awards. Our Duquesne faculty Creative Teaching Award focuses, for example, on innovation in teaching supported by evidence of student learning.

The second criterion reflects Boice's (1991) observation that new faculty who thrive regularly interact with their colleagues about teaching. Research on faculty socialization suggests that this important process begins in the graduate school years (Austin & Wulff, 2004), and that interaction among graduate students, their peers, and their professors in a variety of forms—such as seeking and receiving feedback on teaching practices—is crucial to forging a professional identity (Austin, 2002). Unfortunately, research on graduate student development continually points to a lack of systematic interaction and mentoring in most graduate programs (Austin, 2002). Thus, in order to encourage potential award nominees to seek out these types of socialization opportunities, we have provided a list of what these interactions might include. These range from meeting with incoming TAs, mentoring junior peers, and providing departmental TA leadership, to offering campuswide presentations on teaching.

The final criterion recognizes that teaching is a scholarly activity. Good teachers reflect on their teaching and gather feedback from their students, peers, and faculty. They use feedback to discover their underlying assumptions about teaching and learning, think critically about how their practices are aligned with those assumptions, and develop goals for their future development as teachers (Brookfield, 1995). This criterion ensures that nominees engage in that process, thereby further supporting the formative purpose of the award as a professional development activity.

In order to balance the selectivity of the award between being a high honor, and being attainable to a reasonable number of TAs, the start-up committee established a 1:50 ratio of awards to TAs; that is, 4 awards for roughly 200 TAs. Given the vastly different roles TAs play (e.g., from leading science labs to taking sole responsibility for a course), we chose to address the differences in TA training and level of responsibility by designating a specific number of awards per school: two in the humanities and social sciences, one in natural sciences, and one in pharmaceutical sciences. In so doing, we addressed Menges' (1995) test of representativeness, that "recipients fairly represent the variety of fields and instructional situations" (p. 7).

We structured the nomination process such that nominees who complete the teaching portfolio are publicly honored and receive a letter from CTE detailing the significance of their nomination. The start-up committee intentionally constructed a nomination process worthy of a CV line for entry-level faculty candidates. In addition, the four award winners receive $500 and a letter from the provost. All involved receive a book on teaching, often chosen according to their specific interests.

The award is sponsored by the Office of the Provost and administered by CTE. A representative committee of seven TAs and faculty members evaluate the portfolios, recommend the winners, address procedural questions, and conduct ongoing reflection on the award process. The CTE associate director chairs the committee, and the instructional consultant for TAs serves as advisor; neither has a vote.

The award we designed serves both symbolic and formative purposes. To be nominated in the first place, TAs have to have demonstrated excellence in teaching, but to become eligible to win the award, they must also participate in a process of coaching and feedback by disciplinary faculty as well as CTE staff.

## The Award Dossier

The award process begins with a letter of nomination by a faculty member in the TA's department. The nomination form includes contact information, a confirmation of eligibility, an indication of additional recommendations (optional), instructions for the nomination letter itself, and signatures of the chair and dean. Nominators initial a line saying they have provided the nominee with a copy of the nomination and understand that it will be included in the teaching portfolio. The nomination is not confidential. The details of our award can be found at http://www.cte.duq.edu/awards/taawards/guidelines .html.

We request that the nomination address all three criteria (basic teaching, interactions about teaching, and reflection based on feedback) and that it describe the TA's teaching. Simple rankings and superlative statements are not helpful to a committee choosing winners from a pool of excellent TAs. Nomination letters initiate our TA award process and serve as the leading document of the portfolio. Letters that provide thorough description for each criterion help the evaluating committee make better informed decisions; vague or off-topic letters raise questions and pose difficulty in comparing nominees. Chism (2005) notes that "in 74% of the cases calling for letters of nomination or support, the letter writers are not given any instructions about what their letter should address" (p. 317). We have found that committee members carefully examine the nomination letters, and that nominators are more consistently following our guidelines.

The dossier itself consists of both primary and secondary materials. At the committee's request, we revised the original order so that all secondary materials come first in the portfolio. Though not standard procedure for teaching portfolios, this adaptation makes the dossier easier for committee members to evaluate.

The second required element is a faculty member's observation of the TA teaching. We require a standard form that includes items pertaining directly to the indicators of basic-level teaching excellence: evidence of preparation, organization and use of class time, communication of course content, opportunity for student participation and practice, and specific advice for how the TA might improve his or her teaching. Note the integration of formative processes. Nominees are permitted to include peer observations using the same form. The collaborative nature of our award process was underscored recently when two nominees from the same department observed each other and included the reports in their dossiers.

Primary materials form the majority of the portfolio, beginning with the statement of teaching philosophy. This statement serves as an introduction to the instructor's reflections, presentation of teaching materials, and student evaluation summaries. Ideally, the themes nominees choose to highlight reflect both their teaching practices and the feedback students give them. An exemplary portfolio presents a coherent picture of their teaching beliefs, strengths, and areas for development. Though beyond the nominee's control, ideally this coherence extends to the secondary materials as well.

A descriptive list of postsecondary courses taught provides a context for the TA's teaching experience. Finally, a summary of their professional interactions about teaching indicates the degree to which they engage in public discussions of teaching, and take the opportunity to provide and receive feedback.

The evaluation committee consists of TAs and faculty who generally have no experience in evaluating teaching portfolios. So far, in spite of the considerable work required, they have stepped up to the task and appear to appreciate the rich picture that a portfolio can provide. In order to help the committee evaluate the dossiers, we have created evaluation guidelines (retrievable online at http://www.cte.duq.edu/awards/taawards/evaluation.pdf). The first column indicates the three major criteria (including the six indicators of teaching excellence), the second column tells where evidence of these criteria might be found, and the final column provides samples of what these criteria might look like. Committee members systematically discuss the extent to which nominees have met each criterion.

Two final points bear mentioning. Nominees who do not win the award may be renominated. Sometimes their success is a matter of gaining more experience as teachers. Nominees are welcome to request general feedback on the committee's deliberation after the award celebration. This practice is aligned with the formative purpose of the award. Several TAs have made use of this feedback to improve their portfolios, either after being renominated or in preparing for the job search.

## Ongoing Reflection on Our Award Process

The committee serves not only to evaluate dossiers but to reflect on the process and answer questions posed by various stakeholders. The following is a sample of questions we have addressed in the first three years.

- *Is it truly an award if the nominee has to work so hard?* Upon experiencing the process, the questioners generally come to the conclusion that indeed it is an honor to receive such intense mentoring as well as public recognition.

- *How can we be equitable within schools when TAs have differing roles and training across departments, and some programs only have MA degrees? Do English doctoral students have an unfair advantage because they are more experienced writers and also receive systematic mentoring?* We address this through the guidance provided by CTE in that nominees can consult with CTE staff as often as they want. Because of the clarity and thoroughness of her portfolio, an MA student has won even though she competed with more experienced peers.

- *How can we teach nominees to communicate across the university?* For example, one year, committee members were critical of the attempts nominees made to incorporate metaphors into their teaching philosophies. The nominees had innocently followed basic teaching philosophy how-to articles in using metaphors to think about their teaching. Now we guide nominees away from using metaphors that others may find trite.

- *What counts as teaching?* Our guidelines state, "*Teaching* is broadly defined to include traditional independent teaching of a class, online teaching, lab instruction, recitation leadership, and teaching done in pairs of instructors." The nominator must verify that the nominee has met the criterion of having taught two courses with the official status of TA. Beyond that, our nominees have had teaching experience in various contexts, such as the Writing Center.

- *What if a graduate student has never had a TA position but teaches as adjunct faculty for our department?* In this case, we determined that the person was not eligible because we wanted to maintain the focus on graduate students as teachers and risked opening up the process to all adjunct faculty.

- *Given the high stakes of being a nominee, what happens if a nominee does not complete a full teaching portfolio according to the award guidelines?* In one case, the nominee did not do the most basic work required and was informed behind the scenes that he would not be considered an official nominee.

- *What happens when none of the nominees from a particular school provide indication of excellence in all three criteria in their portfolio?* The committee chose to maintain high standards and, with the provost's approval, to withhold the $500 award from the school that year and instead to honor the TAs only as official nominees. This was a difficult decision because the incompleteness of the dossiers is not completely the fault of individual TAs but can reflect on gaps in their school's mentoring of TAs.

## Initial Evaluation of the Award's Impact

We plan to examine the impact of our award on winners, nominees, committee members, departments, and the institution. We have begun by asking all those involved each year to comment on the value of the award process and to provide suggestions for improving it. In this, the third year, we already see signs of the award's impact.

Awardees and nominees have provided this feedback: They appreciate having three months, including the semester break, to work on the dossier with checkpoints along the way. They are grateful for the mentoring and the opportunity to think about teaching, and are greatly relieved to have begun compiling materials for the job search in advance. One nominee requested that there be more interaction among nominees beyond the introductory meeting because there was too little time to look at each others' work at the ceremony. Another recommended showcasing the portfolios in a library display with excerpts on handouts for people to take and read.

All involved enjoyed the public recognition at the award ceremony and reception. We haven't yet contacted the awardees and nominees once they have left Duquesne, but one reported having successfully used the portfolio to get a position at a well-regarded state university.

Nominees are giving back to the university by providing leadership to their peers in their departments, through CTE, and through the award committee. Award committee members appreciate discussing teaching across disciplines and learning from each others' practices. Also, graduate students have the unique opportunity of serving on a university-wide committee reporting to the provost.

Nominees and committee members alike have returned to their programs requesting increased mentoring, distribution of responsibilities, and systematic feedback from students and faculty on their teaching. This is a slow process but one that can have a dramatic impact on both TAs and the students they teach. The award has also influenced other award programs in the university. For example, one department has required the submission of a teaching portfolio for their TA award, a requirement which was modeled after our university-wide award.

At the institutional level, graduate students are honored for their teaching excellence at the same ceremony as the faculty and receive the same amount of money as a prize. This ceremony is well attended, and we intend to give the message that TAs contribute in significant ways to teaching and learning at Duquesne and that they conduct their teaching and reflection on it in scholarly ways.

## Conclusion

We are fortunate to have had literature on effective teaching awards at our disposal in establishing the Graduate Student Award for Excellence in Teaching at Duquesne University. In the process, however, we have recognized that not all faculty award criteria are appropriate to graduate students. We have thus explored ways in which these criteria might best be adapted to TA awards. Though far from flawless, our TA award serves as an example of one way best practices can be applied both to honor excellent basic-level teaching and to guide graduate students as they seek to enter the professoriate. We are currently planning research that will assess the impact of our TA services overall. In particular, those TAs who have been involved in the award process as nominees, winners, or committee members will be contacted and interviewed about how their involvement with the award has fostered their professional development at Duquesne and beyond.

## Note

We thank Academic Associate Vice President Dorothy Frayer and Provost Ralph Pearson for supporting our TA award, and Steven H. Wells and Fr. David Sedor for their role in its early research and development.

## References

Austin, A. E. (2002). *Assessing doctoral students' progress along developmental dimensions.* Paper presented at the annual meeting of the Association for the Study of Higher Education, Sacramento, CA. Retrieved May 22, 2005, from http://www.carnegiefoundation.org/CID/ashe/Assessing_doctoral_students.pdf

Austin, A. E., & Wulff, D. H. (2004). The challenge to prepare the next generation of faculty. In D. H. Wulff, A. E. Austin, & Associates, *Paths to the professoriate: Strategies for enriching the preparation of future faculty* (pp. 3–16). San Francisco, CA: Jossey-Bass.

Boice, R. (1991). Quick starters: New faculty who succeed. In M. Theall & J. Franklin (Eds.), *New directions for teaching and learning: No. 48. Effective practices for improving teaching* (pp. 111–121). San Francisco, CA: Jossey-Bass.

Brookfield, S. D. (1995). *Becoming a critically reflective teacher.* San Francisco, CA: Jossey-Bass.

Carusetta, E. (2001). Evaluating teaching through teaching awards. In C. Knapper & P. Cranton (Eds.), *New directions in teaching and learning: No. 88. Fresh approaches to the evaluation of teaching* (pp. 31–40). San Francisco, CA: Jossey-Bass.

Chism, N. V. N. (2005). Promoting a sound process for teaching awards programs: Appropriate work for faculty development centers. In S. Chadwick-Blossey & D. R. Robertson (Eds.), *To improve the academy: Vol. 23. Resources for faculty, instructional, and organizational development* (pp. 314–330). Bolton, MA: Anker.

Chism, N. V. N., & Szabo, B. L. (1997). Teaching awards: The problem of assessing their impact. In D. DeZure & M. Kaplan (Eds.), *To improve the academy: Vol. 16. Resources for faculty, instructional, and organizational development* (pp. 181–200). Stillwater, OK: New Forums Press.

Langford, T. A. (1987). Recognizing outstanding teaching. In N. V. N. Chism (Ed.), *Institutional responsibilities and responses in the employment and education of teaching assistants: Readings from a national conference* (pp. 132–133). Columbus, OH: The Ohio State University, Center for Teaching Excellence.

Menges, R. J. (1995). Awards to individuals. In M. D. Svinicki & R. J. Menges (Eds.), *New directions in teaching and learning: No. 65. Honoring exemplary teaching* (pp. 3–9). San Francisco, CA: Jossey-Bass.

Schonwetter, D. J., Sokal, L., Friesen, M., & Taylor, K. L. (2002). Teaching philosophies reconsidered: A conceptual model for the development and evaluation of teaching philosophy statements. *International Journal for Academic Development, 7*(1), 83–97.

Svinicki, M. D., & Menges, R. J. (1995). Consistency within diversity: Guidelines for programs to honor exemplary teaching. In M. D. Svinicki & R. J. Menges (Eds.), *New directions in teaching and learning: No. 65. Honoring exemplary teaching* (pp. 109–113). San Francisco, CA: Jossey-Bass.

# 18

# Expeditionary Learning: A Low-Risk, Low-Cost, High-Impact Professional Development Model

Chris Carlson-Dakes, Alice Pawley
University of Wisconsin-Madison

*We describe a low-risk, low-cost, high-impact professional development program to help faculty, instructional staff, postdoctoral fellows, and graduate students create space in their lives to explore the diversity of their campus community and reflect on beliefs about teaching and learning in higher education. Along with small group discussions, participants have "expeditions" onto campus to explore learning situations and academic life in ways that they have never before experienced. We describe our theoretical model, programmatic and evaluation structure, and some participants' insights into why they participated and what they learned from our first implementation.*

## Introduction

"This program has helped me realize that learning encompasses the mind, body, and the soul. We do a great job of nurturing and developing our students' minds, but how do we nurture their body and soul?" This question was posed by "Greg" after he participated in a semester of expeditionary learning. Expeditionary learning is a small group-based professional development program designed to expose participants to diverse campus resources and approaches to teaching and learning, housed in the University of Wisconsin–Madison's Delta Program for Research, Teaching, and Learning. Greg attributes his insights into this question to his participation in expeditionary learning because, despite his incredibly busy and regimented schedule, this was an opportunity to "treat himself" and permit himself time to open up to new ways of thinking about his teaching and undergraduate learning. Based on his experiences in the program, he proposed to his department's undergraduate curriculum committee including at least a one-credit requirement for undergraduate students to take a course outside the engineering curriculum to nurture more than their "engineering mind," by considering students as whole beings, incorporating care for their intellectual, physical, and emotional growth.

This chapter presents a low-risk, low-cost, high-impact professional development program designed to create opportunities for people like Greg to feel inspired and energized and to bring to life their new insights. The program helps people create a space to reflect on their personal choices of how to balance institutional pressures with a personal need to feel energized about their work. We have been intentional in our efforts to develop a program that requires minimal staff preparation and resources to provide low-risk opportunities to embrace the existing diverse community in a way that has potential for significant impact on individuals and institutions. Small group (seven to nine people) meetings are held once every two weeks for one and one-half hours and require only one facilitator and little preparation. During the off weeks between group meetings, participants venture out on "expeditions" onto our campus to explore learning situations and academic life in ways they have never before experienced.

This chapter describes our underlying model of professional development and details how we have brought it to life through the expeditionary learning program. Accompanying our programmatic structure and experiences as facilitators, we share participants' insights into why they participated, what they learned from the experience, and the impact the experience had on them.

## A Model for Professional Development

The expeditionary learning (EL) program can exist as a stand-alone program or as part of a suite of program offerings. Compared to other models of professional development programs that require large start-up efforts or existing infrastructure, EL is relatively easy to adapt and implement on its own. It can also be easily adjusted to fit within many existing and diverse programmatic structures currently in place on different campuses.

We are fortunate to have it as one part of the core of a group of professional development programs, courses, internships, and other activities known as The Delta Program for Research, Teaching, and Learning (see http://www.delta.wisc.edu), itself part of the National Science Foundation-funded Center for the Integration of Research, Teaching, and Learning. The full spectrum of Delta offerings is designed to provide access to professional development for the widely diverse needs, interests, and levels of commitment for all interested in advancing the teaching and learning culture of science, technology, engineering, and mathematics (STEM) fields. We approach this broad mission by advocating the integration of three key concepts: teaching-as-research, learning community, and diversity.

Our focus on all STEM disciplines is central to our mission, but the EL program can easily be adjusted for a single department or expanded beyond the boundaries of STEM. Similarly, the three concepts of teaching-as-research, learning community, and diversity that form the foundation for our program can be adapted to the cultural and institutional priorities of other institutions. To give context to how we have fit within our cultural and institutional priorities, and to help explain how we have integrated the three concepts into our implementation of the program, each concept is described below. They are presented as independent theoretical concepts, but in practice they are very connected.

## Teaching-as-Research

Teaching-as-research is based heavily in our university culture of research and directly stems from the growing professional development emphasis on the scholarship of teaching (Boyer, 1990). One of our main purposes in Delta is to encourage current and future teachers, consisting of faculty, instructional staff, postdoctoral fellows, and graduate students, to consider teaching as a process of inquiry. This follows a model that builds on their strengths as researchers in the context of teaching and emphasizes the need for teachers to follow four primary steps (see Figure 18.1):

1) Develop and clearly articulate the goals for student learning

2) Plan and implement teaching strategies that help their students meet these goals

3) Design evaluative materials to assess whether students have met these goals

4) Close the loop by revising their teaching based on the information gathered in these evaluations

FIGURE 18.1

Teaching-as-Research Model

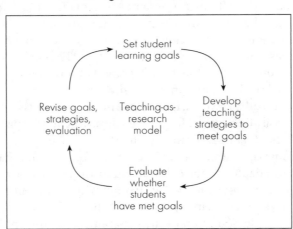

Integrating the teaching-as-research process into the expeditionary learning program builds on the strengths of scientists and engineers as researchers and inquisitive problem solvers, and provides them with a structure and supportive environment to engage these familiar research-based processes in a new environment—that of their teaching.

## Learning Community

Expeditionary learning also incorporates principles of learning community development throughout its design. Our campus has a strong history of undergraduate residential learning communities (e.g., Allen, 1999; Altschuler & Kramnick, 1999; Brower & Laines, 1997; Mattmiller, 1996; Meikeljohn, 1928) that we have built upon through the Delta Program. In particular, we focus on principles of encouraging shared discovery and learning and developing meaningful connections between all participants (graduate students through faculty). Building on these principles as fundamental to the process of learning community development, three structural elements are also critical—the academic, social, and physical space (Brower & Dettinger, 1998). For the expeditionary learning groups, teaching-as-research serves as the academic "content" element, with frequent small group social interactions within a physical setting of the common areas of the Science House, our physical home on campus.

## Diversity

Representatives from higher education and industry have strongly empha-sized the importance of skills related to working in complex and diverse set-tings (see Durand, 2004; Koehler & Miranda, 2004). Faculty and staff play a vital role in preparing students for work and as a safety net for mentoring during a critical time in students' lives. As such, we must be able to teach and model the skills we hope to embody in our students. An often-debated issue in higher education is the question of how to facilitate the development of respect for diverse communities so that we can connect across differences, not be divided by them. We believe one way is to have faculty and staff who are confident in their ability to respond to diverse needs and who model respect, tolerance, equity, and inclusiveness in teaching.

As a large Research-1 university, our campus environment is filled with possibilities for exploring diversity—multiple ways of teaching and learning as well as diverse teachers and learners. But for a variety of reasons, despite the abundance of opportunities, many people working within the university community rarely take advantage of these opportunities. Expeditionary learning is specifically designed to encourage more people to experience and participate in the multiplicity of discussions and learning activities already happening on our campus in order to broaden our collective understandings about each other as colleagues and as people.

Furthermore, our campus community consists of people in multiple roles and career stages. To create inclusive and broad learning experiences, expeditionary learning intentionally brings together graduate students, post-doctoral fellows, instructional staff, and faculty to form program groups, pro-viding everyone with the opportunity to learn from and with each other. The cross-generational nature of this program is just one dimension of diversity that has been structurally integrated into participants' experience.

As part of the larger Delta Program, we explicitly connect expeditionary learning with other related programs, courses, and activities and ensure that participants from diverse backgrounds and experiences feel included. Through our emphasis on learning community principles, we hope that par-ticipants will be inspired to change the isolating and product-oriented char-acter of higher education often found in science and engineering classrooms, particularly at research institutions. We use teaching-as-research, learning community, and diversity together to form the backbone for organizing edu-cational reform in STEM fields. The expeditionary learning program is just one example of how people can creatively build on existing resources to pro-vide a relatively low-cost way to have a significant impact on the teaching and learning culture. We hope that this proves useful for aiding other innovations on other campuses.

## Organization of Expeditionary Learning

The expeditionary learning program stems from the Expeditionary Learning Outward Bound program for K–12 education (Cousins, 1998, 2000) and was modified to be applicable in a higher education setting. We have additionally grounded our program in experiential adult learning theory by emphasizing critical reflection throughout the experience (Apple, 1996; Cunningham, 2000; Henry, 1989; Kolb, 1984; Wilson & Hayes, 2000). The programmatic structure encourages participants to develop new questions about teaching and learning, create methods to explore them, and feel supported by their group in their journey to discover new answers.

### Program Logistics and Structure

Our experience with this and other similar programs shows that community is fostered by forming groups of seven to nine people (including graduate students, postdoctoral fellows, instructional staff, and faculty) that meet semimonthly for one and one-half hour discussions for an academic semester (see Appendix 18.1 for semester schedule). Once every two weeks, individuals, pairs, or groups of participants take a campus expedition to experience a learning activity or environment that would help to stretch their understanding of diverse approaches to learning and teaching. These experiences help participants raise new questions for themselves to discuss with the group the following week. In the weeks between the expeditions, the groups meet to engage in a facilitated discussion of what they experienced the previous week, what they learned, what new questions emerged, and the implications those questions may have on their teaching. Following a talking circle model for group discussion (e.g., Running Wolf & Rickard, 2003), individuals are given an opportunity to share the stories of their expedition *before* the group engages in open discussion of the expeditions. Occasionally, the discussions are supplemented by a short reading.

During the meetings, participants developed and refined ideas for future expeditions based on new insights, questions, and issues that were raised. The influence of the learning community principles of shared discovery and meaningful connections on the experience of participants was evident to us as they discussed their future plans in a public forum with the group. The act of describing their plans in public strengthened participants' commitment to actually do their expedition because members in the group now counted on the others to report back on their experiences and formed their own plans around those of others.

## Recruitment, Participation, and Level of Involvement

Participation is voluntary with no extrinsic rewards. The minimum expectations for participation are to attend and actively participate in all seven group meetings and go on all four expeditions (average of approximately one and one-half hours per week for the entire semester). Recruitment took place through mass emails, personal invitations from the facilitators to those who had expressed past interest, and recommendations from other Delta staff and participants. For the fall 2003 semester, we had two teams of eight participants each (eight graduate students, three postdoctoral fellows, and five faculty). One team had a single facilitator; the other had two co-facilitators.

Based on external circumstances and individual levels of commitment, people took on their own level of engagement with the program. Many attended most meetings; a few missed an expedition. Some representative expeditions from fall 2003 include:

- Visiting a library or campus museum participants had never visited to observe the physical surroundings, glance through research journals from a different discipline, and experience a different environment for learning

- Visiting a resource center for helping students of different abilities

- Interviewing someone in a different professional role about his or her job and position in the university

- Attending a seminar on an unfamiliar topic or from another department

- Visiting and observing the dynamics in a building that houses disciplines different from the participants' own

- Visiting and observing undergraduate hangouts on campus, such as downtown bars or the student union

## Framing Questions to Close the Loop

We modeled the teaching-as-research process for the program the way we hope participants will do for their courses. This process served as the basis of research for this chapter and centered on the following research questions:

- Do participants leave the program "changed" in some lasting way? If so, in what way? If not, why not?

- What aspects of the program were most important to participants' personal experiences?

- In what ways can we improve the program implementation for the next iteration? (For this, we need to know why individuals initially decided to participate, and why they continued their participation throughout the semester.)

## Data Collection

The data collection was largely formative, qualitative, and ongoing (to promote continuous improvement in the program). In addition to weekly facilitation and meeting notes, we conducted formal mid-semester, open-ended written evaluations and end-of-program surveys. The semester following the program completion, we invited all participants to be interviewed to delve deeper into the core issues that emerged from the written evaluations. Eight of 16 participants agreed to 30-minute tape-recorded interviews. We found that these interviews provided the richest, most in-depth data about participants' experiences and changes and serve as the core of the data analysis that follows.

## Data Analysis

We used thematic analysis and pattern formation to analyze the data (Barley, 1990; Glesne & Peshkin, 1992; Robson, 2002). The participants' written feedback, our interview field notes, and weekly facilitator meeting notes led us to the broad categorical themes of:

- Programmatic elements that attracted people to participate

- Reasons people continued their participation

- What participants gained from their experience

Within these three themes that served as a categorical framework, we placed specific comments and observations identifying a subset of common response themes. As with any qualitative study, unexpected themes emerged (e.g., disadvantages of participation and a desire to participate in the program again). The unexpected themes along with the thematic clusters that formed around the central questions were used to construct an outline for the ideas and responses reported next.

## Results

Presented here are the lessons learned about the main themes: programmatic elements that attracted people to participate, reasons people continued their participation, and what they gained from their experience. The first two themes are closely linked and are reported together.

### Programmatic Elements That Attracted People to Participate *and* Reasons People Continued Their Participation

We expected that people would want to participate in EL because the core purpose of the program was to help people feel connected with others interested in teaching and learning, and they wanted to learn about diverse teaching and learning resources and approaches already available on our campus. These reasons did come up frequently in participants' responses, but we did not expect participants to highlight the faculty connection as strongly as they did. Faculty participants indicated their desire to meet other faculty interested in teaching and learning, and several graduate students and postdoctoral fellows said they wanted to hear about the career experiences of the faculty members in their groups.

A common reason identified by participants for initial interest was that the time commitment was not excessive. It is our experience with programs that require similar time commitment that 25%–30% of the people who initially sign up eventually drop out because of schedule conflicts and other priorities. We hypothesized that participants would continue to attend EL meetings if they found the content of the discussions interesting and the expeditions as worthy of their time as other priorities. The importance of the ease and impact of the first expedition was evident as it helped to build commitment to continue with the program. A common reason for continuation was that it was easy to participate, with minimal time commitment and effort for the amount they gained. The semimonthly meetings were frequent enough to develop some group cohesion but not so frequent that attending was a burden. The two weeks between meetings gave participants flexibility to choose an expedition and carry it out within their own schedule constraints.

Several participants said that once they had initially committed to attending EL sessions, the program's structure helped them make time to think about their teaching practices. This activity was something they obviously valued, but without the commitment to the program, even before they knew much about it, they would not have allowed themselves the luxury of this reflection. One senior faculty member noted,

- "I had this assignment, and I had this structure, and I went out and did [the expedition]. And I had to make time to do this. If I wouldn't have had the structure of this program, I wouldn't have made the time. I would have been totally busy with other things and wouldn't have thought to do this. But, given that this is a structure, and it was like treating myself to get out and play with this, that was an enjoyable thing to experiment with."

We were surprised to note that among the personal reasons people gave for continuing, a strong theme of commitment to the group, and a feeling of obligation and accountability to the other participants emerged as the primary reasons for following through with their plans and coming prepared each week. Although it is entirely feasible for individuals to take the initiative to spontaneously pop into libraries they have never visited, attend a seminar from another discipline, or to read articles on teaching and learning, participants said that doing this would have been very uncharacteristic if left to themselves to do it. It was the group setting and sense of accountability they had for the group that propelled them to act in this otherwise unnatural way. Some said it was the sense that they would be letting the group down if they failed to go on their chosen expedition. In reference to the strength of the community, one graduate student participant said that once the program was over, she didn't feel like doing her own expeditions because there was "no one to share it with."

An additional reason people participated was because of reputation and previous positive experiences in other teaching and learning programs led by the facilitators. They noted that the formality of a program run by people whose job it is to structure these sorts of activities gave it credibility and that knowledgeable facilitators opened doors and access to resources the participants didn't even know existed. The presence of knowledgeable facilitators was another reason to continue: they felt as if they could not have made the initial discovery of campus resources on their own, or if they could, they were not able or not qualified to find "good" resources. There was also a feeling that the formally structured program gave participants "programmatic permission" to do things they otherwise would not do. One participant spoke about her reliance on the facilitators and the structure of the program to filter resources to explore:

- "[The expeditions are things] people could do, but they most certainly wouldn't do it . . . they wouldn't be aware of it. You guys go out there and you . . . steer people toward it. [You] have the discussion afterward where people come back and they can say what they thought was really interesting and how they're going to relate it to their own thing. I think that's the extra you get from having a program [to structure these activities]."

Expeditionary learning was also seen as a "fun break" in a relaxed atmosphere different from the working environment of the participants' offices, departments, or labs. Participants talked about finding a sense of adventure and of doing something new: "I'm always looking for something new," "I get to go on expeditions," and "It's an opportunity to treat myself." Again, these opportunities could have been self-generated, but participants pointed to the value of having a group who is counting on them to show up. This constructive peer pressure prompted people to actually take these much-needed breaks that occupational stress research shows are necessary for sustained and more productive work (Salvendy, 1997).

## What They Gained From Their Experience

We expected participants to gain information about the existence of various diverse campus resources, as well as feel as if they were part of a community of people who cared about teaching and learning. Our participants reported that they did personally gain in these two areas, but they were just two among many additional gains. They also pointed to the connections they made with faculty, and others found inspiration to apply to their classrooms the things they had learned from their expeditions and group discussions. Still others shared that they felt they had grown in self-awareness regarding their interest in teaching. One participant wrote in her end-of-semester evaluation,

- "This group has made me seriously reevaluate my job prospects and now teaching is very high on the list whereas before I merely saw it as a backup when other possibilities were exhausted."

Most participants said they had gained an increased awareness and interest in teaching and in different possibilities for reconceptualizing their approaches. Their experiences helped them think about their practice in new and different ways. For example, from something as simple as visiting a library on campus they had never visited before or exploring an unfamiliar part of campus, participants generated many new questions for themselves and their colleagues during group discussions. Some of these included:

- How can I bring art and creativity back into engineering design? (from visiting the art museum)

- What are students' thoughts and feelings of their ethical and social responsibility in education once they leave college? (from walking through the law building)

- The way I've conceptualized education is in conflict with how education works. How can I bridge the gap of this paradox? (from seeing similar challenges in other disciplines)

- What is the environmental impact of the science we do? (from looking differently at the physical environment of the campus)

- What are humanities and social science student perceptions of the sciences in their lives? (from visiting the humanities building)

- How can we nurture the body and spirit as well as we nurture the mind? (from talking with a kinesiology professor)

- How do we learn the different "languages" that other sciences use? (from walking the halls where foreign languages are taught)

- How do introductory science classes influence what undergraduate students think a given field is about? (from sitting in an introductory astronomy course taught by a colleague)

The power of the questions, coming from common program experiences and discussed within a supportive group, catalyzed many participants to move to action on their newfound awareness. In one such discussion, the question was raised of how to get students actively involved in class by having them ask questions. A graduate student participant reflected on how her expeditionary learning group explicitly brought to light a challenge she experienced with student involvement in the course. She knew she was having a problem in her class getting students to be more interactive, but she was not able to put her finger on the real issue. "I have [felt the tension] in class, but I didn't notice [why] until it was pointed out in a[n] [expeditionary learning] meeting and [I saw then that] it's true." With the help of the group, she was able to translate her challenges in the classroom into a new insight of power dynamics in the classroom. She had explicitly recognized and named the problem in such a way that she felt better suited to address the issue in class.

## Future Program Changes: Modeling Teaching-as-Research

The teaching-as-research model emphasizes the need for practitioners to close the loop by revising their teaching based on the information gathered in their formative evaluations. We would be remiss if we didn't model it ourselves with what we have learned about the first run of expeditionary learning. Based on written feedback at the end of the semester, our interviews, and facilitator observations, we have learned many ways to improve the program in future years. Two primary areas of change will be emphasized: more time for discussion and more formalized and defined expeditions.

Discussion time was limited, particularly in one group, because of large group size and scheduling conflicts that dictated a shorter meeting time. The structure for group sharing provided time up-front for each individual to share the story of his or her experience *before* open discussion allowed all to share, but limited time for deeper discussion as a group. There was scarcely enough time to share the basics of each person's expedition before it was time to think about the next expedition. Experience with other similar programs has shown it is not practical to extend meetings beyond one and one-half hours. Instead of lengthening the meetings, we will keep groups smaller in the next iteration (maximum of seven people), and evaluate the timing of storytelling and discussion.

The amount of guidance the facilitators provided the participants intentionally decreased over the course of the semester. We moved from very well-defined expeditions (e.g., visit a library or a museum), to very open-ended assignments (e.g., develop a question of interest about undergraduate learning and go on an expedition to learn more about it). The purpose of this progression was to gradually build group ownership of the program so it was self-directed rather than expert-driven. The feedback we received in both the end-of-semester evaluations and the interviews overwhelmingly indicated that participants wanted more direction and concrete guidance throughout the semester's expeditions. Several reasons participants gave for wanting more direction were ease of participation, an increased chance for "points of intersection" between participants' similar expeditions to facilitate discussions, and the lack of knowledge about what possibilities existed on campus that answered the questions they had developed for themselves.

## Conclusions: Low Risk, Low Resource Needs, but Potential for High Impact

We found the time commitment for facilitators and participants seemed reasonable for those who are truly committed to the teaching mission of their work. The number of people to staff the program and the level of experience for facilitators are minimal compared to many other programs that require either more facilitators or a much higher level of experience and expertise in content knowledge. Because the program builds on existing campus resources, expeditionary learning has no financial cost other than a facilitator's time (roughly two to three hours per week). It is already apparent that a few participants are interested in volunteering their time to facilitate future groups as the program grows. Because of the low resource needs and time commitment, the risk to adopt the program on a trial basis is minimal for both the institution and the individuals who participate.

We do not yet know about the lasting impact of this program on participants. However, it seems that certainly some participants were strongly affected by the insights they gained through their participation. As part of our ongoing learning community development of the broader Delta Program in Research, Teaching, and Learning, we are connecting expeditionary learning to other opportunities to support participants who have acted on their insights, such as Greg, the faculty participant in the chapter's opening story. One of the biggest impacts of the expeditionary learning program may be the future connections that isolated teachers make with each other as they come together to form a diverse community of learners directed toward education reform in science, engineering, and mathematics disciplines.

## Future Work and New Questions

A crucial component of teaching-as-research and ongoing program evaluation is developing new questions for continued inquiry and methods to learn more. Among many other very specific logistical issues we will continue to track, some larger-scale questions we will explore next year include:

- What is the effect of the size of the group on the participants' experience?

- What is the effect of different mixes of participants in the groups (i.e., numbers of faculty, postdoctoral fellows, instructional staff, and graduate students)?

- How is the expeditionary learning experience different for those with teaching experience and those without?

- How is the expeditionary learning experience different for those who are concurrently teaching and participating in the program and those who are not currently teaching?

- How much should the program be participant-driven and how much should be facilitator-driven?

- How can we sustain the program over time (recruitment of participants and facilitators)? How can we help participants sustain the changes they make to their own practice, and to the changes they initiate in their home departments?

These questions will help to guide our ongoing inquiry into the logistics, theory, and implementation of the program. They can guide us on our ongoing expedition and to model for others the process of remaining open to the surprises of this endeavor. A postdoctoral fellow participant commented on the surprises of the program and summed up many of the programmatic themes when she responded to the question "What would you tell someone else about your experience with this program?"

- "It is surprising because you wouldn't necessarily know what you would gain, but you would gain different perspectives that you could apply to your career. [It could help you] if you were interested in teaching, or different ways to look at your research, even different ways to look at yourself. Everyone in the biological sciences goes to lab, does experiments, and does lots of wet bench work. [But] there's a lot of other people on this campus who have a completely different day. [Expeditionary learning] is like a little community of people who are trying to come up with more effective and maybe different, or maybe the same, but effective ways of being teachers and learning about the U[niversity]. If [someone is] interested in teaching, they would gain because of the additional perspectives, but even if they weren't, I think it would be fun."

We close this chapter with a quote from Rachel Naomi Remen, a noted physician who has worked extensively with medical students and practicing physicians to develop comfort with the unexplainable mysteries and surprises of life. She said, "How many people can say 'I don't know' with a sense of adventure rather than a sense of inadequacy?" (Personal communication, September 24, 2003). It is common for self-reflective teachers to have strong feelings of inadequacy without a forum to say safely "I don't know." Expeditionary learning exists for many reasons, not least of which is to encourage, support, and nurture teachers in their journey into the mysteries and surprises of inquiring about learning and teaching.

## Note

This material is based upon work supported by the National Science Foundation under Grant No. 0227592.

## References

Allen, C. (1999). Wiser women: Fostering undergraduate success in science and engineering with a residential academic program. *Journal of Women and Minorities in Science and Engineering, 5*(3), 265–277.

Altschuler, G. C., & Kramnick, I. (1999, November 5). A better idea has replaced 'in loco parentis'. *Chronicle of Higher Education*, p. B8.

Apple, M. (1996). Power, meaning, and identity: Critical sociology of education in the United States. *British Journal of Sociology of Education, 17*(2), 125–144.

Barley, S. R. (1990). Images of imaging: Notes on doing longitudinal fieldwork. *Organization Science, 1*(3), 220–247.

Boyer, E. L. (1990). *Scholarship reconsidered: Priorities of the professoriate*. Princeton, NJ: Carnegie Foundation for the Advancement of Teaching.

Brower, A. M., & Dettinger, K. M. (1998, November/December). What is a learning community? Toward a comprehensive model. *About Campus*, 15–21.

Brower, A. M., & Laines, M. J. (1997). What works and how we found out: An assessment of the Bradley Learning Community. *Talking Stick, 14*(7), 17–19.

Cousins, E. (1998). *Reflections on design principles*. Dubuque, IA: Kendall/Hunt.

Cousins, E. (Ed.). (2000). *Roots: From outward bound to expeditionary learning*. Dubuque, IA: Kendall/Hunt.

Cunningham, P. M. (2000). A sociology of adult education. In A. L. Wilson & E. R. Hayes (Eds.), *Handbook of adult and continuing education* (pp. 573–591). San Francisco, CA: Jossey-Bass.

Durand, B. (2004, April 11). Diversity plans are in effect. *Wisconsin State Journal*, p. B1.

Glesne, C., & Peshkin, A. (1992). *Becoming qualitative researchers: An introduction*. New York, NY: Longman.

Henry, J. (1989). Meaning and practice in experiential learning. In S. W. Weil & I. McGill (Eds.), *Making sense of experiential learning: Diversity in theory and practice* (pp. 29–33). Buckingham, England: Society for Research into Higher Education and Open University Press.

Koehler, T., & Miranda, C. (2004, April 11). Are today's UW–Madison graduates cultural klutzes? *Wisconsin State Journal*, p. B1.

Kolb, D. A. (1984). *Experiential learning: Experience as the source of learning and development.* Englewood Cliffs, NJ: Prentice Hall.

Mattmiller, B. (1996). A new notion of home. *On Wisconsin*, 20–39.

Meikeljohn, A. (1928). *The experimental college.* Madison, WI: University of Wisconsin Press.

Robson, C. (2002). *Real world research: A resource for social scientists and practitioner-researchers* (2nd ed.). Oxford, England: Blackwell.

Running Wolf, P., & Rickard, J. A. (2003). Talking circles: A Native American approach to experiential learning. *Journal of Multicultural Counseling and Development, 31,* 39–43.

Salvendy, G. (Ed.). (1997). *Handbook of human factors and ergonomics.* New York, NY: John Wiley & Sons.

Wilson, A. L., & Hayes, E. R. (2000). On thought and action in adult and continuing education. In A. L. Wilson & E. R. Hayes (Eds.), *Handbook of adult and continuing education* (pp. 15–32). San Francisco, CA: Jossey-Bass.

## Appendix 18.1

# Expeditionary Learning Fall 2003 Semester Schedule

| Week of | Preparation Outside of Meeting | Activity During Meeting |
|---|---|---|
| Sept. 22 | None | *Small group meeting:* introductions, program overview, community agreements, distribute introductory reading |
| Sept. 29 | Read article "Through the Lens of Learning: How Experiencing Learning Challenges and Changes Assumptions About Teaching" (Brookfield, 1996)<br><br>*Roundtable dinner on Wednesday, October 1st, 6:00–7:15 at University Club* | *Small group meeting:* questions, discussion of reading, introduction to expeditions |
| Oct. 6 | Go on expedition 1 | no small group meeting |
| Oct. 13 | Jot down reflections from your expedition and roundtable dinner | *Small group meeting:* discuss expedition 1<br>Choose expedition 2 |
| Oct. 20 | Go on expedition 2 | no small group meeting |
| Oct. 27 | Jot down reflections from your expedition | *Small group meeting:* discuss expedition 2<br>Distribute reading for next week's discussion. (Topic TBA depending on where group is headed) |
| Nov. 3 | Read article given out last week | *Small group meeting:* discuss reading<br>Choose expedition 3 |
| Nov. 10 | Go on expedition 3 | no small group meeting |
| Nov. 17 | Jot down reflections from your expedition | *Small group meeting:* discuss expedition 3<br>Choose expedition 4 |
| Nov. 24 *Thanksgiving* | Go on expedition 4 | no small group meeting |
| Dec. 1 | Jot down reflections from your expedition<br><br>*Roundtable dinner on Wednesday, December 3rd, 6:00–7:15 at University Club* | *Small group meeting:* discuss expedition 4 |
| Dec. 8 | Jot down final program reflections | *Small group meeting:* wrap up discussion, what's next? Plans for next semester? |

# 19

# Learning Communities for First-Year Faculty: Transition, Acculturation, and Transformation

Harriet Fayne, Leslie Ortquist-Ahrens
Otterbein College

*To enhance new faculty members' chances for teaching and career success, Otterbein College piloted a yearlong learning community program and encouraged first-year faculty to participate. Four new faculty members took part in opportunities designed to enhance their teaching, to orient them more fully to a new institution and student body, to foster collegial community, to encourage reflective practice, and to introduce them to the scholarship of teaching and learning. This qualitative case study tracks their developmental trajectory, which led them from an initial concern with self and survival to an eventual focus on student learning.*

## Introduction

There is consensus among higher education professional development scholars that academic careers, while viewed as idyllic from outside of the academy, pose significant challenges, particularly to newcomers. A recent large-scale study (Rice, Sorcinelli, & Austin, 2000) reinforced themes identified in case studies conducted at one or more higher education institutions (Boice, 1991; Menges, 1996; Sorcinelli, 1988). While new faculty members tend to be highly committed and enthusiastic about their choice of career, they often experience negative emotions and obstacles early on that can temper their idealism and reduce their effectiveness. For many, the entry period (lasting from one term to several years) is marked by anxiety, pressure, and stress stemming from ambiguous expectations, a sense of isolation, and a lack of balance between personal and professional life.

Career entry involves learning the explicit and implicit norms, beliefs, and values of three separate cultures: the academy, the discipline, and the particular institution (Lucas & Murry, 2002). Graduate schools socialize their students for the first two years using an apprenticeship model. As research and teaching assistants, future faculty are acculturated into the world of the research university. However, these same well-trained and knowledgeable graduate students become novices in institutions that are likely to be very different from their research universities. Furthermore, preparedness for the classroom varies widely. Despite the increasing availability of TA training and Preparing Future Faculty programs, many new faculty still arrive with limited teaching experience and little or no formal training. The dissonance between the images of the professoriate acquired during the long years of training and the realities of life in comprehensive universities, liberal arts colleges, and community colleges, where one's teaching is often more central than one's research, can be a major source of stress.

Baldwin (1990) outlines several key tasks of the career entry stage. New faculty usually have to design several courses in a limited period of time, some or all of which may be outside of their areas of expertise; they must fine-tune their teaching skills; they must figure out how to continue to stay involved in scholarly pursuits in face of heavy teaching demands; and they must figure out what the institution requires of them in terms of service to the department, college/university, and community.

According to Rosch and Reich (1996), the acculturation process takes place in four sub-stages: pre-arrival (during graduate school), encounter (recruitment and orientation), adaptation (initial period of reconciling expectations and reality), and commitment (settling into routines and finding a niche). It is during the adaptation sub-stage that locally created induction programs can have their greatest impact. Ideally, these programs should help novices acquire new skills, develop an appreciation for the visible and invisible dimensions of institutional culture (Lucas & Murry, 2002) and increase participants' self-knowledge about their place within that culture.

Induction programs to help new faculty adapt come in many different forms (Cox, 1995). Orientation sessions for new faculty have the longest history; they range from one-day meetings to a series of social and educational activities across the first year. Lucas and Murry (2002) report that mentoring programs, a workplace learning model that involves the assignment of a more experienced peer to a beginner, are increasing in popularity.

However, the literature on mentoring practices at the pre-collegiate level offers some cautionary tales to higher education professional developers. Meyer (2000) argues that mentor-mentee relationships tend to be instrumental; pairs focus on the immediate and the particular, often missing opportunities for deeper exploration of the why/why not questions. What's more, inherent in some mentoring programs is a conservative bias. Rather than encouraging new teachers to find their own professional identity or to participate in new initiatives important to the institution, such programs may unintentionally or intentionally indoctrinate rather than acculturate (New South Wales, Department of Education and Training, 2002). In his study of mentoring pairs in higher education, Boice (1992), too, suggests that while highly structured pairings can help newcomers become acculturated more quickly, there can be a "dark side" to mentoring relationships as they are usually practiced. Without external structuring and guidance, the relationship often founders. Even when it doesn't, pairs can get mired in narrow preoccupations related to pragmatic immediacies. Mentors generally hesitate to intervene in truly significant and formative ways unless they, too, are mentored and coached.

## Learning Communities: An Option for New Faculty

How then to develop effective programming that will help new faculty adapt to the specifics of their new positions and new institutions, taking advantage of their plasticity during the third sub-stage of the acculturation process? Junior faculty learning communities provide an alternative model that adds a new dimension to mentorship programs. The Teaching Scholars Program at Miami University Ohio, which began in 1978, has served as a model for other institutions. Miami's program invites faculty in years two through five at the institution to participate. Nine to thirteen participants are selected; activities span across two semesters and include seminars, retreats, attendance at national conferences, work with at least one self-selected mentor, and the completion of a teaching project, usually a course mini-portfolio or an action research project (Cox, 1995). While the program does include individual mentoring relationships, one unique aspect is its emphasis on the cohort group. Program evaluations reveal that the strongest program impact is "colleagueship" and the strongest outcome is "participants' interest in the teaching process" (Cox, 1995, p. 291). Across the two semesters, new faculty move from "discussions of 'how to' topics led by experts to more controversial or philosophical topics, such as ethical dilemmas in teaching, often led by a member of the group" (p. 294).

If a junior faculty learning community has such a profound impact on participants, why not include first-year faculty in the mix? Cox (1997) advises against this: "First year faculty are not eligible for the Teaching Scholars Program because the Program's designers believed that a professor's initial year is necessarily focused on adjusting to and getting comfortable with the department" (p. 259).

In preparing to introduce the learning community model at Otterbein College, the director of the Center for Teaching and Learning decided, based on institutional context and needs, to break the mold and not only invite but strongly encourage first-year faculty to participate. While Cox's choice at Miami involved conceiving of the department as the first and primary context for induction—a choice which may make sense at a research-oriented institution with large departments—this model seemed less satisfactory for helping new faculty adapt quickly to the culture of a small comprehensive college with a strong regional character, a multitude of first-generation students, and a strong liberal arts tradition—all of which is likely to be new to many incoming colleagues.

Furthermore, the decision to include first-year faculty rested on concerns about classroom incivilities that may plague and derail them and about the lasting patterns of success and failure established for many in the first year. Boice (2000) points out that it is during that first year when faculty are most likely to experience classroom incivilities that "make or break us as teachers" (p. 81). He lists the following as examples of student incivilities that many new faculty find themselves poorly prepared to deal with: cutting class, arriving late, cheating, distracting the instructor or classmates, refusing to participate, and coming to class unprepared. A learning community provides a forum to discuss these incivilities and to learn how to address them promptly. Facilitators and other early career faculty, particularly "quick starters" who have no trouble establishing rapport with their students and have relaxed, effective teaching styles (Boice, 1991), could be helpful in identifying ways to address or prevent them. If department chairs or senior department colleagues are acting as mentors, new professors may be less likely to disclose frustrations and failures, as these colleagues will eventually evaluate their work.

Equally significant, although not as immediate as classroom management issues, was the need to provide opportunities for new faculty to reflect upon beliefs, assumptions, and actions with the intent of encouraging more self-awareness. Robertson (1999), in his developmental model of college teaching, posited that faculty in their early years at an institution are likely to be egocentric, teacher-centered, and content-driven. Without a safe place to analyze "teaching failures" (p. 278), they may not move beyond "egocentrism" to learner-centeredness and finally to an understanding of the "intersubjective dynamics among learners and teachers" (p. 282). Key readings and conversations would pair with reflections on classroom experience to help shift new faculty members from an intense concern with self and survival to a focus on teaching strategies and fostering student learning. Self-evaluation skills that would be critical for long-term success (McMillin & Berberet, 2002) could be developed and encouraged. The mutuality and trust established in learning communities might encourage conversation and risk-taking (Harper, 1996) and allow for "reflection-in-action" (Schön, 1987).

The decision to open the pilot junior faculty learning community to new hires was likely to impact both process and product, and it remained to be seen whether first-year faculty would benefit from such an induction experience. We thus designed a qualitative case study to address the following questions about the value and effectiveness of the learning community as an induction experience and in terms of its ability to encourage development as reflective practitioners:

- Was the New Faculty Professional Learning Community (PLC) able to induct its members into the larger campus community by providing a vehicle for acculturation, skill acquisition, and reflection?

- Did the group's conversation begin with a survival focus, move to a task orientation, and culminate in discussions about impact as would be predicted by career development theory?

- Did individual teaching projects demonstrate "reflection-in-action"?

## Context

Otterbein College is a private, co-educational comprehensive college located in a suburb of Columbus, Ohio. While the vast majority of the student body of approximately 3,000 comes from the surrounding part of the state, in 2003–2004, students were drawn from 28 states and 24 foreign countries; 2,096 of those enrolled were full-time undergraduate students; 578 were part-time students; and 358 were graduate students enrolled in master's programs in business, education, and nursing. Approximately 35% of freshmen are first-generation students (a figure that has remained relatively constant over the past several decades), and 90% receive some sort of financial aid.

In May 2003, the Center for Teaching and Learning received a grant from the McGregor Fund to support seven PLCs over a three-year period. One track annually is open to a cohort of five to eight junior faculty members who are in their first three years at Otterbein, and incoming faculty members are especially encouraged to participate. This sustained development opportunity is designed to reach significantly beyond the new faculty orientation and mentoring programs that have already been in place at Otterbein for a number of years.

## Participants

While five individuals applied and were selected for participation, only four could truly be called new or junior faculty. One participant, a student affairs administrator, had been with the college for fifteen years but was embarking on a new journey by agreeing to teach a section of freshman English. Though she was an "apprentice" teacher, she knew the local culture well and had a firm grounding in student development theories. She was thus able to serve as a translator of campus culture, acting as a de facto co-facilitator for the group with the CTL director, who facilitated this learning community.

The four new faculty members came together from different disciplines—art history, communication, English, and mathematics, representing four of the five academic divisions at the college—and brought a wide range of preparation and prior teaching experiences to the table. One newcomer had had only limited experience and essentially no formal training in pedagogy. The other participants had had more preparation and experience, ranging from teaching assistant training during graduate school to faculty development opportunities while serving as visiting professors elsewhere. One participant was a graduate of a teacher education program before returning to graduate school to pursue her Ph.D.; another had participated in a Preparing Future Faculty program as part of her graduate experience. Two of the newcomers had some prior experience teaching at Otterbein: one had taught a summer course, and the second had completed her first year on a tenure-track line.

## Life Cycle of the New Faculty Learning Community

### Fall Term: Survival

From the outset, the group developed and progressed collaboratively and democratically, choosing target readings, activities, projects, and conference attendance by consensus. Responsibility for developing questions and leading discussion at meetings rotated among members as did hosting of the meetings in participants' homes. The decision to meet in a home setting helped to distinguish learning community sessions from formal meetings or seminars held on campus. It also provided a context that allowed participants to get to know one another as people, not just as colleagues.

As focus texts for the year, the members selected Brookfield's (1995) *Becoming a Critically Reflective Teacher* (1995) and Bransford, Brown, and Cocking's (2000) *How People Learn: Brain, Mind, Experience, and School.* In addition, they read a range of articles contributed by members of the group as these became relevant, and they consulted two reference texts for assessment and teaching ideas: Angelo and Cross's (1993) *Classroom Assessment Techniques: A Handbook for College Teachers* and Davis's (1993) *Tools for Teaching.* The group spent approximately half of each meeting discussing the texts. Readings on active learning strategies by Nelson (1997), Frederick (1989), and Angelo (1993) proved to be very useful, as did one by Lewis (1994) about soliciting ongoing student feedback. Less well received, particularly early on in the life of the community, were more theoretical selections.

Group members quickly learned to value the sense of connection and belonging they felt in the learning community. While not initially part of the proposed structure for the group, participants in the learning community found it extremely important to dedicate half of each meeting to a sharing of teaching highs and lows from the past two weeks. Doing so helped these newcomers to the institution (or to teaching) work through the adjustment to a new culture, a new student body, and new expectations—in a safe and supportive context. At the same time, gradual self-disclosures and risk-taking in sharing failures and challenges as well as successes built a strong foundation of trust. It was particularly helpful for them to experience support and collegiality with others in the same phase of adjustment and with colleagues from outside of their department contexts.

All four new faculty members found the students in their classrooms at Otterbein significantly different from previous students they had taught during their graduate programs. During fall quarter, new faculty brought stories to the group that often involved classroom incivilities or other perplexing situations. Serving as a cultural tour guide, the student affairs administrator, with years of experience at the institution, provided feedback as to whether the behaviors described were typical or atypical at Otterbein. In turn, participants and the facilitator provided instructional ideas, relevant readings, and moral support. Conversations also included discussions of department cultures and experiences serving on college committees; participants considered how to navigate the politics of the institution. Collegial and mutually supportive relationships began to emerge as the learning community members checked in with one another regularly and followed one another's progress in addressing old problems, meeting new challenges, and experiencing new successes. Frequently, this informal time of catching up and exchanging experiences was interwoven with thoughtful observations gleaned from the day's scholarly readings.

A key shared experience for the members of this community involved attendance at the Lilly Conference on College Teaching in Oxford, Ohio. Rather than use learning community stipends of $250 for the academic year to support their individual teaching projects, the participants unanimously decided to attend the conference together in November. This experience proved pivotal, first, because it gave members a good opportunity to get to know one another better, and second, because the presentations on college teaching and student learning were of high quality. It was the first time any of the participants had attended a conference devoted solely to college-level pedagogy. One participant reflected on several sessions where, as she put it, "the light came on" and there were "moments that encouraged a more mindful pedagogical stance. I was grateful for the opportunity to attend the conference. Holistically, it was a register of the kind of research, professional development, and teaching the learning community can nurture."

## Winter Term: Getting Down to Business

Trying to understand first-generation college students was a major focus of discussion during the winter term. Otterbein considers itself a college of opportunity, attracting sizable numbers of traditional and adult students who have limited exposure to the culture of the academy. Learning community members discussed the impact of background on classroom behavior and disconnects between their expectations of typical college students and realities encountered in their classes. By midyear, group members realized that their assumptions had been based in large measure on their own student identities, which were quite different than their students'. One perplexed participant, whose wry, ironic humor was at odds with her students', posted the following on the PLC discussion board: "I sometimes think that I seem way too strange to these students."

As group members became more comfortable with one another (and more exhausted), the tone of the meetings shifted, taking on a marked note of frustration and a relatively exclusive focus on student behavior and challenges posed by students: How can we get our jobs done when we have troublesome students who challenge our right to assign analysis papers, refuse to participate in group activities, and write scathing criticisms on course evaluations? Are we required to modify assignments for adult students? Why aren't majors willing to accept challenges in their field of study? Why do my students overreact when they have trouble with directions? How do I get students to read my comments and take them seriously?

The facilitators gradually introduced participants to the literature on student developmental theory, and, in so doing, helped them conceive of their students developmentally. Rather than see their students in a monolithic fashion, participants were freed to think of behaviors as representative of developmental positions or stages. In tandem with the chapter from Brookfield (1995) on seeking to see oneself as a teacher from a student's perspective, the facilitators asked the members to use at least one classroom assessment technique in their classes and to bring results back to the group. As the new faculty collected data, they gained new insights into their own assumptions and into students' behaviors and perspectives; they became empowered and consequently began to shift from a teacher-centered to a student-centered perspective. There were positive discussions of ways to improve learning. The group was back on track. They were ready to look at Brookfield—and at themselves in relationship to the students—through a new lens. The author's ideas, while deemed controversial by some, prompted important talk and a few "a-ha" experiences. One of the new faculty members posted the following in March:

- "For me, a big breakthrough moment came when Brookfield pushed us to consider the assumptions on which we teach (e.g., discussion circles are democratic, pop media can clarify difficult concepts, etc.). Naming and identifying these assumptions . . . has helped me to develop more goal-centered teaching strategies and to make these strategies more 'transparent' to myself and to my students."

## Spring Term: Impact

Using assessment to shape instruction proved to be a crucial practice for all of the members. Across the year, members experimented with assessment techniques in their classes and debriefed during meetings. Formative assessment was helping participants gain an understanding of and appreciation for their students. By getting to know their students, participants were getting to know themselves better at the same time. At different points, each of the four recognized that they needed to be more explicit about the "whys" as well as the "how-to's" that shaped their class activities, assignments, and grading policies. A participant posted the following comment on the discussion board in April:

- "Although I've always strived to help my students become reflective learners, I've realized that I was not being reflective about my own teaching. Over the past year, I've devoted a greater percentage of my prep time to process. Why am I presenting the material in this fashion? What do I hope students take away from the lesson? Am I modeling good problem solving? How does this fit into the big picture? What I struggle with still is making my teaching transparent—sharing my process with students."

Participants recognized that there had been growth both individually and collectively. For one, the PLC provided a forum to learn sound teaching techniques. "Teaching is not taught in graduate school, yet somehow we all have to start out our careers being able to teach effectively." The faculty member in her second year not only felt better able to address the needs of freshmen with limited backgrounds in her discipline, but also more "connected to the larger campus community." Her colleagues in the learning community had encouraged her to venture out into campus committee involvement, something she had been uncertain about before. A third noted that the group had moved from serving primarily an affective function for its members to providing all of them with "pedagogical insights. . . . There is this wonderful sense of shared wisdom, this great exchange of ideas that has made me a more confident, reflective teacher." A fourth, while still "fuzzy" on institutional expectations and a bit confused by student responses, concluded that participation in the PLC had energized her and helped her to recognize that teaching was valued across the campus. She regretted that the group would be disbanding; by spring term, individuals really trusted one another and were able to "discuss things in greater depth."

## Projects: Reflection-in-Action

Each participant in the learning community was required to undertake a project related to teaching: either a course mini-portfolio documenting the instructor's approach to a key course component or a small action research project. Two faculty members elected to create course mini-portfolios. One chose to revise assessments and connect them to course objectives. Her focus emerged from student feedback: students had found her expectations unclear during fall and winter terms. She intended to pilot her revisions during the summer quarter. Her central question was: How can I provide direction without compromising my goal of encouraging creativity and originality? The second member had struggled during fall and winter terms with the diverse academic backgrounds of students in her survey courses. She wanted to explore various innovations in assignments and then determine their effectiveness across the term using classroom assessment techniques and student evaluations. Her central question was: How can I meet the radically different needs of majors and nonmajors in the same section of a survey course?

The other two junior faculty members opted to do action research projects. One project involved students' necessary but weak algebra competencies in a college trigonometry course. By integrating regular opportunities for practice and review throughout the course rather than providing an isolated algebra review at the beginning and by giving mastery quizzes on Blackboard over key algebra topics across the term, the instructor saw significant growth on a basic skills posttest. The second action research project was designed to assess the impact of a service-learning component on student attitudes in a freshman-level English course. The English instructor collected field reports and summative self-assessments in addition to classroom assessment techniques throughout the term in order to address the following questions: What do students gain from service-learning assignments tied to course content? Do education majors find the course more relevant than they have in the past because of the field-based assignments?

## Conclusions

Was the pilot New Faculty Professional Learning Community a success? Information collected for the external evaluation of the grant-funded project in the form of anonymous surveys and focus group interviews left no doubt as to participants' satisfaction with their experiences as learning community members in their first or second year at the college. In response to the survey question "Would you recommend participation in a learning community to a new faculty colleague and why or why not?" participants replied enthusiastically in the affirmative. PLC members felt that they had avoided a sense of isolation, so common and potentially devastating to newcomers. They were able to gain a better understanding of the institutional culture and its expectations—learning about the "intangible aspects of the college," in one participant's terms; they became more aware of resources available to them than they could in a one-day orientation session. They valued a sense of being part of a "faculty"—rather than simply part of a department—because of the close collegial relationships, and even friendships, they had developed in this multidisciplinary group.

Not only did a sense of community and collegiality flourish, but within the context of the group, participants were able to help each other get off to a "quick start." The fall term initiated members into possibilities for the learning community as well as into literature on teaching and learning. While it seemed during the winter quarter—the second phase of the community's development—that what PLC members wanted most were ways to tailor their habitual practices and prior convictions about teaching and learning to the Otterbein context, they were able, through supportive and challenging dialogue, use of formative classroom assessments, and construction of an inquiry project, to move beyond a teacher-centered perspective toward a more firmly grounded learning-centered perspective. By the end of the spring quarter, collegial relationships were cemented, and participants had emerged as thoughtful and reflective practitioners. They were at home in a new context, savvy about institutional culture, and willing and able to consider their long-term place within it.

## Note

A generous three-year grant from the McGregor Fund has supported a learning community initiative at Otterbein College, with emphases on new faculty, the scholarship of teaching and learning, diversity, and undergraduate research to date. The case study described in this chapter is part of ongoing assessment underwritten by grant funds.

## References

Angelo, T. A. (1993). A "teacher's dozen": Fourteen general, research-based principles for improving higher learning in our classrooms. *AAHE Bulletin*, 45(8), 3–13.

Angelo, T. A., & Cross, K. P. (1993). *Classroom assessment techniques: A handbook for college teachers* (2nd ed.). San Francisco, CA: Jossey-Bass.

Baldwin, R. G. (1990). Faculty career stages and implications for professional development. In J. H. Schuster & D. W. Wheeler (Eds.), *Enhancing faculty careers: Strategies for development and renewal* (pp. 20–40). San Francisco, CA: Jossey-Bass.

Boice, R. (1991). Quick starters: New faculty who succeed. In M. Theall & J. Franklin (Eds.), *New directions for teaching and learning: No. 48. Effective practices for improving teaching* (pp. 111–121). San Francisco, CA: Jossey-Bass.

Boice, R. (1992). *The new faculty member: Supporting and fostering professional development*. San Francisco, CA: Jossey-Bass.

Boice, R. (2000). *Advice to new faculty members*. Needham Heights, MA: Allyn & Bacon.

Bransford, J. D., Brown, A. L., & Cocking, R. R. (Eds.). (2000). *How people learn: Brain, mind, experience, and school* (Expanded ed.). Washington, DC: National Academies Press.

Brookfield, S. D. (1995). *Becoming a critically reflective teacher.* San Francisco, CA: Jossey-Bass.

Cox, M. D. (1995). The development of new and junior faculty. In W. A. Wright & Associates (Ed.), *Teaching improvement practices: Successful strategies for higher education* (pp. 283–305). Bolton, MA: Anker.

Cox, M. D. (1997). Long-term patterns in a mentor program for junior faculty: Recommendations for practice. In D. Dezure & M. Kaplan (Eds.), *To improve the academy: Vol. 16. Resources for faculty, instructional, and organizational development* (pp. 225–268). Stillwater, OK: New Forums Press.

Davis, B. G. (1993). *Tools for teaching.* San Francisco, CA: Jossey-Bass.

Frederick, P. J. (1989). Involving students more actively in the classroom. In A. F. Lucas (Ed.), *New directions for teaching and learning: Vol. 37. The department chairperson's role in enhancing college teaching* (pp. 31–40). San Francisco, CA: Jossey-Bass.

Harper, V. (1996). Establishing a community of conversation: Creating a context for self-reflection among teacher scholars. In L. Richlin & D. DeZure (Eds.), *To improve the academy: Vol. 15. Resources for faculty, instructional, and organizational development* (pp. 251–266). Stillwater, OK: New Forums Press.

Lewis, K. G. (1994). *Using on-going student feedback to increase teaching effectiveness and student learning.* Retrieved May 22, 2005, from the University of Texas at Austin, Division of Instructional Innovation and Assessment web site: http://www.utexas.edu/academic/diia/gsi/assessment/ongoing.php

Lucas, C. J., & Murry, J. W., Jr. (2002). *New faculty: A practical guide for academic beginners.* New York, NY: Palgrave.

McMillin, L. A., & Berberet, W. G. (2002). *A new academic compact: Revisioning the relationship between faculty and their institutions.* Bolton, MA: Anker.

Menges, R. J. (1996). Experiences of newly hired faculty. In L. Richlin & D. DeZure (Eds.), *To improve the academy: Vol. 15. Resources for faculty, instructional, and organizational development* (pp. 169–182). Stillwater, OK: New Forums Press.

Meyer, T. (2000). *Finding a voice and place in a normative profession.* Paper presented at the 80th annual meeting of the American Educational Research Association, New Orleans, LA. (ERIC Document Reproduction Service No. ED 440970)

Nelson, C. (1997). Tools for tampering with teaching's taboos. In W. E. Campbell & K. A. Smith (Eds.), *New paradigms for college teaching* (pp. 51–77). Edina, MN: Interaction Book Company.

New South Wales, Department of Education and Training. (2002). *Educational leadership and practice: A review of the literature and an exploration of mentoring practices.* Retrieved May 25, 2005, from the New South Wales, Department of Education and Training web site: http://www.schools.nsw.edu.au/edu_leader ship/prof_read/mentoring/intro.php

Rice, R. E., Sorcinelli, M. D., & Austin, A. E. (2000). *Heeding new voices: Academic careers for a new generation* (New Pathways Working Paper Series No. 7). Washington, DC: American Association for Higher Education.

Robertson, D. L. (1999). Professor's perspectives on their teaching: A new construct and developmental model. *Innovative Higher Education, 23*(4), 271–294.

Rosch, T. A., & Reich, J. N. (1996). The enculturation of new faculty in higher education: A comparative investigation of three academic departments. *Research in Higher Education, 37*(1), 115–131.

Schön, D. A. (1987). *Educating the reflective practitioner: Toward a new design for teaching and learning in the professions.* San Francisco, CA: Jossey-Bass.

Sorcinelli, M. D. (1988). Satisfactions and concerns of new university teachers. In J. Kurfiss, L. Hilsen, S. Kahn, M. D. Sorcinelli, & R. G. Tiberius (Eds.), *To improve the academy: Vol. 7. Resources for faculty, instructional, and organizational development* (pp. 121–134). Stillwater, OK: New Forums Press.

# 20

# Faculty Competency by Design: A Model for Institutional Transformation

Helen M. Clarke, Philip E. Bishop
Valencia Community College

*For a decade, Valencia Community College has striven for a faculty development program with direct impact on student learning. The college succeeded by designing faculty learning with the same logic we apply to student learning. Valencia's program for new tenure-track faculty focuses on significant faculty learning outcomes, a learning-centered pedagogy, high standards of scholarship, and continuous program assessment. The college's Teaching/Learning Academy and a coordinated tenure process have cultivated new learning leaders and created a fresh partnership among deans and faculty members. This developing process of new-hire faculty development has been pivotal to Valencia's learning-centered transformation.*

## Introduction

In 1997, a task force at Valencia Community College resolved to create a competency-based culture at the college. The group sought to define competencies for students, faculty, and staff, and maybe even trustees. After a year of study and deliberation, the task force had created the first part of their vision: a draft of Valencia's Student Core Competencies placing *think, value, communicate,* and *act* at the heart of Valencia's curriculum. This, by itself, was a considerable achievement. Even so, at the group's celebratory final meeting, a vice president reminded them, "Of course, we still need competencies for faculty and staff." The group murmured its agreement and officially disbanded.

By fall 2001, a different college group had been charged with reforming Valencia's induction program for newly hired tenure-track faculty. At its first meeting, the group recalled the unfinished business of faculty competencies and saw the chance to realize another part of the competency-based vision. And so, Valencia embarked on an intriguing path to design a learning program for faculty with the same logic it had applied to students. In principle, at least, what worked for student adult learners ought to work for faculty. Following that logic, the design group imagined:

- A faculty development program that focused on significant learning outcomes and promoted lifelong professional mastery

- A learning-centered pedagogy that would challenge a broad range of faculty learners

- Learning work that reflected high standards of scholarship and met explicit criteria of assessment

- An assessment process that fed back into improved faculty learning and enhanced program design

As it turned out, pre-tenure faculty members weren't the only ones who benefited from Valencia's reform. Good design involves a good bit of discovery, too, and all the participants discovered there were things for us to learn about faculty development. We were about to go through the messy process by which a healthy organization creates, and continuously must recreate, programs of faculty vitality.

## Learning Leaders

Circumstances do sometimes conspire. In 2000, a new Valencia president, Sanford Shugart, engaged the college in broad conversations about strategic goals, including the aim of developing "learning leaders" across a large, multi-campus college. At the same time, the college was realizing that its existing faculty induction program, called the Faculty Academy, didn't suit the varied needs of Valencia's newly hired faculty. When it was instituted in the early 1990's, the Faculty Academy had been an important stepping stone. It moved Valencia from scattered professional development for tenure-track faculty to a portfolio evaluation model. But it consisted mostly of a one-size-fits-all program and measured a participant's progress by seat time. Sincere efforts to improve it had failed to quiet faculty dissatisfaction. Finally, a steering committee recommended that the Faculty Academy be scrapped and replaced by something entirely new. The committee's recommendations were simple: Focus on teaching and learning. Tailor the program to faculty candidates' individual needs. Foster peer interaction.

What better place to develop learning leaders than in a new faculty induction program? Valencia was ready for the task. In summer 2001, President Shugart and the elected faculty leadership had authorized a wholesale redesign of the Faculty Academy and designated a full-time coordinator from faculty ranks. As fall term began, the coordinator convened a group of faculty members who were grounded in the college's emerging learning-centered initiative. They were faced with a daunting challenge: to reengineer the faculty induction program (now renamed the Teaching/Learning Academy, or TLA) that would be simultaneously implemented for faculty newly hired in 2001. From the outset, the redesign had to involve the college's 22 deans, who at Valencia combine the functions of department chair and division dean. The deans have extensive individual contact with their faculty and a large stake in the success of their tenure-track faculty. In 2001, these deans would start guiding about 45 newly hired faculty members through a three-year pretenure process—a process that didn't exist yet. As the design team and the deans developed the TLA, its design would have to be endorsed by faculty governance leaders and executive administrators. Above all, the new program had to be in tune with the college's commitment to the learning paradigm.

Valencia's readiness to take on this challenge wasn't just a matter of circumstance. It was an effect of culture. Through the 1990s, with the support of federal and private grant programs, the college had become more collaborative and collegial in its way of working and better educated in the emerging national conversation on learning. Faculty and administrators were used to speaking frankly while working collectively toward shared goals. Leaders in faculty governance were often also leaders in curriculum and program innovation. The learning paradigm had taken root, not everywhere, but in patches where its appeal and utility were becoming more visible. Now this collaborative culture was about to be tested.

## Competency by Design

In tradition-bound places like colleges, we're not often handed a blank slate. With the new Teaching/Learning Academy, Valencia had the chance to design a learning process from the inside out, something everyone recommends but college educators seldom have the opportunity to do. For a few furious months in fall 2001, the ad hoc faculty design team and the college deans set to the gritty work of designing for learning. Their work addressed a thorny cluster of questions:

- What essential professional abilities did we seek in a faculty educator (a term that includes teaching faculty as well as counselors and librarians of faculty rank)? How should these faculty competencies reflect Valencia's aim to become a learning college, as Tagg (2003) has termed it? Could we design faculty competencies that for now might only apply to new-hire faculty development but eventually be accepted as the center of all faculty development?

- How could each tenure candidate's learning program be individualized and tailored to both his or her professional learning needs and the department's needs, while also promoting broader and consistent development of professional competencies?

- Who should design and lead the TLA learning program? What should be its core curriculum and how should it encourage deep learning in a supportive and collaborative process?

- How would the candidate's learning be demonstrated, documented, and assessed? How could assessment enhance the candidate's learning without getting tangled up in pre-tenure anxiety? How would the assessment process be documented in ways that held the stakeholders accountable to core principles?

- How would a candidate's progress through the TLA program be related to the tenure decision-making process?

Valencia's answers to these questions took shape over several months of intensive dialogue among members of the entire academic community. The TLA design group led a series of summer workshops with the college deans. Not only were deans highly vested in the new program's success, they also had their own ideas about the development of new faculty. Some were justifiably anxious about a new tenure process that promised to redefine their role. As summer turned to fall and ideas became more coherent, they were presented to the faculty-at-large and the Faculty Association Board, where a valuable feedback loop among the principal stakeholders continued to shape the design.

From these discussions emerged the components of a workable faculty development program. Its cornerstones were a set of essential competencies for faculty educators (the equivalent of student core competencies) and an individualized plan of professional learning. Its programs—a curriculum, the campus roundtables, the portfolio, and the assessment process—emerged as the necessary stimulus to and support for faculty learning. As a result of these efforts, the following components are currently in practice at Valencia.

## Essential Competencies of a Valencia Faculty Educator

Tenure-track faculty members are required to demonstrate core abilities of a learning-centered educator and, in turn, develop them during their post-tenure professional practices. The following essential competencies define broad areas in which Valencia educators strive to improve: learning-centered teaching strategies, Valencia Student Core Competencies (*think, value, act, communicate*), LifeMap (Valencia's brand name for developmental advising), assessment, inclusion and diversity, scholarship of teaching and learning, and professional commitment (see Appendix 20.1 for competency statements and indicators). These competencies synthesized the substantial literature on the reform of teaching and learning (Gardiner, 1996) and were collaboratively developed among all the principal stakeholders within Valencia's academic community.

## Individualized Learning Plan (ILP)

Newly hired tenure-track faculty members, in collaboration with their deans, design a two-and-a-half year learning program to meet the candidate's most urgent learning needs. The ILP defines individualized and often specific learning outcomes that reflect one or several essential competencies (see Figure 20.1). Take, for example, this learning outcome from a mathematics professor's ILP: "Improve the level of Intermediate Algebra students' critical thinking skills by developing learning-centered teaching strategies that correspond with higher-order testing methods." This learning outcome involves the essential competencies of employing learning-centered teaching strategies, assessing for learning, and teaching for the student core competency *think*. The ILP also establishes a set of activities and projects to achieve and demonstrate learning targeted by the faculty member. Each ILP includes a schedule of formative assessments by tenured faculty peers.

## The TLA Curriculum

The Teaching/Learning Academy offers, on an annual cycle, professional instruction, mentoring, roundtable discussions, and individualized learning. The TLA curriculum is geared to developing the essential competencies and supporting TLA candidates in their progress through their learning plans. The TLA web site, http://faculty.valencia.cc.fl.us/development/Programs/TLA_academy, functions much like a textbook and course manual, offering support through online mini-courses, samples of action research projects, professional portfolios and links to faculty development resources. The TLA workshops often employ nationally recognized leaders in teaching and

FIGURE 20.1

## Individualized Learning Plan (ILP): What Does It Mean?

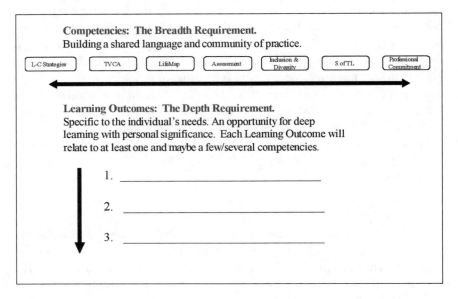

**Competencies: The Breadth Requirement.**
Building a shared language and community of practice.

| L-C Strategies | TVCA | LifeMap | Assessment | Inclusion & Diversity | S of TL | Professional Commitment |

**Learning Outcomes: The Depth Requirement.**
Specific to the individual's needs. An opportunity for deep learning with personal significance. Each Learning Outcome will relate to at least one and maybe a few/several competencies.

1. _____

2. _____

3. _____

learning research but also rely on in-house expertise that has developed over 10 years of largely grant-funded faculty development programs (Nellis, Clarke, DiMartino, & Hosman, 2001). The graduated cycle of TLA support leads the candidate toward successful completion and a tenure decision based on a full view of the candidate's current professional mastery and potential for professional growth (see Figure 20.2).

## Professional Portfolio

The professional portfolio gathers qualitative evidence of the candidate's achievement of ILP learning outcomes and appropriate mastery of the essential competencies. In a format they choose, candidates collect and present materials documenting the "clear and concise evidence of the quality" of their professional practices (Seldin, 2004). Typically, candidates augment paper portfolios with CDs, audiotape, and/or videotape. Increasingly, candidates are finding advantage in online portfolios. Regardless of format or organization, all candidates are required to provide the same portfolio elements (see Appendix 20.2) and adhere to the same standards of scholarship as expressed in the evaluation rubric (see Appendix 20.3).

FIGURE 20.2

## Cycle of TLA Support

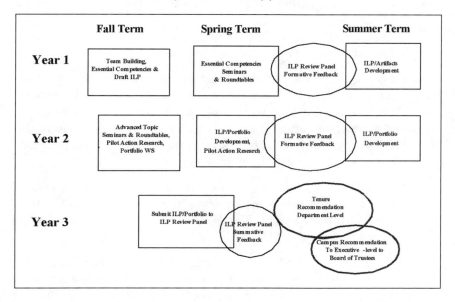

| | **Fall Term** | **Spring Term** | **Summer Term** |
|---|---|---|---|
| **Year 1** | Team Building, Essential Competencies & Draft ILP | Essential Competencies Seminars & Roundtables | ILP Review Panel Formative Feedback | ILP/Artifacts Development |
| **Year 2** | Advanced Topic Seminars & Roundtables, Pilot Action Research, Portfolio WS | ILP/Portfolio Development, Pilot Action Research | ILP Review Panel Formative Feedback | ILP/Portfolio Development |
| **Year 3** | Submit ILP/Portfolio to ILP Review Panel | ILP Review Panel Summative Feedback | Tenure Recommendation Department Level | Campus Recommendation To Executive -level to Board of Trustees |

### ILP Review Panel

A panel consisting of the dean and three tenured faculty members provides formative assessment of the candidate's ILP and his progress toward completion. Formal ILP review occurs on a graduated cycle (see Figure 20.2), but usually deans and often peer reviewers offer informal feedback as the candidate's work develops. The panel's formal reviews are summarized in writing and become part of the candidate's portfolio. This public assessment aids deans in their decisions about continuation of contract during the pre-tenure period. Besides the traditional devices of student evaluations and classroom observations, deans now have evidence in the developing ILP of the candidate's focus on student learning. For the candidates, the ILP review process provides a model of assessment for improvement and an authentic opportunity to discuss pedagogy with their dean and faculty peers.

### Faculty Coordinator and Campus Facilitators

The full-time, college-wide faculty coordinator and a team of tenured faculty members from different disciplines and from each campus support tenure candidates as they develop their learning plans. Facilitators lead campus roundtables, stimulating peer interaction and collaboration among members of each new-hire class. Facilitators also design and present workshops and provide campus liaison to faculty and deans on each of Valencia's four campuses.

## Results: A Continuous Program Assessment Process

From the earliest days, the TLA leadership has been committed to continuous, evidence-based program assessment. Eventually, the program adopted Astin's (1991) Inputs-Environments-Outcomes model as a basic framework. Not only do we systematically assess participants' learning, we have also assessed TLA programs and ILP processes. Currently, the assessment process consists of the following multiple program evaluation measures:

- Candidate's assessment of professional needs consist of TLA-generated surveys, *Teaching Goals Inventory* (Angelo & Cross, 1993), *A Guide for Composing Teaching Philosophies* (Nuhfer, Krest, & Handelsman, 2003), and candidate self-reflection.

- Pre- and post-surveys in Year-1 measure a candidate's understanding of the essential competencies and tenure process, and constructing appropriate learning outcomes (LOs). For the class of 2007 Year-1 (see Figure 20.3) the percentage of respondents who reported confidence in constructing a LO increased from 88% to 95% of participants. Those who reported having a good idea for their LOs increased from 58% to 100% of the participants. The percentages of the class who reported they understood the competencies and the tenure process increased by more than 10%.

- Pre- and post-surveys in Year-2 measure candidates' understanding of constructing a competency-based portfolio and using student feedback to improve teaching, counseling, or librarianship. The data (see Figure 20.4) indicate a dramatic increase in percentage of candidates reporting that they understand these key components of creating a portfolio: creating evidence-based artifacts, accurately assessing an artifact, evaluating a reflective critique, planning the organizational structure of a portfolio, writing an analysis of an essential competency, and assessing the outcomes of an action research project. In each category, at least 60% reported they understood the component. These skills and understandings are critical for the successful completion of a portfolio.

- Retention rates (course dropout rates) and mean GPAs for students of TLA graduates will be compared to those of experienced faculty mem-

FIGURE 20.3

## Class of 2007 Year-1, Pre- and Post-Survey

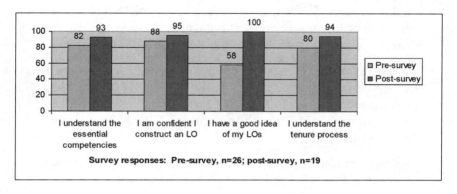

Survey responses: Pre-survey, n=26; post-survey, n=19

FIGURE 20.4

## Class of 2006 Year-2, Fall 2004 Pre- and Post-Survey

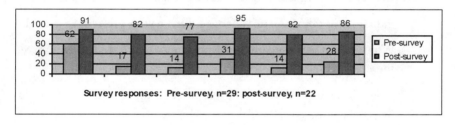

Survey responses: Pre-survey, n=29: post-survey, n=22

bers and common discipline-area faculty with extensive experience. This project will begin in summer 2005.

- Faculty portfolios provide qualitative evidence of a candidate's integration of the essential competencies in his or her practice via the individualized learning outcomes. Forty-five candidates started in the initial tenure class, and of those, 39 submitted final portfolios. All final portfolios were judged either acceptable or exemplary using the Valencia Faculty Portfolio Rubric (see Appendix 20.3).

- The action research projects demonstrate a candidate's scholarly approach to the investigation and improvement of teaching, counseling, or librarianship and learning. Action research engages both practitioners and students in the collaborative study of learning in the particular daily context of their own classrooms (Cross & Steadman, 1996). Ninety-eight percent of all candidates include action research projects in their portfolios.

- Student engagement comparisons (Year-1 compared to Year-3) using the Classroom Climate Assessment Tool will begin in the 2005–2006 academic year.

- Surveys of the ILP review panel experience measure the "customer service" aspects of the process and gauge the ripple effect of the reviews. It is promising that more than 70% of all participants (candidates, deans, and peer reviewers) agreed with the prompt "The ILP review process improved my practice."

- The program conducts appreciative inquiry into the ILP/portfolio review processes as a way of improving reviews and reporting.

- Third-party focus groups were implemented in spring 2005 to query recent TLA graduates about the impact of TLA on their professional practices and student learning. Focus groups employed these prompts:

  ~ Explain how your practice changed during your pre-tenure period.

  ~ What events, people, and/or experiences facilitated or supported these changes?

  ~ How did your professional development efforts influence your students' learning, growth, and/or development?

While the responses have not been fully analyzed at the point of this writing, early reports indicate that the TLA has had a highly positive impact on faculty behavior. One recent TLA graduate stated, "I've been teaching many years at Valencia, but never really understood the importance of developmental advising. Now that I better understand LifeMap, I realize that not only are my students accountable, but so am I."

TLA leaders use this evidence to inform the continuous refinement and revision of TLA and ILP review processes. The TLA coordinator also makes annual formal reports to the college's governing councils. It's a concentrated effort to answer the learning college's two fundamental questions: What have learners learned? How do we know? In fact, the effort is so central to the TLA work that a faculty facilitator has been assigned to coordinate TLA program assessment.

We're glad to report that, after three years of progressive design and implementation, Valencia's Teaching/Learning Academy works. Many members of the graduating TLA classes of 2004 and 2005 have just gained tenure. The coherence and consistency of the TLA design do evidently create a ripple effect beyond the tenure process. For example, a mathematics professor from the recent graduating class has organized a community of practice for instructors of a critical college preparatory math course. The community of practice is implementing a methodology designed as part of an ILP, clear evidence that the TLA stimulates professional development beyond tenure. Several recent TLA graduates have published journal articles, presented at national conferences, and attended scholarly institutes reporting on their ILP work. The colleges' deans are, more than ever, living the learning paradigm. All are actively engaged in collaborative learning design with their new hires, participating hands-on in the kind of competency-based learning program that Valencia envisions now for both students and faculty.

## Development by Discovery

The TLA design proceeded, and succeeded, from what we believed and understood as a learning college. But we never know enough at the beginning. Some things are better discovered. For example, we had to discover the proper relationship between a formative faculty development process and a tenure decision process. Following the advice of Peter Seldin (2004), TLA leaders tried to distance the faculty development program from the often high-anxiety process of evaluation for tenure. But a complete divorce was impossible. The candidate's ILP and portfolio work needed to count somehow in the "final grade" of the tenure decision.

To address this issue, the college convened a series of tenure summits in the TLA's first design year, led by our chief learning officer. While vetting the new program to a college-wide meeting of leaders, the summits simultaneously aimed to redefine the tenure process. The summits involved some 50 active participants, comprising the college president, general counsel, academic affairs executives, campus provosts, and college-wide faculty governance leaders, as well as the TLA design group, college deans, and anyone else wanting to sit in. They raised a knot of tough questions: How would the ILP review panel's formative assessments count in the record for summative decisions about tenure? Besides the tenure candidate's ILP/portfolio, how should the tenure decision weight the other contents of a candidate's dossier like student evaluations, annual performance evaluations, and similar records? What role should tenured department faculty play in the tenure evaluation, which before had formally involved only the dean and provost? How should the

TLA's formative assessments, designed to promote learning, be insulated from the summative process of recommending for tenure?

In one summit, the college's president broke a logjam by suggesting that the ILP review panel make a final assessment "to the record," a last report on the candidate's ongoing professional development. Although some had emphasized that review panelists' feedback should be formative right to the very end, nevertheless, as part of the record, the review panel's assessments would carry substantial weight with tenure decision-makers. In fact, a strong portfolio and positive review panel assessments have become a necessary, though not sufficient, condition for tenure recommendation.

We determined that a tenure review committee comprised of the dean and two senior department faculty members (elected by their peers) should review the candidate's portfolio and the other evidence of professional ability. Using the portfolio as a substantial and telling evidence of ability, the tenure review committee advises the dean, who then makes a tenure recommendation to the provost, chief learning officer, and president. The tenure committee's decision process provides a transparency that tenure decisions had sometimes lacked before. Having had its first implementation in spring 2004, this process is already being adjusted and refined. Valencia has discovered ways of balancing the need for an effective professional development program and evidence-based faculty performance evaluation.

Another discovery was the serendipitous but significant learning that the ILP review process fostered among veteran faculty members and deans. ILP and portfolio reviews prompted significant discussions of the essential competencies, philosophical and discipline perspectives, and the challenge of defining and assessing learning outcomes. For some veteran faculty, service on ILP review panels was their first serious engagement in outcomes-based programs, and the TLA staff led mini-seminars to brief review panelists on their roles as formative assessors. Across three years of implementation, we've learned that the interdisciplinary and intercampus membership of the review panels stimulates rich dialogue and appreciation for multiple perspectives. Ultimately, we have found that the ILP review process is a rich learning experience for all involved.

We've also learned that even experienced college educators sometimes struggle with the concept of learning outcomes. The first round of individual learning plans tended to state learning outcomes as tasks or activities, rather than intended professional learning. For example, a new English professor's first draft ILP defined an outcome as "Identify, read, and discuss a representative selection of works of poetry." To remedy her limited background in poetry, the candidate planned to keep a reading journal and have regular discussions about poetry with two senior colleagues. As a plan of action, this was reasonable and it helped the dean and candidate answer the urgent question "What must she do to get tenure?" It was a neat analogy to the student's question "What must I do to make an 'A'?"

However, students often get an "A" without learning anything significant. For both students and college educators, a well-stated learning outcome needs to define the deeper and enduring learning that will result from a learning program. In the case of the new-hire English professor, it wasn't clear that her poetry study would enable her to incorporate poetry more effectively into literature classes. She eventually restated her ILP learning outcome as "Develop learning-centered teaching strategies that reflect my understanding and appreciation of poetry as a resource for teaching literature." The ILP reading program, what she would now do to earn her "A," would be the foundation of a new and, it is hoped, career-long interest in teaching poetry. Her appreciation of poetry would endure beyond the timeframe of her learning plan and continue to develop, just as we hope that students' learning will endure beyond the work of academic courses.

Another important institutional instance in the TLA design process emerged. We discovered an active tension around teaching faculty members' responsibility for supporting LifeMap, Valencia's elegant program for developmental advising of students (Tagg, 2003). Although Valencia teaching faculty members have no formal responsibility for advising students, executive leaders had declared that every Valencia professor was responsible for supporting LifeMap. Yet in 2001, as we were designing TLA, veteran teaching faculty members had not fully endorsed the new idea that they do "advising" in their courses. Given this gap in expectations, we asked what level of competence in and commitment to developmental advising did we expect of teaching faculty members?

Addressing that question has actually helped Valencia resolve concern around LifeMap. The public commitment to LifeMap in the essential competencies encouraged newly hired faculty members to think intentionally about their advising roles. As a result, after three years of TLA, support for developmental advising is more effectively integrated into faculty responsibility.

## Conclusion: TLA as a Model for Organizational Transformation

It's a credit to Valencia's collaborative institutional culture that we saw the challenges of TLA as opportunities for discovery. The challenges are likely to be different at different institutions. But any authentic process will require institutional leadership and collaborative dialogue around core values. One reason for TLA's success has been this institutional commitment to asking tough questions and working our way toward honest and workable answers.

Clearly, the TLA innovation benefited from Valencia's sense of urgency about its growing need to increase faculty positions. These new instructors, counselors, and librarians will become the next generation of Valencia faculty, replacing faculty members who were founders of the college. The college's budgetary commitment to a full-time faculty coordinator and eventually to a team of faculty facilitators, partially reassigned to the TLA from their teaching duties, reflected this priority. Without urgency and supportive executive leadership, there is little chance that large and largely successful institutions can change as they need to. Without urgency, Valencia may not have overcome the barriers it faced—inertia, myopia, and the occasional discomfort of public assessment.

At a retreat in 2004, the college's executive leadership reflected on three years of TLA and asked themselves, "How is TLA a successful model for institutional change?" The discussion revealed that even administrators from the far reaches of the organization, outside academic affairs, recognized TLA's impact on organizational learning. These executive leaders were interested in ways that the lessons of TLA might be applied in other administrative domains. They saw that the college's investment in new faculty had created high expectations, commitment and responsibility among faculty, clearly a wise use of college resources. The peer review process had broadened understanding of the essential competencies, effectively connecting individual and organizational goals. Perhaps most important, all stakeholders had a hand in the program's design. As one executive leader put it, "The TLA bears the fingerprints of its users." In sum, Valencia had managed to fashion a continuous quality improvement process that nurtured lasting community relationships. The retreat ended with the executives exchanging ideas about competencies for themselves and speculating on other improvements to staff and professional development throughout the college.

Valencia's successful moment of organizational learning arose above all from its examination of student learning and faculty development through the same lens. The cultural transformation that began by our defining student competencies has now grown to competencies for our new faculty. As we began to "model the model," to "practice what we teach," applying the same principles of good teaching that we encourage in our classrooms, libraries, and counseling offices to our own learning, we could see the powerful potential of our new learning paradigm.

As learners, students and faculty are different, but surely not that different. We all seek to act in the world with assured competence. The challenge is to design our colleges in ways that promote the learning that leads to the competencies we seek.

## References

Angelo, T. A., & Cross, K. P. (1993). *Classroom assessment techniques: A handbook for college teachers* (2nd ed.). San Francisco, CA: Jossey-Bass.

Astin, A. W. (1991). *Assessment for excellence: The philosophy and practice of assessment and evaluation in higher education.* New York, NY: American Council on Education/Macmillan.

Cross, K. P., & Steadman, M. H. (1996). *Classroom research: Implementing the scholarship of teaching.* San Francisco, CA: Jossey-Bass.

Gardiner, L. F. (1996). *Redesigning higher education: Producing dramatic gains in student learning* (ASHE-ERIC Higher Education Report, 23[7]). Washington, DC: George Washington University, Graduate School of Education and Human Development.

Glassick, C. E., Huber, M. T., & Maeroff, G. I. (1997). *Scholarship assessed: Evaluation of the professoriate.* San Francisco, CA: Jossey-Bass.

Nellis, P., Clarke, H., DiMartino, J., & Hosman, D. K. (2001). Preparing today's faculty for tomorrow's students. In D. Lieberman & C. Wehlburg (Eds.), *To improve the academy: Vol. 19. Resources for faculty, instructional, and organizational development* (pp. 149–168). Bolton, MA: Anker.

Nuhfer, E., Krest, M., & Handelsman, M. M. (2003). Developing in fractal patterns III: A guide for composing teaching philosophies. *The National Teaching and Learning Forum, 12*(5), 10–11.

Seldin, P. (2004). *The teaching portfolio: A practical guide to improved performance and promotion/tenure decisions* (3rd ed.). Bolton, MA: Anker.

Tagg, J. (2003). *The learning paradigm college.* Bolton, MA: Anker.

## Appendix 20.1

# Essential Competencies and Indicators of a Valencia Educator

Indicators provide examples of how competencies can be demonstrated in an Individualized Learning Plan.

### Demonstrate Learning-Centered Teaching Strategies

Valencia educators will utilize diverse teaching and learning strategies that accommodate the learning styles of students and that promote acquisition and applications of knowledge and understanding.

- Employ active learning techniques (punctuated lectures, discussion, experiential learning, scenarios, role-play, case study, problem-based learning)
- Encourage students to challenge ideas
- Use cooperative learning strategies
- Integrate concrete, real-life situations to analyze
- Invite student input on course outcomes (goals for course outcomes; choice among assignment topics; in-progress student feedback)

### Measure Valencia's Core Competencies: Think, Value, Communicate, Act

Valencia educators will facilitate student growth in thinking critically and creatively across different contexts and domains of human understanding; communicating effectively in different modes and across different settings; articulating personal values and those of the various disciplines and appreciating the values of others; and applying learning and understanding effectively and responsibly in their lives as educated adults.

- Engage students in construction of knowledge
- Facilitate the discovery and use of the ways of knowing in the discipline
- Design assignments and assessments that demonstrate student growth in the core competencies
- Align course outcomes and learning activities with core competencies
- Document student growth in the core competencies
- Collaborate with colleagues and the dean to assure and demonstrate progression of student learning across courses and programs

### Incorporate LifeMap Concepts as Tools for Learning

Valencia educators will design learning opportunities that promote student life skills development while enhancing discipline learning. Through intentional inclusion of growth-promoting strategies, instructors, counselors, and librarians will facilitate the students' reflection, knowledge, and appreciation for self and others; gradual assumption of responsibility for making informed decisions; and formulating and executing educational, career, and life plans. As a result, students can transfer those life skills to continued learning and planning in their academic, personal, and professional endeavors.

- Foster social connections in classroom, library, and counseling environments
- Help students to continue clarifying and developing purpose (attention to life, career, and education goals)
- Establish rapport via student-faculty contact
- Establish student services-faculty connections
- Employ electronic tools to aid student contact (Atlas, MyPortfolio, WebCT, email)
- Seek out struggling students and identify options through dialogue (and appropriate referrals)

### Use Assessment as a Tool for Learning

Assessment strategies used by Valencia educators will enable student growth through consistent, timely, formative measures, and promote students' ability to self-assess. Assessment practices will invite student feedback on the teaching and learning process as well as on student achievement.

- Employ formative feedback loops early and often (both to and from students)
- Provide students with written or face-to-face comments on the strengths and weaknesses of their performance(s)
- Give timely feedback on class activities, exams, and papers
- Design activities to help students refine their abilities to self-assess learning
- Integrate self-assessment into course processes
- Align summative evaluations with course outcomes and learning activities (appropriate to level of thinking; appropriate levels of performance)
- Make assessment criteria public to students and colleagues
- Evaluate effectiveness of assessment strategies and grading practices
- Vary assessment measures and techniques to form a more complete picture of learning

### Form an Inclusive Learning Environment That Respects Diverse Talents and Ways of Learning

Valencia educators will design learning opportunities that acknowledge, draw upon, and are enriched by student diversity. An atmosphere of inclusion and understanding will be promoted in all learning environments.

- Design learning experiences that address students' unique strengths*
- Design learning experiences that address students' unique needs*
- Develop reciprocity and cooperation among students (interdependence and teamwork)

- Include content well suited to Valencia's diverse student population
- Establish connections among students in and out of the classroom (learning communities)
- Vary assessment measures and techniques to engage cognitive diversity
- Create learning atmospheres that encourage all students to share viewpoints
- Use diverse perspectives to engage and deepen critical thinking (diversity as learning resource)
- Develop student self-awareness (learning styles, personality types, assumptions)

*Note: Diversity has many dimensions (culture, gender, race/ethnicity, socioeconomic circumstances, learning style, education background, skill level, etc.)

### Engage in the Scholarship of Teaching and Learning (SoTL)

Valencia educators will continuously examine the effectiveness of their teaching, counseling, librarianship, and assessment methodologies in terms of student learning. They will keep abreast of the current scholarship in the fields of teaching and learning.

- Produce professional work that meets the Standards of Scholarship* (course designs, conference presentations, action research projects, publications)
- Build upon the work of others (consult literature, peers, self, students)
- Be open to constructive critique (by both peers and students)
- Make work public to college and broader audiences
- Demonstrate the relationship of SoTL to improved teaching and learning processes

*Note: Valencia's Standards of Scholarship: Clear goals, adequate preparation, significant results, appropriate methods, reflective critique, and effective presentation are adapted from Glassick, Huber, and Maeroff (1997).

### Demonstrate Professional Commitment

Valencia educators will stay current and continually improve their knowledge and understanding of their discipline. They will participate in activities that promote Valencia's learning mission, including serving on campus and college-wide groups, attending professional conferences, and involvement with community or other organizations.

- Contribute to discipline/academic field
- Participate actively on department, campus, and college committees/task forces
- Engage with faculty governing bodies
- Access faculty development programs and resources
- Stay current in discipline (professional organizations; journals and other literature)
- Collaborate with colleagues in the department/discipline
- Expand knowledge of college connections to wider communities (Focus on Workplace; student development activities; trends in business and government)

## Appendix 20.2

# Required Elements of a Valencia Faculty Portfolio

**Clear Goals**
- Individualized Learning Plan
- Philosophy of teaching, counseling, or librarianship (evidence of philosophy should be reflected in the support section)
- Educational and professional background

**Supporting Artifacts Documentation for Each Learning Outcome (LO)**
**Candidates Usually Have Three LOs**

*Adequate Preparation*
- What the faculty candidate was trying to learn, achieve, or accomplish
- What the faculty candidate did to learn, achieve, or accomplish (workshop, book, article, conversations, etc.)

*Significant Results*
- What evidence and explanation demonstrate that the faculty candidate has learned, achieved, or accomplished the learning outcome objectives (supporting artifacts)?
- What evidence has the faculty candidate used from students and about student learning that documents the goals of the learning outcome (not necessarily relevant to all LOs)?

*Appropriate Methods*
- Analysis and evidence of how the faculty candidate demonstrated essential competencies in this LO

*Other Essential Competencies Not Addressed in Learning Outcomes*
- Descriptive narrative
- Supporting artifacts

**Reflective Critique**
- What the faculty candidate might do to more effectively integrate the essential competencies as his or her career progresses
- What the faculty candidate learned during his or her pre-tenure experience
- Future professional development
- Professional goals
- Year-1 and Year-2 ILP review panel feedback

## Appendix 20.3

# Valencia Community College Portfolio Evaluation Rubric

*Criteria for Quality Professional Teaching Portfolios/Artifacts*

| Standards of Scholarship | Not Yet Acceptable | Acceptable | Exemplary |
|---|---|---|---|
| Clear Goals<br>Introduction<br>1) Individualized Learning Plan<br>2) Professional Philosophy<br>3) Background Information | 1) ILP not included in the portfolio and/or does not relate to teaching and learning<br>2) Philosophy not included in portfolio; philosophy either not clearly stated or does not support teaching and learning<br>3) Background information not included in portfolio; not well organized | 1) ILP included in portfolio; relates to teaching and learning<br>2) Philosophy included in portfolio; philosophy clearly stated and supports teaching and learning<br>3) Background included in portfolio; information well organized | 1) Acceptable and clearly reflected in portfolio documentation/ artifacts<br>2) Acceptable and clearly reflected in portfolio documentation<br>3) Acceptable and documents educational and professional experiences that contribute to professional commitment |
| Appropriate Methods<br>Essential Competencies<br>• L-C Teaching Strategies<br>• Core Competencies (TVCA)<br>• LifeMap<br>• Assessment<br>• Inclusion and Diversity<br>• Scholarship of Teaching and Learning<br>• Professional Commitment | One or more competency not addressed; little or no analysis of teaching and learning related to faculty candidate's classroom/professional practice | Each competency addressed with an analysis of teaching and learning that relates to the faculty candidate's classroom/professional practice | Acceptable and insightful analysis for each demonstrated competency; results described and explained |

| Standards of Scholarship | Not Yet Acceptable | Acceptable | Exemplary |
|---|---|---|---|
| Reflective Critique | Little or no relevant discussion of teaching and learning related to faculty candidate's teaching/professional practice; future professional development and goals | Discusses how the results of pre-tenure/ILP work have affected faculty candidate's teaching and learning as it relates to his or her own teaching/professional practice, will likely affect future professional development, and professional goals | Acceptable and insightful analysis |
| Adequate Preparation Supporting Artifacts Documentation | One or more learning objectives not demonstrated; little or no evidence of teaching and learning related to faculty candidate's professional practice | Each learning objective demonstrated; evidence of teaching and learning related to faculty candidate's professional practice | Acceptable and results indicate understanding of relevant scholarship/pedagogy |
| Significant Results Supporting Artifacts Documentation | One or more learning objectives not demonstrated; little or no evidence of teaching and learning related to faculty candidate's professional practice goals; no evidence of student feedback/work, if applicable | Each LO demonstrated; evidence of teaching and learning related to faculty candidate's classroom/professional environment goals, including student feedback/work, if applicable | Acceptable and results described and explained; opens additional questions for further exploration, if applicable |
| Effective Presentation Publication | Not clearly written; not professionally presented and edited | Clearly written; professionally presented and edited | Acceptable, insightful, and comprehensive |

# Bibliography

Abdal-Haqq, I. (1998). *Professional development schools: Weighing the evidence.* Thousand Oaks, CA: Corwin Press.

Alire, C. A. (2002). The new beginnings program: A retention program for junior faculty of color. In T. Y. Neely & K.-H. Lee-Smeltzer (Eds.), *Diversity now: People, collections, and services in academic libraries* (pp. 21–30). Binghamton, NY: Haworth.

Allen, C. (1999). Wiser women: Fostering undergraduate success in science and engineering with a residential academic program. *Journal of Women and Minorities in Science and Engineering, 5*(3), 265–277.

Allen, K. E., & Cherrey, C. (2000). *Systemic leadership: Enriching the meaning of our work.* Lanham, MD: University Press of America.

Altschuler, G. C., & Kramnick, I. (1999, November 5). A better idea has replaced 'in loco parentis'. *Chronicle of Higher Education,* p. B8.

Amabile, T. M. (1982). Social psychology of creativity: A consensual assessment technique. *Journal of Personality and Social Psychology, 43,* 997–1013.

Amabile, T. M., DeJong, W., & Lepper, M. R. (1976). Effects of externally imposed deadlines on subsequent intrinsic motivation. *Journal of Personality and Social Psychology, 34,* 92–98.

Ameen, E. C., Guffey, D. M., & Jackson, C. (2002). Evidence of teaching anxiety among accounting educators. *Journal of Education for Business, 78*(1), 16–22.

Anderson, L. W., & Krathwohl, D. R. (Eds.). (2001). *A taxonomy for learning, teaching, and assessing: A revision of Bloom's taxonomy of educational objectives* (Abridged ed.). New York, NY: Longman.

Angelo, T. A. (1993). A "teacher's dozen": Fourteen general, research- based principles for improving higher learning in our classrooms. *AAHE Bulletin, 45*(8), 3–13.

Angelo, T. A., & Cross, K. P. (1993). *Classroom assessment techniques: A handbook for college teachers* (2nd ed.). San Francisco, CA: Jossey-Bass.

Apple, M. (1996). Power, meaning, and identity: Critical sociology of education in the United States. *British Journal of Sociology of Education, 17*(2), 125–144.

Arnold, M. (1865). The function of criticism at the present time. In *Essays in criticism* (pp. 1–41). London, England: Macmillan.

Arreola, R. A., Aleamoni, L. M., & Theall, M. (2001). *College teaching as meta-profession: Reconceptualizing the scholarship of teaching and learning.* Paper presented at the 9th annual American Association for Higher Education Conference on Faculty Roles and Rewards, Tampa, FL.

Arreola, R. A., Theall, M., & Aleamoni, L. M. (2003). *Beyond scholarship: Recognizing the multiple roles of the professoriate.* Paper presented at the 83rd annual meeting of the American Educational Research Association, Chicago, IL.

Astin, A. W. (1991). *Assessment for excellence: The philosophy and practice of assessment and evaluation in higher education.* New York, NY: American Council on Education/Macmillan.

Austin, A. (1990). *To leave an indelible mark: Encouraging good teaching in research universities through faculty development.* Nashville, TN: Peabody College of Vanderbilt University.

Austin, A. E. (2002). *Assessing doctoral students' progress along developmental dimensions.* Paper presented at the annual meeting of the Association for the Study of Higher Education, Sacramento, CA. Retrieved May 22, 2005, from http://www.carnegiefoundation.org/CID/ashe/Assessing_doctoral_students.pdf

Austin, A. E. (2002). Preparing the next generation of faculty: Graduate school as socialization to the academic career. *Journal of Higher Education, 73*(1), 94–122.

Austin, A. E., Sorcinelli, M. D., Eddy, P. L., & Beach, A. L. (2003). *Envisioning responsive faculty development: Perceptions of faculty developers about the present and future of faculty development.* Paper presented at the 83rd annual meeting of the American Educational Research Association, Chicago, IL.

Austin, A. E., & Wulff, D. H. (2004). The challenge to prepare the next generation of faculty. In D. H. Wulff, A. E. Austin, & Associates, *Paths to the professoriate: Strategies for enriching the preparation of future faculty* (pp. 3–16). San Francisco, CA: Jossey-Bass.

Baldwin, R. G. (Ed.). (1985). *New directions for higher education: No. 51. Incentives for faculty vitality.* San Francisco, CA: Jossey-Bass.

Baldwin, R. G. (1990). Faculty career stages and implications for professional development. In J. H. Schuster & D. W. Wheeler (Eds.), *Enhancing faculty careers: Strategies for development and renewal* (pp. 20–40). San Francisco, CA: Jossey-Bass.

Bandura, A. (1997). *Self-efficacy: The exercise of control.* New York, NY: W. H. Freeman and Company.

Barefoot, B. O., Gardner, J. N., Cutright, M., Morris, L. V., Schroeder, C. C., Schwartz, S.W., et al. (2005). *Achieving and sustaining institutional excellence in the first year of college.* San Francisco, CA: Jossey-Bass.

Barley, S. R. (1990). Images of imaging: Notes on doing longitudinal fieldwork. *Organization Science, 1*(3), 220–247.

Battistoni, R., Gelmon, S. B., Saltmarsh, J., Wergin, J., & Zlotkowski, E. (2003). *The engaged department toolkit.* Providence, RI: Campus Compact.

Baxter Magolda, M. B. (2000). Teaching to promote holistic learning and development. In M. B. Baxter Magolda (Ed.), *New directions for teaching and learning: No. 82. Teaching to promote intellectual and personal maturity: Incorporating students' worldviews and identities into the learning process* (pp. 88–98). San Francisco, CA: Jossey-Bass.

Beckhard, R. (1969). *Organization development: Strategies and models.* Reading, MA: Addison-Wesley.

Belshaw, C. S. (1974). *Towers besieged: The dilemma of the creative university.* Toronto, Canada: McClelland and Stewart.

Bennis, W. (1973). An O.D. expert in the cat bird's seat. *Journal of Higher Education, 44*(5), 389–398.

Bernstein, D. A. (1983). Dealing with teaching anxiety: A personal view. *Journal of the National Association of Colleges and Teachers of Agriculture, 27,* 181–185.

Besterfield-Sacre, M. E., Atman, C. J., & Shuman, L. J. (1997). Characteristics of freshman engineering students: Models for determining student attrition in engineering. *Journal of Engineering Education, 86*(2), 139–149.

Birnbaum, R. (2001). *Management fads in higher education: Where they come from, what they do, why they fail.* San Francisco, CA: Jossey-Bass.

Birnbaum, R. (2002, Fall). The president as storyteller: Restoring the narrative of higher education. *The presidency,* 33–39.

Black, A. E., & Deci, E. L. (2000). The effects of instructors' autonomy support and students' autonomous motivation on learning organic chemistry: A self-determination theory perspective. *Science Education, 84,* 740–756.

Bland, C. J., & Bergquist, W. H. (1997). *The vitality of senior faculty members: Snow on the roof–fire in the furnace* (ASHE-ERIC Higher Education Report, 25[7]), Washington, DC: George Washington University.

Bloom, A. (1987). *The closing of the American mind.* New York, NY: Simon & Schuster.

Bloom, B. S. (Ed.). (1956). *Taxonomy of educational objectives: Book 1. Cognitive domain.* New York, NY: Longman.

Boice, R. (1991). Quick starters: New faculty who succeed. In M. Theall & J. Franklin (Eds.), *New directions for teaching and learning: No. 48. Effective practices for improving teaching* (pp. 111–121). San Francisco, CA: Jossey-Bass.

Boice, R. (1992). *The new faculty member: Supporting and fostering professional development.* San Francisco, CA: Jossey-Bass.

Boice, R. (1993a). Early turning points in professorial careers of women and minorities. In J. Gainen & R. Boice (Eds.), *New directions for teaching and learning: No. 53. Building a diverse faculty* (pp. 71–80). San Francisco, CA: Jossey-Bass.

Boice, R. (1993b). New faculty involvement for women and minorities. *Research in Higher Education, 34*(3), 291–341.

Boice, R. (2000). *Advice to new faculty members.* Needham Heights, MA: Allyn & Bacon.

Boyer, E. L. (1990). *Scholarship reconsidered: Priorities of the professoriate.* Princeton, NJ: Carnegie Foundation for the Advancement of Teaching.

Boyer, R. K., & Crocket, C. (1973). Organizational development in higher education: Introduction. *Journal of Higher Education, 44*(5), 339–351.

Bransford, J. D., Brown, A. L., & Cocking, R. R. (Eds.). (2000). *How people learn: Brain, mind, experience, and school* (Expanded ed.). Washington, DC: National Academies Press.

Breneman, D. W. (1994). *Liberal arts colleges: Thriving, surviving, or endangered?* Washington, DC: The Brookings Institution.

Brookfield, S. (1993). Through the lens of learning: How the visceral experience of learning reframes teaching. In D. Boud, R. Cohen, & D. Walker (Eds.), *Using experience for learning* (pp. 21–32). Buckingham, England: Society for Research into Higher Education and Open University Press.

Brookfield, S. D. (1986). *Understanding and facilitating adult learning.* San Francisco, CA: Jossey-Bass.

Brookfield, S. D. (1987). *Developing critical thinkers.* San Francisco, CA: Jossey-Bass.

Brookfield, S. D. (1990). *The skillful teacher: On technique, trust, and responsiveness in the classroom.* San Francisco, CA: Jossey-Bass.

Brookfield, S. D. (1995). *Becoming a critically reflective teacher.* San Francisco, CA: Jossey-Bass.

Brookfield, S. D. (2005). *The power of critical theory: Liberating adult learning and teaching.* San Francisco, CA: Jossey-Bass.

Brower, A. M., & Dettinger, K. M. (1998, November/December). What is a learning community? Toward a comprehensive model. *About Campus,* 15–21.

Brower, A. M., & Laines, M. J. (1997). What works and how we found out: An assessment of the Bradley Learning Community. *Talking Stick, 14*(7), 17–19.

Browning, J. E. S., & Williams, J. B. (1978). History and goals of black institutions of higher learning. In C. V. Willie & R. R. Edmonds (Eds.), *Black colleges in America* (pp. 68–93). New York, NY: Teachers College Press.

Buber, M. (1961). *Between man and man.* New York, NY: Routledge and Kegan Paul.

Burd, S. (2005, January 7). Change in federal formula means thousands may lose student aid. *Chronicle of Higher Education,* p. A1.

Campus Compact. (2001). *Planning document for the engaged department institute.* Providence, RI: Author.

Campus Compact. (2002). *Intermediate institutes on the engaged department.* Providence, RI: Author.

Carusetta, E. (2001). Evaluating teaching through teaching awards. In C. Knapper & P. Cranton (Eds.), *New directions in teaching and learning: No. 88. Fresh approaches to the evaluation of teaching* (pp. 31–40). San Francisco, CA: Jossey-Bass.

Chaffee, E. E., & Jacobson, S. W. (1997). Creating and changing institutional cultures. In M. W. Peterson, D. D. Dill, & L. A. Mets (Eds.), *Planning and management for a changing environment: A handbook on redesigning postsecondary institutions* (pp. 230–245). San Francisco, CA: Jossey-Bass.

Chism, N. V. N. (1998). The role of educational developers in institutional change: From the basement office to the front office. In M. Kaplan & D. Lieberman (Eds.), *To improve the academy: Vol. 17. Resources for faculty, instructional, and organizational development* (pp. 141–153). Stillwater, OK: New Forums Press.

Chism, N. V. N. (2005). Promoting a sound process for teaching awards programs: Appropriate work for faculty development centers. In S. Chadwick-Blossey & D. R. Robertson (Eds.), *To improve the academy: Vol. 23. Resources for faculty, instructional, and organizational development* (pp. 314–330). Bolton, MA: Anker.

Chism, N. V. N., & Szabo, B. L. (1997). Teaching awards: The problem of assessing their impact. In D. DeZure & M. Kaplan (Eds.), *To improve the academy: Vol. 16. Resources for faculty, instructional, and organizational development* (pp. 181–200). Stillwater, OK: New Forums Press.

Clotfelter, C. T. (1999). The familiar but curious economics of higher education. *Journal of Economic Perspectives, 13*(1), 3–12.

Cohen, I. B. (1994). *Interactions: Some contacts between the natural sciences and social sciences.* Cambridge, MA: MIT Press.

Cohen, L. (1993). Anthem. In *Stranger music: Selected poems and songs* (pp. 373–374). Toronto, Canada: McClelland and Stewart.

Cohen, M. D., & March, J. G. (1974). *Leadership and ambiguity: The American college president.* Boston, MA: Harvard Business School Press.

Cohen, M. D., March, J. G., & Olsen, J. P. (1972). A garbage can model of organizational choice. *Administrative Science Quarterly, 17*(1), 1–25.

Commission on the University of the 21st Century. (1989). *The case for change.* Richmond, VA: Commonwealth of Virginia.

Cook, P. J., & Frank, R. H. (1993). The growing concentration of top students at elite schools. In C. T. Clotfelter & M. Rothschild (Eds.), *Studies of supply and demand in higher education* (pp. 121–144). Chicago, IL: University of Chicago Press.

Cooke, A. (1952). *One man's America.* New York, NY: Alfred A. Knopf.

Cooper, J. (1990). Cooperative learning and college teaching: Tips from the trenches. *The Teaching Professor, 4,* 1–2.

Cooper, J. L., Robinson, P., & Ball, D. (Eds). (2003). *Small group instruction in higher education: Lessons from the past, visions of the future.* Stillwater, OK: New Forums Press.

Cousins, E. (1998). *Reflections on design principles.* Dubuque, IA: Kendall/Hunt.

Cousins, E. (Ed.). (2000). *Roots: From outward bound to expeditionary learning.* Dubuque, IA: Kendall/Hunt.

Cox, M. D. (1995). The development of new and junior faculty. In W. A. Wright & Associates (Ed.), *Teaching improvement practices: Successful strategies for higher education* (pp. 283–305). Bolton, MA: Anker.

Cox, M. D. (1997). Long-term patterns in a mentor program for junior faculty: Recommendations for practice. In D. Dezure & M. Kaplan (Eds.), *To improve the academy: Vol. 16. Resources for faculty, instructional, and organizational development* (pp. 225–268). Stillwater, OK: New Forums Press.

Cranton, P. (2001). *Becoming an authentic teacher in higher education.* Malabar, FL: Krieger.

Cranton, P., & Carusetta, E. (2004). Perspectives on authenticity in teaching. *Adult Education Quarterly, 55*(1), 5–22.

Cross, K. P., & Steadman, M. H. (1996). *Classroom research: Implementing the scholarship of teaching.* San Francisco, CA: Jossey-Bass.

Cross, T. (2003). The nation's colleges show a modest improvement in African-American graduation rates, but a huge racial gap remains. *Journal of Blacks in Higher Education, 41,* 109.

Cunningham, P. M. (2000). A sociology of adult education. In A. L. Wilson & E. R. Hayes (Eds.), *Handbook of adult and continuing education* (pp. 573–591). San Francisco, CA: Jossey-Bass.

Curzan, A., & Damour, L. (2000). *First day to final grade: A graduate student's guide to teaching.* Ann Arbor, MI: University of Michigan.

Cuseo, J. B. (2003). Critical thinking and cooperative learning: A natural marriage. In J. L. Cooper, P. Robinson, & D. Ball (Eds.), *Small group instruction in higher education: Lessons from the past, visions of the future* (pp. 63–74), Stillwater, OK: New Forums Press.

Cutright, M. (1999). *A chaos-theory metaphor for strategic planning in higher education: An exploratory study.* Unpublished doctoral dissertation, the University of Tennessee, Knoxville. (ERIC Document Reproduction Service No. ED457931)

Cutright, M. (Ed.). (2001). *Chaos theory and higher education: Leadership, planning, and policy.* New York, NY: Peter Lang.

Davis, A. M., & Smith, M. J. (2004). Embracing diversity in pursuit of excellence. *Report of the President's Commission on Diversity and Equity.* Retrieved May 20, 2005, from the University of Virginia, Voices of Diversity web site: http://www.virginia.edu/uvadiversity/embracing_report04.html

Davis, B. G. (1993). *Tools for teaching.* San Francisco, CA: Jossey-Bass.

Davis, S., & Botkin, J. (1994). *The monster under the bed: How business is mastering the opportunity of knowledge for profit.* New York, NY: Simon & Schuster.

Dawkins, R. (2003). *A devil's chaplain: Reflections on hope, lies, science, and love.* New York, NY: Houghton Mifflin.

Deci, E. L. (1975). *Intrinsic motivation.* New York, NY: Plenum.

Deci, E. L., Koestner, R., & Ryan, R. M. (1999). A meta-analytic review of experiments examining the effects of extrinsic rewards on intrinsic motivation. *Psychological Bulletin, 125*(6), 627–668.

Deci, E. L., & Ryan, R. M. (1985). *Intrinsic motivation and self-determination in human behavior.* New York, NY: Plenum.

Deci, E. L., & Ryan, R. M. (1991). A motivational approach to self: Integration in personality. In R. A. Dienstbier (Ed.), *Perspectives on motivation* (pp. 237–288). Lincoln, NE: University of Nebraska Press.

Deci, E. L., & Ryan, R. M. (2000). The "what" and "why" of goal pursuits: Human needs and the self-determination of behavior. *Psychological Inquiry, 11,* 227–268.

Deci, E. L., Vallerand, R. J., Pelletier, L. G., & Ryan, R. M. (1991). Motivation and education: The self-determination perspective. *Educational Psychologist, 26,* 325–346.

Dewey, J. (1916). *Democracy and education: An introduction to the philosophy of education.* New York, NY: Macmillan.

Dewey, J. (1938). *Experience and education.* New York, NY: Touchstone.

DeZure, D. (2002). *Priorities/concerns of faculty at several career stages.* Paper presented at a University of Michigan Faculty Seminar, Ann Arbor, MI.

Dolence, M. G., & Norris, D. M. (1995). *Transforming higher education: A vision for learning in the 21st century.* Ann Arbor, MI: Society for College and University Planning.

Donald, J. G. (2002). *Learning to think: Disciplinary perspectives.* San Francisco, CA: Jossey-Bass.

Drewry, H. N., & Doermann, H. (2001). *Stand and prosper: Private black colleges and their students.* Princeton, NJ: Princeton University Press.

DuBois, W. E . B. (1961). *The souls of black folks.* Greenwich, CT: Fawcett.

Durand, B. (2004, April 11). Diversity plans are in effect. *Wisconsin State Journal,* p. B1.

Einstein, A. (1961). *Relativity: The special and general theory.* New York, NY: Crown Publishers.

Fantuzzo, J. W., Dimeff, L. A., & Fox, S. L. (1989). Reciprocal peer tutoring: A multimodal assessment of effectiveness with college students. *Teaching of Psychology, 16*(3), 133–135.

Fantuzzo, J. W., Riggio, R. E., Connelly, S., & Dimeff, L. A. (1989). Effects of reciprocal peer tutoring on academic achievement and psychological adjustment: A component analysis. *Journal of Educational Psychology, 81*(2), 173–177.

Farr, G. (1988). Faculty development centers as resource centers. In E. C. Wadsworth (Ed.), *A handbook for new practitioners* (pp. 35–38). Stillwater, OK: New Forums Press and Professional and Organizational Development Network in Higher Education.

Fayol, H. (1984). *Administration industrielle et générale.* Paris, France: Denod.

Felder, R. M. (1994). Things I wish they had told me. *Chemical Engineering Education, 28*(2), 108–109.

Field, K. (2005, January 7). Pork crowds out the competition. *Chronicle of Higher Education,* p. A33.

Fink, L. D. (1988). Establishing an instructional development program. In E. C. Wadsworth (Ed.), *A handbook for new practitioners* (pp. 21–25). Stillwater, OK: New Forums Press and Professional and Organizational Development Network in Higher Education.

Fink, L. D. (1992). Orientation programs for new faculty. In M. D. Sorcinelli & A. E. Austin (Eds.), *New directions for teaching and learning: No. 50. Developing new and junior faculty* (pp. 39–50). San Francisco, CA: Jossey-Bass.

Fink, L. D. (2003). *Creating significant learning experiences: An integrated approach to designing college courses.* San Francisco, CA: Jossey-Bass.

Finkelstein, M. J. (2003). The morphing of the American academic profession. *Liberal Education, 89*(4), 6–15.

Finkelstein, M. J., Seal, R. K., & Schuster, J. H. (1998). *The new academic generation: A profession in transition.* Baltimore, MD: Johns Hopkins University Press.

Fisher, J. L. (1994). Reflections on transformational leadership. *Educational Record, 75*(3), 54, 60–65.

Florence, C. W. (1932). Critical evaluation of present policies and practices of Negro institutions of higher education. In T. E. McKinney, *Higher education among Negroes* (pp. 39–58). Charlotte, NC: Johnson C. Smith University.

Foner, E. (1989). *Reconstruction: America's unfinished revolution, 1863–1877.* New York, NY: Perennial.

Franklin, J. H., & Moss, A. A., Jr. (1994). *From slavery to freedom: A history of African Americans* (7th ed.). New York, NY: Alfred A. Knopf.

Frantz, A. C., Beebe, S. A., Horvath, V. S., Canales, J., & Swee, D. E. (2005). The roles of teaching and learning centers. In S. Chadwick-Blossey & D. R. Robertson (Eds.), *To improve the academy: Vol. 23. Resources for faculty, instructional, and organizational development* (pp. 72–90). Bolton, MA: Anker.

Frederick, P. J. (1989). Involving students more actively in the classroom. In A. F. Lucas (Ed.), *New directions for teaching and learning: Vol. 37. The department chairperson's role in enhancing college teaching* (pp. 31–40). San Francisco, CA: Jossey-Bass.

Freire, P. (1982). Creating alternative research methods: Learning it by doing it. In B. Hall, A. Gillette, & R. Tandon (Eds.), *Creating knowledge: A monopoly* (pp. 29–37). New Delhi, India: Society for Participatory Research in Asia.

Freire, P. (1984). *Pedagogy of the oppressed.* New York, NY: Continuum.

Frye, N. (1969). *The ethics of change.* Toronto, Canada: Canadian Broadcasting Corporation.

Frye, N. (1988). *On education.* Toronto, Canada: Fitzhenry & Whiteside.

Gardiner, L. F. (1996). *Redesigning higher education: Producing dramatic gains in student learning* (ASHE-ERIC Higher Education Report, 23[7]). Washington, DC: George Washington University, Graduate School of Education and Human Development.

Gardner, L. E., & Leak, G. K. (1994). Characteristics and correlates of teaching anxiety among college psychology teachers. *Teaching of Psychology, 21,* 28–32.

Gartner, A., Kohler, M. C., & Riessman, F. (1971). *Children teach children: Learning by teaching.* New York, NY: Harper & Row.

Gell-Mann, M. (1994). *The quark and the jaguar: Adventures in the simple and the complex.* New York, NY: Henry Holt and Company.

Gere, A. R. (1987). *Writing groups: History, theory, and implications.* Carbondale, IL: Southern Illinois University Press.

Giamatti, A. B. (1990). *A free and ordered space: The real world of the university.* New York, NY: W. W. Norton & Company.

Glaser, B. G., & Strauss, A. L. (1967). *The discovery of grounded theory: Strategies for qualitative research.* Chicago, IL: Aldine.

Glassick, C. E., Huber, M. T., & Maeroff, G. I. (1997). *Scholarship assessed: Evaluation of the professoriate.* San Francisco, CA: Jossey-Bass.

Gleick, J. (1987). *Chaos: Making a new science.* New York, NY: Penguin.

Glesne, C., & Peshkin, A. (1992). *Becoming qualitative researchers: An introduction.* New York, NY: Longman.

Greenblatt, S. (2004). *Will in the world: How Shakespeare became Shakespeare.* New York, NY: W. W. Norton & Company.

Grolnick, W. S., & Ryan, R. M. (1987). Autonomy in children's learning: An experimental and individual difference investigation. *Journal of Personality and Social Psychology, 52*, 890–898.

Grubb, W. N., & Associates. (1999). *Honored but invisible: An inside look at teaching in community colleges.* New York, NY: Routledge.

Hale, F. W., Jr. (Ed.). (2004). *What makes racial diversity work in higher education: Academic leaders present successful policies and strategies.* Sterling, VA: Stylus.

Harackiewicz, J. M., Manderlink, G., & Sansone, C. (1984). Rewarding pinball wizardry: The effects of evaluation on intrinsic interest. *Journal of Personality and Social Psychology, 47*, 287–300.

Harper, V. (1996). Establishing a community of conversation: Creating a context for self-reflection among teacher scholars. In L. Richlin & D. DeZure (Eds.), *To improve the academy: Vol. 15. Resources for faculty, instructional, and organizational development* (pp. 251–266). Stillwater, OK: New Forums Press.

Hativa, N., & Goodyear, P. (2002). *Teacher thinking, beliefs and knowledge in higher education.* New York, NY: Springer.

Heidegger, M. (1962). *Being and time* (J. Macquarrie & E. Robinson, Trans.). New York, NY: Harper & Row.

Henry, J. (1989). Meaning and practice in experiential learning. In S. W. Weil & I. McGill (Eds.), *Making sense of experiential learning: Diversity in theory and practice* (pp. 29–33). Buckingham, England: Society for Research into Higher Education and Open University Press.

Herrnstein, R. J., & Murray, C. (1994). *The bell curve: Intelligence and class structure in American life.* New York, NY: Free Press.

Hilsen, L., & Wadsworth, E. C. (1988). Staging successful workshops. In E. C. Wadsworth (Ed.), *A handbook for new practitioners* (pp. 45–52). Stillwater, OK: New Forums Press and Professional and Organizational Development Network in Higher Education.

Hollis, J. (1998). *The Eden Project: In search of the magical other.* Toronto, Canada: Inner City Books.

Holton, S. A. (1995). Where do we go from here? *New Directions for Higher Education, 92*, 91–95.

Howard Hughes Medical Institute. (2004). *Making the right moves: A practical guide to scientific management for postdocs and new faculty.* Chevy Chase, MD: Author.

Innes, J. (1996). Planning through consensus building: A new view of the comprehensive planning ideal. *Journal of the American Planning Association, 62*(4),
460–472.

Jarvis, P. (1992). *Paradoxes of learning: On becoming an individual in society.* San
Francisco, CA: Jossey-Bass.

Jensen, E. (2000). *Brain-based learning: The new science of teaching and training*
(Rev. ed.). San Diego, CA: The Brain Store.

Johnson, D. W., Johnson, R. T., & Smith, K. A. (1991). *Cooperative learning: Increasing college faculty instructional productivity* (ASHE-ERIC Higher Education Report No. 4). Washington, DC: George Washington University, School of Education and Human Development.

Jung, C. (1971). *Psychological types.* Princeton, NJ: Princeton University Press.
(Original work published 1921)

Kadison, R. D. (2004, December 10). The mental-health crisis: What colleges must
do. *Chronicle of Higher Education,* p. B20.

Kahneman, D., & Tversky, A. (1979). Prospect theory: An analysis of decision under
risk. *Econometrica, 47*(2), 263–291.

Kalivoda, P., Sorrell, G. R., & Simpson, R. D. (1994). Nurturing faculty vitality by
matching institutional interventions with career-stage needs. *Innovative Higher
Education, 18*(4), 255–272.

Karpiak, I. E. (2001). Midlife: The "second call" for faculty renewal. *The Department
Chair, 11*(4), 11–12.

Keller, G. (1983). *Academic strategy: The management revolution in American higher
education.* Baltimore, MD: Johns Hopkins University Press.

Keller, G. (1988, February). Academic strategy: Five years later. *AAHE Bulletin,* 3–6.

Keller, G. (2004). *Transforming a college: The story of a little-known college's strategic
climb to national distinction.* Baltimore, MD: Johns Hopkins University Press.

Knapper, C. (2004). *Research on college teaching and learning: Applying what we
know.* Paper prepared for the Teaching Professor Conference, Philadelphia, PA.
Retrieved May 17, 2005, from http://teachingprofessor.com/conference/sun
daypaper.html

Knowles, M. S. (1970). *The modern practice of adult education: Andragogy versus pedagogy.* New York, NY: Associated Press.

Koehler, T., & Miranda, C. (2004, April 11). Are today's UW–Madison graduates
cultural klutzes? *Wisconsin State Journal,* p. B1.

Kolb, D. A. (1976). *The learning style inventory: Technical manual.* Boston, MA: McBer.

Kolb, D. A. (1984). *Experiential learning: Experience as the source of learning and development.* Englewood Cliffs, NJ: Prentice Hall.

Kuhn, T. S. (1970). *The structure of scientific revolutions* (2nd ed.). Chicago, IL: University of Chicago Press.

Lakoff, G., & Johnson, M. (1980). *Metaphors we live by.* Chicago, IL: University of Chicago Press.

Langford, T. A. (1987). Recognizing outstanding teaching. In N. V. N. Chism (Ed.), *Institutional responsibilities and responses in the employment and education of teaching assistants: Readings from a national conference* (pp. 132–133). Columbus, OH: The Ohio State University, Center for Teaching Excellence.

Leaming, D. R. (1998). *Academic leadership: A practical guide to chairing the department.* Bolton, MA: Anker.

Leamnson, R. (1999). *Thinking about teaching and learning: Developing habits of learning with first year college and university students.* Sterling, VA: Stylus.

LeDoux, J. (1996). *The emotional brain: The mysterious underpinnings of emotional life.* New York, NY: Putnam.

Levesque, C., Zuehlke, A. N., Stanek, L. R., & Ryan, R. M. (2004). Autonomy and competence in German and American university students: A comparative study based on self-determination theory. *Journal of Educational Psychology, 96*(1), 68–84.

Levin, B. H., Lanigan, J. B., & Perkins, J. R. (1995). *Strategic planning in a decentralized environment: The death of linearity.* Paper presented at the 24th annual Conference of the Southeastern Association for Community College Research, Asheville, NC.

Lewis, K. G. (1994). *Using on-going student feedback to increase teaching effectiveness and student learning.* Retrieved May 22, 2005, from the University of Texas at Austin, Division of Instructional Innovation and Assessment web site: http://www.utexas.edu/academic/diia/gsi/assessment/ongoing.php

Lincoln, Y. S., & Guba, E. G. (1985). *Naturalistic inquiry.* Newbury Park, CA: Sage.

Litwack, L. F. (1998). *Trouble in mind: Black southerners in the age of Jim Crow.* New York, NY: Alfred A. Knopf.

Lorenz, E. N. (1993). *The essence of chaos.* Seattle, WA: University of Washington Press.

Love, P. G., & Estanek, S. M. (2004). *Rethinking student affairs practice.* San Francisco, CA: Jossey-Bass.

Lucas, C. J., & Murry, J. W., Jr. (2002). *New faculty: A practical guide for academic beginners.* New York, NY: Palgrave.

Mangan, K. S. (2005, January 14). Berkeley law dean calls for partial privatization of his school. *Chronicle of Higher Education,* p. A25.

Marino, J. (1995). Clearcutting in the groves of academe. In G. Laxer & T. Harrison (Eds.), *The Trojan Horse: Alberta and the future of Canada* (pp. 209–222). Montreal, Canada: Black Rose Books.

Martin, J., & Samels, J. E. (2001). Lessons learned: Eight best practices for new partnerships. In A. Kezar, D. J. Hirsch, & C. Burack (Eds.), *New directions for higher education: No. 116. Understanding the role of academic and student affairs collaboration in creating a successful learning environment* (pp. 89–100). San Francisco, CA: Jossey-Bass.

Martini, K. (1999a). *Making service count (a little): Guiding principles for junior faculty.* Retrieved May 20, 2005, from the University of Virginia web site: http://www.people.virginia.edu/~km6e/Papers/service-essay-99.html

Martini, K. (1999b). *Making your case: Strategies for an effective tenure package.* Retrieved May 20, 2005, from the University of Virginia web site: http://www.people.virginia.edu/~km6e/Papers/make-case/

Marton, F., Hounsell, D., & Entwistle, N. (1997). *The experience of learning: Implications for teaching and studying in higher education* (2nd ed.). Edinburgh, Scotland: Scottish Academic Press.

Marzano, R. J., Pickering, D. J., & Pollock, J. E. (2001). *Classroom instruction that works: Research-based strategies for increasing student achievement.* Alexandria, VA: Association for Supervision and Curriculum Development.

Master Teaching Team. (2004). Becoming Jonas: Reflections from the team. In D. M. Qualters & M. R. Diamond (Eds.), *Chalk talk: E-advice from Jonas Chalk, legendary college teacher* (pp. 11–20). Stillwater, OK: New Forums Press.

Mattmiller, B. (1996). A new notion of home. *On Wisconsin,* 20–39.

Mazur, E. (1997). *Peer instruction: A user's manual.* Upper Saddle River, NJ: Prentice Hall.

McAlpine, L., & Weston, C. (2002). Reflection: Issues related to improving professors' teaching and students' learning. In N. Hativa & P. Goodyear (Eds.), *Teacher thinking, beliefs and knowledge in higher education* (pp. 59–78). New York, NY: Springer.

McGraw, K. O., & McCullers, J. C. (1979). Evidence of a detrimental effect of extrinsic incentives on breaking a mental set. *Journal of Experimental Social Psychology, 15*, 285–294.

McGregor, D. (1960). *The human side of enterprise.* New York, NY: McGraw-Hill.

McKinney, T. E. (1932). *Higher education among Negroes.* Charlotte, NC: Johnson C. Smith University.

McMillin, L. A., & Berberet, W. G. (2002). *A new academic compact: Revisioning the relationship between faculty and their institutions.* Bolton, MA: Anker.

McTighe, J. (1992). Graphic organizers: Collaborative links to better thinking. In N. Davidson & T. Worsham (Eds.), *Enhancing thinking through cooperative learning* (pp. 182–197). New York, NY: Teachers College Press.

Meikeljohn, A. (1928). *The experimental college.* Madison, WI: University of Wisconsin Press.

Menges, R. J. (1995). Awards to individuals. In M. D. Svinicki & R. J. Menges (Eds.), *New directions in teaching and learning: No. 65. Honoring exemplary teaching* (pp. 3–9). San Francisco, CA: Jossey-Bass.

Menges, R. J. (1996). Experiences of newly hired faculty. In L. Richlin & D. DeZure (Eds.), *To improve the academy: Vol. 15. Resources for faculty, instructional, and organizational development* (pp. 169–182). Stillwater, OK: New Forums Press.

Merriam, S. B., & Caffarella, R. S. (1999). *Learning in adulthood: A comprehensive guide* (2nd ed.). San Francisco, CA: Jossey-Bass.

Meyer, T. (2000). *Finding a voice and place in a normative profession.* Paper presented at the 80th annual meeting of the American Educational Research Association, New Orleans, LA. (ERIC Document Reproduction Service No. ED 440970)

Meyers, C., & Jones, T. B. (1993). *Promoting active learning: Strategies for the college classroom.* San Francisco, CA: Jossey-Bass.

Mezirow, J. (1991). *Transformative dimensions of adult learning.* San Francisco, CA: Jossey-Bass.

Miles, M. B., & Huberman, A. M. (1994). *Qualitative data analysis: An expanded sourcebook* (2nd ed.). Thousand Oaks, CA: Sage.

Millis, B. J. (2002). *Enhancing learning—and more!—through cooperative learning* (IDEA Paper No. 38). Retrieved May 22, 2005, from the Kansas State University, IDEA Center web site: http://www.idea.ksu.edu/papers/Idea_Paper_38.pdf

Millis, B. J., & Cottell, P. G., Jr. (1998). *Cooperative learning for higher education faculty.* Phoenix, AZ: American Council on Education/Oryx Press.

Moody, J. (2004). *Faculty diversity: Problems and solutions.* New York, NY: Falmer.

Morgan, G. (1986). *Images of organization.* Newbury Park, CA: Sage.

Morgan, G. (1997). *Images of organization* (2nd ed.). Thousand Oaks, CA: Sage.

Morrison, J., Wilkinson, G., & Forbes, L. (1999). *Common sense management for educational leaders.* Retrieved May 13, 2005, from http://horizon.unc.edu/projects/CSM/

Morrissey, S. (2002). Academic diversity. *Chemical and Engineering News, 81*(34), 24.

Mullinix, B. B. (2004). *Tapping technology to facilitate a faculty-centered approach to faculty development.* Paper presented at the 2nd annual Technology in Education Conference, Plainsboro, NJ.

Mullinix, B. B., & Harr, C. (2003). *Faculty-centered program development.* Paper presented as Bright Idea Award Winner at the 28th annual meeting of the Professional and Organizational Development Network in Higher Education, Denver, CO.

Mullinix, B. B., & Harr, C. (2004). *Build it for them, they will come: Interest-based and scheduled faculty development.* Paper presented at the 84th annual meeting of the American Educational Research Association, San Diego, CA.

Mullinix, B. B., & Sarsar, S. (2002). *Institutional proposal for establishing a center for excellence in teaching and learning at Monmouth University* [Internal report]. West Long Branch, NJ: Monmouth University, Office of Academic Program Initiatives.

Mullinix, B. B., & Savoth, W. (2004). *Technological tools of our trade: Managing and assessing faculty development.* Pre-conference workshop at the 29th annual meeting of the Professional and Organizational Development Network in Higher Education, Montreal, Canada.

National Center for Education Statistics. (2003). *Digest of education statistics, 2002.* Retrieved May 13, 2005, from http://nces.ed.gov/pubsearch/pubsinfo.asp?pubid=2003060

National Center for Higher Education Management Systems. (2000, August). *The competency standards project: Another approach to accreditation review.* Washington, DC: Council for Higher Education Accreditation.

National Research Council. (2003). *Evaluating and improving undergraduate teaching in science, technology, engineering, and mathematics.* Washington, DC: National Academies Press.

National Science Foundation. (2000a). *GEO 2000 full report (NSF 00–27)*. Retrieved May 20, 2005, from http://www.nsf.gov/geo/adgeo/geo2000/geo_2000_full_report.jsp

National Science Foundation. (2000b). *Women, minorities, and persons with disabilities in science and engineering: 2000*. Retrieved May 20, 2005, from http://www.nsf.gov/sbe/srs/nsf00327/start.htm

Nellis, P., Clarke, H., DiMartino, J., & Hosman, D. K. (2001). Preparing today's faculty for tomorrow's students. In D. Lieberman & C. Wehlburg (Eds.), *To improve the academy: Vol. 19. Resources for faculty, instructional, and organizational development* (pp. 149–168). Bolton, MA: Anker.

Nelson, C. (1997). Tools for tampering with teaching's taboos. In W. E. Campbell & K. A. Smith (Eds.), *New paradigms for college teaching* (pp. 51–77). Edina, MN: Interaction Book Company.

Nelson, C. E. (2004). *Responding to diversity: Three pedagogical changes that can make a real difference in ANY college classroom.* Paper presented at the 24th annual Lilly Conference on College Teaching, Oxford, OH.

Neumann, A., & Larson, R. S. (1997). Enhancing the leadership factor in planning. In M. W. Peterson, D. D. Dill, & L. A. Mets (Eds.), *Planning and management for a changing environment: A handbook on redesigning postsecondary institutions* (pp. 191–203). San Francisco, CA: Jossey-Bass.

New South Wales, Department of Education and Training. (2002). *Educational leadership and practice: A review of the literature and an exploration of mentoring practices.* Retrieved May 25, 2005, from the New South Wales, Department of Education and Training web site: http://www.schools.nsw.edu.au/edu_leadership/prof_read/mentoring/intro.php

Nuhfer, E., Krest, M., & Handelsman, M. M. (2003). Developing in fractal patterns III: A guide for composing teaching philosophies. *The National Teaching and Learning Forum, 12*(5), 10–11.

Olsen, D., & Sorcinelli, M. D. (1992). The pretenure years: A longitudinal perspective. In M. D. Sorcinelli & A. E. Austin (Eds.), *New directions for teaching and learning: No. 50. Developing new and junior faculty* (pp. 15–25). San Francisco, CA: Jossey-Bass.

Organization Development Network. (1998–2005). *Principles of practice.* Retrieved May 10, 2005, from http://www.odnetwork.org/principlesofpractice.html

Orton, J. D., & Weick, K. E. (1990). Loosely coupled systems: A reconsideration. *Academy of Management Review, 15*(2), 203–223.

Palmer, P. J. (1997). The renewal of community in higher education. In W. E. Campbell & K. A. Smith (Eds.), *New paradigms for college teaching* (pp. 1–18). Edina, MN: Interaction Book Company.

Palmer, P. J. (1998). *The courage to teach: Exploring the inner landscape of a teacher's life.* San Francisco, CA: Jossey-Bass.

Parker, D., & Stacey, R. (1994). *Chaos, management and economics: The implications of non-linear thinking* (Hobart paper 125). London, England: The Institute of Economic Affairs.

Perkins, J. R., Lanigan, J. B., Downey, J. A., & Levin, B. H. (2001). Chaos theory applied to college planning: A case study in defense of ten propositions. In M. Cutright (Ed.), *Chaos theory and higher education: Leadership, planning, and policy* (pp. 79–112). New York, NY: Peter Lang.

Peterson, M. W. (1997). Using contextual planning to transform institutions. In M. W. Peterson, D. D. Dill, & L A. Mets (Eds.), *Planning and management for a changing environment: A handbook on redesigning postsecondary institutions* (pp. 127–157). San Francisco, CA: Jossey-Bass.

Pintrich, P. R. (2003). A motivational science perspective on the role of student motivation in learning and teaching contexts. *Journal of Educational Psychology, 95,* 667–686.

Portland State University. (1996). *Policies and procedures for the evaluation of faculty for tenure, promotion, and merit increase.* Retrieved May 17, 2005, from www.oaa.pdx.edu/documents/pt.doc

Priesmeyer, H. R. (1992). *Organizations and chaos: Defining the methods of nonlinear management.* Westport, CT: Quorum Books.

Prigogine, I., & Stengers, I. (1984). *Order out of chaos: Man's new dialogue with nature.* New York, NY: Bantam Books.

Prochaska, J. O., DiClemente, C. C., & Norcross, J. C. (1992). In search of how people change: Applications to addictive behaviors. *American Psychologist, 47,* 1102–1114.

Professional and Organizational Development Network in Higher Education. (2002). *What is faculty development?* Retrieved May 10, 2005, from http://www.podweb.org/development/definitions.htm

Ray, P. H., & Anderson, S. R. (2000). *The cultural creatives: How 50 million people are changing the world.* New York, NY: Three Rivers Press.

Rhem, J. (1995). Close-up: Going deep. *The National Teaching and Learning Forum, 5*(1), 4.

Rice, R. E., Sorcinelli, M. D., & Austin, A. E. (2000). *Heeding new voices: Academic careers for a new generation* (New Pathways Working Paper Series No. 7). Washington, DC: American Association for Higher Education.

Richards, L. (1999). *Using NVivo in qualitative research.* Thousand Oaks, CA: Sage.

Robertson, D. L. (1999). Professors' perspectives on their teaching: A new construct and developmental model. *Innovative Higher Education, 23*(4), 271–294.

Robertson, D. R. (2000). Professors in space and time: Four utilities of a new metaphor and developmental model for professors-as-teachers. *Journal on Excellence in College Teaching, 11*(1), 117–132.

Robertson, D. R. (2003). *Making time, making change: Avoiding overloads in college teaching.* Stillwater, OK: New Forums Press.

Robson, C. (2002). *Real world research: A resource for social scientists and practitioner-researchers* (2nd ed.). Oxford, England: Blackwell.

Rogers, E. M. (1962). *Diffusion of innovations.* New York, NY: Free Press.

Rogers, T. B., Kuiper, N. A., & Kirker, W. S. (1977). Self-reference and the encoding of personal information. *Journal of Personality and Social Psychology, 35,* 677–688.

Rosch, T. A., & Reich, J. N. (1996). The enculturation of new faculty in higher education: A comparative investigation of three academic departments. *Research in Higher Education, 37*(1), 115–131.

Ruelle, D. (1991). *Chance and chaos.* Princeton, NJ: Princeton University Press.

Running Wolf, P., & Rickard, J. A. (2003). Talking circles: A Native American approach to experiential learning. *Journal of Multicultural Counseling and Development, 31,* 39–43.

Ryan, R. M., & Deci, E. L. (2000). Self-determination theory and the facilitation of intrinsic motivation, social development, and well-being. *American Psychologist, 55*(1), 68–78.

Salvendy, G. (Ed.). (1997). *Handbook of human factors and ergonomics.* New York, NY: John Wiley & Sons.

Sandberg, K. (2003). Senior professors, too, sometimes need a helping hand. *The Department Chair, 14*(1), 26–27.

Schein, E. H. (1992). *Organizational culture and leadership* (2nd ed.). San Francisco, CA: Jossey-Bass.

Schmidt, P. (2003, December 19). Accept more state control or go private. *Chronicle of Higher Education,* p. A24.

Schön, D. A. (1983). *The reflective practitioner: How professionals think in action.* New York, NY: Basic Books.

Schön, D. A. (1987). *Educating the reflective practitioner: Toward a new design for teaching and learning in the professions.* San Francisco, CA: Jossey-Bass.

Schonwetter, D. J., Sokal, L., Friesen, M., & Taylor, K. L. (2002). Teaching philosophies reconsidered: A conceptual model for the development and evaluation of teaching philosophy statements. *International Journal for Academic Development, 7*(1), 83–97.

Scott, S. (1998). An overview of transformation theory in adult education. In S. Scott, B. Spencer, & A. Thomas (Eds.), *Learning for life: Canadian readings in adult education* (pp. 178–187). Toronto, Canada: Thompson Educational Publishing.

Seldin, P. (2004). *The teaching portfolio: A practical guide to improved performance and promotion/tenure decisions* (3rd ed.). Bolton, MA: Anker.

Selingo, J. (2003, February 28). The disappearing state in public higher education. *Chronicle of Higher Education,* p. A22.

Senge, P. M. (1990). *The fifth discipline: The art and practice of the learning organization.* New York, NY: Currency Doubleday.

Seymour, E. (2002). Tracking the processes of change in U.S. undergraduate education in science, mathematics, engineering, and technology, *Science Education, 85*(6), 79–105.

Seymour, E., & Hewitt N. M. (1997). *Talking about leaving: Why undergraduates leave the sciences.* Boulder, CO: Westview Press.

Sharp, D. (1995). *Who am I really? Personality, soul and individuation.* Toronto, Canada: Inner City Books.

Sharp, D. (1998). *Jungian psychology unplugged: My life as an elephant.* Toronto, Canada: Inner City Books.

Showalter, E. (2003). *Teaching literature.* Malden, MA: Blackwell.

Shulman, L. S. (1993). Teaching as community property. *Change, 25*(6), 6–8.

Silberman, M. (1998). *Active training: A handbook of techniques, designs, case examples, and tips* (2nd ed.). New York, NY: Wiley.

Sorcinelli, M. D. (1988). Encouraging excellence: Long-range planning for faculty development. In E. C. Wadsworth (Ed.), *A handbook for new practitioners* (pp. 27–31). Stillwater, OK: New Forums Press and Professional and Organizational Development Network in Higher Education.

Sorcinelli, M. D. (1988). Satisfactions and concerns of new university teachers. In J. Kurfiss, L. Hilsen, S. Kahn, M. D. Sorcinelli, & R. G. Tiberius (Eds.), *To improve the academy: Vol. 7. Resources for faculty, instructional, and organizational development* (pp. 121–134). Stillwater, OK: New Forums Press.

Sorcinelli, M. D. (1992). New and junior faculty stress: Research and responses. In M. D. Sorcinelli & A. E. Austin (Eds.), *New directions for teaching and learning: No. 50. Developing new and junior faculty* (pp. 27–39). San Francisco, CA: Jossey-Bass.

Sorcinelli, M. D. (2002). Ten principles of good practice in creating and sustaining teaching and learning centers. In K. H. Gillespie, L. R. Hilsen, & E. C. Wadsworth (Eds.), *A guide to faculty development: Practical advice, examples, and resources* (pp. 9–23). Bolton, MA: Anker.

Sorcinelli, M. D., Austin, A. E., Eddy, P. L., & Beach, A. L. (2006). *Creating the future of faculty development: Learning from the past, understanding the present.* Bolton, MA: Anker.

Springer, L., Stanne, M. E., & Donovan, S. S. (1999). Effects of small-group learning on undergraduates in science, mathematics, engineering, and technology: A meta-analysis. *Review of Educational Research, 69*(1), 21–51.

Srivastva, S., & Cooperrider, D. (1990). *Appreciative management and leadership: The power of positive thought and action in organizations.* San Francisco, CA: Jossey-Bass.

Strauss, A., & Corbin, J. (1998). *Basics of qualitative research: Techniques and procedures for developing grounded theory* (2nd ed.). Thousand Oaks, CA: Sage.

Svinicki, M. D. (2004). *Learning and motivation in the postsecondary classroom.* Bolton, MA: Anker.

Svinicki, M. D., & Menges, R. J. (1995). Consistency within diversity: Guidelines for programs to honor exemplary teaching. In M. D. Svinicki & R. J. Menges (Eds.), *New directions in teaching and learning: No. 65. Honoring exemplary teaching* (pp. 109–113). San Francisco, CA: Jossey-Bass.

Tagg, J. (2003). *The learning paradigm college.* Bolton, MA: Anker.

Taylor, C. (1991). *The malaise of modernity.* Toronto, Canada: House of Anansi Press.

Taylor, F. W. (1911). *The principles of scientific management.* New York, NY: Harper & Row.

Theall, M., & Arreola, R. A. (2001). *Beyond the scholarship of teaching: Searching for a unifying metaphor for the college teaching profession.* Paper presented at the 81st annual meeting of the American Educational Research Association, Seattle, WA.

Thompson, D. C. (1978). Black college faculty and students: The nature of their interaction. In C. V. Willie & R. R. Edmonds (Eds.), *Black colleges in America* (pp. 180–194). New York, NY: Teachers College Press.

Tompkins, J. (1996). *A life in school: What the teacher learned.* New York, NY: Perseus.

Trow, M. (1970). Reflections on the transition from mass to universal higher education. *Daedalus, 99,* 1–42.

Trow, M. (1971). Admissions and the crisis in American higher education. In W. T. Furniss (Ed.), *Higher education for everybody? Issues and implications* (pp. 26–52). Washington, DC: American Council on Education.

U.S. Department of Education. (2003). *Status and trends in the education of blacks* (NCES 2003–034). Retrieved May 15, 2005, from http://nces.ed.gov/pubs2003/2003034.pdf

U.S. Department of Education. (2004a). *Historically Black Colleges and Universities, 1976 to 2001* (NCES 2004–062). Washington, DC: Government Printing Office.

U. S. Department of Education. (2004b). *White house initiative on Historically Black Colleges and Universities.* Retrieved May 15, 2005, from http://www.ed.gov/about/inits/list/whhbcu/edlite-index.html

Vallerand, R. J. (1997). Toward a hierarchical model of intrinsic and extrinsic motivation. In M. P. Zanna (Ed.), *Advances in experimental social psychology* (Vol. 29, pp. 271–360). San Diego, CA: Academic Press.

Walvoord, B. (2004). *Teaching well, saving time.* Keynote address presented at the 24th annual Lilly Conference on College Teaching, Oxford, OH.

Washington, B. T. (1974). *Up from slavery.* New York, NY: Dell.

Webb, N. (1983). Predicting learning from student interaction: Defining the interaction variable. *Educational Psychologist, 18*(1), 33–41.

Webb, N. (1991). Task-related verbal interaction and mathematics learning in small groups. *Journal of Research in Mathematics Education, 22,* 366–389.

Weick, K. E. (1976). Educational organizations as loosely coupled systems. *Administrative Science Quarterly, 21,* 1–19.

Wenger, E. (1998). *Communities of practice: Learning, meaning, and identity.* Cambridge, England: Cambridge University Press.

Wheatley, M. J. (1992). *Leadership and the new science: Learning about organization from an orderly universe.* San Francisco, CA: Berrett-Koehler.

Whitman, N. A. (1988). *Peer teaching: To teach is to learn twice* (ASHE-ERIC Higher Education Report No. 4). Washington, DC: Association for the Study of Higher Education.

Wiggins, G., & McTighe, J. (1998). *Understanding by design.* Alexandria, VA: Association for Supervision and Curriculum Development.

Wilson, A. L., & Hayes, E. R. (2000). On thought and action in adult and continuing education. In A. L. Wilson & E. R. Hayes (Eds.), *Handbook of adult and continuing education* (pp. 15–32). San Francisco, CA: Jossey-Bass.

Wilson, R. (2004, December 3). Where the elite teach, it's still a man's world. *Chronicle of Higher Education,* p. A8.

Zohar, D. (1997). *ReWiring the corporate brain: Using the new science to rethink how we structure and lead organizations.* San Francisco, CA: Berrett-Koehler.

Zull, J. E. (2002). *The art of changing the brain: Enriching the practice of teaching by exploring the biology of learning.* Sterling, VA: Stylus.